WITHDRAWN

DATE DUE			

The Notorious Dr. Bahrdt

Dr. Carl Friedrich Bahrdts
Geschichte
seines
Lebens, seiner Meinungen
und Schicksale.

Von ihm selbst geschrieben.

Vierter und letzter Theil.

Berlin, 1791.
bei Friedrich Vieweg, dem älteren.

The title page from Volume IV of Dr. Bahrdt's autobiography.

The
NOTORIOUS

{ **Dr. Bahrdt** }

Sten Gunnar Flygt

VANDERBILT

Nashville MCMLXIII

The type face used for the text of this book is Baskerville, named after the designs of John Baskerville, the eighteenth-century English printer who was the greatest type founder of his time. It is a transitional form between Old Style and Modern faces. The title page is set in a combination of Baskerville, Goudy Hand-tooled, and Engraver's Old English. The Goudy faces are the work of the great twentieth-century American type founder, Frederic W. Goudy. Engraver's Old English is representative of the earliest forms of blackletter type, which prevailed in German printing until very recently.

Composed, printed, and bound by the Parthenon Press
Nashville, Tennessee, United States of America
Library of Congress catalogue card number 63–14648

FOREWORD

In our day almost the only association we make with the name of Carl Friedrich Bahrdt is that he was satirized in Goethe's little farce, *Prolog zu den neuesten Offenbarungen Gottes,* and also, without being named, in Part One of *Faust.* But in his own day Bahrdt was one of the most controversial and influential champions of the Enlightenment. He was known to every person of importance in the intellectual life of Germany and was closely associated with some of them for a longer or shorter time. More than this, he had a great popular following: books by him or about him were sure to be best sellers, and his sermons and lectures directly affected hundreds—even thousands—of people. Indeed, it might even be maintained that it was Bahrdt as much as anyone, not excepting Lessing and Nicolai, who in Germany, at any rate, popularized the rationalistic and critically evaluative attitudes toward the Bible and religion that have since been so commonly accepted. His relation to the intellectual giants (both actual and imagined) of the time provided the point of impact upon which many of their lives and careers turned. Bahrdt was deeply involved in that precursor of modern, "progressive" education known as the Philanthropinical movement. He was no less involved in the inner workings of the affairs of the petty monarchies of his day. First and foremost, though, he was a theologian and a university man, whose academic career, in the years when the modern character of the German universities was being established, affords a vivid insight into the reality behind their façade of pomp and erudition.

It has, therefore, seemed a legitimate undertaking to attempt to state Bahrdt's claim to being remembered for his controversial importance. It has been my purpose in stating this claim to present a concrete and rounded picture of him as a man of the *Aufklärung* in relation to his contemporaries and against his specific background. I have emphasized the real, the actual, and the individual; the interaction of people contending for power, prestige, and even truth. It is my hope that by sketching Dr. Bahrdt engaged in lively debate, earnest discussion, bizarre undertakings, and a serious struggle for existence in the midst of the people who admired and hated, helped and damned him, the result may be a readable and informative book.

All translations from the German are my own.

STEN GUNNAR FLYGT

Vanderbilt University
Nashville, May 1963

CONTENTS

vii

ILLUSTRATIONS

The title page from Volume IV of Bahrdt's autobiography
Frontispiece

Vignettes from title pages of Bahrdt's autobiography
Facing pp. 186–87

ACKNOWLEDGMENTS

My thanks are due first and foremost to the John Simon Guggenheim Memorial Foundation, whose generous grant made it possible for me to devote a full year to collecting, sorting, and organizing materials for this study. Thanks are due also to Vanderbilt University for its grant of sabbatical leave, as well as for funds for summer travel and research. The library of the University of Tübingen (Depot der ehemaligen Preussischen Staatsbibliothek) very kindly furnished me with a microfilm of the unpublished letters of J. A. Eberhard to Friedrich Nicolai.

I wish to acknowledge my appreciation of the kind encouragement and suggestions offered by various friends who have read all or portions of the manuscript. Among these are Professor Jack M. Stein of Harvard University, Professor T. C. Dunham of Wesleyan University, and my former teacher, Professor T. M. Campbell. I am especially indebted to Professor Heinrich Meyer for numerous suggestions and comments.

I must also acknowledge a debt of gratitude to my wife (who has greatly helped me with proofreading) and children for respecting the sanctity of my study as much as they did.

S. G. F.

I have often asked myself how characteristics, seemingly ir-reconcilable, can exist in the same person. I have known crooks who were capable of self-sacrifice, sneak-thieves who were sweet-natured and harlots for whom it was a point of honour to give good value for money. The only explanation I can offer is that so instinctive is each one's conviction that he is unique in the world, and privileged, that he feels that, however wrong it might be for others, what he for his part does, if not natural and right, is at least venial.

From *The Summing Up*
W. Somerset Maugham

I

⟨CHILDHOOD⟩

THE NOTORIOUS Dr. Bahrdt was born early in the reign of Frederick August II, Elector of Saxony, who was also King August III of Poland, and one of the 354 children whom August II, modestly surnamed the Strong, was rumored to have sired before going to his last reward. Dr. Bahrdt's achievements, it must be admitted, were not in any respect so spectacular as the achievements of August the Strong, but they were arresting in their way, and they moved some of his contemporaries, notably the clergy of orthodox persuasion, to denounce him with a fury that could scarcely have been more indignant if he had flagrantly seduced and despoiled the seven hundred ladies, more or less, who had lent August their gentle but effective assistance in the production of his brood.

There is some doubt as to the exact date when Dr. Bahrdt was born: he himself says it was the twenty-fifth of August 1741, but Professor Bel, who wrote the biographical sketches of the students who received the degree of *Magister* from the University of Leipzig in 1761, gave the date as 1740. There is no doubt, however, as to the place in which he was born: it was the small town of Bischofswerda in Lusatia, a part of the Electorate of Saxony where Bahrdt's father occupied the post of *Diakonus,* the first rung in the ladder of his climb to theological and academic honors. Johann Friedrich Bahrdt, the son of an advocate of very moderate circumstances, had taken this first step with the aid of a very substantial boost from a Count von Holzendorf, who had influence in Dresden, the capital city. The Count had conceived an exaggerated and unshakable notion of the genius of the elder Bahrdt, who, in

1

his capacity as a private tutor in the house of a Count Flemming, had been present at a wedding banquet at which Count Holzendorf was a guest. When Bahrdt was unexpectedly called upon to make a speech in honor of the bridal couple, he extemporized upon a daring theme with such skill, discretion, and success that Count Holzendorf then and there decided to make the young man's fortune and promptly secured for him the position in Bischofswerda, thereby unwittingly and indirectly making a contribution, however questionable it might be considered, to the cause of religious enlightenment in Germany. For it was in Bischofswerda that the elder Bahrdt met and married a girl of fifteen, who became the mother of Carl Friedrich Bahrdt, the so-called *enfant terrible* of the *Aufklärung*.

Count Holzendorf did not forget the man whose clever elocution had so impressed him. Very soon he secured for him a pastorate in Schönefeld, near Dresden, and then, after two years, he got him the appointment of *Superintendent* in Dobrilug, for he had determined that his favorite should attain to the high honor and dignity of a university professorship. The fact that the elder Bahrdt had not prepared himself for a scholar's career and did not possess the necessary erudition was no disqualification in the eyes of the Count, who was guided by the principle that a man of talent could readily pick up whatever information might prove to be indispensable. Thus it came about that the erstwhile tutor was propelled through a series of distinctions that made him the pastor of St. Peter's in Leipzig—*Baccalaureus, Magister, Professor Extraordinarius, Doctor Theologiae,* and *Professor Ordinarius* of the University. He also received other honors and offices such as that of *Domherr* in Meissen and *Superintendent* in Leipzig.

Whereas Count Holzendorf's intentions were surely good (though his motives were probably somewhat egotistical) it cannot be said that the results of his benevolence were altogether happy. Indeed, it might with some show of justice be maintained that the Count must bear part of the ultimate responsibility for some of the unfortunate aspects of the notorious Dr. Bahrdt's character, for his determination to force the older Bahrdt into positions for which he was not ready entailed certain consequences which he did not foresee or would have disregarded if he had foreseen them.

A consequence that could easily have been foreseen was that the colleagues and competitors of the elder Bahrdt became envious of his undeserved success and eager to collect evidence of his incompetence. He, on the other hand, well aware that he was vulnerable to their attacks, proceeded to make a scholar of himself. He brushed up on his Latin to acquire fluency in lecturing and elegance in writing in that language; he deepened his knowledge of the various branches of theology, notably church history; improved his knowledge of Hebrew; learned Chaldaic, Syriac, and Arabic. The younger Bahrdt tells us that his father never ceased to study and strove to the end of his life to broaden his intellectual horizons. But however admirable this earnest resolution to perfect his knowledge may have been, it necessarily made extraordinary demands upon his time and energy and must have isolated him to a considerable degree from his growing family of seven children.

The schooling of small children, at least in Protestant Germany during most of the eighteenth century, was badly managed. Luther and Melanchthon, following the model of the Catholic church, had made the clergy responsible for public instruction, but the pastors were frequently inclined to turn this duty over to the church sexton or some other semiliterate assistant. A conscientious parent in the upper and professional classes was therefore faced with the necessity of either teaching his children himself or employing tutors, who usually lived in the household and occupied a more or less menial position. In fact, older children and even young people of university age had their private tutors, and this method of instruction with its attendant evils was a social phenomenon conspicuous enough to become the subject of the sensational play *Der Hofmeister oder Vorteile der Privaterziehung* (1774), by Jacob Michael Reinhold Lenz.

Thus it was not unusual that the young Bahrdts were given private schooling at home, and the experience need not have been unfortunate. What made it at least questionable were the facts that Bahrdt Senior was so engrossed in his pursuit of scholarship that he exercised almost no supervision whatever and that he was too poor to engage young men who merited the confidence he reposed in them. After one had demonstrated his unfitness he was dismissed and another engaged, but the chances were slight that the new one would be an improvement on the one just leaving. Bahrdt himself believed that some of his traits of character were established through the influence of his tutors and house servants, though he protests, perhaps not very convincingly, that he was too young and innocent to be much affected by what was told him of erotic matters. The explanation he gives of the persistent optimism, not to say levity, with which he later advanced from one disastrous experience to another, is sufficiently interesting to summarize: a servant named Ernst, who was employed for two years, regaled him with numberless unrealistic plans for making a fortune, attaining fame and position, and so on. Every day was unrolled some new fabrication in which the hero, whom the boy always identified with himself, achieved a brilliant success without effort. Thus was strengthened and made ineradicable, so Bahrdt says, his native tendency to minimize difficulties, to look past the unpleasant reality close at hand to some happy unreality in the imagined future.

The anecdotes about Bahrdt's childhood cannot readily be either confirmed or disproved, but it is not hard to believe that he was an alert, inquiring, and enterprising boy and that, as he himself says, he missed no opportunity to visit all sorts of places, such as the various craftsmen's workshops, where he learned what he could by observation. By the time he was ten, for instance, he had learned enough of the hairdresser's trade to make up his tutor's wig every Saturday evening so that it would be stiff with tallow and freshly powdered for the Sunday service and the following week. The practical bent which he manifested in this way, even a matter-of-fact readiness to work with his hands in the performance of tasks considered menial, persisted and even increased throughout his life and furnished one more occasion of scandalized amazement to many contemporaries and later literary historians, who seemed to see in it an affront to the dignity of the learned professions.

If it is not hard to believe this anecdote which he reports himself, it is also at least not impossible to believe certain other anecdotes, much less creditable, which he does not report, and it is likely that his protestations of boyhood innocence are at least exaggerated. But it is very interesting and valuable to have direct testimony as to his character from one of the two or three tutors whom Bahrdt himself singles out as capable and praiseworthy in every respect. This man, a certain Hofmann, who at the time of Bahrdt's death was one of the senior masters of the Thomasschule in Leipzig, is quoted in Schlichtegroll's *Nekrolog* (the supplementary volume for the years 1790 to 1793) as saying that he speedily discovered that the young Bahrdt was intelligent and good-hearted, although seriously deficient in certain subjects. Hofmann's predecessor had not tried to reason with the boy but had been severe and even harsh, a mistaken procedure when dealing with such an alert and lively mind.

He immediately retained everything he heard [said Hofmann] and asked questions about everything that did not seem convincing to him. He made objections which were acceptabe to me and useful to him. He continued to occupy himself with what he had heard and did not cease until he was completely satisfied.

Hofmann concludes his remarks with the observation,

Because of his affection for me he readily obeyed me in everything, and I have nothing to reproach him for.

Such was the child whom his father, as his circumstances improved, resolved to send to one of the well-known public schools, the Nikolaischule of Leipzig, perhaps to save him from utter ruin at the hands of his tutors. If it was the elder Bahrdt's hope that his son would now be taught by informed and competent men, it was apparently a mistaken one. To be sure, the great Johann Jacob Reiske, so Bahrdt says,[1] was rector of the school at that time, but, according to Bahrdt's account, his overwhelming erudition was an encumbrance rather than an asset in teaching young boys the elements of Latin and Greek. Bahrdt says that Reiske was unable to impart any of his immeasurable wealth of scholarship to his classes and that one almost literally had to pump him for information. Says Bahrdt,

His mind resembled a stomach that could not be unburdened save by means of an enema.

The man whom Bahrdt so drastically characterizes was one of
the most remarkable and unhappy scholars of his age, whom some
historians of classical philology rank perhaps even higher than
C. G. Heyne and F. A. Wolf. Here, if anywhere in the annals
of scholarship, we find a man who pursued knowledge for its own
sake and almost completely ignored the promptings of worldly
ambition. It is quite possible that he desired fame above all else
as the just recognition of knowledge, and he very probably was
possessed by a fierce pride in his accomplishments that caused him
to become jealous of the regard in which the learned world held his
amanuensis and wife, Ernestine Christine, who led a life of un-
fulfilled yearning for love and cherished an unrequited passion
for Gotthold Ephraim Lessing. At the time Reiske became rector
of the Nikolaischule, however, he had just been rescued by the
intervention of Providence, as he believed, from a long struggle
against poverty and lack of recognition and had not yet gotten up
the courage to marry. The only really remunerative position he
ever held was the rectorship of the Nikolaischule, to which he was
appointed not for his real qualifications, but because of the more
or less accidental circumstance that he had deciphered the inscription on a semiprecious stone owned by a Count von
Wackerbart, who was so gratified that a little later he wrote to
Bürgermeister Born of Leipzig that the Electoral Prince would
be pleased if Reiske were appointed to the vacancy. Thus one of
the most learned men of his time became responsible for the
schooling of small boys, much to the disappointment and envy of
the associate rector, *Konrektor* Adami, who did everything he
could to undermine Reiske's authority.[2]

The melancholy and hermetical Reiske was not the man to
exert a salutary influence upon the mettlesome, inquiring, and
impatient young Bahrdt, even if he had been old enough to be in
Reiske's classes. As for Adami, the associate rector, he seems to
have been the butt of the children's ridicule. At any rate, at the
end of a year Carl Friedrich and his brother were enrolled in the
most famous of the three Saxon so-called "princely academies,"
Schulpforta. Carl Friedrich must have been fourteen or fifteen
at the time. Bahrdt Senior took the two boys to Pforta, entrusted

them to the care of Rector Freytag, and returned to Leipzig, no doubt convinced that he was doing everything in his power to ensure their happiness and welfare. Carl Friedrich, so he tells us, did not long remain sad because of parting from his home and parents: Freytag inspired in him a sense of trust and confidence, and besides, the boy's active imagination was soon busy with all sorts of interesting possibilities. Throughout his life he displayed an astonishing capacity to erect new, fascinating, complicated, and practical-impractical dream structures on the basis of the disagreeable present, and so we can readily imagine that the pangs of separation became quickly less perceptible as he contemplated the future.

The future, however, proved to be very trying in many respects, at least so Bahrdt says. For one thing, the domestic economy of the school was mismanaged: in theory the pupils had a great variety of excellent food, but in practice they were served a monotonous fare of inferior meat with very few greens, and the steward pocketed an illicit profit. For another thing, except for Rector Freytag, the teaching staff was only mediocre at best, and at least one, the mathematics instructor, was scandalously incompetent and senile. Moreover, the pupils themselves were governed by a brutal hazing system: all the seniors had the authority to discipline the younger boys and some of them had special powers, so that every breach of the code was punished by kicks and blows; those who suffered most were of course the boys who in any way seemed to be teacher's pets. The "hell week" of some present-day American college fraternities lasted a whole year at Schulpforta, every year as long as the boy was an underclassman. Moreover, sexual malpractice was common: if we can believe Bahrdt, masturbation, homosexuality, and pederasty were endemic, and he himself avoided entering into unnatural relations with an older boy only because of his failure to comprehend what was desired of him.

Is Bahrdt's picture of life at Schulpforta in his time just and fairly accurate? Some of his contemporaries were, of course, incensed by his account and said that he was defiling his own nest in vindictive anger at having been expelled from the school and that, moreover, if he had been allowed to remain and had accepted the discipline, he would very possibly have gone the way of so many solid scholars who had received their preliminary training there. Other equally trustworthy commentators, however, write that Bahrdt was not exaggerating very much and that conditions were probably as he describes them. To the modern, more disinterested reader it would seem that Bahrdt's account has a certain air of verisimilitude, whatever may be the truth as to the reason he left the school. And we know, of course, that sexual aberrations constituted a great problem in Basedow's Philanthropinum in Dessau a few years later and that for this reason Salzmann, who had observed conditions in Dessau, took especial precautions in his own institution in Schnepfental.[3]

Wherever the truth may lie, it is certain that young Bahrdt's experience in Schulpforta was not very much more fortunate than most of his previous schooling had been. After two years he left Pforta. Whether he was withdrawn from the school by his father at his own request, as he himself says, or whether he was expelled, as some hostile contemporaries affirm, cannot now be ascertained. He did return to Leipzig, however, and became a student at the University. He says that he was scarcely fifteen years old when he began attending lectures, but for a number of reasons with which we are already familiar it seems likely that he was at least sixteen and perhaps even seventeen. He would live at home, to be sure, but at the University it would be presumed that he had advanced sufficiently in knowledge, maturity, and wisdom to pursue his studies without further guidance. One might say that he had now really been set adrift on the ocean of learning.

II

❬STUDENT YEARS❭

THE PROFESSOR at a German university, presumably after communing for some time with himself, decides what he would like to lecture on. He informs no one of his intentions until the semester is about to begin. Then he condescends to have a scrap of paper, which he has signed, affixed to the general bulletin board. The bulletin board is full of such scraps of paper, each one announcing, often in illegible script, to expectant youth the time, place, and subject of the professors' lectures. The student approaches the bulletin board, studies the various slips of paper, makes a note of what he thinks might interest him, goes at first to all the lectures he can squeeze into a full day, and then begins to stay away from an ever-increasing number of them, until finally his task of elimination is perfect. This means that he now has time enough to glean the information he wants from the books he can beg, borrow, steal, or even buy.

It was such a bulletin board as has just been described before which young Carl Friedrich Bahrdt stood one day, making a chaotic selection from the confused display before him. His father had given him no advice except to suggest philosophy as a subject and to recommend Dr. Crusius as a professor. This advice was given without any regard to the fact that he was by no means prepared to follow the intricacies of logic or mature enough to maintain a wholesome skepticism toward the so-called "mystical tendencies" of Crusius, whose devoted disciple he became.

Christian August Crusius (1715–1775) and Johann August Ernesti (1707–1781) were the rallying points of two opposing factions in the University of Leipzig during the middle of the

9

century. The issue in dispute between these two factions was the philosophy of Christian Wolff (1679–1754), which by the middle of the eighteenth century was sweeping the learned world, to the dismay of the orthodox Christian clergy, who rightly sensed that Wolff's kind of philosophical rationalism had implications not only for formal theology but also for simple and unquestioning faith that could very well undermine them both.[1] To undermine religious faith had surely not been Wolff's intention. From early youth he had had a great need to find a way not only to end his own doubts and questions concerning revealed religion but to establish theology on a basis of irrefutable certainty. To this end he studied theology and philosophy and also natural sciences and especially mathematics, for which the great Leibniz suggested that he was peculiarly well suited. But Wolff had been so impressed by the certainty of mathematical method and syllogistic reasoning that he proceeded to construct a closed system of philosophy that would explain everything through a chain of reasoning from axiomatic and incontrovertible principles: the principle of identity and contradiction ("A thing cannot both be and not be") and the principle of sufficient cause ("Everything must have its sufficient cause"). From Wolff's general position followed certain consequences, of which two are of especial interest in the present context. The alarmed theologians perceived that Wolff's principle of sufficient cause would lead to a rigid determinism that excluded the possibility of divine intervention in human life and history, either through revelation or through miracles. Although Wolff himself as a pious gesture allowed for the possibility of miracles, belief in them was not consistent with his system, and he gave assurances that his was really a loftier conception of God because miracles presuppose only God's power to suspend the laws of nature momentarily, whereas the eternal causal flow of natural events presupposes not only God's omnipotence in creating the world but also his omniscient knowledge of everything that would follow from that creation. The other consequence of Wolff's general position with which we are here concerned could well escape the notice of the theologians. In fact, the insidious thing about it was that Bible scholars could agree to it and work according to it without at first realizing where it would take them, since it was merely a restatement of already accepted philological method. This is his theory of concepts (*notiones*), which he classifies as clear and obscure, adequate and inadequate. Concepts were, of course, inevitably associated with words—their meanings, their combinations in propositions, syllogisms, and other figures of logic and valid reasoning. The long self-evident principle, that a good textual reading must be established before a document can be understood, caused no discomfort as long as it was applied to secular Greek and Latin writings, but when applied to Holy Writ, as it had already been applied by Richard Simon in his *Histoire critique du Vieux Testament* (1678), it was bound to alter the perspective from which the Good Book was scrutinized. The Wolffians did not hesitate to profess orthodoxy, accepted the Bible as the inspired Word of God, and affirmed by oath that they believed literally in such articles of dogma as the Virgin Birth and Eternal Damnation, then proceeded to examine the Word of God as though it were the word of man, oblivious of what their procedure entailed, until they found that they really had made it impossible for themselves to accept orthodox doctrine. The internal dialectic of Wolffianism, like that of Cartesianism, led to discomfiting conclusions. The anti-Wolffians, however, had an intuitive distrust of subjecting the actual words of the Bible to an uncommitted philological scrutiny, which, as they foresaw, would soon lead to the disturbing inquiry into questions of interpolation, textual authenticity, multiple authorship, and the like.

This was precisely the direction taken in Leipzig by J. A. Ernesti, who was capable of affirming his belief in Eternal Damnation without turning a hair and, in general, maintained the posture of devoutness. Ernesti had put in his academic apprenticeship as rector of the Thomasschule in Leipzig, a post which he seems to have filled very ably at the same time he was making a name for himself as a scholar. As a schoolman he was known for the elegance of his Latin style and for his pupils' mastery of Latin, which they acquired by the method of reading extensively for accurate comprehension, rather than by the method of grammatical analysis. As a scholar he so distinguished himself that, contrary to established

practice, he was elevated to the dignity of a university professorship. Indeed, for a while he held a double professorship: that of
eloquence, which comprehended not only rhetoric and Greek and
Latin literature but also ancient history and classical archaeology;
and that of theology, which he eventually made his main interest.
He had, of course, already demonstrated his competence in theology by writings in which he brought the learning and critical
method of the philologist to bear upon this discipline. But this
meant that in order to obtain a true understanding of the Bible—
and it must be remembered that after the rise of Protestantism
with its various branches and sects, the conflict of opinion as to
the meaning of the Word of God made the establishment of incontrovertible proof of opinion a matter of eternal moment—
he naturally resorted to grammatical and linguistic methods. From
this it became clear that the Greek of the New Testament had
its own peculiarities of syntax, idiom, vocabulary, and style. That
is, the Word of God was not a fixed and immutable thing to
which one needed only the right key to attain salvation, but it
was subject to the vicissitudes of human conditions. Now it must
not be supposed that Ernesti singlehandedly revolutionized New
Testament scholarship; his work would probably have had no effect
if scholars had not already been working along his general lines,
but it has been stated that his little book, *Institutio interpretis
Novi Testamenti* (1761), marks a decisive turn in scholarship
towards general acceptance of the philological, as opposed to the
theological, basis of New Testament exegesis and hermeneutics.

If it was possible for such men as Ernesti and Semler, of whom
we will hear more later, to proceed with their investigations without being aware of, or perhaps disregarding, the radical implications for their professed faith and for orthodox doctrine, their
opponents sensed the danger and hastened to the attack, thereby
perhaps making *their* contribution to the cause of enlightenment,
for there is nothing like an attack to stimulate a counterattack. At
Leipzig, as has been said, the opponents of enlightenment rallied
around Christian August Crusius.

Crusius is now as much forgotten as Bahrdt. Therefore it may
be well to recall that no less an intellect than Immanuel Kant had

words of appreciation for him.[2] His philosophical views have often been called mystical, but mysticism does not seem an appropriate label for a philosophy which is derived systematically from certain premises, even though the basic premise, that everything which is of necessity conceived as true must be true, and everything which is of necessity conceived as false must be false, rests upon assumptions that seem contrary to empirical knowledge. His whole method of procedure seems very rationalistic: full of definitions, classifications, inferences, and syllogistic reasoning. His attack on Wolff's principle of sufficient cause was not a mystical rejection of it; in fact, he accepted the basic notion, introduced certain distinctions, and then proceeded, using Wolff's method, to reach the foregone conclusions which he desired and which were in contradiction to Wolff's. This was necessary in order to provide for indeterminism within his system—that is, for the belief in freedom of the will—and was done by distinguishing between sufficient cause and necessarily determining cause. The same principle could also account for direct, arbitrary, almost whimsical, divine intervention in human affairs, temptation by the devil, and the work of evil spirits. These and related apocalyptic matters constituted the subject of his theological system.

Looking back on his work under Crusius, Bahrdt acknowledges a great debt to him: the effort required to follow the intricacies of his philosophical system schooled Bahrdt in logical and syllogistic thinking. Crusius as a philosopher, says Bahrdt, was an excellent thinker, but as a theologian he was a wild visionary. Bahrdt explains this by pointing out that there are cases of only partial insanity or derangement centered upon a fixed idea: the patient seems completely normal until something is mentioned which pertains to the illusory world which he has constructed and then his utterances lose all contact with reality. So it was with Crusius, who was perfectly rational in all matters that were not connected with religion. In this area, however, he held the wildest beliefs, even going so far as to interpret all Old Testament passages which described an evil and dangerous personage as referring prophetically to Antichrist, that is, the Pope. But at the time that Bahrdt was attending Crusius's lectures he accepted everything his pro-

fessor said, hated the Pope, looked to the Second Coming, and
hoped with confidence for the conversion of all Jews. In his autobiography he gives a sample of his own theologizing at this time
while he was so completely under the influence of Crusius, and
it may be interesting to cite it here as a sample of "unenlightened"
rationalism. He had developed a metaphysical proof of the Trinity
based upon the principle of activity and pleasure by reasoning that
if God is and has been through eternity active and blissful, then He
must also through eternity have had an object of His blissful activity. Now since in eternity, as contrasted with time, no created
thing existed, this object must have been present in God Himself.
That is, there must have been Persons in God so that He could
have an object of His activity, love, and blissfulness. But since
one additional Person would have been too boring and more than
three, unnecessary, there must therefore be a Trinity.[3]

Of course, not all Bahrdt's time and energies were occupied
during his student days by such idle speculation: he had experienced seduction and, a little later, puppy love. The story of his
seduction is the not unusual tale of a very young and inexperienced
boy being the semi-victim of a much older and unattractive
woman, in this case, a servant in the household. The anecdote
does not contribute much to our understanding of Bahrdt: it is
possible that he was not, at the age of seventeen, as innocent and
passive in this affair as he says, but it is at least equally possible
that he was.

The story of puppy love is more interesting, however, not because the episode was in any way unique, but because of the comment which the mature Bahrdt makes upon it. Briefly, the young
man decided to have a real sweetheart and his choice fell upon
the daughter of a distinguished professor of law, to whom he had
not been introduced. He arranged to go with a friend to the girl's
home to call, and in preparation for the meeting composed and
practiced a number of gallant speeches, carefully selected his costume, studied himself in the mirror, and practiced facial expressions which were intended to create the effect of dignity, languish-
ing love, ironical superiority, and so on. Of course, everything
went wrong: he got such acute stage fright that he forgot his

speeches, made every conceivable wrong move in going to greet the girl's brother, whom he knew, and retired in extreme confusion. But the effects of this humiliation did not last long. In looking back upon the episode Bahrdt comments that his characteristic levity prevented him from learning the lesson which his humiliation should have taught him.

It concealed from me [he writes] the true cause of my failure, which lay in my childishness and inexperience, and persuaded me that my game had been spoiled by the fortuitous circumstance that there had been too many onlookers.

One wonders whether Bahrdt, when he wrote this, was still not deceiving himself, still not able to see that the real lesson he should have learned was the vanity of pretense, sham, and posing. As we trace his life story we will find many instances of sham and pretense. An interesting question will be whether, as his enemies said, he was all sham, all pretense, and motivated solely by the basest desires, or whether at the center of his personality there was a solid core.

At the time of which we are writing, to be sure, the solid core at the center of his character, if there was one, was not much in evidence. What was in evidence, in addition to childishness, were, he says, a fiery temper and a tendency toward foppishness. As for his temper, we will have several occasions to observe him in angry defiance of the world, but it is most interesting to learn that his foppishness and vanity had as a sort of corollary a strong impulse to neatness and cleanliness, for neatness and cleanliness, even though perhaps originally necessary only to help him sustain a pose and create an impression, necessarily involve a certain kind of self-awareness and, in this case, suggest a drive to be that which he wished to seem. It is not inconceivable that this kind of physical neatness might have an intellectual parallel, one that made him uneasy once he had become aware that certain facts or truths would not fit neatly into his logical scheme. His strong practical bent, his sense of *things*—for things are not altered by wishful logic-chopping—would not allow him to make himself blind to the flaw or to belabor it with dialectic until it seemed to support the argument it really denied.

Be this as it may, the ferment of extreme youth took some time
to work itself out. The various anecdotes from this time need de-
tain us only briefly; similar anecdotes can be told about the late
adolescence of many persons both more and less distinguished
than Bahrdt. They concern a foolish admiration for a woman
twice his age, a reprehensible flirtation with the wife of a pastor
who gave him his first chance to preach, some innkeepers who
were duped by Bahrdt and three young friends, and the like.
But one of the anecdotes is rather amusing as an account of some
unreasonable antics in the Age of Reason.

An impoverished student had stolen a manuscript of *Fausts
Höllenzwang,* which was a book of practical instructions on the
conjuring up of spirits. Young Bahrdt was seized with the desire
to possess a copy of it but could not pay the price which the student
demanded. He therefore persuaded the student to come with the
book to the Bahrdt home where, he said, a Prussian officer would
be waiting to examine the book in a private room, since he did
not wish it to become known that he was interested in buying
it. The ruse worked: Bahrdt took the manuscript into the room
next to his and then left the house for a safe place, where he and his
brothers spent a few days copying it. They eventually returned
the manuscript to its unrightful owner, whose anguish can be
imagined, and were severely reprimanded by their father. Then
Carl Friedrich proceeded to try to raise a few spirits. He thought
at first of exorcising one of the major powers of the spirit world,
one of the Electoral Princes—their political system seemed to
parallel that of the Holy Roman Empire—in order to

learn dogmatics, polemics, prophetical theology, church history, and the
history of heresy, everything that was necessary to become a great man.

After reading a while he decided that this would involve as much
work as learning all those subjects in the usual way, and that he
would do well to settle on one of the minor spirits, the one who
would give him luck at cards and gaming. He therefore bought
some white virgin parchment and procured a white dove. Then,
while muttering mysterious incantations, he tore off the dove's
head, caught the blood, and used it to write certain characters on
the parchment as the book directed. The parchment thus in-

scribed, he secured it to the bare skin under his left arm, put on his best clothes and sallied forth to a party where there was gambling, played for high stakes, and lost all his money. Despite this disappointment he continued his attempts to get at least one spirit in his power until, after many unsuccessful experiments, it dawned on him that the whole thing was a fraud. From that moment on, he says, he ceased to put any trust whatever in stories of the manifestation of spirits and ghosts, and he was firmly convinced that all such stories were obvious lies.[4]

Bahrdt tells this anecdote not merely to entertain his readers but also to trace from the very beginning the progress of his enlightenment.

To be sure [he says] I did not for this reason cease to believe in the existence of ghosts and devils, for Crusius had too deeply impressed me with that by means of his explications of the Bible. But nonetheless, as a result of this affair the first germ of enlightenment sprouted within me. My reason, so to speak, for the first time took its seat on the judgment bench of truth. And even though for a long time afterward I remained deprived of its full light and was in many respects an out and out visionary, nevertheless a spark had been struck which gradually grew bigger and bigger, received more and more fuel and, before long, illuminated a good many cells in the mass of my ideas.

Some of the fuel which fed the first feeble flame of Bahrdt's enlightenment was probably furnished by Christian Adolf Klotz (1738–1771). Klotz came to the University of Leipzig late in Bahrdt's career as a student, probably 1760. Only a few years older than Bahrdt, Klotz had an astounding facility in the composition of Latin, both prose and verse, and was loud in his praises of Greek and Latin as the only fountainhead of intellectual culture. He influenced Bahrdt to study Latin composition under Hentsch, one of Ernesti's pupils. Bahrdt later continued his study under Ernesti himself. The friendly relations which first prevailed between Bahrdt and Klotz were soon disturbed, however, by their dispute as to the value of studying the Greek and Latin authors. Bahrdt, as a true disciple of Crusius, took the position that a Christian had nothing to learn from the pagans and wrote a Latin essay praising modern writers and taking a few digs at Klotz. Klotz became offended and later, after he had become an extremely influential professor and editor, attacked and ridiculed Bahrdt's writings in his journals. Bahrdt must have felt the whiplash of his ridicule very keenly and was probably stung by it into an uneasy feeling that his pious Crusian system really was vulnerable. That early spark of enlightenment was at least not dampened by his relations with Klotz.

It must have been from a sense of invulnerability, however, that he decided to present himself as a candidate for the degree of *Magister*. Looking back upon that decision Bahrdt writes that he is amazed at his own effrontery, for he had no solid knowledge at all, merely the reputation for knowing a great deal, and this reputation came only from the bold glibness with which he would debate any given subject in Latin. His fluency and air of self-assurance passed for learning even during the examination, though Ernesti shook his head doubtfully at some of the revelations of ignorance in the written extempore interpretation of classical authors. In the oral part of the examination Bahrdt answered very promptly and tried to guess what he didn't know, always formulating his answers so obscurely that his examiners were left with some doubt as to whether perhaps he didn't really have the information after all. Furthermore, he was aided by the fact that the examiners were too lazy to change their stock questions and were satisfied with an answer that seemed approximately right. They were, of course, prompt to give the right answer themselves if the candidate started off wrong. But the biggest inducement the examiners had to pass the candidates, says Bahrdt, was the fact that they received a substantial sum of money for conducting the examination. They reasoned, therefore, that if they were too severe, the poorly prepared and stupid candidates would not present themselves and thus this academic rite would become less lucrative.

All things therefore conspired to favor Bahrdt's candidacy, and he was especially aided by the fact that a student who really knew all the answers was able to prompt him. He was then, not so surprisingly, one of the young men whom the dean of the theological faculty admitted to the degree of *Magister,* praising them as most worthy and most learned. This took place in the year 1761, the year when Bahrdt's father was rector of the University.

III

⟨ THE YOUNG SCHOLAR ⟩

BAHRDT APPARENTLY enjoyed the ceremonies that inaugurated him and his companions into their new dignity, or rather, solemnized their wedding to the Lady Philosophia. The procession of successful candidates was led by a dean in full academic regalia into the great auditorium, which had been appropriately decorated for the occasion and was filled with spectators, some proud and happy, others full of envy and derision. After a number of orations had been delivered, the academic marriage took place:

Every candidate for the degree of *Magister* had a folio volume before him which was supposed to represent Aristotle. (Mine was a lexicon, one neighbor had an old chronicle, and another had a volume of funeral sermons.) He also had a ring and a beret before him, the symbols of marriage. The master of ceremonies descended, placed the beret on the head of one after the other, put the ring on his finger, gave him a kiss, opened the volume of Aristotle and uttered various Latin words which were supposed to signify the wedding with Madame Sophia. As he opened the book he said, "Aperio tibi librum," and exhorted us to study Aristotle with diligence and to acquire wisdom.

If Bahrdt had enjoyed the ceremony, he enjoyed even more the rights, privileges, and distinctions which the new degree conferred upon him. Chief among these was his new title itself:

Cicero did not experience so much inward celestial joy upon receiving the news of Catiline's flight as I felt when that bald *Herr* or even *Musge* [*Monsieur*] Bahrdt was suddenly banned and *Herr Magister* had taken its place. How often I looked into the mirror on this day! How often I looked at my sword, to see whether it was still keeping up with me as it should! How often I put a question to the rabble in order to hear the answer: "Yes —No—Right away, *Herr Magister!*"

19

Vanity demanded also that the young scholar appear in public to display his erudition and enhance his dignity. He attended all academic functions, lectures, and disputations, especially the latter, for he excelled in public debate not only because of his forensic and oratorical gifts, but also because of a stratagem that he found greatly to his advantage. The stratagem was simple: at a public disputation or defense of an academic thesis he bided his time until the disputant showed signs of fatigue from replying to his interrogations. When he deemed the moment to be ripe, young Bahrdt would arise, fresh, eager for the fray, to demolish his opponent's arguments with fluent ridicule. But when it came to delivering his own lectures at the University, he fared somewhat less well, even though his subject was dogmatics, which at that time in Leipzig required no more of its professors than that they deliver pious sermons on the cardinal points of orthodox belief. Bahrdt's training had been too sketchy for him to be well grounded even in this superficial discipline, and he would eventually have met utter failure if the elder Bahrdt had not concealed himself within earshot of his son's podium and presented him with a list of his errors and shortcomings at the end of each lecture. Thus Bahrdt was somewhat shakily embarked upon the path to traditional academic success.

A fine advance in this direction was marked by his becoming in 1762 *Katechet* at his father's church, St. Peter's. Although the remuneration was small, the office gave him great social and professional advantages: he had certain pastoral duties, but he had also the frequent opportunity to deliver sermons, and preaching was his glory. There is abundant testimony from every period of his life to his magnificent powers of oratory and his ability to sway an audience as he wished. His father was also a very popular preacher, but even at this early time the young Bahrdt's sermons were preferred by the congregation to those of the elder Bahrdt. And these sermons were strictly traditional and orthodox in content. Indeed, they breathed such militant piety that *Hauptpastor* Götze of Hamburg (now known chiefly because of his famous dispute with Lessing, which produced Lessing's great manifesto of liberal religious belief *Nathan der Weise*) somewhat later invited young

Bahrdt to Hamburg for the purpose of delivering a trial sermon in connection with a position which had fallen vacant. Bahrdt declined, presumably because the future looked too promising in Leipzig. Götze's expression of interest must have been convincing evidence that he needed only to persist in the course he had chosen to attain distinction and security in the fold of the orthodox.

At this very time, however, Bahrdt was indulging in a few pranks that were destined, even though not designed, to take him outside those comfortable bars.

For one thing, the extent of his ignorance made it impossible for him to rely on notes he had taken in lectures and on the authority of texts he had studied. In order not to be exposed as an utter ignoramus he had to work up the material afresh. It seems likely that for this very reason he had to make sure of his ground and therefore studied his Bible much more closely and critically than he might have done otherwise. Thus he speedily attained the insight that many Old Testament passages commonly interpreted as referring prophetically to the New Testament clearly referred only to the contemporary Old Testament situation, Isaiah 7 and 53, for example. It will be recalled that his insight did not constitute a new and original discovery by Bahrdt and that this was precisely the line taken by Ernesti, the great opponent of Bahrdt's teacher, Crusius. It is interesting that with Bahrdt, as indeed with Ernesti himself, the attainment of such an insight was not incompatible with a continued adherence to orthodoxy, an adherence which, in Bahrdt's case, continued for a considerable time after the point when, as he says,

the light of reason broke through the hard crust of his rigid belief and the new-born child of enlightenment was able to grow, although, to be sure, very gradually and slowly, and ripen into manhood.

It may be doubted that Bahrdt's account of what he calls his conversion is altogether accurate, but it probably is true in a general way, for if it were not true, it would be very difficult to understand why he should first jeopardize and then throw away the highly successful career which seemed within his grasp. To be sure, his enemies and detractors have always said that he espoused the cause of enlightenment for gain; this explanation might be acceptable if he had given no indication of doing so before his frivolous conduct had made it possible for his enemies to thwart his ambitions for advancement in Leipzig as a theologian. But his own statement that it was his philological interest that opened his eyes to the impossibility of literally accepting orthodox dogma is supported by the titles of many of his earliest publications dating from the years before the public scandal which drove him from Leipzig in 1768. For example, his very first publication, *De usu linguae arabicae ex comparatione cum hebraea* (1758), although it was so trifling and unoriginal that it was dismissed by its reviewers as being a mere private exercise book, clearly demonstrates the philological bent, as do also his *Compendium der hebräischen Grammatik* (1765), *Observationen zum 2., 8. und 36. Psalm* (1766), and *De locorum V. T. in nova accommodatione orthodoxa* (1766), although it must be said that the last work represented a pretty violent effort to twist New Testament significance out of Old Testament passages in an orthodox sense. Thus there seems to be no real reason to doubt Bahrdt's statement that his enlightenment took place gradually, slowly, and even involuntarily.

In Bahrdt's gradual and involuntary progress along the road of enlightenment we have one of those interesting examples of how serious search for objective evidence in support of a cherished belief may often produce evidence which will destroy the belief. Other examples may be cited from earlier in the eighteenth century as well: Johann Jakob Scheuchzer, seeking for evidence that would prove the Bible story of Noah's flood, discovered in 1705 fossilized bones which completely disproved it—although to be sure, Scheuchzer himself died in happy ignorance of that fact. And the great Linnaeus, who had based his *Systema Naturae* of 1735 on the principle that the "number of species is the same as that which existed at the start of creation" and made it his life's task to classify all living creatures in demonstration of this principle, was finally forced by the evidence of what he saw to postulate that life had originated at a "single initial point from which creation began and gradually spread" and to strike from the *Systema Naturae* of 1759 the statement of his original basic principle of the immutability of species. The story of Bahrdt's "conversion" is therefore both plausible and typical, even though we do not have to accept in its entirety Bahrdt's own generalization that a person who is

resolved to examine church theology and put it to the touchstone of reason and philology, can, if he has the necessary talent and perseverance, not persist in his faith, but he must, if he pursues this path, finally lose his faith; that is, at the end of his investigation he will have nothing left except the religion of reason, and the positive rubbish will finally burst like soapbubbles.

Bahrdt says that his defection from the faith began when a young friend named Topf persuaded him to attend the lectures of Johann Friedrich Fischer (1728–1799). At the time Bahrdt heard his lectures, Fischer was *Ausserordentlicher Professor* of theology at the University and also one of the instructors in the Thomasschule, of which Ernesti had only recently been rector. When Ernesti gave up the rectorship of the Thomasschule for a professorship at the University he was not succeeded by Fischer, who had expected the appointment. For eight long years Fischer continued in a subordinate position, full of bitterness that his merits had not been recognized as he thought they should. This disappointment, as was natural, only increased Fischer's fanatical devotion to the letter of the classical and biblical texts he taught and confirmed him in his character of one of those painfully conscientious schoolmen who cite all the parallels for every word of the text. In this respect Fischer's knowledge was probably unexcelled and, since he had taken Ernesti as his master and model, it can readily be understood that his interpretation of the New Testament would be uncompromisingly philological. This was the man whom Topf praised to Bahrdt as offering the key to absolutely certain knowledge of the meaning of the Scriptures.

When Bahrdt began attending Fischer's lectures Fischer was discussing First Corinthians in his usual way. When he came to the third chapter, in which Paul upbraids the Corinthians for being divided into sects, saying in the eighth verse, "Now he that planteth and he that watereth are one," Fischer pointed out that this obviously meant that Paul and Apollos are in agreement, and he adduced many passages from various Greek writers in which it was said of different people that they were one, meaning that they had the same belief or intention or purpose. Having thus established what both Greek and Hellenistic writers meant by the phrase "to be one," he directed his hearers' attention to I John 5:7, "For there are three that bear record in heaven, the Father, the Word, and the Holy Ghost: and these three are one," and added gruffly that they could now see what value this passage would have as proof of the doctrine of the Holy Trinity even if it were genuine.

> It was [says Bahrdt] as though a clap of thunder shook me. I turned pale and my heart began to pound, as if I had seen a friend in danger of being burned up. "Good heavens," I thought to myself, "not genuine, and even if it were genuine, valueless as proof?"

This attack upon the classic passage of greatest authority in support of the doctrine of the Trinity caused Bahrdt much concern for a long time. In fact, the thought that a Biblical passage might not be genuine seems never to have occurred to him, and he hurried to ask his father how this could be. The latter then informed him, meanwhile reproving him for never having heard lectures on textual criticism, that ancient copyists had sometimes incorporated mere marginal notes into the Bible text, but that the consensus was that I John 5:7 was authentic, even though it was missing in some old manuscripts. Bahrdt, however, was far from reassured, for it seemed to him that if there was the slightest doubt about the authenticity of the passage it could have no value as proof of a cardinal point of faith. Thus he continued his discussions with his father and pursued his philological studies in order to confirm his faith by scriptural evidence that could in no way be questioned or doubted. As for I John 5:7, even if there could be no question of its authenticity, it would have lost its value as proof for Bahrdt merely on philological grounds, for no matter how many passages the elder Bahrdt could cite in which Jesus spoke of his being one with the Father, there seemed to the younger Bahrdt to be no completely compelling reason to take I John 5:7 as signifying identity of being, for the usage of the Greek writers, both scriptural and profane, left open the other possibility, that of mere moral or intellectual agreement. So long as in every other known instance of its use the phrase "to be one" did not signify identity of person, there was no compelling reason to take it as signifying identity of person in I John 5:7. And, indeed, there was no compelling reason to take Jesus' own statements that he and the Father were one as signifying anything beyond moral and spiritual harmony. Clearly the foundations of good Lutheran faith had to be shored up by compelling proof, and once Bahrdt had begun looking for philological proof he had to go on, for his doubts had to be resolved. But, as is now readily understandable and as he was warned, especially by Crusius, the path of philology led only to further questioning, doubt, and finally disbelief.

It was a long time, however, before he finally came to the point of actually disbelieving his old articles of faith, and he continued to preach and write in the fiery orthodox vein which attracted the favorable attention of Pastor Götze. In this, of course, he was not perfectly honest, but it is not unusual—in fact, it is readily understandable—that a person who has undergone a change of belief will continue for a while to maintain the outward defense of positions which he has almost abandoned: Nietzsche, for example, continued to use his pen in behalf of Wagner for some time after he had inwardly broken with that "old sorcerer." What we can criticize in Bahrdt is not the fact but the excess and also the manner of his continued defense of orthodoxy.

Martin Crugot (1725–1790), who came of a respectable Huguenot family and had been appointed court preacher to the Prince of Schönaich-Carolath, wrote in 1758 a book of devotions entitled *Der Christ in der Einsamkeit,* unctuous and inoffensive in tone, which proved to be extraordinarily popular and immediately ran through several editions. But it was so mild and gentle and, it might be added, so influential among pious ladies that it attracted the unfavorable attention of the orthodox clergy. The pastor of the Nikolaikirche in Leipzig, Dr. Eichler, condemned it roundly, and Christoph Christian Sturm wrote an improvement entitled *Der wahre Christ in der Einsamkeit* (1761). Bahrdt apparently thought that he could turn this controversy to his own advantage and published a book which he entitled *Der wahre*

Christ in der Einsamkeit. Verbessert und mit etlichen neuen Abhandlungen vermehrt von M. C. F. Bahrdt (1763). Bahrdt "improved and augmented" Crugot's book by inserting omitted points of Lutheran doctrine at various appropriate intervals, sometimes expanding the original sentences, and sometimes composing whole new passages which were incorporated into the book. Although Bahrdt's publication was popular and sold well, it brought him reproof from various responsible persons, including Johann Caspar Lavater, the pious physiognomist of Zürich, who published anonymously *Zwei Briefe an Herr M. K. F. Bahrdt, betreffend seinen verbesserten Christen in der Einsamkeit* (1764). Bahrdt, of course, took up the challenge and wrote an anonymous satire addressed to himself: *Etwas an Herrn M. K. F. Bahrdt, seinen Verbesserten Christen in der Einsamkeit betreffend* (1764). All these maneuvers served to focus public attention on Bahrdt and to increase his reputation as a fiery traditionalist. In fact, it was the Crugot affair which brought Bahrdt the invitation from Pastor Götze to deliver a guest sermon in Hamburg.

But if, on the one hand, the Crugot affair helped to advance Bahrdt's career along orthodox lines, it may also be considered one of those incidents that helped to put him eventually outside the pale of comfortable orthodoxy. For he became identified in the public eye with the most intolerant of the orthodox, and this had certain indirect but far-reaching results. It can readily be supposed that Bahrdt would not have been seriously affected by, for instance, Moses Mendelssohn's exclamation of thankfulness that God was more merciful than Trescho, Ziegra, and Bahrdt, but ridicule cut deeper, perhaps the more so because of his growing suspicion that the faith which drew support for orthodox doctrine from the text of the Bible was in practice blind. Thus, when Klotz, whose facile mind Bahrdt admired, held him up to scorn in his journal, *Acta Litteraria,* as being an orthodox simpleton of the same stamp as Götze, Ziegra, and Friedrich Teller, Bahrdt writhed with humiliation and resolved that he must find incontrovertible and unquestionable biblical proof of orthodox doctrine. To this end in his *Laute Wünsche eines stummen Patrioten* (which Bahrdt says was written in 1767 but not published until

1769, when he was engaged in a bitter controversy with his colleagues at the University of Erfurt) he castigated the theologians for the wretched inadequacy of their proofs, and to correct this failing he urged the study of philology, the very subject which was bound to undermine the kind of proof he wanted.

Meanwhile, however, Bahrdt had been making good progress toward comfort, security, and eminence among the traditionalists. In 1766 he was appointed *Adjunkt* at St. Peter's and *Ausserordentlicher Professor* of religious (*geistlich*) philology at the University. The road was open to the highest offices, honors, and dignities of his profession. At this very time, however, Bahrdt committed an indiscretion which, although it did not produce in him an immediate radical change of doctrine, ejected him with ignominy from the fold of the true believers.

IV

∮ A CHANGE OF SCENE ∮

THE STORY OF THE downfall and disgrace that cost Bahrdt his
position and prospects in Leipzig begins quite innocuously
in his account of how,

in the year 1767, in the fall, there came a knock at my door, and upon my
"Come in!" there appeared a woman, quite respectable in appearance, who
asked for permission to speak with me privately.

The mere facts of the case are that Bahrdt became involved
with a prostitute who was to have a child, presumably Bahrdt's,
and who obtained his written promise to pay her a certain sum
of money. The affair became public, the promissory note was
undeniable evidence, and Bahrdt was compelled to give up his
posts in the church and on the theological faculty of the University.

According to Degenhardt Pott, who later was one of Bahrdt's
associates but broke with him and, while Bahrdt was in prison,
wrote a sensational biography,[1] Bahrdt had been a regular visitor
at the house of a Madam Godschevsky, the woman who knocked
at the door in Bahrdt's account quoted above. In fact, Pott affirms that Bahrdt continued to frequent the place even after he
had signed the note and that the note itself was taken from him
in Madam Godschevsky's house by a policeman, who informed
the authorities. Just why the note should have been confiscated
remains obscure. Bahrdt's version of the story, however, makes
much better use of the dramatic possibilities afforded by the
situation, especially the promissory note, and is designed to elicit
sighs of compassion for the inexperienced young man who stum-
bled just once and fell.

As Bahrdt tells the story, Madam Godschevsky came to press
claims of paternity against him on behalf of one of the women

whom she harbored. Bahrdt, however, professes that he had never
seen Madam Godschevsky before and was baffled by the whole
situation. Finally however, he recalled that during the preceding
summer, when he was returning to his home in the evening after
various social occasions, he had rather often seen a very nicely
dressed woman who seemed to be arranging these chance encounters. Eventually, he says, it occurred to him that she might have
taken a fancy to him, but, since she was obviously only middle-
class, considerations of social rank—for university people, it will
be remembered, constituted a kind of secondary aristocracy—prevented him from striking up an acquaintance. But then came one
fateful evening when he was returning home somewhat exhilarat-
ed by the consumption of excellent Rhine wine. This time the
woman brushed up against Bahrdt as she quickly walked past
him and said very respectfully, "Pardon me, Sir!" Bahrdt was so
unnerved by the encounter that he replied, quite involuntarily,
"Good evening." Thus one thing led to another and before
Bahrdt knew what he was about, he had escorted her to her abode
and made himself vulnerable to the charges which she was even
then plotting to bring against him.

For, as Bahrdt says he discovered later, the whole thing was
a plot of *Hofrat* Bel, his father's enemy. Carl Andreas Bel was
Professor of Poetry at the University, and it was one of his duties
to distinguish public occasions with Latin verse. This, however,
was beyond his powers, so he paid more talented people (for instance, his student and protégé, Klotz) to compose poems for him
to read in public as his own. The practice had not become as respectable as it is in modern times, and Bel was grievously offended
by an anonymous booklet which Bahrdt and Johann Friedrich
Teller [2] had published satirizing Bel and that "vainglorious idiot"
Gottsched. For this reason, so we are supposed to believe, Bel had
promised Madam Godschevsky ten *louis d'or* if she could lure
young Bahrdt into a trap. It was, therefore, to spring the trap in
which her victim now sat in perfect innocence and ignorance that
Madam Godschevsky knocked at Bahrdt's door and demanded
that he provide for the poor girl whom he had brought to such
a sad state. Bahrdt, ignorant, so he says, of the ways of the world

and too poor to make a cash payment that would have settled the thing quietly and decently, wanted only to have done with the whole affair and therefore signed that accursed promissory note. Madam Godschevsky, all smiles and friendliness, left in triumph, and Bahrdt dismissed the matter from his mind.

Tranquility had been restored to Bahrdt for only a few days, however, for very soon a student came to see him, not an innocent freshman, but one who had already spent many semesters at the University and was prepared to spend many more. This student had heard, presumably from unimpeachable sources, that Madam Godschevsky had outsmarted Professor Bahrdt and he was stirred by a fellow feeling. For this reason he had come to offer his services in the execution of a stratagem that would remove Bahrdt from the embarrassment in which he now found himself. The plan was for Bahrdt to invite Madam Godschevsky to a meeting place on the pretext of paying off the note. As soon as she had produced the note the student would come forth from hiding and tear it up, and Bahrdt would keep his money. The student assured Bahrdt that this plan would succeed because he, the student, knew positively that Bahrdt had not brought the misfortune of paternity upon himself as Madam Godschevsky pretended, and besides, he had so much incriminating information about the Godschevsky establishment that she would never dare to take action. Bahrdt gratefully accepted the plan of his would-be benefactor, but events took an unforeseen turn. The student did not abide by the plan but carried on the negotiations himself while Bahrdt remained concealed. Madam Godschevsky suspected a trap and refused to produce the note until she had the cash counted out before her. The student lost his temper, drew his sword, threatened her with it, then began to beat her, and finally took the note away by force. After all this Bahrdt felt that he had gained his point and once more dismissed the matter from his mind. But Madam Godschevsky, in her infamous way, created a public scandal, the situation could not be saved, and Bahrdt's career as a churchman and theologian in Leipzig was blasted. In his own words,

The lovely cedar had been felled, not by the mighty arm of some noble person but by a procuress and a drunkard.

Bahrdt follows the lengthy account of his downfall in his autobiography with some animadversions upon conventional morality.
How hypocritical, he exclaims, to say nothing about the countless
cases in which it is either certain or most likely that the sanctity of
wedlock has been violated because the violations have had no
visible outward consequences, and to set up a great hue and cry
of indignation if by chance visible outward consequences do occur.
How unjust are the laws which afford equal satisfaction to an
innocent young woman who has been wickedly seduced and to
a woman of the streets who urges unprovable claims against some
pillar of society who may perhaps have moved off his base just
once. What makes us smile at this moralizing is not the absurdity
of the principles, for they do, after all, have something to recommend them, but Bahrdt's bland assumption that the irregular
things that he himself did somehow or other did not count and
that he, that is, his real self was not actually involved. It was, of
course, the trait in him which his contemporaries quite naturally
denounced as *Leichtfertigkeit* (frivolousness). This was a permanent trait of character, but it would be a mistake to suppose,
as his contemporaries did and his biographers have done, that he
was completely unprincipled. As we will see, there were some
matters which Bahrdt felt with all his soul involved his real self
and his integrity. Unfortunately for his reputation, the matters
on which Bahrdt would not compromise his beliefs were matters
which, to the orthodox and the conventional, seemed only to constitute additional proof of his depravity.

The turn which events now took in Bahrdt's life, however, could
only confirm him in his frivolous attitudes, for what happened next
seemed to him to have been ordained by Providence for his benefit. And indeed, it was one of a number of occasions during his
life when he was unexpectedly rescued from a situation that had
become impossible.

This time it was Bahrdt's old enemy Klotz, who sent word that
he had been moved to sympathy by the story of Bahrdt's misfortune and that he was ready to help him, if he would only have
confidence in him.

I could not restrain my tears of joy [writes Bahrdt]. The speedy help of

Providence on the one hand and the unexpected magnanimity of my enemy on the other pierced my soul. . . . I immediately went to Halle, to Herr Klotz and stayed in his house for four weeks.

This kind of hospitality and generosity on the part of Klotz was not unusual, so we are informed by Carl Renatus Hausen, who was a friend and colleague of Klotz and the author of a biography[3] which is one of the main sources of our information about this rather puzzling figure. Klotz, whose extraordinary reputation and influence had brought him the very remunerative appointment from Frederick the Great as *Professor Ordinarius* of secular philosophy and eloquence with the title of *Geheimrat,* was able to entertain visiting scholars very graciously, and it was his pleasure to do so, thus rather munificently representing the University and increasing his coterie of friends and partisans, who sustained his reputation and increased his influence.

Klotz was at this time, although only thirty years old, at the height of his almost awesome fame and power. He had been born in Bahrdt's native city, Bischofswerda, in 1738, had had his schooling in Meissen, and then gone to the University of Leipzig under the protection of Carl Andreas Bel. Although he was far from persevering and thorough in his study, he had such quickness of perception, ease of assimilation, and fluency of expression that he dazzled his contemporaries, including such men as Lessing and Herder, into supposing that his attainments were more substantial than they actually were. Moreover, his peculiar kind of dilettantism was favored by the growing interest of scholars and philosophers in aesthetics as a branch of secular philosophy (which had been neglected by Christian Wolff) and in the aesthetic aspect of classical letters. In fact, it was the age when classical philology in the wide sense of being the study of Greek and Roman literature, art, archaeology, and civilization was established, culminating in the demand of the illustrious Friedrich August Wolf that the goal of the classical philologian be the complete knowledge of ancient humankind. This liberal and enlightened approach to classical philology had received an early impetus long before Klotz from Johann Mathias Gesner (1691–1761), professor of poetry and eloquence at the newly founded University of Göttingen, and especially, from Johann Friedrich Christ (1700–1756) at the University of Leipzig. Klotz was particularly indebted to Christ, whose attainments were not only those of an erudite professor and collector but also those of at least an amateur painter, etcher, and sculptor. In his concern with the aesthetic aspect of classical civilization Christ was a forerunner of Winckelmann, Lessing, Heinse, and Goethe, to mention only a few. To this man and to Winckelmann, Klotz owed a very great deal, for his whole striving, insofar as he can be said to have striven for anything beyond adulation, was directed toward informing classical studies with aesthetic appreciation. Indeed, while he was still teaching at Göttingen, before going to Halle, his lectures were officially listed as explaining the rules of good taste and criticism according to the models of Greek and Latin poets.[4] In this respect, of course, he paralleled that other Göttingen professor, Christian Gottlob Heyne, who perhaps did more than anyone except F. A. Wolf to incorporate matters of aesthetics and general civilization into the field of classical philology.[5]

It would be interesting to know just why Klotz offered to become Bahrdt's protector and friend. Hausen writes in his biographical sketch of Klotz that the two were reconciled in the year 1768 but that "the particulars of the reconciliation can be passed over in silence," and Bahrdt himself gives no details. Perhaps no further explanation is needed than Klotz's well-known practice of encouraging and helping talented younger people to make a start and find a foothold.[6] But this very practice seems to bear the mark of an inward uneasiness, of a rather effeminate and compulsive concern with the impression he made on others, just as does the petty spitefulness to which he was moved when he felt himself slighted. At the time of which we are writing he had just launched a new journal, *Die deutsche Bibliothek der schönen Wissenschaften*,[7] largely for the purpose of weakening the position of Nicolai's *Allgemeine deutsche Bibliothek*, which had unfavorably reviewed a collection of his Latin poems, and for the purpose of attacking Nicolai and his collaborators and friends, among whom was Gotthold Ephraim Lessing, who had offended Klotz by taking no notice of the latter's flattering review of Lessing's *Laokoon*.

By Easter 1768, Lessing, who had previously had a good opinion of Klotz and had respectfully differed with him on a minor point in the *Laokoon,* had decided that he would try to demolish his influence and reputation. The occasion was the publication of Klotz's *Über den Nutzen und Gebrauch der alten geschnittenen Steine* (Altenburg, 1768), an antiquarian causerie of little originality. Lessing made a comprehensive study of the subject of ancient cameos, not from the viewpoint of the appreciative amateur but from that of the specialist. In his *Briefe antiquarischen Inhalts,* the first part of which appeared at the end of September 1768, he revealed so much of what Klotz did not know about cameos, the technique of cutting the stones, the references made to them in the writings of antiquity, the history of their use through the Middle Ages and so on, that Klotz's professional reputation was completely and permanently ruined. As a result the name Klotz and *Klotzianismus* (coined by Lessing) have become epithets of opprobrium in the history of German literature.

But the blow that felled Klotz, although imminent, had not yet been struck at the time he extended a helping hand to Bahrdt, and we can readily imagine that time passed very pleasantly for the young reprobate during the four weeks in Halle. It seems not unlikely that Klotz expected that Bahrdt would aid him in his literary feuding by contributing to his journals. And Bahrdt was probably flattered and impressed by being in the center of the professional manipulations which were designed to provide him with a suitable position. For Klotz did go to work energetically and found an academic berth for Bahrdt at an institution where he had already been able to place his friends, Friedrich Justus Riedel and Johann Georg Meusel,[8] namely at the ancient and also decrepit University of Erfurt.

It is likely that not even so skilled a manipulator as Klotz could have secured positions for three friends on the philosophical faculty of one university within a period of less than two years, save for the fact that an attempt was being made to rehabilitate and reform the whole University and particularly the philosophical faculty. Everyone who knew anything about Erfurt and its University was convinced that something should be done: the population of the city had shrunk within its fortified walls to about 16,000, and the approximately one hundred fifty-eight students who chose to attend the University there did not have the best academic qualifications. Moreover, the University itself was governed to a great extent by antiquated traditions and a constitution that served largely to give the appearance of sanctity to selfish interests.

At the time of which we are speaking, Erfurt, although a mixed Catholic and Protestant city not far from Jena, was part of the domains of Emmerich Joseph, Archbishop of Mainz and Prince Elector of the Holy Roman Empire, and administered for him by his vicegerent Baron von Breidbach-Büresheim, a nephew of the Archbishop. Emmerich Joseph, who some four years previously had crowned Emperor Joseph II in the ceremonies which Goethe describes so vividly in the fifth book of *Dichtung und Wahrheit,* seems to have shared the Emperor's zeal for enlightenment and reform. But Emmerich Joseph's reforms in Erfurt, like those of Joseph II throughout the Empire, were impeded and thwarted by his system of government by remote control: Baron von Breidbach-Büresheim was more interested in keeping his cellars full of good wine than he was in the affairs of the University. In fact, he delegated full responsibility for the University to *Regierungsrat* Genau, who had neither the strength of character nor the perspective to be a wise administrator and to carry out the excellent intentions of the Elector. Moreover, the citizens of Erfurt were openly discontented with their government and even sought redress of grievances from the Empire.

The spark which set off the University reform program in which Bahrdt now became involved was the petition of a certain Christian Heinrich Vogel that the University, serving, as it did, an area with a substantial number of Protestants, have Protestant as well as Catholic professors of theology and that he, Vogel, be given the first Protestant appointment. The tolerant and enlightened Emmerich Joseph agreed. In fact, he appointed *two* Protestant theologians, Vogel and Johann Balthasar Schmidt. These men, far from reflecting the humane and liberal outlook of their sovereign, were strictly and militantly orthodox. They and Bahrdt later became the center of a violent conflict.

The Elector now directed his attention to the philosophical faculty, which was probably the branch of the University most in need of reform. Not, to be sure, in its own eyes, for it enjoyed a semi-independent status, had its own endowment, and the right to select its own members. Unfortunately, however, the endowment had shrunk so much that no one could afford to accept a professorship unless he had some other employment or source of income. Besides, since the faculty was a self-perpetuating body constituted from the citizenry of Erfurt, merit and scholarship were the qualifications most likely to be overlooked in the selection of a new professor. To remedy this situation it was resolved to appoint several new professors, but the Elector did not make use of his sovereign powers to give the University a new constitution which would have enabled his appointees to maintain themselves in the struggle that was bound to ensue. The Electoral Professors, also called *Professores Novae Fundationis* in distinction from the Faculty Professors or *Professores Antiquae Fundationis,* received good salaries, an arrangement that naturally aroused the resentment of the Faculty Professors, but they did not become regular, that is, voting members of the Academic Council, and had no voice in the internal government of the University or the granting of degrees. Moreover, it was of course contrary to the vested interests of the established professors to accept the appointment of a distinguished and able scholar. Thus, when it was proposed to extend a call to Professor Darjes, then at the University of Frankfurt an der Oder, Professor Nunn of the medical faculty at Erfurt, was able to prevent this appointment by pointing out that for the salary which Darjes expected, eight hundred *Reichstaler,* it would be possible to appoint three other instructors. As a result of Nunn's operations the appointment went to Klotz's friend Friedrich Justus Riedel.

Riedel, whose modest but promising attainments lay in the field of aesthetics, quickly became a great favorite with *Regierungsrat* Genau and through him, of the vicegerent, Baron von Breidbach. The traits that endeared him to these men were his conviviality, boisterous humor, and partiality to good wine. Thus Riedel came to be one of the most influential professors at the University and obtained an immunity from attacks made upon him for his riotous living and loose associates, both among the students and in a certain class of society in the city which was dominated by *Kammerrat* Bolmann and his wife. Bolmann had made a fortune in the Seven Years' War and had obtained the post of Counsellor of the Exchequer in Erfurt. He and the *Frau Kammerrat* prided themselves upon providing the most lavish and the most indelicate entertainment in Erfurt. Sumptuous repasts, conversation spiced with indecent jests, and daring dress (on occasion none at all) were the attractions that made the Bolmanns' home the talk of the town. This was the circle in which Riedel shone most brilliantly and into which he soon introduced Bahrdt by flinging open the door of the salon and crying out to the hostess and her guests, "Here you have the limb of Satan!"

V

{THINGS SOCIAL AND DOMESTIC}

F RAU BOLMANN greeted him with the exclamation, "Come,
liebes Bahrdtchen, we have been looking forward to seeing
you for a long time," and embraced and kissed him so that his
head swam. On this occasion, he says, he was so bewildered that
his attempt to meet the challenge failed. It did not take many
weeks, however, for him to acquire the kind of social graces that
could distinguish him in this society, and life went on very merrily
for some time among the notables of Erfurt, for it seems that almost everybody, including such people as Jordan Simon, the
Augustine Father who was one of the leaders of the conservative
faction in Erfurt, came to the Bolmanns' entertainments.

Perhaps one of the reasons that the Bolmanns were so popular
was that life was boring in Erfurt. Catholics and Protestants tended
to be reserved with each other and besides, there were no pleasant
parks and public places where people could meet informally. As
a place to live, Erfurt had only one thing to recommend it: it was
easy to find adequate housing there for little money. This was
very important to Bahrdt, for he had at first no salary at all and
when Genau obtained a salary for him it amounted only to one
hundred *Taler*. Therefore, in order to satisfy his needs and wants,
he had to seek to augment his income in various ways. Incidentally,
he was faced with this necessity all his life and compelled by it
not only to resort to doubtful journalism but also to undertake
speculative ventures of one sort or another, which frequently
ended in failure.

The project which he now undertook was probably suggested to
him by the very fact that he had comfortable quarters and good

kitchen facilities. It was, very simply, to set up a boardinghouse for his unmarried colleagues and friends. Since he himself was also unmarried at this time, the undertaking was viewed with disfavor by the sober citizens of Erfurt and has ever since been one of the things to which his biographers have pointed with indignation as being a flagrant violation of academic propriety. His paying guests, however, such as Meusel and the parsimonious Herel and others, seem to have fared pretty well at Bahrdt's table, for he was, as he says, an excellent chef. Before his lectures began he doled out to his cook the food that was to be prepared, gave her precise instructions as to cooking time, temperature, and so on, and when he returned after his lectures were over,

I donned an apron and did the important things, such as sautéing the vegetables and preparing the sauces myself, in order to have everything really tasty. To be sure, all three courses were delicious every time, but at the end of the year I was 250 *Taler* in debt.

Apparently something more radical had to be done to secure the creature comforts he desired, so Bahrdt decided that it would be a good thing to be married to a rich woman and he set out to find one.

At this point in his autobiography Bahrdt makes an observation about himself that deserves some attention, especially because it has been so vehemently denied. He remarks that it is strange that never in his life has he met a woman who was able to inspire a compelling passion in him.

That fiery, indestructible love which takes possession of the entire soul, such as the passionate love of infatuation is apt to be, I have never known. . . . I have never been really in love. And, of course, the reason is that I am not capable of any real passion. In anger as well as in joy, [but] certainly not in grief, I can mount to the limits of passion, but it is only for a moment. It's over in a flash. My soul is not in tune with prolonged, intense, and intoxicating feelings.

This assertion was often ridiculed by Bahrdt's enemies, especially his brother-in-law, who wrote a commentary on Bahrdt's autobiography.[1] But the question is whether Bahrdt was not right, after all, and whether he was not a true rationalist of a certain type, incapable of the ardent self-surrender which he rather wistfully felt sure was experienced by others. And it does seem that the way he set about getting married points to the rather simple assumption on his part that he could live in wedlock without being profoundly and vitally affected. To be sure, many people have thus lived in wedlock, but Bahrdt was to discover later that his inmost self really was so involved and affected that he was unable to entertain the thought of conciliation and compromise.

But at the age of twenty-eight he could feel that marriage was a rather impersonal arrangement of convenience and that he had only to make up a list of desirable properties (and property) and soon he would find somebody to fit it.[2] Several women were called to his attention and for each one he felt his ardor flame at the mention of the fortune that had been left by a deceased husband. But then, just as he was about to propose marriage, some defect would be revealed: the match looked ridiculous in the eyes of his friends, certain personal qualities were too unpleasant, or else the lady did not have a clear title to the money she had inherited.

But one day an acquaintance spoke to him of a beautiful widow, twenty-two years old, with a fortune of six thousand *Taler*. To be sure, she lived in Gotha, but this was only a slight obstacle to making a match, for after all, would not six thousand *Taler* invested at five per cent bring in three hundred *Taler* a year, or three times Bahrdt's salary? The prospect was too delightful, and Bahrdt resolved to drive to Mühlhausen to visit his former teacher Reinhold for a week. Since the road to Mühlhausen, where the lovely widow's family lived, passed through Gotha, what could be more natural than for Bahrdt to inform the widow Kühn that he had by chance learned that she had friends in Mühlhausen and to inquire respectfully whether she might wish to avail herself of this opportunity to make the trip in a private equipage? Frau Kühn accepted with alacrity and when Bahrdt called for her he saw that she really was young, blooming like a rose, had large blue eyes, delicate complexion, and a good figure. His mind was made up and within a few weeks their marriage was celebrated quietly and decorously in Erfurt.

The beginning was not auspicious, however. For one thing, during the first twenty-four hours, so Bahrdt tells us, he found himself, for some reason he could not understand, unable to enjoy the privileges and to fulfill the duties of a husband. For another thing, when he turned the conversation to the subject of the six thousand *Taler* he discovered them "in the negative." The late lamented Herr Kühn had left his widow only 3,333 *Taler* in the first place; moreover, the widow had lent her brother two thousand for the lease of an estate, but the brother had been a poor manager and lost everything. Frau Bahrdt had only her personal possessions and no more than eight hundred *Taler*, which, of course, barely sufficed to pay her new husband's old debts. In fact, at the end of the first six months it became necessary to sell the silverware to meet the bills.

Nonetheless, so Bahrdt says, the marriage could have been made fairly happy and agreeable because of his own sanguine temperament, if his wife had not had certain traits that were destined to estrange them more and more. She loved him, of course, even to the point of adoration. In fact, she loved him too much. As Bahrdt phrases it:

She had certain needs which were so powerful that she watched with the greatest attentiveness for anything which even remotely suggested that there might be a diminution of that which was so indispensable to the satisfaction of those needs and which she wished to be in no wise diminished.

Moreover, her predisposition to jealousy could only be strengthened by the questionable behavior of the society to which she was introduced. On the occasion of her first visit to the Bolmanns, for example, Mme Bolmann embraced and kissed Bahrdt with her customary fervor, while the *Herr Kammerrat* devoted himself to Frau Bahrdt, who was so plainly unnerved by the whole evening that Mme Bolmann found occasion to whisper to Bahrdt that he had made a stupid choice in marrying this hysterical woman.

Of course, Bahrdt's own shortcomings are revealed in almost every line he writes about his marriage, and yet it is probably true that in the early years he made some attempt to be agreeable to his wife and to find understanding and indulgence for her. He may even have loved her in a certain fashion, for his brother-in-law, Pastor Volland, writing in 1791, says that a great change had come over Bahrdt: whereas he had once been a loving and obliging husband, he had more recently become one of the lowest of men. Volland, of course, was offended by the immodest discussion in the autobiography of Bahrdt's marriage and the defamation, as Volland saw it, of his sister's character. Incidentally, Volland's book can only have done further injury to her character, for his method of defense and vindication is to reprint long sections of the autobiography which dealt with the marriage difficulties. Then, after quoting an injurious passage at length, he says merely, "This is, of course, not true, as everybody knows." Indeed, if we can judge Frau Bahrdt by her brother, we can readily believe that she was as stupid as her husband said she was, and her stupidity, according to him, was well nigh unendurable.

As examples of her stupidity Bahrdt cites her sense of humor and her sense of pride in her virtue. As for the first, he found it hard enough to control his irritation when she was vexed and reproached him for being unable to supply her with the means of satisfying her feminine vanity in dress, but things were much worse when she was in a cheerful and communicative mood. Her conversation was as devoid of entertainment as her jesting was of wit.

Her outbursts of merriment were restricted to five or six turns of phrase which she had brought along from Mühlhausen and in which one could find no sense, nor could one understand how they were appropriate to the situations in which she used them. Thus, for example, she could be heard to say daily on every occasion when she wished to describe something humorously, "Das ist Frikassee a la Brasch [fricasée a la brioche?]." She laughed heartily at herself every time and in a tone that pierced one's ears.

As for her sense of pride in her virtue, she took the word in its narrowest sense of female virtue, namely strict avoidance of any sign of extramarital tenderness. This would have been all well and good had she not felt that her undisputed possession of virtue in this sense gave her dispensation for cultivating any other amiable traits such as neatness or industriousness. In fact, her virtue made her angry with her husband, intolerant of others, and generally avoided by society. The upshot was that Bahrdt received invitations to produce himself at social gatherings without his wife, and he was not loth to accept them.

VI

⟨ STRUGGLE FOR POWER ⟩

A T FIRST THE university reform instituted by Emmerich Joseph
did not threaten seriously the position of the *Professores
antiquae fundationis*. To be sure, the appointment of Protestant
theologians was an innovation that must have excited some dismay
and wonder, but Schmidt and Vogel were, after all, neither outsiders nor innovators in any radical sense. Riedel, Meusel, and
Herel, of course, posed a different problem, even though they
were young and without reputation, for as has been said, Riedel
soon became a favorite of both Genau and Baron von Breidbach
and thus a power behind the throne. Bahrdt also strengthened the
radical party, for he also became a friend of Genau and besides,
he was a popular lecturer. Nonetheless, the position of the old professors was still fairly secure, for Andreas Nunn was *Rector
Magnificus* in 1768 and Father Jordan Simon, considered a marvel
of erudition, had lost none of his power. It was clear that if the
reform were to have a chance of succeeding, a really brilliant appointment had to be made. Such an appointment was not long in
coming.

At the very time that Bahrdt began his lectures in the fall of
1768, Emmerich Joseph, at the suggestion of Count Stadion, was
exploring the possibility of appointing to the post of *Professor
Primarius Philosophiae* an illustrious alumnus with an interna-
tional reputation as a poet and *bel esprit*, Christoph Martin Wieland. Wieland was at that time groaning under the burden of civic
affairs in his native town of Biberach and eager to find a more
congenial occupation. He had indeed hinted to Riedel, with whom
he carried on an active and cordial correspondence, that he would
be happy for an appointment to the University of Erfurt. Riedel,

who foresaw that Wieland would eclipse him at the University, undertook nothing on behalf of his friend until it seemed likely that the highest authorities would make the appointment. Then he did everything he could to secure the best possible conditions for Wieland, including a salary of six hundred *Taler*. Wieland arrived in Erfurt to take up his position on the first of June 1769.

Wieland and Bahrdt became key figures in the struggle which ensued, a struggle which the Elector had provoked by his program of reform, which was itself apparently a part of a larger design, namely to lessen the dependence of German Catholicism on Rome. Emmerich Joseph's "enlightenment," whatever else may be said of it, probably had its political aspects, a consideration which helps to explain why the foremost Catholic prelate of Germany so singularly favored a Protestant who wrote graceful and rather frivolous verse and was known to be something of a free thinker.

Bahrdt had already aroused the ire of the Protestant theologians of Erfurt by trespassing on their preserves. As Professor of Biblical Antiquities he was not authorized to lecture on theological subjects but this did not deter him from announcing in 1769 in his *Nachricht an das Publikum, meine akademischen Vorlesungen betreffend* that he would lecture on the following subjects: a dogmatic and moral system of religion, exegesis of the Old and New Testaments in the original languages, theory of criticism and philology of the Old and New Testaments, history of theological literature, church history, a practicum in homiletics and catechetics, pastoral theology, logic, metaphysics, physics, ethical philosophy, Hebrew, Syriac, and Arabic. Moreover, his lectures were not free of a certain heretical tinge. For example he had said that a good many theologians exaggerated the doctrine of original sin and painted far too black a picture of man's innate wickedness. And he had also said that the Symbolic Books[1] of the Lutheran church were both in error in some respects and also were too diffuse to be a convenient norm of faith. The indignant theologians sent spies to Bahrdt's lectures as Christian Wolff's colleagues at Halle had once sent spies to Wolff's lectures, in order to make notes of his heresies. The spies found enough material to enable Schmidt and Vogel to draw up a bill of particulars charging

Bahrdt with 150 errors in doctrine and requesting the ministry to dismiss him from his post (July 19, 1769).

Bahrdt was not slow to defend himself and decided to publish his lectures so that everyone could see whether his teachings were, in fact, as heterodox as Schmidt and Vogel said they were. He went to work on his *Versuch eines biblischen Systems der Dogmatik*, which appeared late in September 1769. He also presented his side of the case to the Elector and reinforced it by a petition to protect the innocent Dr. Bahrdt against the intrigues of his colleagues. This petition bore the names of Bahrdt's students but also, it was said, the names of students who had nothing to do either with Bahrdt or with Erfurt and even of students who had never existed anywhere. The defense and the petition, together with helpful reports by Genau and Breidbach, produced the desired effect: the Elector decreed in favor of Bahrdt, at the same time warning him to be more discreet, and severely admonished the Senate of the University not to pursue the matter further. The Senate, however, in order to justify itself, sent in the entire file of documents pertaining to the case. This produced an even more severe reproof and the imposition of a fine of one hundred *Taler* on the group. Bahrdt had momentarily triumphed over his enemies.

Meanwhile much the same thing had been happening to Wieland. His favored position and generous salary plus his status as an outsider had, quite understandably, roused the envy and resentment of the old guard. Andreas Nunn felt that his influence as former rector and friend of the vicegerent was being undermined, and Jordan Simon felt that the presence of Wieland, the enlightened Protestant and popular poet, greatly increased the attractiveness of the naturalistic religious philosophy which he, Simon, so earnestly detested. Nunn and Simon thus became the leaders of a faction which actively opposed Wieland and sought to discredit him. They too had their spies or, at least, friends among the students attending Wieland's lectures and were quick to seize upon reports of liberal or free-thinking sentiments in order to manufacture charges that would discredit Wieland in the eyes of the Elector.

Although Wieland was a cautious man he had spoken in his lectures about the consequences of ignorance and about the barbarousness of those people who were still deprived of the light of the sciences and of sound philosophy. He had asserted that such ignorance led to the crassest and most debasing kind of superstition and had gone so far as to cite in proof of this the practice of certain tribes to venerate the excrement of their Lama as a holy relic. Nunn and Jordan Simon interpreted this as a veiled attack upon Catholicism and made it the basis of their denunciation, an unbelievable charge, for, as Wieland wrote to Sophie La Roche, he could certainly not be so stupid as to blaspheme publicly against the religion of the sovereign who employed him.

The denunciation of Nunn and Simon was sent in to the Elector along with other complaints of the old guard against Wieland. Chief among these complaints was the charge of academic incompetence because Wieland did not have a proper university degree. Wieland, at this time about thirty-six years old, had taken up this matter in his correspondence with Riedel and confessed a reluctance to having himself examined by the faculty to which he was being appointed. Besides, Wieland had been created a *Comes Palatii Caesarei,* an honorary office of the Free Imperial City of Biberach which brought with it the privilege of conferring academic degrees. Wieland was therefore inclined to treat the matter of university degrees rather lightly and to feel that such outward signs and trappings could be dispensed with in his case.

In this respect also there was a striking parallel between Bahrdt and Wieland. Not only were they said by their enemies to be in favor of Enlightenment and thus dangerous to the established order but also that they were not formally qualified for their posts, and lack of such formal qualification, as is well known, can always be used as evidence of unfitness when all else fails. Bahrdt had not acquired a doctorate of theology and now that he came under attack in Erfurt realized that he would be well advised to make up for this omission, especially since he hoped that the story of his fall from grace in Leipzig would soon lapse into half oblivion and that he might receive a call to be pastor of a church in Erfurt.

So now the problem for Bahrdt was where to obtain the doctorate. Leipzig was out of the question because of that unfortunate episode; Wittenberg and Göttingen were impossible because Schmidt and Vogel had requested of these two faculties an opinion as to whether Bahrdt's teachings could be tolerated as conforming to strict belief; Halle was not a good place because the theologians there hated Bahrdt's friend Klotz; Giessen was dominated by Dr. Johann Hermann Benner, who was death on everyone who did not swear literal faith in every word and letter of the Symbolic Books; and the faculty of Jena seemed unfavorably disposed toward Bahrdt also. Then Bahrdt Senior remembered Dr. Kiesling in Erlangen "who needed money and was glad to accept it if he could come by it honestly." Kiesling proved to be ready to do his old friend, the elder Bahrdt, a favor which entailed a profitable business arrangement. Accordingly, the theological faculty of the University of Erlangen sent the younger Bahrdt a list of weighty questions on dogmatics, polemics, church history, and criticism which he was to answer in writing. He was also required to take an oath before a judge that he had received no help on the examination. He then made a public defense of his thesis and received from the faculty in Erlangen a large doctoral diploma,[2] which he showed to the Electoral administration and by this demonstrated that he was entitled to lecture on any theological subject whatever and was in every respect the equal of the regular professors. All this without leaving Erfurt!

This method of earning a degree could scarcely appease the *Consilium Academicum* of the University which had been collecting a number of grievances against the new professors. But, on the other hand, the government had apparently also been biding its time for signs of some serious internal conflict which would justify its taking drastic action against the recalcitrant and reactionary *Professores antiquae fundationis*. The time seemed ripe: there had been the trouble about Bahrdt, and now Wieland was openly attacked. Riedel was also denounced for being associated with Klotz in the publication of the satirical *Briefe scurrilischen Inhalts* which had offended the Erfurt professors. Accordingly Breidbach and Genau went to Steinheim to report on University matters to the Elector and his *Grosshofmeister* von Groschlag. Genau, Riedel's intimate friend, who was of a more resolute character than his superior von Breidbach, found the means of securing a private interview with Emmerich Joseph. As a result the *Consilium Academicum* was the recipient of an Electoral communication dated the twentieth of September, 1769, the so-called Steinheim Decree.

The terms of the decree must have brought consternation to the hearts of the reactionary party: Nunn, who had just finished a term as *Rector Magnificus* of the university and had also been *Bürgermeister* of the city, and Jordan Simon, the erudite cleric, were summarily dismissed from the university; the old guard were commanded to cease their agitation and intrigue against the new professors; Wieland and Riedel were appointed *Assessores Consily academici et facultatis phylosophicae extraordinarios cum sessione et voto;* and a limit of three days was set for payment of the fine which had been incurred in the Bahrdt affair.

Wieland was overjoyed and prophesied in a letter to Sophie La Roche that the University would be radically reformed and that he and Riedel would be placed at the head of it. In this respect at least, Wieland was a false prophet. After a few years the new professors vanished from the scene; Emmerich Joseph died, vexed and weary of the constant bickering. Subsequent attempts to breathe new life into the University also failed and it eventually (1816) gave up the ghost.

The Steinheim Decree had by no means tied the hands of the reactionary party, even though its leaders had been deprived of their official position. The attacks upon Wieland now (January 1770) took the form of legal action against one of Wieland's protégés among the students, a certain Heinrich Schwarz, who was accused of blasphemy. The story of Wieland's successful defense of Schwarz and of the persecution which Schwarz later endured does not belong here.[3] What concerns us is the effect of the experiences in Erfurt upon the shaping of Bahrdt's outlook and the hardening of his convictions, for the attacks made upon him chiefly by Schmidt and Vogel forced him to examine his assumptions and beliefs more closely and to make the choice whether to advance further along the road of Enlightenment or to retreat from it. And it must be remembered that he had as yet not made that choice, for he was still looking for philological support of Lutheran dogma and finding it, for example, in the argument that the Hebrew plural *Elohim* was proof of the Trinity.

Bahrdt says that he feels sure he would have remained faithful to orthodox belief all his life and employed his talents "to reinforce the crumbling structure and whitewash it with philological wisdom" if he had not had to endure such hostility from the theologians.[4] This is indeed at least conceivable, though Bahrdt is surely guilty of a certain one-sidedness when he goes on to say that orthodox belief makes its adherents delight in persecution, implying that there is no intolerance among people of his own liberal persuasion. At any rate, it was at this time, he says, that he felt the

first stirrings of hatred for priests and the religion of priests, which subsequently took root ever deeper and finally became the indestructible driving mechanism of all my active life.

To be sure, Bahrdt did nothing to appease and mollify his opponents. Instead, he was always ready to state his position explicitly and to ridicule anyone who might be so obtuse as not to agree with the voice of reason, that is, Bahrdt's own voice. Bahrdt had none of the caution of a Wieland, who could trim his sails to the wind. Bahrdt's reaction when accused of having lapsed from true belief was to draw up a statement of faith and publish it, regardless of consequences. As we have seen, he did this as soon as Schmidt and Vogel charged him with heresy and he was to do it again at a time when his position and his future were at stake; whatever else may be said against Bahrdt it cannot justly be said that he lacked courage. At the time of which we are writing, when Bahrdt was planning his *Versuch eines biblischen Systems der Dogmatik,* in which he took the same position on doctrine as Ernesti, the latter advised him not to publish. Bahrdt did not heed this counsel of prudence. He was convinced that the articles of faith had to be improved and corrected in certain respects if they were to be proof against the attacks of the skeptics and unbelievers, and he was further convinced that he was a really qualified defender of Divine Revelation.

When any interpretation of doctrine seemed questionable to

him he looked for support or lack of it in the Scriptures. Thus, he had come to feel that the accepted idea of original sin was exaggerated.

By the use of reason I had found that it was mad to consider God the Creator of mankind and at the same time ascribe to man an innate hostility to God and an ingrained inclination towards everything evil. Consequently, I later discovered that this exaggerated idea is not taught in the Bible. . . . I assumed the truth of the doctrine, took the innate corruption of man to be scriptural truth, derived it from the fall of man etc. Only my reason softened the idea and thus softened I discovered it in the Bible.

Thus, Bahrdt began to turn from dogmatic faith to scriptural faith, making the customary naïve assumption that the truth is "in the Book," to be discovered by any who will read correctly. For Bahrdt reading correctly meant discarding Luther's inadequate translation and going back to the original text. At this point, of course, as Bahrdt had begun to learn in Leipzig, philology poses its unsettling questions about authenticity of text, interpolations, alternate readings, multiple authorship, and so on. Furthermore, as Bahrdt learned later, the light of reason by which the truth of the Scriptures was to be illuminated, was not pure, single, and universal, but prejudiced, manifold, and limited, and he had really been deceiving himself.

For this is the way things are in the world. People always find in the Bible whatever their reason has recognized as true. For, of course, nobody will find anything unreasonable in the Bible, that is, anything which seems to his reason to be contrary to good sense. Consequently, everybody will explain the Bible according to reason, that is, in every passage he will become aware of such [i.e., reasonable, *vernünftig*] meaning, and will explain it reasonably, that is, in accord with the religious teachings which have been accepted as true by his reason.

It need scarcely be said that Bahrdt is not here using the term *Vernunft* in Kant's sense of the word, but the observations he makes on the rationalization of preconceived belief are shrewd and telling. It should be added, however, that Bahrdt never learned to view his current beliefs with the same detachment as he here looks back upon his Biblical system of doctrine.

In setting up his Biblical system, which also expressed reservations about certain other articles of belief such as the doctrines of three distinct Persons in one God, justification by faith alone, salvation and redemption, Bahrdt, of course, only fed the flames of his enemies' zeal to prove him guilty of heresy. Schmidt presented the case against Bahrdt to the theological faculties of Wittenberg and Göttingen, requesting an answer to two questions: First, did Bahrdt's system of doctrine not contain many teachings which manifestly deviate from the basic articles of faith of the Symbolic Books? Second, was it permissible for a minister of the church to expound such teaching publicly without offense to the church, and was he entitled to remain in office? The Wittenberg theologians declared Bahrdt to be guilty of various heresies and to have put himself beyond the pale of the Lutheran church even as a lay member. The response from Göttingen was not nearly so drastic. In fact, it said that Bahrdt's suggestions and criticisms affected only the form and not the substance of faith, but Schmidt hastened into print with his *Actenmässige Erzählung und Nachricht an das Publikum und abgenöthigte Vertheidigung wider Herrn Dr. und Prof. Bahrdt* (1770). Schmidt, however, instead of printing the full text of the Göttingen opinion, as the title of his publication implied he had done, printed only an excerpt out of context together with certain other unfavorable opinion.

Bahrdt wrote an energetic rebuttal, *Abgenöthigte Vertheidigung gegen ein unüberlegtes und widerrechtliches Responsum der Wittenberger Theologen* (1770), in which he abused the Wittenberg faculty as being composed of incompetent dunces. Interestingly enough, Bahrdt must have made a fairly good case, for the Wittenbergers received a reproof from their government for having made a public response to an unauthorized request, and they were forbidden to engage in further controversy with Dr. Bahrdt. Bahrdt was much more moderate in his discussion of the Göttingen response, the full text of which he had come by, despite Schmidt's opposition.

Meanwhile Bahrdt, who was something of a Till Eulenspiegel, had played a prank that threatened for a while to have serious consequences for him. It will be recalled that he had, or so he says, already written a book called *Laute Wünsche eines stummen Patrioten* but had not published it. In this book he attempted to defend the faith against its own adherents, that is, against the orthodox and their insistence upon literal belief in what seemed to Bahrdt to be manifest absurdities. This book he decided to modify a bit so that it would apply to the situation in Erfurt and ridicule Bahrdt's enemy Johann Balthasar Schmidt. To this end he had an engraving[5] made for the title page of the book showing a clergyman before whom a crowd of people were kneeling in open-mouthed awe of his supposed wisdom. This was intended to represent Schmidt and the congregation which admired the nonsense he preached. Bahrdt did not dare, however, to have this figure depicted wearing the regular clergyman's ruff, but "disguised" him by giving him a bishop's mitre. The clue to what was meant was supplied by the inscription II Timothy 4:14-18: *Alexander der Schmidt hat mir viel Böses getan: Gott vergelte ihm nach seinen Werken.*[6] To Bahrdt's dismay the disguise was too good and the reading public interpreted the picture to be directed against the Archbishop-Elector, Emmerich Joseph. Bahrdt was summoned before a board of inquiry, had to admit that he was satirizing Schmidt, cited the Bible verses to prove his contention, and was let off with a fine. Thus he emerged from this fray somewhat poorer but, as we will see, no wiser.

During all this time Bahrdt had been busy with various professional and scholarly or semischolarly publications, not only out of pure dedication to learning but with an eye on augmenting his income. He put out a reasonably priced pocket edition of Origen's *Hexapla*[7] into which he incorporated variants and fragments which he had discovered in a manuscript of the Septuagint in Leipzig. This work, although it was based upon the edition of Montfaucon and therefore had no claim to originality, won the approval of such scholars as Kennecot and Semler. Bahrdt himself was disappointed in it, for it netted him only eighty *Taler*. A work of Old Testament exegesis failed in every respect; Bahrdt did not have the philological training required for this effort. The *Versuch eines biblischen Systems der Dogmatik,* which has already been mentioned, was more successful, however, and was favorably received by Ernesti.[8] But his hastily written *System der Moraltheologie,*[9] which was based on a collection of his father's sermons, brought him only scanty reward and recognition.

None of these publications was comparable in scope and significance to a project that was suggested to his ingenious mind by his controversy with Schmidt and Vogel and their accusations of heresy. It had become plain to him from all the conflicting opinions as to his orthodoxy that no judgment of heresy could be generally accepted until all the theologians had reached an explicit agreement as to what were essential truths of religion and what were still controversial matters of theology. As we will see later, this distinction is much like the distinction made by Semler between personal religious feeling and the conceptual or theological formulation of religious belief. Bahrdt, with his practical bent, wanted to have the whole matter codified. Moreover, he made a proposal that was as simple as it was audacious: he invited the most distinguished theologians to engage in a published correspondence with him and with each other in order to reach a consensus. Bahrdt, of course, was to be the editor, and the basis of the discussion would be his own system of doctrine and of ethics. Bahrdt would be the indispensable heart and brain of this extraordinarily important venture. He would, in fact, institute a new Reformation with himself as the Reformer, and he would not have to pay his correspondents for their contributions. Two volumes were published under the title *Briefe über die systematische Theologie zur Beförderung der Toleranz*,[10] but after a year and a half the venture collapsed. Established scholars had no interest in contributing to the glory of a questionable upstart.

While Bahrdt was thus struggling, with indifferent success, to maintain tranquility at home, increase his reputation abroad, fend off the attacks of his enemies, and earn enough money to make both ends meet, the forces of reaction, which had received a severe blow in the Steinheim Decree, had been recovering strength and renewed their efforts to discredit the new professors and undermine their position. The indictment of Heinrich Schwarz for heresy, as has been mentioned, was actually a blow struck at Wieland, about whom many harmful rumors were launched, and by the fall of 1770 there were various indications that the reform of the University was endangered. In October Baron von Breidbach fell ill, an event that precipitated a tragicomic struggle for power behind the scenes, for Breidbach engaged as his physician none other than Andreas Nunn, who had so recently been dismissed from the medical faculty. Nunn began to suggest to Breidbach that his illness was divine retribution for Breidbach's support of the godless new professors. The city was in a turmoil; Breidbach seemed ready to undo everything that had been accomplished; Wieland was close to despair. To counter the influence of Nunn he and Genau prevailed upon Emmerich Joseph to send a more "enlightened" physician, Wieland's friend Dr. Arand, from Mainz to devote himself to the care of the vicegerent. This bit of strategy seems to have had the desired effect, but Wieland and his party did not breathe easily again until Breidbach died in December.

Bahrdt, however, was able to regard the renewed struggle for power with a certain sense of detachment. In the very month when Breidbach fell ill, on the twenty-seventh of October 1770, to be exact, Professor Bechtold of the University of Giessen wrote a letter to Bahrdt that caused hot tears of gratitude for the intervention of Providence to course down his cheeks. Bechtold's letter was an inquiry as to whether Bahrdt would be interested in accepting a professorship of theology at the University of Giessen.

VII

┌THE ENLIGHTENMENT COMES┐
└ TO GIESSEN   ┘

G RADUALLY, and over a period of some years, that habit of mind and scholarly inquiry which called itself "enlightened" had been exhibited by a growing number of professors at the German universities. Everywhere, to be sure, they had to contend with the established authority of orthodox and pietistic theologians, and many of them, like Ernesti, shut their eyes to the necessary consequences of their fundamental position. But their number was increasing, and by 1770 there were not many universities where students would be in no danger of being exposed to "enlightened" views. Even Erfurt, which had been stagnating for so long, had been stirred up by Emmerich Joseph's reform professors, especially Bahrdt. But one stronghold remained where orthodoxy had only temporarily receded before a wave of Pietism and returned with renewed force. This stronghold was the University of Giessen.

The city of Giessen belonged to the Landgravate of Hessen-Darmstadt, which was ruled until 1768 by Landgrave Ludwig VIII. Ludwig had fallen under the influence of Pietism, especially as represented by one Christoph Matthäus Pfaff, for whose intellectual and moral gifts Ludwig had a deep and abiding admiration. In 1756 Pfaff was made Chancellor of the University, despite the indignation of the professors, who, far from sharing Ludwig's admiration, considered him an intriguer and a hypocrite. Their opposition was fruitless, however, for the Landgrave had given him great powers to effect a reform. Orthodoxy was thus eclipsed, but only temporarily, for the old professors were not dismissed but merely unable to veto new appointments and guide University policy.

Johann Hermann Benner was the most important and most influential member of the orthodox party. He had been born in 1699, the son of a poor baker. He was gifted and erudite—even Bahrdt calls him *ein wahres Genie, ein guter Lateiner*—but undoubtedly narrow and inflexible, a man whose entire life had been lived in Giessen, where he had gradually attained to all the dignity and eminence which his profession could bring him in the Landgravate of Hessen-Darmstadt. He had also amassed a considerable fortune: his estate amounted to nearly 100,000 *Gulden*. He had been appointed to the theological faculty in 1735, was known to everybody in Giessen, and was respected by countless ministers and learned theologians who had received their training under him. Whether he was also as calculating and hypocritical as Bahrdt says he was is doubtful, but if Bahrdt can be believed, Benner always arranged to be out promenading in the streets of Giessen when the prayer bell rang. At the first stroke of the bell he would be galvanized into immobility, devoutly cover his face with his hat, and give at least four minutes to prayer wherever he happened to be standing.[1] However this may be, there seems to be no doubt that Benner's vast influence formed a bulwark of defense against the tide of liberalism and enlightenment. Upon his death in 1782 a member of the faculty of law, Professor Gatzert, who later became minister of state, wrote triumphantly to correspondents in Darmstadt, "Der grosse Pan ist tot!"

It was the relatively insignificant Johann Georg Bechtold (1732–1805) who did more than anyone else to counter Benner's influence, not by opposing him but by arranging for the appointment of Dr. Bahrdt.[2] Bechtold became a great favorite of Chancellor Pfaff, who saw to it that Bechtold received speedy advancement despite the opposition of the older professors, who had only contempt for Bechtold's attainments. In 1759 Bechtold was advanced to the rank of *Ausserordentlicher Professor* on the philosophical faculty, and in May 1760, he became Pfaff's administrative assistant in charge of stipendia and grants-in-aid. Even Pfaff's death in November 1760 did not impede Bechtold's advance: Ludwig VIII, devoted to the memory of the deceased chancellor and wishing to carry out his intentions, overruled the faculty on every point and gave him a succession of new appointments, culminating in the junior or fourth regular professorship of theology in 1765. Bechtold now had a solid base on which to rear the structure of his ambitions ever higher. He had always been cautious and careful to catch a favorable wind from whatever quarter it might be blowing; as long as Pfaff lived he was devoutly pietistical and after Pfaff's death his writings took on a more orthodox cast in deference to his colleagues on the theological faculty. Meanwhile his true private belief seems to have been of the "enlightened" variety.

The year 1768 was a year of upheavals for the University of Giessen. The first and third theological professorships fell vacant through death. It was inevitable that Benner, who had held the second chair, would be advanced to the first, but it was not at all inevitable that Bechtold would be advanced as well, for death had taken Landgrave Ludwig VIII also, and his successor, Ludwig IX, was a man of different stamp altogether, who professed a sense of loathing for hypocrites, bigots, and whited sepulchers.

Bechtold repressed his ambitions for a while and allowed events to take their course—a wise proceeding, for his opportunity was not overlong in coming, although it arrived by a devious route. At first the University made a proposal to reduce the number of the theological faculty from four to three. This would save money, reward a deserving professor of oriental languages by giving him the second place, and keep Bechtold on the lowest rung of the ladder while nominally advancing him to third place. This suggestion was not accepted by the new Curator of the University (the title of the responsible government administrator seems to have varied), Andreas Peter von Hesse, who informed the University that the appointment of professors to the first and second positions was the sole prerogative of *Serenissimus* the Landgrave. Furthermore the government felt that it was incompatible with the glory of the University to have only three professorships of theology. Therefore the University was asked to suggest a candidate for the third position only, for Bechtold was to be left in the fourth. The University complied with these instructions and proposed that Professor Nösselt in Halle be sounded out as to his readiness to accept the third position. On the twenty-eighth of September 1770, the Landgrave gave his formal approval, and Bechtold's enemies rejoiced that a stop had apparently been put to his further advancement.

Bechtold, however, decided that the time had come for him to take action, made the trip to Darmstadt, where he spoke with influential friends in government circles and was consulted by the Privy Council as to how the vacancies on the theological faculty at Giessen should be filled. As the result, on the twelfth of October, *Serenissimus* issued a new decree revoking the decisions he had published only two weeks before and commanding that Bechtold be advanced to the third professorship, Nösselt be asked whether he would be ready to accept the second, and Bahrdt be sounded out as to the fourth. More than this, Bechtold had suggested who might be considered as a candidate for the Professorship of Eloquence, which he had also held but which he would now relinquish. His list of candidates consisted of Wieland, Riedel, and a certain Schmitt, who was also a reform professor at Erfurt. It therefore seems evident that Bechtold, the erstwhile Pietist turned orthodox, had become a kind of Trojan Horse of the Enlightenment.

Benner, of course, sprang into action and petitioned the Rector of the University and the Landgrave to undo the threatened mischief, and the Landgrave so far acceded as to enjoin the University to prepare a formal opinion on Bahrdt's orthodoxy. The professors set about this task with the customary academic dilatoriness, so that weeks passed, during which Bechtold and von Hesse, whom Bechtold had convinced of Bahrdt's suitability, were able to bolster their cause impressively.

Since all the objections to Bahrdt's appointment were based on the charge of heresy,[3] it was plain that these objections would have to be refuted by the voice of some recognized authority. As has been mentioned, Ernesti had favorably reviewed Bahrdt's *System der Dogmatik,* and therefore Bechtold suggested that the government officially request Ernesti to prepare an opinion as to Bahrdt's orthodoxy. This was done, so that when the University report was finally sent in with all the professors except Bechtold voting against Bahrdt, Hesse was able to counter that they had in fact, as Benner officially recorded,[4] acted under the influence of Benner, whose opinion could not be considered impartial, for Ernesti had declared that he did not consider Bahrdt to be heretical and unfit to occupy a professorship of theology. Although, Ernesti went on to say, he could not consider Bahrdt to be correct on every point, the questionable matters were either minor or expressed carelessly, and this was an inexactness that could be excused in an enthusiastic young man, especially since he wrote in German, a language lacking in dogmatic precision. But Hesse had been dealt another trump card, namely favorable opinion by the illustrious Johann Salomo Semler, and that had come about in this way. When Nösselt had refused the second professorship, the Privy Council had asked Michaelis in Göttingen, Ernesti in Leipzig, and Semler in Halle to make suggestions. Semler had proposed two names and then written:

I do not hesitate to make special mention of Dr. Barth [sic] in Erfurt also. He came to see me last summer and despite a good many tales which have been picked up from Leipzig, I am actually trying to get him to our country. His mode of thinking is very good, without timidity, his discernment already great, and his outward bearing very agreeable.

Armed with these two documents the Privy Council advised Ludwig IX that there could be no reason to hold the decree appointing Bahrdt to the fourth position in suspension any longer. The University was therefore overruled and Bechtold had the pleasure of informing Bahrdt that the campaign had been won.

Bahrdt's pleasure at being called away from Erfurt was probably no greater than the delight of Schmidt and Vogel at his leaving. At least one person was dismayed, however, that the cause of enlightenment and reform had been dealt such a severe blow, and that man was Christoph Martin Wieland. Since it has become almost obligatory among scholars who have occasion to mention Bahrdt to deny that he had any positive qualities whatever, Wieland's opinion, which he expressed in a forceful letter to the Academic Council of Erfurt, is especially interesting and sufficiently important to warrant some discussion here.

To be sure the name of Wieland is not by itself a sufficient guarantee of sound and impartial judgment, but evidence exists which compels us to acknowledge the competence and objectivity of his judgment of conditions at the University of Erfurt. This evidence is in the form of a long letter[5] to Dalberg, who succeeded Breidbach as vicegerent of Erfurt. This letter was written in 1778 in reply to an inquiry by Dalberg whether Wieland could not be persuaded to leave Weimar and return to Erfurt as director of the University. Wieland refused, but he very thoroughly discussed the entire situation in Erfurt, and made sound and incisive suggestions for an effective reform, together with shrewd characterizations of the professors. The points that interest us most can be summed up very briefly. The basic condition for reform, says Wieland, is the radical revision of the constitution and administrative apparatus. Then, generous funds should be appropriated for stipends to attract good students and to offset the drawing power of the neighboring universities. Moreover, all the professors should be paid proper salaries so that they would have no reason to regard their academic duties as secondary. Of course, excellent professors must be brought in who will enhance the reputation of the University and effect the desired reform, but they must be established scholars who will be able to devote themselves to the welfare of the University because they have no need of making a name for themselves. Moreover, the new appointees should not receive extraordinarily generous salaries and conditions of tenure, which can only arouse the envy and excite the bitter opposition of the older professors.

It is therefore of considerable significance when Wieland writes to the Academic Council on the eighteenth of April 1771:

Dr. Bahrdt is a man of excellent and unusual talents, a famous and popular writer and a splendid teacher.[6]

Wieland then goes on to say that various eminent theologians consider Bahrdt to be no heretic, and that the accusation has been made against him in Erfurt by orthodox blockheads and peevish heretic hunters, whose presence at the University is positively harmful. The machinations and denunciations of Schmidt and Vogel have injured the glory of the University and are now about to deprive it of Bahrdt's services.

People who injure the University as much by the malice of their will as by the stupidity of their brain should be cut off from the University, if men who do us honor are to remain and be encouraged to devote their talents to its advancement.

Wieland also suggests that possibly Bahrdt can still be induced to remain and gives it as his opinion that a salary of three to four hundred *Taler* would not be too high a price to pay.

The price was not paid, however, and therefore Bahrdt was not tempted to refuse the offer from Giessen, which included the pastorate of St. Pankratius. He sold all his goods at auction, took his wife with him to Leipzig, where his mother would be able to be helpful in the birth of their first child, and after six weeks set off for his new post in a city where Bechtold was his only friend, and the inhabitants, including his future parishioners, shuddered at the thought of his heresy.

The shudders, however, were soon transformed into thrills of admiration, for Bahrdt realized from his conversations with Bechtold that he would not be able to maintain himself in the hostile atmosphere of Giessen unless he could win people over to his side. Therefore it was extraordinarily important that Bahrdt's inaugural sermon not only give no offense but that it make a good impression. Accordingly, Bahrdt prepared a pious sermon "à la Lavater," as he says, in which the name of Jesus was often called upon to give unctuousness to an exposition of major uncontroversial matters of doctrine.

When Bahrdt appeared in the pulpit to deliver this sermon, his church was crowded beyond capacity. People had come from outlying villages to hear the notorious heretic and were forced to stand on the street, straining to catch his words.

When I began my prayer in a slow and solemn voice, [he writes] and exalted devoutness shone in my eyes and was audible in my quivering voice, a silence came over the crowded multitude, an attentiveness and immobility, as though everyone had turned to stone. None shifted his position, none cleared his throat, none took his eyes off me. Many even shed a tear . . . thus, by a single sermon the whole congregation was stirred up and won over. . . . Only a few hours before, my name had been a stench in everyone's nostrils . . . and now I would not have advised anyone to speak a word against me on that day: the populace would have stoned him.

VIII

╎LIFE IN A LANDGRAVATE╎

THE LANDGRAVATE of Hessen-Darmstadt boasted three important cities: Giessen, the seat of the University, Darmstadt, the
seat of government, and Pirmasens, the seat of *Serenissimus* the
Landgrave.

None of these places was impressive as an urban center. Indeed,
Friedrich Nicolai, in his *Beschreibung einer Reise durch
Deutschland und die Schweiz*, has little more to say about
Darmstadt, the capital, than that drums were beaten every two
hours, an observation which, however, was certainly less than just
to the very lively intellectual and emotional life of certain circles
in Darmstadt at the very time of which we are speaking. For
Darmstadt was the residence of Karoline, the Great Landgravine of
Goethe's remarkable friend, Johann Heinrich Merck, and of a
circle of sentimental literary enthusiasts, for whom the Landgravine caused the first collection of Klopstock's odes and elegies to
be published and who are still remembered for their connection
with Herder and Goethe.

All the emotional and literary ferment of Darmstadt seems, quite
naturally, to have made no impression upon Dr. Bahrdt, who
found life in Giessen absorbing enough. Looking back upon the
years in Giessen he realized that they were probably the most
pleasant and comfortable years of his life despite the fact that
the city itself was small and possessed very few, not more than a
dozen, comfortable modern houses. The streets and alleys were
narrow and crooked and the city was surrounded by a wall which
towered above the houses and cut off the circulation of air from

62

the great manure piles which lay just outside many a front door. Bahrdt makes the observation that the walls should have been razed and transformed into gardens so that the whole town might have had air and sunshine! But in spite of these disadvantages, Bahrdt says, Giessen was a good place to live, because it was not expensive: his salary, together with income from his books and certain perquisites of office such as vegetables and firewood, enabled him to maintain a household which consisted of himself and his wife, three children, a nursery maid, a cook, a coachman, two horses, and a carriage. The horses and carriage attracted considerable attention and provoked much criticism of Bahrdt's luxurious and extravagant mode of life, criticism which probably did not affect him very much when he found that he had fifty *Gulden* to spare every year and reflected upon the wealth that his colleague and enemy Benner had amassed.

Perhaps this prosperity was due to the fact that the University had a good endowment which was controlled by the nineteen professors themselves, with the help of an administrative secretary. *Serenissimus* the Landgrave, who had the power of appointment and dismissal, might have wanted to divert some of the funds to his soldiers, but he was not allowed to do so by the constitution of the University, a very fortunate provision, because the students, some two hundred in number, were mostly penniless native sons. For this reason most of the lectures were free: any professor who insisted upon collecting the tuition that was his due would have found himself lecturing to empty seats. Although Bahrdt followed custom in this respect, his lectures were not very popular, probably because the students realized the necessity of having the support of Professor Benner if they were to prosper professionally.

The poverty of the students did not, however, prevent them from spending much time in various taverns, consuming vast quantities of beer. The practical necessity of securing the preparation and backing required to obtain the various ecclesiastical posts to which they aspired did not prevent them from passing much, if not most, of their time in riotous amusements of one kind or another, for student life in Giessen was modelled upon student

life in Jena, which had the reputation of being the veriest den of
dissoluteness.

A very vivid and, in the perspective of history, amusing account
of student activities in the Giessen of Bahrdt's day can be found
in the autobiography of F. C. Laukhard (1758–1822?), an unprincipled adventurer with considerable journalistic talent, whose
path occasionally crossed Bahrdt's.[1] From Laukhard we can learn
a good deal about the intellectual and moral level of the students
to whom Bahrdt sought to bring the light of reason. For example,
one of the *Burschenschaften* carried on a regular feud with a poor
citizen named Euler. Euler had once aspired to an ecclesiastical
career but had fallen by the wayside because of a liaison with his
father's maidservant who had borne him a child. Disappointed in
his ambitions, he had settled for a position as a teacher in a local
girls' school and augmented his meager salary by performing
various unimportant church duties. According to Laukhard he
was pitiable and ridiculous in appearance and the natural butt
of student humor. The feud had begun when a student who lived
across the alley from Euler noticed that he had left his apartment
with a window open. The student had a brilliant idea: he procured
a long pole, by means of which he was able to empty his chamber
pot in Euler's room. Euler, quite naturally, complained to the
University authorities, with the only result that the entire fraternity to which the student belonged resolved to persecute Euler.
The campaign of persecution was simple: every fraternity member was bound to go once a week to Euler's house, strike his sword
on the pavement, and cry out "Pereat!," the regular procedure
of issuing a challenge to a duel. Since there was no hope that
Euler would accept the challenge the students also looked for
opportunities to throw stones and break Euler's windows. Whenever Euler had proof of a culprit's identity he would complain
to the Rector of the University, with the result that the student
had to pay for the window and spend a day or two in the University jail, but he also had the satisfaction of knowing that the
Rector was really rather amused by the whole business.

This sort of thing went on for years and constituted only a
small part of similar academic diversions that gave a tone of

extreme coarseness to the University. It is therefore not too difficult to believe that Bahrdt may very well have sought to tickle the prevailing sense of humor by vulgar antics in his lectures. Thus, it is reported that, in order to vex Benner, he gave a course on ethics, using Benner's book as a text. On one occasion he is reported to have said,

The author, for whom (and here he cleared his throat and spat audibly) I have the greatest respect, is in error on this point.

This kind of behavior was, of course, not calculated to appease the hostile orthodox camp.

This camp, as Bahrdt well knew, was very powerful, so powerful that one wonders how Bahrdt was able to be as foolhardy in displaying his contempt for them as he seems to have been. Benner alone was a redoubtable enemy but his strength was multiplied many times over by the large number of clerics who owed their livelihood to him or hoped to attain a position with his aid. And, of course, there were a good many other professors of the University who were actively opposed to Bahrdt. Thus, if Bahrdt's audacity had any foundation other than his unthinking belief in himself and his good fortune, it may have been the assumption that he enjoyed the favor and protection of more powerful forces than those that were mustered against him.

For this assumption there were good grounds. One of his very best friends was the Chancellor[2] of the University, a professor of law named Koch, and another was the Curator, Hesse, who has already been mentioned. Hesse's early good opinion of Bahrdt had been further strengthened by Wieland, who visited Giessen in May 1771, shortly after Bahrdt had sworn to his faith in the Symbolic Books. Wieland had been fervent in his praise of Bahrdt and informed Hesse that Erfurt would be glad to take him back if he should not find the situation in Giessen to his liking. Hesse made special mention of this in a report to *Serenissimus,* who liked what he heard and remained well disposed towards Bahrdt during most of Bahrdt's tenure of office. Bahrdt must have known this but in his autobiography he passes over the Landgrave's support rather lightly and instead makes much of the friendship and protection of the Great Landgravine.

My greatest support [he writes in his autobiography] was the Great Landgravine of Hessen-Darmstadt, whom Frederick the Great himself admired
and acknowledged to be one of the wisest and most excellent of her sex.
She lived separated from her weak spouse and magnanimously tolerated
his mistresses. . . . This lady was my warmest friend. I still treasure the
letters which she wrote me as something sacred.[3] As long as she lived and
maintained her influence no persecution could harm me and no calumny
find an ear at court. And never, never would I have left Giessen if she had
not so soon departed this life and if the chameleonlike Moser had not assumed control.

In this passage it seems fairly obvious that Bahrdt wishes to
make the most of his relations with Karoline, whom Frederick
the Great considered one of the four most remarkable women of
the time, the other three being the Electress Antonie of Saxony,
Maria Theresa, and Catherine the Great. Indeed, upon the death
of the Landgravine, Frederick dedicated to her memory an urn
inscribed with her name, the dates of her birth and death, and the
Latin motto "Femina sexu, ingenio vir." Bahrdt undoubtedly
hoped that some of the great esteem in which Karoline was so
generally held would redound to his credit and so it is very probable that he is here exaggerating her interest in him and minimiz-
ing the support and protection of the Landgrave, for the general
opinion of Landgrave Ludwig IX was rather dubious and, insofar
as he is not completely forgotten, has remained so to the present
day. However this may be, Bahrdt is perfectly correct in attributing his downfall to Moser, and he may have had some, but probably very incomplete and distorted, awareness of the interplay
of forces and interests in the highest circles of the petty monarchy
in which he lived. Since the tensions among these forces, as they
affected Bahrdt, were resolved in a way that had a decisive effect
upon his career and outlook, it can be said that the spread of religious enlightenment in Germany was influenced in some degree
by the personalities of Ludwig, Karoline, and Moser.

The interplay of these three personalities is extremely interesting in and of itself and deserves to be more fully explored
than it has been hitherto. The easy, traditional appraisal of them
exalts Karoline and Moser at the expense of Ludwig, who is apt
to be dismissed as a childish nonentity who often thwarted the

noble designs of his consort and prime minister. That he often did thwart their designs is undeniable, as it is undeniable that his ruling passion overrode all other considerations and made him a noteworthy eccentric in an age of eccentric monarchs. But the question will remain whether the Great Landgravine herself must not bear some, perhaps a good deal, of the blame for the confirmation and hardening of the grotesque aspects of his personality.

The eighteen-year-old heir to the domains of Hessen-Darmstadt and Hanau-Lichtenberg who paid court to the young daughter of the Dowager Duchess of Zweibrücken seems to have been an attractive, simple youth who combined an exaggerated sense of his own importance with a capacity and need for affection and friendship. There is no mistaking the tone of wonder and wholehearted love in his diary entries from the years of courtship and early marriage. Nor is there any mistaking the tone of frosty irony in Karoline's replies to his ardent letters.[4] It was apparently not within the power of the elegant, subtle, and cultivated princess, who cherished a strong attachment to her mother, to open her heart to the naïve and somewhat crude, but far from stupid young man who needed her so desperately. It may even have been, at least partially, to solace his growing sense of disappointment that Ludwig established his famous military colony in Pirmasens, and it surely suited Karoline to restrict her relations with Ludwig to the distant politeness of letters exchanged between Pirmasens and her own residences in Buchsweiler and Darmstadt. On rare occasions the obligations of her status required of her a visit to Pirmasens. How repugnant this necessity was to her can be learned from a letter to her dear friend, Princess Amalie of Prussia:

Ma santé est très passable, je commence à prendre l'air après un mois du prison; vous ai-je dit, Madame, que l'on prétend, que je suis grosse? Mais je ne puis le croire. Si je le suis, les femmes ne sont que des automates, des machines; je n'ose entrer dans d'autres détails vis-à-vis de votre Altesse.[5]

Ludwig's attachment to Pirmasens and his soldiers grew to fantastic proportions and caused the town itself to grow from an insignificant village of thirty-eight houses to a city whose population of eight thousand rivalled the nine thousand of Darmstadt, the

capital, which Ludwig almost never visited. Because he refused
to leave his personal capital, all affairs of state that required
Ludwig's attention had to be transacted by means of couriers. Not
even when his father suddenly died did Ludwig come to Darmstadt. He remained in Pirmasens and informed Karoline, who had
taken up residence in Darmstadt a few years before, of his will by
letter. It seems possible that this behavior was dictated by a mor-
bid fear of the capital, for the castle there was haunted and Ludwig
was a ghost-seer.[6] Karoline, of course, treated this idiosyncrasy of
her husband with mock seriousness and deference but in reality
despised him for his weakness.

Ludwig's mode of living in Pirmasens was simple, unpretentious,
and monotonous to an extreme. Whereas his father had been
deeply devoted to Maria Theresa and the House of Habsburg,
Ludwig cherished an intense admiration for Frederick the Great
and Frederick's father, the royal drillmaster of Prussia. Having
neither the means nor the gifts to emulate the Philosopher-King,
he found his fulfillment in becoming the princely drillmaster of
Hessen-Darmstadt and making his regiments the best trained and
most impressive looking troops in Europe. They were not, however, allowed to smell powder, for their sole function was to drill
and march for the pleasure of their master, who devised maneuvers,
personally put them through their paces, and composed marches
for them. Indeed, Ludwig was one of the most prolific composers
of whom there is any record, the number of his marches exceed-
ing one hundred thousand. He was also one of the greatest virtuosi
of his time—on the drum. This explains, of course, why drums
were beaten every two hours in Darmstadt, as was noted by Nicolai;
in Pirmasens the uproar must have been constant. Grotesque
though this mania for soldiers undoubtedly was—Ludwig occupied his rather frequent periods of illness by studying and devising uniforms and playing with some six thousand wooden soldiers—it had at least one redeeming aspect, namely that Ludwig
really loved his troops. He could very handily have filled his empty
coffers by selling his men to the British for service in the colonies,
as his kinsmen in Hessen-Kassel did, but they were far too precious
to expose to this or any other martial danger.

It is a pity that circumstances apparently conspired to stimulate Ludwig's great love to take on the force of uncontrollable passion, for in matters that did not affect his soldiers he was reasonable, just, and, according to Goethe's friend Merck, perspicacious in his judgment of character. He was concerned for the welfare of his subjects and found numerous occasions to issue edicts and proclamations designed to combat injustice and intolerance. For example, he issued a rescript enjoining his officials to see that legal decisions were quickly made, lest the lawyers impoverish their clients by protracted argument, and he wrote on the margin of the rescript in his own hand the characteristic blunt lines:

Krieg, Pestilenz, und theure Zeiten sind grosse Land-Plagen, Setzt man die Advokaten bey, so kann man ohne Furcht und Scheu, Von ihrer vieren sagen.[7]

In the matter of religion he took a liberal stand as was evidenced by his Edict of Toleration of 1755 for his domains of Hanau-Lichtenberg. In this edict he accorded the Reformed church completely equal rights with the Lutheran church, a step that was apparently stubbornly resisted by the entrenched powers, for he wrote no less than four marginal notes in his own hand (*Manu clementissima scriptum*) to impress the earnestness of his intention upon his government.[8] That this decree was not the expression of mere immature liberalism can be seen in the fact that soon after he succeeded his father as Landgrave he granted the same privileges to the Reformed church in his new domains also (1770). Even in financial matters he had the right impulses, but here, of course, his soldiers were involved and the voice of reason could not be heard.

It was precisely in financial matters that the voice of reason should have been heeded, for Hessen-Darmstadt had long been on the verge of bankruptcy. Ludwig's grandfather, Ernst Ludwig, had squandered great sums in alchemistic experiments, and his father, Ludwig VIII, had squandered equally large sums on the great stables, kennels, and retinue required to satisfy his passion for hunting. The situation had become so grave that only the intervention of Maria Theresa herself on behalf of her old friend Ludwig VIII prevented the naming of an imperial bankruptcy

commission to take over the affairs of Hessen-Darmstadt. The
threat of such a commission became actual, of course, when Ludwig IX, the friend of Prussia, came to power. To his credit it
must be said that Ludwig immediately effected retrenchments and
economies with unmitigated severity. The hunt was abolished,
horses sold, pages and retainers dismissed, and the personal expenditures of the princely family reduced to a modest sum. But
Ludwig made one thing clear from the outset: he would counte-
nance no proposal whatever to reduce military expenses.

It must therefore have been the occasion for surprised comment
when on the eleventh of April 1772, not quite four years after he
had succeeded his father, Ludwig appointed to the office of
Präsident, that is, prime minister, none other than Friedrich
Karl von Moser, the celebrated author of *Der Herr und der
Diener,*[9] a book that had made no little sensation for its veiled
but understandable description of intolerable conditions in many
petty courts and for its outspoken condemnation of militarism
as the chief cause of so much misery in the small states of Germany.
Dr. Bahrdt may very well have been both surprised and disturbed
by this appointment, for his friend, Hesse, had been made subordinate to the new minister and therefore could no longer advise
Serenissimus officially. Accordingly, Bahrdt made haste to write
Moser a letter of congratulation upon his re-entry into the services
of the Landgrave and to present him with a collection of sermons.
He could scarcely have sought a more inept way to sway Moser
in his favor: the new minister, rationalist and man of enlightenment though he was in political thought, when it came to matters of religious faith, was a devout and ardent Pietist. Moser became Bahrdt's nemesis in Giessen.

IX

⟨A FORMIDABLE ENEMY⟩

WHAT A STROKE of irony it was that the forces of reaction in
Giessen should be helped to victory over Bahrdt by a man
who had earned widespread acclaim as a champion of liberalism
and enlightenment in the style of Frederick the Great and Joseph
II. Indeed, it may be said that the life work of Moser and Bahrdt
was directed to the same ends, the one in practical politics, and
the other in practical religion. This suggestion would have been
indignantly rejected by Moser, however, who, as has been clearly
established,[1] opposed Bahrdt from the first and persisted in his
opposition until he eventually forced Bahrdt to resign his professorship, thus setting him irrevocably upon the path that led to
his becoming the notorious *enfant terrible* of the German Enlightenment.

The interesting question is: why did Moser set out to destroy
Bahrdt or at least to neutralize his influence? Did he act out of
lofty and disinterested concern for the welfare of university,
church, and state? If so, his hatred of Bahrdt may reflect upon
Bahrdt's character and ability in a way far less to Bahrdt's credit
than if this were not the case. But an examination of Moser's career
and of the opinion of him held by many of his close associates reveals that it would be unwise to see in Moser's enmity of Bahrdt
a confirmation of the latter's unworthiness.

Frederick Karl von Moser was undoubtedly a man of great
ability, energy, and resoluteness—qualities that were evident also
in his equally famous father, Johann Jakob Moser, who had suffered arbitrary imprisonment for his political views by command
of the despotic Duke Karl Eugen of Würtemberg. Interestingly

71

enough, even though Friedrich Karl von Moser was deeply affected
by this injustice done his father, his zeal for political reform did not
take the radical shape that led to the Revolution in France, but instead followed the lines of legitimacy, constitutionality, and responsibility. Moser's ideal of government pointed away from the autocratic rule of the monarch toward rule by minister, for he distrusted genius upon the throne almost as much as he distrusted
tyranny. He was thus one of the shapers of the bureaucratic system as well as an extraordinarily able fiscal expert.

It was no doubt his talent for finance that made him seem so
valuable to the Great Landgravine and at least acceptable to the
Landgrave. He had first (1752) come to the favorable attention of
the court of Hessen-Darmstadt for his services in settling a dynastic
dispute between Ludwig VIII and the ruling House of Hessen-
Kassel. Ludwig VIII then employed him from 1756 to 1763 in the
adjustment of other differences between himself and the House of
Hessen-Kassel regarding the succession in the County of Hanau.
It was during this time that Moser wrote his most famous work,
Der Herr und der Diener, and entered into close relations with
Karoline and the hereditary prince, later Ludwig IX, who was
already the ruling Count of Hanau-Lichtenberg. Indeed, the young
couple made private arrangements with Moser for him to conduct
affairs of state for them upon the death of the old Landgrave, and
Moser attained a settlement with Kassel that pleased Karoline and
her consort more than it did Ludwig VIII.

The relations between Moser and the future ruler of Hessen-
Darmstadt were not completely cordial, however, and it was presumably due to Karoline's influence that Ludwig gave Moser a
secret commission to draw up plans for economic reforms to be
put into effect as soon as the old Landgrave should die. That
Ludwig did so is testimony both to the urgent need he foresaw
for straightening out the tangled finances of the country and to
his belief in Moser's ability to do what nobody else could, for
only about four months before he gave Moser this commission
(May 1762), he had instructed *Regierungsrat* Hesse to draw up
a blistering criticism of Moser's *Der Herr und der Diener.* The
criticism was really designed to force Moser out of his employ and

would have had that effect then and there if Moser's services had not been so desperately needed.

The book that so deeply stirred up Ludwig's suspicions of Moser's plans and purposes was one of the most popular treatises of its kind, appearing in many printings and in translations into French and Russian. In general tone and spirit it depended a good deal upon Montesquieu's *L'esprit des Lois* and Frederick the Great's *Anti-Machiavel,* that is, it was a re-formulation of ideas that were of intense interest and growing general acceptance by "enlightened" political thinkers. Fragmentary and unsystematic in method, it offered a mélange of insights, generalizations, maxims, and practical suggestions for improving the conduct of government. These were all corollary to the axiom that Frederick the Great not only propounded as theory but also, in his fashion, exemplified in his reign, that the monarch should be the foremost servant of his people. Perhaps what made it so very popular, even sensational, was the vigorous, rather crude style and the tone of disrespect toward the petty monarchs whose transgressions and foibles were mercilessly, though anonymously, pilloried. Indeed, it was said of Moser that he cured the Germans of their canine servility. The impression made by the book upon a modern reader is somewhat the same as the impression made by much of what Bahrdt wrote: the ideas have become so commonplace that one is amazed that they should ever have caused such a stir, but at the same time this very sense of amazement is striking evidence, if any were needed, of how completely the achievements of the Enlightenment have been absorbed into the fabric of contemporary Western thought.

The rift between the master, Ludwig, and the servant, Moser, revealed by the publication of this book, was glossed over for a time, however, for the prince undoubtedly believed that he could bend Moser to his will, and Moser hoped he could bring Ludwig to a realization of the ruinous folly of his passion for building up his battalions. Ludwig gave Moser renewed instructions to draw up detailed plans for sweeping reforms in government, and Moser complied to the apparent satisfaction of both Ludwig and Karoline, who received him together in Pirmasens and had private discussions with him about ways and means of saving the country from bankruptcy. Upon Karoline he made an indelible impression which confirmed the opinion she had already formed that he alone could manage the involved affairs of Hessen-Darmstadt, an opinion to which she seems to have clung even after she was, as evidence apparently shows, in some way cruelly betrayed by him. Ludwig, however, alternated in confidence and distrust and never, of course, lost sight of his main goal, to secure enough money to maintain and expand his small army. Eventually Moser came to feel that he was being thwarted in his aims and asked for his dismissal, which Ludwig, influenced by Karoline, was at first unwilling to grant. Eventually, however, the impression grew upon Ludwig that Moser intended to take the reins of effective power into his own hands, and in December 1768, he allowed Moser to leave his service.

The next stage in Moser's career had been prepared for by his last activity in behalf of Ludwig, for he had sought to effect a *rapprochement* between Ludwig and the Imperial government in Vienna. This activity and certain other commissions had paved the way for his entry into the service of the House of Habsburg. This step signified an about-face for the former enthusiastic admirer of Frederick the Great and probably is one of the reasons why Bahrdt characterized him as chameleonlike (*der allfarbigte Moser*). In fairness to Moser, however, it should be added that he had probably experienced a genuine disappointment in Frederick, partially because of the latter's power-politics but perhaps even more because of his indifference to religion. There had been no echo from Berlin to such passages in *Der Herr und der Diener* as this one in which Moser writes, probably thinking of himself,

A God-fearing minister gives lustre to the entire government of a ruler, and if a ruler had several such, one might very well say that even if he personally had little greatness about him (save for the dignity of his birth), he would be bathed in their light just like ordinary glass balls filled with water at illuminations, which send out rays from the fire burning all around them, rays which they would never be able to produce by themselves.[2]

The Catholic court of Vienna was of course not indifferent to religion and was glad of the opportunity to fit Moser, even though he was a Protestant, into its intricate machinery. In the long run, however, playing a subordinate role proved to be not to Moser's liking. The young Emperor Joseph II was too impetuous and flighty, and, quite naturally, Moser grew less popular in Vienna. In the year 1770 he was therefore made administrator of the Imperial County of Falkenstein, a minute territory not far from the domains of his former master, who had now become Ludwig IX of Hessen-Darmstadt.

Moser was at the time a mature and experienced man of forty-seven with a good many futile struggles and disappointments behind him. His naturally energetic and resolute temperament had hardened into intolerance tinged with bitterness. Everywhere he had encountered inertia, indifference, inefficiency, and resentment of his reform plans. Nobody ever had done anything right except himself, and so he felt justified and compelled to gather all authority into his own hands. For this reason the administration of Falkenstein, where he had very little less than absolutely sovereign powers, might have been the ideal task for him. As it turned out, however, he overestimated the extent of his sovereignty and became embroiled in what amounted to a tiny war with his powerful neighbor, the Elector Palatine, whose territories completely surrounded the divided area comprising Falkenstein. Without waiting for instructions from the Emperor, Moser on his own authority but in the name of Joseph II undertook negotiations with the Elector. The Imperial Court was incensed and deliberated the necessity of calling Moser to account for this and other acts that had caused the populace of Falkenstein to turn against him. This was very early in March 1772. By April the decision had been reached to take no action against him, but his administratorship was formally terminated on the thirtieth of April. On the eleventh of April Moser had re-entered the service of Hessen-Darmstadt as chancellor and president of all deliberative and executive councils of the state.

This, in brief, was the history of the man whose favorable regard Bahrdt sought to win by his diplomatic letter and the presentation of his sermons. That Moser's latest experience in the service of Austria had made him more embittered and autocratic than ever Bahrdt probably did not know. The knowledge would undoubtedly have done him no good, however, for Moser had become no less despotic than the titled monarchs of his day and was determined to rule as though in his own right. This resolve was made manifest in two decrees which he caused to be promulgated shortly after he was appointed to his new post. The first isolated the Landgrave from his subjects by denying them direct access to him whether by petition or in audience. The second gave Moser the right to discharge any state official whatever for negligence or misconduct of office without first having to notify the Landgrave. Ludwig's feelings in signing these decrees can only be surmised, but there is little reason to doubt that he agreed to them in the hope that the time thus spared from the performance of onerous duties could be gained for his soldiers. If Karoline urged upon him that only Moser could manage affairs of state, then let Moser manage them, providing he could find money for military expenditures. Ludwig did not, however, completely lose touch with what went on within his land, as will be seen from the role he played in the struggle led by Benner but lent force by Moser to eject Bahrdt from the University.

Before we turn to a consideration of this struggle, however, it will be of interest to glance briefly at the further course of Moser's career up to and beyond April 1775, when Bahrdt was finally forced out of the university, for a man may be known as well by the enemies he makes as by the company he keeps.

It is not, however, the intention to examine closely the governmental reorganization that Moser undertook. In some measures he was highly successful, but in others much less so. His financial reforms seem to have been brilliant and effective,[3] but an attempt to revise the economy of the country by compelling the peasants to plant new crops and use different methods resulted in dismal failure. In this and other matters he seems actually to have employed thoroughly incompetent and even dishonest people, and it is certain that he instituted a reign of terror among the established officials. One of these officials was Goethe's friend, Johann Heinrich Merck, whose hatred of and contempt for Moser knew no bounds. That the relations between the two men should have been strained was only natural because, for one thing, Merck was careless in the performance of his duties and, for another, he had nothing but scorn for Moser's religiosity, which he considered hypocritical. But nevertheless the loathing and hatred which are manifest in Merck's utterances concerning Moser even before his alleged betrayal of the Great Landgravine are not readily explained away, for Merck, even though his ironical and incisively critical turn of mind made him a model for Goethe's Mephisto, seems to have been a generous, sensitive, and forgiving soul.[4] In this connection it must also be remembered that Merck had opportunities to observe Moser very closely, especially on one occasion that dearly touched the heart of the Landgravine and the interests of the Landgrave as well as the political designs of two of the greatest monarchs of the time, Frederick the Great and the Empress Catherine of Russia.

For some time Catherine had been concerned to find a suitable consort for her son, Grand Duke Paul, and had by 1772 been persuaded of the soundness of Frederick's advice that no one could be more suitable than a daughter of the Great Landgravine of Hessen-Darmstadt. Frederick had already (1769) allied his house with that of Hessen-Darmstadt through the marriage of his nephew and successor to Princess Friederike and hoped now to establish dynastic relations between Russia and Prussia. Since there seemed to be general agreement that such a match as the one envisioned had much to recommend it, Catherine invited Karoline and her daughters to visit her in St. Petersburg, in the hope that a marriage could be arranged. Furthermore, since the depleted treasury of Hessen-Darmstadt would not permit Karoline and her daughters to make such a long journey in the style that befitted their station, the Empress placed a generous sum of money as well as ships at their disposal.

On the sixth of May 1793, Karoline, accompanied by three daughters and a modest retinue, which included Merck but not Moser, set out for Russia. On the eighth of June they were in Travemünde where three ships were awaiting them, and by the twenty-fifth, after a difficult voyage, they had all reached port. In

the course of the lavish entertainment which followed, a bond of
inclination was formed between Grand Duke Paul and Princess
Wilhelmine, but one obstacle remained to a formal betrothal:
it was necessary for the Princess to take her future husband's religion. This was a serious step which had caused the Landgravine
and her daughter some concern, but the decision had been made
to take it. Wilhelmine was instructed in her new faith, received
into the Russian church on the twenty-sixth of August, and on
the following day solemnly betrothed to the future ruler of all
the Russias.[5] On the twenty-eighth of August, just too late to
accomplish his mission, Moser arrived in St. Petersburg.

Had Moser arrived only three or four days earlier than he did,
his presence would have been a source of great embarrassment to
both parties, for he had been sent by Ludwig to object to Wilhelmine's conversion to the Russian church. It seems that when
the Landgravine was exchanging letters with Ludwig about
Catherine's proposition she had glossed over the fact that a change
of faith was a necessary condition to any such marriage as was
contemplated. When Ludwig later learned of this he decided to
intervene, probably hoping to gain some material concessions by
magnifying the seriousness of his objection. Indeed, according
to Merck, it was Moser who suggested to Ludwig that political and
financial advantages were to be gained by having his prime
minister present in St. Petersburg. Even though Moser had arrived too late to make representations in the matter of faith and
was therefore an almost completely superfluous witness, he took
his own role very seriously in the formalities that followed. Moreover, he hoped that by making a favorable impression upon the
Empress and her counsellors he might receive an offer to enter
the service of the Russian government and to play a great part
among the leading figures of European diplomacy. These hopes
came to nothing. Whereas all honor was shown to Karoline and
her circle, Moser was made to feel out of place, since Karoline kept
the management of what was primarily a family and dynastic
matter in her own hands. More than that, his obsequiousness and
his obvious interest in gold and honor made him unpopular among
the Russian nobility, and Catherine, although she expressed her

esteem for his writings, did not grant his request for a title and pension. His only real success was in earning a sizable commission for assisting a Count Wittgenstein to obtain payment of his claim against the Russian court. All these circumstances apparently combined to embitter Moser so deeply that upon his return to Hessen-Darmstadt he is said to have complained to Ludwig that the change of faith had not really been necessary and that Karoline had, by consenting to it, thrown away all the concessions that might have been wrung from the Russian court. Indeed, Moser is said to have used this same accusation to sow seeds of discord between Karoline and her mother, who was ardently devout and to whom the Landgravine was so deeply attached.

Karoline returned to Darmstadt at the end of December 1773, weary, ill, and already marked by death, to face the humiliating accusations made against her by Moser. What happened is best described in the words of Merck, about which there must be some reservations, however, because, as we have seen, Merck was far from impartial:

He [Moser] now put sole blame for the failure of his negotiations on behalf of his master upon the Landgravine and shamelessly accused her not only of having done nothing for him and his mission, but also of having deliberately put obstacles in his way. The Landgrave, with his well-known perspicacity, saw through this and believed none of it whatsoever, but transmitted Moser's fine papers to the Landgravine in the original. The Landgrave placed the traitor's fate in the hands of his consort and declared himself ready to dismiss him at once. However, the Landgravine was too magnanimous to accept this sacrifice, because she had made it an unshakable rule that no one should experience misfortune because of her. She even suppressed the letter in which she intended to confront him with the recital of his base actions and left him to be punished by his own guilty conscience. In her testament she mentioned him as the only person in this world whom she had found to be her enemy.[6]

Not long after this, on the thirtieth of March 1774, Karoline died, allowing Moser, as Bahrdt says, to exercise power almost completely undirected, for Pirmasens was far away and Ludwig could not tear himself from his soldiers but was unbelievably and understandably content to leave things in the hands of the Prime Minister. But if it suited Ludwig's purpose to forgive and forget as Karoline had urged him to, it seems not to have suited Moser's purpose to exhibit a comparable generosity towards those who had enjoyed Karoline's esteem and protection or towards the memory of Karoline herself. If Merck can be believed, soon after the death of the Landgravine, Moser renewed his attacks upon her character and persecuted those who had enjoyed her favor. That Bahrdt was one of these there is, as we shall see, some reason to believe, and there is no doubt that Ludwig regarded him highly. It is also a fact that about a year after the Landgravine's death Moser had made Bahrdt's position untenable, thus accomplishing a purpose that he had undoubtedly had in mind from the first.

The rest of Moser's career, astounding and even puzzling though it is, must be briefly told. Suddenly, on the ninth of June 1780, he was dismissed from his post. The news amazed everyone who was familiar with the situation and delighted many, especially of course, Merck, who supplied Goethe and Duke Karl August of Sachsen-Weimar,[7] Ludwig IX's son-in-law, with the details. The immediate cause of the dismissal was Ludwig's reversal of an ordinance prohibiting lotteries—Ludwig wanted the income from the lotteries for his soldiers. Moser flew into a rage and sent in his resignation from office. Ludwig accepted it and proceeded to name new ministers whom he instructed to study Moser's fiscal policies and methods, for, as he pointed out, it was Moser alone who had been able to save the state. Gradually, however, Moser's enemies determined upon revenge and brought charges of malfeasance of office against him. Ludwig's attitude towards Moser slowly underwent an inexplicable change from grudging admiration to implacable hatred; he confiscated Moser's property and fortune—Moser had lived in luxury and magnificence—and systematically persecuted and impoverished him. The once proud, powerful, and arrogant man suffered the miseries of the damned until Ludwig's son succeeded his father (1790), dropped the charges against Moser, and made it possible for him to spend his remaining years in relative comfort.

To draw a parallel between Moser and Bahrdt is not only interesting for its own sake but may be instructive as well. It is certainly quite possible to do so, paradoxical as the idea may seem at first glance, for, as we have seen, Moser was a representative of the Enlightenment in practical politics as Bahrdt was in practical religion. They were both very productive and very popular writers, not original and revolutionary, but they proclaimed ideas that were in the air with such force and appeal and with a flourish so disrespectful of authority that the layman understood and was convinced. In a way, both men were successful because their ideas have gained general acceptance: the war in which they were captains has been won and need not be fought again. The personal misfortune which both men suffered was, to a considerable degree, of their own making, for they were rash and blameworthy in many respects—Bahrdt in his rather puckish way and Moser with the deadly self-importance of the bureaucrat. In any balanced view they must both be regarded as questionable characters, and there seems no reason to doubt that among their contemporaries Moser made at least as many enemies as Bahrdt, probably more. Why then are they apt to be described in such a contrasting set of clichés, Bahrdt as a monster of iniquity and Moser as a paragon of virtue? Perhaps it is, as Gustav Frank implies,[8] because Bahrdt's enemies, the orthodox and the Pietists, were so voluble, articulate, vindictive, and persistent.[9]

X

{ VENDETTA }

As in Erfurt, the opposing forces had lost no time in preliminaries to combat: the orthodox party, which included most of the University, was intent on immediately depriving Bahrdt of power and influence, and he made the very act of moving to Giessen symbolic of the open warfare that was to be waged for the next four years.

As soon as Bahrdt's appointment was confirmed, leading church laymen petitioned the Landgrave to relieve him of the duties of preaching or giving instruction to children. (One suspects the influence of Benner behind this move to defend the purity of the faith, as the petitioners put it.) The petition had no effect on Ludwig except to make him feel annoyed that the appointment should be questioned. As for Bahrdt, no sooner had he arrived in Giessen than he presented the University with an augmented bill for moving expenses: he had gone from Erfurt to Giessen by way of his native city of Leipzig, a roundabout route, to say the least, and now demanded payment of the expenses which were incidental to moving his possessions from Leipzig to Giessen. When the University Senate quite naturally refused, he appealed to the Landgrave, who ordered the University to pay Bahrdt in full, since he, Ludwig, did not like to see the reputation of the University suffer because of shabby treatment of distinguished professors whom he had seen fit to appoint. The Senate was reluctant to comply, however, but finally agreed to a compromise which was acceptable to Bahrdt as well.

For about a year after this preliminary skirmish the advantage lay with Bahrdt, thanks to the backing of Bechtold, Hesse, and Landgrave Ludwig. Hesse had been strongly influenced by Wieland's praise of Bahrdt, as we have already seen, and did what he could to improve Bahrdt's position and salary. In fact, Bahrdt's salary was almost doubled immediately but at the expense of a certain Ouvrier, who became one of Bahrdt's bitterest and most active enemies. Ouvrier had been Court Chaplain and tutor of the princely family but when Ludwig upon coming to power had reduced expenses by eliminating many court positions, Ouvrier had become superfluous. Nevertheless, Ludwig felt that Ouvrier could not just be turned out into the street and decided that he could be put on the University budget in the theological faculty. Ouvrier was therefore shoved into the third position between Bechtold, who had the second, and Bahrdt. Although Ouvrier was made superior to Bahrdt in rank, he was given a salary no greater than Bahrdt's, for Hesse reapportioned the total sum allotted to the three lower ranks in Bahrdt's favor, a maneuver that was certain not to inspire Ouvrier with friendly feelings towards his colleague.

By January 1772, Bahrdt felt that he had been in Giessen long enough to secure some influence in the management of ecclesiastical affairs and sought appointment to the Giessen consistory. Ludwig, to whom Bahrdt had addressed his petition, turned the question over to the Privy Council, which passed it along to the consistory itself for action. In the consistory only Bechtold favored admitting Bahrdt; the others, led by Benner, resolutely opposed such action and persuaded the Privy Council to recommend denying the petition. Ludwig, however, disagreed, and on the second of May 1772, commanded the consistory to accept Bahrdt as a member. He had been sufficiently impressed by the representations of the opposition, however, to make the provision that Dr. Bahrdt should be instructed to move the introduction of no innovations contrary to the accepted constitution on pain of losing his vote in the matter. After this concession to the reactionary party, Ludwig went on to point out that it was his personal conviction that Bahrdt was right in his main theses that the clergy had interpolated many things into religion for which there was no biblical authority.[1]

Benner was, of course, the member of the consistory who most actively opposed Bahrdt's admission to it. In the written opinion which he had composed on the subject he had indicated that he intended soon to publish a rebuttal of Bahrdt's proposals for revising Lutheran dogma in the spirit of the Enlightenment.[2] Benner's book, *Pflichtmässige Erwägungen, die Religion betreffend,* however, was just one of a large number of books and pamphlets that appeared in 1772 attacking Bahrdt indirectly or openly denouncing him as a heretic.[3] This storm of attack and abuse was directed specifically against Bahrdt's publications of the year 1771 which included, in addition to the proposals for revising dogma, one popular book published anonymously in Halle[4] and two more technical studies in Latin.[5] All of them, of course, reflected Bahrdt's ever-increasing doubts about the supernatural mysteries of Lutheran doctrine and his growing tendency to see in Jesus a human teacher, rather than the incarnate God, to distinguish between the religion that Jesus taught and the religion that grew up about him. These writings were addressed to specific objective questions; it was the reactionary party that first indulged in personal polemics, at least in print.

Bahrdt's first move in countering the personal attacks made upon him was to address a letter to the Landgrave. In this letter he complained of the charges of heresy and perjury made against him by Benner and his helpers and requested Ludwig to make known his pleasure: whether he might undertake a detailed refutation of the charges made by his enemies or whether he must suffer in silence.[6] This letter was written April 12, 1772. On the preceding day (April 11) Friedrich Karl von Moser had taken up his duties as the all-powerful minister of state, superseding Hesse and quickly promulgating the decrees by which he intended to isolate the Landgrave from his subjects and his officials. Thus, it is possible that Bahrdt's request for instructions may never have come to Ludwig's personal attention, for the action that was taken, as will be described later, seems to have been calculated to give Bahrdt's enemies a chance to lodge formal complaints and charges against him. The attacks on Bahrdt continued to increase in number and in bitterness, with the result that he addressed two more letters to Ludwig, on the nineteenth and the twenty-ninth of July, in which he complained that almost all the preachers in Hessen-Darmstadt were denouncing him from their pulpits and that Schwarz (who was *Professor extraordinarius*) and Ouvrier had delivered sermons to demonstrate that it was

Christ's righteousness and not the love of God and one's neighbor which makes us happy and blessed.

The two had made it very plain that they were attacking Bahrdt's "so-called errors" and Schwarz had said in so many words that he

intended to refute the opinion of his colleague, who taught that love was the source of blessedness.

To this letter Bahrdt attached documentary evidence that Schwarz had publicly boasted that he would soon succeed in getting Bahrdt removed from his position. The reply to these two letters was a sharp admonition to refrain from injuring the University by publishing heretical views. This admonition was, of course, the work of Moser, who did not bring it to Ludwig's attention.

A matter that did come to Ludwig's attention, however, injured Bahrdt in his estimation. This was a quarrel with a Colonel Müller, who was in charge of military and other official buildings. Müller had spread it abroad that when Bahrdt had moved out of his old apartment he had left it in a disgustingly filthy condition. Bahrdt called the colonel an infamous liar and the colonel demanded a public formal apology. When it was reported to the Landgrave that the honor of one of his officers had been impugned he quite naturally was incensed and commanded Bahrdt to make amends to the Colonel in the presence of the Commandant and Major General von Rothberg.[7] Bahrdt, acting on the advice of certain colleagues who felt that a representative of the University should be present also at the meeting between Bahrdt and the Colonel, insisted that Chancellor Koch be called in as a witness. Then the Colonel refused to meet Bahrdt face to face and demanded a written apology, but agreement could not be reached on a formula. At this point Ludwig lost patience and commanded Bahrdt to apologize in person before the entire regiment and officer corps before a specified date. Bahrdt had no recourse but to endure this public humiliation. It must have alarmed him very seriously to realize that he had gravely jeopardized the favorable regard in which Ludwig had held him, especially since his appeal of April twelfth for Ludwig's protection seemed about to produce unforeseen disastrous results.

What had happened was that in response to Bahrdt's complaint about the intrigues of Benner and his friends the government had asked the Giessen consistory for an opinion. When the consistory was unable to respond quickly and completely, the same request was made of the University. It is plain that neither the consistory nor the University could make an impartial judgment, for both the consistory and the theological faculty were composed of the very men against whom the complaint was lodged. This was a procedure that put the defendants in the jury box to deliberate upon their own guilt. Small wonder if the verdict turned out to be that the plaintiff should be hanged. And that was exactly what happened. Benner and Ouvrier composed opinions that would give the hostile judge, Moser, grounds to ruin Bahrdt. And, what was even more dangerous, Bahrdt was accused of having written a slanderous review of a disputation by Schwarz in the *Erfurter Gelehrte Zeitung*. Moser in fact took it for granted that Bahrdt was the author of the review and reprimanded him publicly and severely for dishonesty so grave that it amounted to attempted perjury. Thus, during the summer of 1772 Bahrdt's position was very shaky indeed.

He managed to recover lost ground, however, in two ways. First, in a letter to the Landgrave he declared himself ready for the sake of restoring tranquility and harmony to restrict his publications to exegetical and historical problems, provided that his enemies be commanded to observe complete silence on what both sides had said and done up to then. It was, in other words, a sort of promise to wipe the slate clean and begin again. The hook concealed by this bait, however, was the simple fact that historical and exegetical research could not help touching upon matters of dogma, as became abundantly clear even in so unoriginal a work as the church history that Bahrdt published in 1773. The Landgrave rose to the bait nonetheless, conferred with Moser on the matter, and enjoined the professors of the University and all the pastors in his realm to desist from further polemical writing or preaching against Bahrdt. The Landgrave's decree was dated August 31, 1772. Not long after this date, on the second of November, Bahrdt had the further satisfaction that the Privy Council vindicated him completely in the case of the anonymous attack on Schwarz in the *Erfurter Gelehrte Zeitung*. The man responsible for the review, Professor Schulz, had come forward and admitted his connection with the case, and the reproof which Moser had administered was formally reversed. This was a triumph for Bahrdt but not one that left the choleric minister of state in a conciliatory mood.

The Professor Schulz who turned out to have been the man responsible for the review which Bahrdt was blamed for having written was *Professor ordinarius* of oriental languages (Greek and Hebrew) on the philosophical faculty. He seems to have been ambitious, versatile, and talented—but superficial, a dabbler in many things which he did not take the time or pains to master. He had received his training in Göttingen under Michaelis, from whom he had learned his exegetical method and critical approach to the text of the Scriptures while rejecting his teacher's timid profession of orthodox belief. He and Bahrdt were drawn together by the similarity of their views, and for a while Schulz seemed to be Bahrdt's faithful supporter and true friend. This happy relationship came to an end in the summer of 1772, however, not, as Bahrdt says it did, because Schulz married Benner's daughter.[8] Rather it was because he took advantage of Bahrdt's helpless position to gain a post to which they both aspired, namely the directorship of a seminary for preachers, which was about to be established, apparently as the result of a suggestion by Bahrdt. Schulz had persuaded Bahrdt that the whole idea should be dropped and then had pushed for it and gotten himself appointed to the directorship.[9] Bahrdt, of course, was not the man to forget and forgive an act of this kind, but he waited until an opportunity might present itself to even up the score a bit. Thus, as the year 1772 drew to a close, the situation resembled an uneasy cease-fire between two bands of snipers: as soon as one or the other exposed himself or could train his sights on the enemy, a lively exchange of shots was sure to follow.

Quite unexpectedly in December 1772, Bahrdt was put into a strategic position: *Hofrat* Deinet offered him the editorship of the *Frankfurter Gelehrte Anzeigen*. Goethe's friend Merck, who had had a large share of editorial responsibility for this journal, especially during the earlier part of the year 1772, had become less and less active and had finally resigned completely from the enterprise, and there was nothing to hold together the circle of contributors which had included Goethe, Herder, and Schlosser as well as Merck and a few others.[10] Someone was urgently needed to breathe life back into the expiring journal, and Bahrdt seemed to be the man who could do it. In fact, Deinet urged Bahrdt to begin his duties by furnishing the first numbers of the year 1773 with some reviews that were sure to receive attention, and Bahrdt was glad to comply, for Ouvrier, Schulz, and Schwarz had laid themselves open to attack in recent publications.

Schwarz had written an outline of church history which, according to Bahrdt's unsigned review, was totally without merit, full of faults and mistakes of all kinds. There seems no reason to doubt the correctness of Bahrdt's judgment. As for the books by Ouvrier and Schulz, they were discussed at greater length, likewise in unsigned articles, which, although negatively critical, are objective and moderate in tone.

Ouvrier had written a Latin *Programmschrift* for the Nativity. After pointing out mistakes and infelicities in the Latin, Bahrdt went on to discuss more substantive matters, attacking the whole problem from the viewpoint of textual criticism. In tone the review is clever and ironical but not abusive, and the method it employs is the effective and legitimate one of pointing out what conclusions follow from certain basic premises. Thus Ouvrier had attempted to prove that in the Epistle to the Galatians Paul used the term νόμος to signify moral law. Bahrdt points out with devastating effect that if the Greek word were so used by Paul, then Chapter Five of the Epistle would constitute an exhortation to licentiousness, for Paul urges the Galatians not to be "entangled again with the yoke of bondage." It is quite plain, Bahrdt concludes, that νόμος means the law of the Hebrews which has been superseded by the Christian dispensation.[11]

As for Schulz, he had published an announcement of the new seminary for preachers complete with a description of courses, aims, and methods. In his notice of the publication Bahrdt says that he was not greatly troubled by the fact that Schulz himself had none of the qualifications of a good public speaker. After all, a person may know how something ought to be done and be totally unable to do it himself. But what did dismay Bahrdt was the description of courses and methods, which made it plain that the new seminary was not new at all, but merely a duplication of the same old unsatisfactory institutes which had failed to give adequate training in public speaking; that it was just an ordinary *Collegium homiletico-practicum*. Bahrdt then quotes directly from the announcement to show that the students would be required to do very little else than read aloud from already published collections of sermons, to memorize standard homiletical precepts and recite them. He points out what could and should be done to train future preachers in lucid composition and effective delivery, matters that were completely ignored in Schulz's new seminary.[12] The review, in other words, although entirely negative, is reasonable, objective, and relatively mild in tone, despite the concluding sentence: "Hier fiel uns vor Schrecken die Feder aus der Hand." It was this sentence that Bahrdt's enemies pounced upon as flagrant evidence of personal abuse.

Chief among Bahrdt's enemies was, of course, Moser, who had been looking for some way to repay Bahrdt for the defeat which he had suffered when it was proved that Schulz and not Bahrdt had written the scurrilous review of Schwarz's disputation. Moser sent to the Privy Council a copy of the *Frankfurter Gelehrte Anzeigen* which contained the articles just described with the proposal to discover whether a certain professor in Giessen might not have written them, for they disclosed not the "carping tone of a pedant but of a learned *bon vivant*." [13] The investigation quickly revealed that Bahrdt was indeed the author of the reviews and led to a fine of one hundred *Reichsthaler* being imposed upon Deinet the publisher. Deinet immediately warned Bahrdt of the danger threatening him, and Bahrdt turned to his friend Chancellor Koch for help. Koch advised him to seek the help of the University Curator von Hesse. All these steps seemed useless, however, for Moser was putting pressure on the Privy Council to take legal action against Bahrdt that would entail not only the prohibition of all similar publications but also some serious penalty. The penalty was apparently to be imposed on Bahrdt for having dared to criticize a decision of the Landgrave, the founding of the seminary for preachers. In a letter to the Landgrave, dated February 3, 1773, Bahrdt solemnly disclaimed any intention of offending the Majesty of Ludwig IX and begged for clemency. Ludwig, who had apparently not been told by Moser of what was going on, promptly (February 10) informed the Privy Council of his views on the subject, and these views were absolutely contrary to Moser's plans and purposes. Ludwig minced no words in giving it as his opinion that the whole affair was just a matter of inconsequential scholarly logomachy and that he knew from conversation with the two of them that Bahrdt had more sense in his little finger than Ouvrier had in his whole body.[14]

Moser, thwarted and furious, informed the Privy Council that Bahrdt, relying on the favor of both Ludwig and Karoline, had escaped the condign punishment that Moser had hoped to inflict upon him.[15] It was therefore Moser's suggestion that a memorandum be sent to the Landgrave on the necessity of humbling Bahrdt, this to be sure learned but much too proud and contentious man. The memorandum had little effect: Ludwig replied that no legal action should be taken against Bahrdt unless he refused to obey another admonition to keep silence. Bahrdt's reply to this renewed admonition was a long and circumstantial letter in which he ably defended himself against the charges that his reviews were scurrilous lampoons and pointed out that the Attorney General had not taken action either against various writers and preachers who had publicly vilified him or against such people as Schulz, who had both defamed Schwarz and injuriously deceived him, Bahrdt. Moser could only turn Bahrdt's communication over to the Attorney General for a formal reply, which, together with all the other documents in the case, was then filed away.

The year 1773, which had begun so stormily, was destined to

end in a relative quiet which lasted until the beginning of 1775. Once again there was a tacit cease-fire, but not before Bahrdt had suffered two minor defeats: he had unsuccessfully petitioned to be appointed Court\Chaplain, a position that would have taken him away from Giessen, and a written complaint of Ouvrier and Benner had produced an official admonition to heed his own promise to refrain from lecturing on dogmatics and from propagating heterodox principles. It must not be supposed that Bahrdt was idle during this brief period of relative tranquility, however. It was, on the contrary, a time of great literary activity for him and of progressive estrangement from orthodoxy; and of the books and articles that poured from his pen, one, his paraphrase of the New Testament, was destined to catapult him into a storm of controversy that raged far beyond the bounds of Hessen-Darmstadt.

XI

{PLAIN WORDS AND SIMPLE TRUTH}

As WE HAVE SEEN, Bahrdt was aware of how much his theological and philosophical outlook was influenced by practical experience and by his associates, whether friendly or hostile. In Giessen, of course, the enmity of Benner and the other theologians caused him to look for flaws in the orthodox position and thus to grow rapidly more skeptical of many articles of Lutheran faith. But this trend of his inner development was aided by friendly associates also, especially by Johann Wilhelm Baumer, who at the time Bahrdt knew him was the senior professor of medicine and a member of the council of mines.

Baumer, of whom Bahrdt writes with warm appreciation, was one of the three friends Bahrdt had at the University, the other two being Chancellor Koch and *Regierungsrat* Adolphi, a pupil and devoted associate of Koch. Baumer took no part in the quarrels and dissensions that rocked the University, but lived for his teaching, his medical practice, and research. He enjoyed good food and wine but preferred the stimulating conversation of a few friends to large noisy gatherings. He and Bahrdt visited each other every two or three weeks and Bahrdt says that he owed much of his "enlightenment" to his conversations with Baumer.

Baumer was a good deal older than Bahrdt, having been born in 1719, was well established, and had his period of inner turmoil behind him. He was, therefore, a sufficiently impressive personality to affect Bahrdt considerably, especially since his religious convictions had undergone a change from orthodoxy to deism. Since he was also gifted in many ways and accomplished to the point of professional competence in several different fields, he is himself a representative minor figure of the Enlightenment. Moreover, he had the best possible opportunity for observing and evaluating the feuding parties on the theological faculty and found that he preferred Bahrdt to Benner, Schwarz, and Ouvrier. For all these reasons it may be helpful for our understanding of Bahrdt to inquire a little further into the character and personality of Baumer.

He had begun his intellectual and professional career as a student of theology and philology at the Universities of Halle and Jena and had lectured for a very brief time at the latter university. Then, in 1742, he had been called to a pastorate in Krautheim in Baden, where he remained for four years. For reasons of health he resigned from his post and went to Halle in order to receive medical treatment and also to take up the study of medicine professionally. He received his doctorate in medicine in 1748 and shortly thereafter moved to Erfurt, where he was appointed to the philosophical faculty of the University to lecture on philosophy and Latin style. The conflict in his thinking between religious supernaturalism and empirical naturalism was solved early in his life in favor of religion but later in favor of empiricism. The course of his development is not only indicated by the fact that he switched from theology and philology to medicine, physiology, chemistry, and mineralogy, but it is also, so to speak, epitomized in the subjects of two of his publications. His *Habilitationsschrift,* written when he joined the philosophical faculty of Erfurt, had the title *De nexu rerum hypothetice necessario libertatem moralem non auferente,* but about six years later (1755) he wrote a *Programma de Electricitatis effectibus in corpore animali.*

The very considerable influence that he exerted upon the development of the natural sciences in both Erfurt and Giessen was strongly in the direction of empirical and practical methods. He made the dissection of human cadavers a much more significant and regular part of the medical student's training at Erfurt than it had been before his time. Indeed, before the university reform instruction in anatomy had become so excellent that it was one of the very few drawing cards the University could boast. Despite this fact, Baumer, who enjoyed the highest regard of Emmerich Joseph's predecessor, met with bitter opposition from the old

guard, who deeply resented his influence and his resolute modes
of procedure. When, therefore, Prince Elector Johann Friedrich
Karl died and Baumer received a call to the University of Giessen,
he was probably no less delighted than Bahrdt was later to escape
from the stagnant backwaters of Erfurt. In Giessen Baumer was
much more successful than Bahrdt was destined to be. He had
the first full professorship of chemistry at the University, a position to which Justus Liebig succeeded in 1824, and he reformed
and strengthened instruction throughout the natural sciences.
The geology field trips which he had been the first to sponsor in
Erfurt and which became a permanent feature of instruction in
Giessen may serve as an indication of how he pushed the natural
sciences along the paths of practical activity and firsthand observation. He became, in short, a shrewd and skeptical student of nature,
a careful observer and classifier, a sober and cautious thinker, and
an enemy of superstition and mysticism.

It was this man who became Bahrdt's friend and associate, with
whom he talked of all the many things that interested them both,
who injected a strong dose of skepticism into the current of Bahrdt's
thinking. Their conversations often turned to human folly, ignorance, and superstition. The last was a subject which seems to
have exercised Baumer very much. As a sworn foe of supernaturalism he once had the opportunity to put his convictions to the test
and to expose what had been thought to be an authenticated instance of haunting. In Erfurt there was a house that was worth
about four thousand *Taler* but which could not be sold because of
the unearthly noises that were heard there nightly. Baumer
bought the house for seven hundred *Taler* and went with a servant
to spend the night and lay the ghost. In due time they heard the
sounds: human beings seemed to be chasing one another and up-
setting tables and chairs. But when the two observers retained
their composure and watched closely they were able to discern a
number of fitchets playing in the moonlight. When Baumer
destroyed their nesting place the house ceased to be haunted and
it was acknowledged that he had done a very profitable bit of
business. Bahrdt tells this story with evident admiration as much
for Baumer's financial gain as for his intrepid skepticism and the

lesson to be drawn from the story, namely, the unreliability of the senses and the justified doubt of supernatural explanations. Furthermore, there can be little question that Bahrdt very quickly saw what the implications of Baumer's justified skepticism of the supernatural were for the tales of miraculous cures and super-natural happenings in the Bible. Indeed, Baumer's own position in religious matters was one that reduced the compelling reason for belief in God to the beneficial moral effect which such a belief, in his view, had upon mankind. His philosophy was a Wolffianism of the oversimplified sort which explained everything in terms of immediate human purpose. And in his psychology reason was a composite of the senses and memory: a sound healthy body al-lowed the senses to function with clarity and the memory to recall stored-up sense impressions with accuracy.

If [he wrote in an essay on the existence of God] we always had clear sense perceptions and were able to recall them with the very same clarity, we would always be in possession of our reason. We would know nothing of sleep, dreams, errors, or passions.

Small wonder that he constantly challenged Bahrdt to produce compelling evidence in favor of the supernatural mysteries of re-ligion, not only the miracles of the New Testament, but also such articles of faith as the doctrines of the Trinity and of atonement.

These two dogmas seem to have caused Bahrdt much concern during the time with which we are dealing now. Of the two, it was the doctrine of the Trinity which Bahrdt first rejected, as can very readily be understood if Bahrdt was impressed by Baumer's ideas of what constituted reasonable thinking. Bahrdt says that he gave up this article of faith out of sheer weariness, convinced, moreover, that the name of the Trinity was not known in the earliest church. Having once given up his belief in the Son and the Holy Spirit as Persons of the Godhead, Bahrdt found it necessary to find a substitute rationalization. The upshot of his thinking was that Christ was a man directly inspired by God. Jesus was declared to be God's Son in a metaphorical sense, God proclaiming Jesus as, so to speak, begotten of him, as his Representative among men. And if, as Bahrdt says, any tyro could refute the scriptural proofs of the personal nature of the Holy Spirit, then the Holy

Spirit must be a designation of God's power, which is present in
all creation. Bahrdt had not at that time hit upon the idea (which,
incidentally, found such a wry echo in the "Bergidylle" of the
self-styled last of the Romanticists, Heinrich Heine) that the Spirit
—the Spirit of God, the Spirit of Christ—was nothing more than
reason enlightened by the teaching of Jesus.

The doctrine of atonement or redemption, however central to
Christian belief faith in the Redeemer might be, gradually became
just as difficult for Bahrdt to understand and accept as the doctrine
of the Trinity. The corrosives that eventually destroyed his faith
in this doctrine were once again the drive to seek a rational understanding of it and insistence on incontrovertible philological
evidence in favor of it.

Doubts began to set in when he asked himself in what way the
sacrificial death of Christ had released mankind from guilt and
from punishment for sin. This was, of course, a very important
question, for belief in the redemption was impossible without an
understanding of how the redemption was effected. But on this
point Bahrdt found the writings of the Apostles to be silent.
There were, of course, many assurances that the death of Christ
had secured for us forgiveness of sins and had reconciled us with
God, but, says Bahrdt, he could not find a single passage which
satisfactorily explained the manner in which this was done. Nowhere could he find clear explanation of Christ's merits, of man's
appropriation of these merits, or of Christ's vicarious passion.
Whenever he subjected to philological scrutiny those passages of
Scripture which were taken to be proof, for example, of the imputation of Christ's righteousness to sinful man, he found that the
language of the passage was not free from ambiguity. Since, as we
have seen earlier, he had come to the conclusion that no passage
which was in any way ambiguous or subject to question of any
sort could be said to prove anything, he found that one *dictum
probans* after the other failed to explain just how man is redeemed
by Christ.[1] But for a while he was not compelled to discard the
supernatural interpretation of redemption because of a passage
which seemed to be a clear proof of the imputation of Christ's
merits to mankind, I John 2:2:

And He is the propitiation of our sins: and not for our sins only, but also for the sins of the whole world.

He was, he says, very happy when the force of this passage dawned upon him, for it refuted the Socinian heresy that the death of Jesus on the cross made possible man's redemption by virtue of its inspirational effect. At the same time the passage seemed to be a refutation of the narrow orthodox views, for the merits of Christ must, so Bahrdt reasoned, be imputed not solely to one sect or denomination of Christians and not even solely to Christians, for the language plainly says that Christ is the "propitiation not for our sins only, but also for the sins of the world." At this time, he says, he was so overjoyed to find support for a broadly tolerant view of redemption by Christ that he overlooked the fact that the corollary of imputation is the active acceptance of the Redeemer by the sinner. In other words, the righteousness of Christ cannot be imputed to the whole world, but only to those professing Christ.

It was, however, inevitable that Bahrdt would wholeheartedly embrace the Socinian heresy of redemption through the moral influence of Christ's example, since, like Baumer, he had a powerful drive to dispel mystery and rationalize the supernatural. This drive was necessarily strengthened by his choice of friends and intimates, with whom he would, of course, debate the questions that concerned him. With one of his freethinking friends who came to visit him in Giessen just at the time that he was trying to get some light on the problem of redemption he had a long conversation, which, so he says, had a very great influence on his development.

To this friend Bahrdt admitted that he was plagued by doubts which threatened his mental and spiritual tranquility. The friend professed himself unable to understand how these particular doubts, which did not affect faith in the existence of God, in revelation, or in the immortality of the soul, could be so disquieting and challenged Bahrdt to explain what consolation he derived from the doctrine of redemption. When Bahrdt fell back upon what the friend called the "usual pulpit oratory" about the unworthiness of sinful man who can be redeemed only through the merit of Christ, the friend confronted him with a new challenge, to

state what ground of consolation was to be found exclusively in
the doctrine of redemption, to state whether he could believe in
all earnestness that the righteousness of Christ could entail re-
mittance of the punishment for sins. When Bahrdt, somewhat
hesitatingly replied that this was what Scripture taught, his friend
asked a question which is a kind of epitome of the spirit of enlightenment: "Can your Bible contradict experience?" If experience is consulted it is plain that the most enthusiastic acceptance
of the merits of Christ does not prevent the drunkard from getting
a headache or the spendthrift from becoming impoverished. When
Bahrdt replied that these "natural" punishments of transgression
were necessary for the moral betterment of man, the friend inquired whether Bahrdt believed in arbitrary (*i.e.*, unnatural)
punishments or torments. The logical conclusion to be drawn from
Bahrdt's denial was, of course, that there was no such thing as
remission of punishment through the merits of Christ, for natural
punishments must be acts of kindness and arbitrary punishments
nonexistent. As for punishment in the hereafter, the righteousness
of Christ cannot be imputed to an incorrigibly wicked man, and
God can certainly not damn a man who has reached the highest
degree of moral goodness attainable by him. Therefore, concluded
Bahrdt's friend, the doctrine of redemption is empty and can be
replaced by the philosophical insight into the true consolation of
belief in the unchanging love of an infinitely loving God.

It need not, of course, be assumed that Bahrdt's account of this
conversation just summarized is literally true. Indeed, it probably
is not. Nevertheless, there is no reason to doubt that it is an
authentic reflection of his thinking on this subject. We know from
various letters written to him by prominent theologians at this
time that he was very deeply concerned with the whole question
of redemption in its different technical aspects. For instance, J. G.
Töllner[2] wrote to him at great length on both the Trinity and
redemption, expressing agreement but with certain reservations.
The general line taken by "enlightened" theologians of the age
is indicated by Töllner's admission that the *substitutio vicaria* entails great difficulties and that he himself would be inclined to
the explanation that Christ through his death, which was the high-

est stage of his passive obedience, had attained a special right to be heard in his intercession for sinful man. Because God does accede to Christ's plea for mercy to be shown to repentant sinners it may be said that man gains redemption through the death of Christ.

As a result of the conversation with his freethinking friend, Bahrdt says he felt as though a blindfold had suddenly been taken from his eyes. He no longer felt pangs of conscience because he was compelled to question supernatural theories of redemption and had no scruples about subjecting to rational examination the various passages that were always adduced in evidence of the doctrine of redemption. Thus, for example, I John 2:2, which he had once taken as proof of the imputation of Christ's righteousness to all the world, he now felt to be no such thing, for in the context John is plainly speaking of moral reformation. The passage is an exhortation to renounce moral depravity and an expression of faith that if anyone sins Christ will lead him back to the Father through moral regeneration, for he can make us and the whole world pleasing to God.[3]

Thus I found very soon [he says] that all the passages which ascribe the effect of forgiveness of sin to the death of Jesus can be explained as being mediate, namely that the death of Jesus effects forgiveness not immediately but mediately, inasmuch as by his teaching, which is sealed by his blood, Jesus reforms men and makes them pleasing to God, thus delivering them from sin which had previously brought so much misery (death) upon them.

Once the idea had come to him that Christ's redemption of man was effected by moral regeneration, Bahrdt says, he found corroborative evidence everywhere in Scripture. For instance, when Paul writes in Romans 11:11 that by the fall of the Hebrews salvation came to the Gentiles, the meaning is that because the Jews rejected the Gospel the Apostles had occasion to bring Christ's teaching to the Gentiles, who then, from being depraved heathens, became reformed men, pleasing to God.[4] Or again, when Paul writes in Colossians 1:24,

Now I rejoice in my sufferings for your sake and fill up on my part that which is lacking of the afflictions of Christ in my flesh for his body's sake, which is the church [5]

he plainly refutes the theory of redemption:

The Apostle is speaking of his sufferings for truth. He compares them with the sufferings of Jesus. He represents them as, so to speak, a supplement to Jesus' sufferings, a continuation of them. And so it is plain that the sufferings of Jesus can have had no other purpose than the one which the sufferings of the Apostles had. They were sacrifices for the instruction and moral regeneration of humanity.

After this it was a matter of piling up evidence for his point of view, and the method Bahrdt hit upon is completely characteristic. It was to make a collection of passages bearing upon the point and to classify them into two groups, literal and figurative. The figurative passages Bahrdt felt to be a legacy from the metaphorical language of Hebrew religion. The task was, therefore, to look for clear and unmetaphorical passages which dealt with the matter. If no such passage could be found which ascribed the effect of immediate redemption to the death of Jesus, then, of course, the figurative passages must be merely obscure language disguising the plain truth of the unmetaphorical passages. The result of the investigation was that where the purpose of Christ's sufferings was described in clear and unadorned language, it was plain that He died for the moral regeneration of man.[6] Since he found a great many such passages, Bahrdt had no hesitation in coming to the conclusion that all the other passages which seemed to justify supernatural interpretation were really metaphorical distortions of the simple truth. He was confirmed in this conviction when he examined all the passages once more to see whether any general distinction could be drawn between what Jesus himself said about redemption and what the Apostles said.

Now I became completely convinced [he says] that, because Jesus never spoke about the mercy seat, atonement, justification, and all those things, but always insisted only upon virtue and rectitude, and described this as true worship and devoutness, the whole doctrine of redemption had arisen from misunderstood expressions of the Apostles, who had accustomed themselves to speak with Jews in Jewish imagery.

The turn taken by Bahrdt's thinking was, quite naturally, reflected in his publications, for, as we know, he was always ready to rush into print with his views. The year 1773 was particularly fruitful, since in the course of it Bahrdt published, in addition to the highly controversial translation of the New Testament, a number of minor works which followed the general lines of thought which have just been discussed.

There was, for example, a textbook in church history,[7] which was the result of lectures on this subject which he was commanded to give because none of the other professors had any interest or competence. Bahrdt had no competence in the subject either, but as long as he had no choice in the matter, he worked up a course of lectures in outline fashion and decided to publish it. Both his father and Ernesti tried to dissuade him, pointing out that he had almost no independent knowledge of the subject and that the field of church history was one of the most difficult of all to master. Even Dr. Walch in Göttingen, who had been occupied for many years writing a church history and had all the necessary books at his disposal, occasionally made "gruesome blunders" such as creating new historical personalities because he had not read all the sources systematically and with perfect knowledge of the various languages.[8] These warnings had no effect on Bahrdt, who dedicated his book to Ludwig IX in the customary flowery style. In his foreword, however, Bahrdt specifically disclaims originality and learning, pointing out that his work was based on Rechenberg's *Compendium,* which he had supplemented and corrected partly by some limited investigation of his own but mostly by reading Semler's *Capita Selecta.* The book is, therefore, quite frankly a text such as students would buy to cram for examinations and must for this reason have been considered particularly dangerous by Benner and his friends. For Bahrdt in his introduction stated explicitly in simple German what had become the guiding principles of such scholars as Ernesti and Semler in transferring the methods of historical research in classical philology to the study of the Bible, the history of dogma, and the church.

Historical knowledge [he says] must be not only clear and correct but also pragmatic.[9] It must depict the mores and the characters of its heroes. It must discover the way events came to pass, and their origins, means, and consequences. Especially in church history it must be concerned with the history of beliefs and of the interpretation of doctrine and the changes that have been made in the latter. Its value will be shown in the study both of the ritual and the dogmas of the church and in the evaluation of the contentions which have arisen about these matters; it will give us wisdom and good sense in our affairs and deeper insight into the ways of Providence. It will have a very great influence upon the *humaniora*, civil history and jurisprudence, our knowledge of canon law, and on biblical philology and criticism.

The thesis of the book is that in the course of the centuries the teachings of Jesus were corrupted by meaningless speculations and quarrels about matters that were extraneous to them. The purpose of Jesus' coming among men, whether Jews or Gentiles, was to elevate them to a higher degree of morality and thus help them to attain bliss. Jesus' ethical teachings differed from the contemporary pagan and Jewish systems in that he made love, even of one's enemies, the maxim of social behavior and prayer the best means of confirming oneself in faith. In order to lead men closer to moral perfection and the happiness that such perfection would entail, Jesus tried to teach them more correct ideas about God and more rational principles of worship: that God is a spirit and must be venerated as a spirit, that God is love, and that the human soul is immortal and will be reunited with the resurrected body for reward or punishment. Jesus' death upon the cross was the necessary consequence of his absolute obedience to the will of God and the price he paid to redeem humanity. His Passion and Resurrection constitute the great example and inspiration to men to follow him.[10]

The book then goes on to say that this clear and simple doctrine became overlaid by metaphysical and theological obscurities beginning with the second century, when most of the learned men of the church were of the Neoplatonic school. It is to the Neoplatonic philosophy that we owe the ideas about the value of fasting, celibacy, monogamy, and all mysticism. The baneful influence of Neoplatonism was aided by the fact that the New Testament writings were not generally available but were in the possession of only a few priests and that incautious use was made of the apocryphal books, which fanned the fires of fanaticism. The Gnostics, too, contributed a great deal of nonsense to the stream of Christian thought. In the fourth century fresh and powerful impetus was given to useless speculation about free will and grace by St. Augustine.[11] Thus, in short, the history of the church is seen to be the history of the proliferation of irrational delusions and of a hierarchy that was the antithesis of the early Christian community. Eventually, Martin Luther tried to restore Scripture as interpreted by reason to the place of authority, but his successors were indolent and merely patched up the traditional system and subordinated Scripture and reason to the Symbolic Books.

The hostility to "obscure language," "mysticism," and "useless speculation," which characterizes the church history is the dominant note in other publications of the year 1773 also, chief of which was the already mentioned translation of the New Testament. Bahrdt had, of course, been occupied with the thought of making his own improved version of the New Testament for some time. He had preached on the subject and now published his sermons.[12] He also published his criticisms[13] of the German version of the Old Testament by J. D. Michaelis, which had begun to come out in 1769. He found that Michaelis's style was obscure and unidiomatic and that the poetic passages had been watered down and transformed into something dark and dismal. Bahrdt therefore very plainly intended his translation of the New Testament to be a major work. This in a certain sense it did indeed turn out to be, although not at all in the way Bahrdt hoped.

Although after the translations, paraphrases, and commentaries of Heumann (1748), Michaelis, Ernesti, and Semler, it had ceased to be felt almost a sacrilege for anyone to try to deviate from the translation of Martin Luther, the appearance of Bahrdt's New Testament produced an almost pristine sense of shock among the orthodox. This was, of course, the learned doctor's intention, for he entitled it "The Most Recent Revelations of God in Letters and Narratives, put into German by Doctor Carl Friedrich Bahrdt." [14] This was a title, he said in his preface, which he had no need of defending, for experts would realize immediately that it truly expressed the meaning of the Greek.

In the preface Bahrdt also says that his aim was to produce a translation which "friends of the most lovable religion" would be able to understand without a commentary and use for confirmation in their faith. For this purpose a literal translation such as that by Michaelis, however accurate it may be said to be, is useless, for it may be truly described as "Greek or Hebrew in German letters." The reader for whom Bahrdt was translating is interested only in the content and not the form. Such a reader can be only confused and annoyed by Greek or Hebrew turns of phrase. What he wants is plain down-to-earth German. Anyone who feels that this kind of translation takes forbidden liberties with the text is asked to consider three things: first, that the authors of the New Testament were uneducated people, who were unable to organize their material or to use choice language and were sometimes so excited that they actually became incoherent; second, that the "Oriental" turns of phrase in Luther's translation have done much to perpetuate the mysticism, ambiguity, and obscurity of dogma; third, that the Greek of the New Testament is a hybrid language, the flavor of which is not worth retaining in a translation.

A good example of how Bahrdt "cleared up" the obscurity of the oriental figurative language is afforded by his translation of Matthew 12:19-20, the passage about the servant:

He shall not strive nor cry; neither shall any man hear his voice in the streets. A bruised reed shall he not break, and smoking flax shall he not quench, till he send forth judgment unto victory.

Bahrdt's version has:

He will perform his duty with love and gentleness, will not secure obedience by severity or compel respect with haughty noise. Modest virtue and noble meekness will mark every step of his life.

A footnote to the first of these two verses reads: "Like a consul with his lictors," and to the second:

According to the Greek, he will walk so softly that he will not crush a reed which has already been broken and so easily that a wick which is merely glimmering will not be blown out by the passing of his garment.[15]

This, of course, is not translation but paraphrase and commentary, as is in fact the entire book. Another striking example of the same tendency is found in Matthew 3:2, which reads (referring to John the Baptist) : "And saying, Repent ye: for the kingdom of heaven is at hand." According to Bahrdt the passage means:

In brief the substance of his teaching was this: Reform, for God is about to establish a new religious society in which virtue may anticipate rewards which will extend into eternity, but depravity, inconceivable misery.

If this passage seems surely to be more Bahrdt than the Baptist it has still been acknowledged by such a scholar as Karl Aner[16] that Bahrdt's rendering of μετανοεῖτε as "Bessert euch" hits the sense of the Greek better than Luther's "Tut Busse." Furthermore, Aner says, Bahrdt's New Testament embodies results of scholarly interpretation and his adaptation of Scripture to the mode of feeling of the age[17] humanized the Bible in the same way that scholarly research did: the Bible was taken down from the pedestal of absolute dogmatic authority on which it had been placed by orthodoxy.

Both things—placing the biblical books in their historical milieu and the transposition of the texts into contemporary modes of feeling—meant a humanization of the contents of Scripture.

There is no doubt that humanization was Bahrdt's very deliberate intent and aim, and he could with some justice point out that his treatment of the original text was in principle not so very different from Martin Luther's. This intention to humanize had been made plain in the preface to the first part of his translation (the Gospels of Matthew, Mark, and John) and the comparison with Luther was explicitly stated in the preface to the second part (Luke, Acts) as part of his defense against the attacks made upon his version. The defense is not addressed to scholars and theologians but to simple and devout readers of the Bible, who would be expected to buy and read the book with greatest profit to themselves and to Bahrdt.

In the preface such a simple devout reader is represented as objecting that Bahrdt's translation is not really the Bible, but some newfangled book in which everything is unfamiliar.

I want the words of Jesus and the Apostles, [he is made to say] they have the power which speaks to the heart. "Woman, what have I to do with thee? Mine hour is not yet come." See, that is sonorous, pithy speech.

To this fictitious critic Bahrdt concedes that the words of Jesus and the Apostles really are more pithy than anything that can be found in the usual devotional readings. But, he goes on, the devout reader is mistaken in supposing that Bahrdt had robbed him of the very words of Jesus and the Apostles, for those words were in Greek, a language that the reader does not know. If the devout

reader is to understand the words of Jesus and the Apostles, those
words must be rendered in German, and Bahrdt is no more guilty
of depriving the reader of the very words of Jesus than was Martin
Luther, for Luther's translation is by no means always literal, as
can be seen very well in the example from John which the simple
reader cited.

If Jesus said, "τί ἐμοὶ καὶ σοί, γύναι," Luther's translation doesn't contain what
is contained in the words of Jesus. Indeed, Luther's version cannot be considered a literal translation, for the Greek actually says, "What [is it] to me
and thee, woman?"

Thus, Bahrdt declares the sense of the passage to be something like
"It is of no concern to us," and he justifies his own rendition:

He, however, asked her not to concern herself with the matter at all. She
was not to worry about it in the least: he would carry out his intentions at
the proper time.

In this version the direct quotation has been discarded because
such direct quotation is merely a part of the "Oriental" narrative
technique which Bahrdt has abandoned for the sake of greater
clarity. If, says Bahrdt, he has made mistakes in his interpretation,
then he is in the excellent company of Martin Luther himself,
who also made mistakes, although in respect of general faithfulness
to the original, Luther's text is unimpeachable. Bahrdt's own
version, however,

has this advantage over Luther's Bible—that it is modern, intelligible, and pure in expression, and, most important of all, it is fluent and
coherent. On the other hand, you will find a hundred passages in your
German Bible which will have no meaning to you whatever, or even if you
understand the individual expressions, there is not even the shadow of connection or coherence.

Out of fairness to Bahrdt, however, it should be added that he
was not altogether devoid of reverence for the mighty work of his
great predecessor, for he writes in the preface which we have
just cited:

I must tell you that that person who, like me, makes a new translation of
the Bible is by no means entitled to supplant the old one. And he cannot
do it either: let him be the most respected theologian in Germany, nonetheless, his will always be a private work, and he will never cause Luther's
Bible to be discarded and his own put in its place.

The publication of this book let loose a flood of protests, denunciations, diatribes, and satires, many of them, like that of Pastor Götze,[18] vehemently accusing Bahrdt of intentionally falsifying his text. Indeed, Götze who, it is interesting to recall, had once been so favorably impressed by Bahrdt as to try to secure a handsome appointment for him, turned upon him the full fury of his wrath, accused him of blasphemy, and expressed the hope that severe legal action might be taken against such a translation and its author. This attack brought to Bahrdt's side a staunch defender who, while specifically refusing to comment on the merits or demerits of the translation, pointed out that any Lutheran who questioned the legal or moral right of Bahrdt or any other to make and publish his own translation of the Bible was really attacking the basis of his own faith, for Luther himself had no more right to translate the Bible than had Bahrdt. This defender was none other than Gotthold Ephraim Lessing, whose controversy with Götze gave rise indirectly to what has ever since been considered one of the noblest monuments of religious enlightenment, *Nathan der Weise*.[19]

Sober evaluations of Bahrdt's work by other representative men of the Enlightenment can be found in the *Allgemeine deutsche Bibliothek*. For example, the review of Götze's attack on Bahrdt criticizes Götze's call for inquisitorial censorship much as Lessing does. It points out, however, that Bahrdt failed to feel his way into the spirit of the original and imposed his own way of thinking upon it by his arbitrary changes and alleged improvements, that his language was not serious and dignified, and that he paid no attention to the quality of the particular writer he was translating but jumped from serious to playful, to witty, or to precious style. Another reviewer, writing about Bahrdt's translation of the epistles of Paul,[20] finds much to praise but finds it amazing that

a man who often sees the sense of the Apostle so vividly, grasps it so felicitously, and translates it into German so naturally, suddenly becomes inconsistent and violates the correct principles of translation which he himself has recognized and exemplified.

All of this was wittily summed up by Goethe in his little sketch

Prolog zu den neuesten Offenbarungen Gottes,[21] in which the four
Evangelists are represented as calling on Bahrdt, who finds their
company very embarrassing, for he is on his way to a garden party,
where his visitors, with their rough cloaks and untrimmed beards,
with Mark's lion and Luke's ox, would be sure to cause consternation. Bahrdt informs them that if they wish to go with him they
will have to become more civilized. Since they do not accept his
suggestion, Bahrdt resumes his work on their writings, to which,
it may be inferred, he can give the elegance the writers themselves
lacked. The most memorable lines in the sketch are the shrewd and
penetrating self-characterization which Goethe puts on Bahrdt's
lips and which may be paraphrased:

Now here's an idea I call pretty nice: that's what I'd say if I were the
Christ.[22]

Hot though the fires of indignation blazed immediately upon
the publication of the New Testament, the flames merely singed
Bahrdt, whose professional status was at first not noticeably affected. But hidden fires had also been set smoldering which were
destined, several years later, to have the most serious consequences.

XII

⟦THE TRAP AND THE MOUSE⟧

FOR A TIME immediately following the publication of his New
Testament, however, Bahrdt feared that he might have kindled
a blaze that could destroy him, for he had received a warning from
a friend which made him look to none other than Moser for protection. On the twenty-fourth of April 1774, he sent Moser a letter[1] which was apparently intended to subtly flatter Moser's sense
of power and his pietistic devoutness. Bahrdt wrote:

A letter from an intimate friend which I received in today's mail and of
which I enclose a copy of the important passage imposes upon me the duty
of informing Your Excellency of an imminent danger which is threatening
me. I really do not know how much there is to the whole affair or whether
it is really true, but this much I know, that God will preserve me in the
tempest. It would, however, give me even greater comfort if Your Excellency
at your convenience would inform me of the proper way to regard the matter
and also reassure me of the sweet hope that in this instance also I would find
in Your Excellency a worthy instrument of the God who watches over me.

The extract from the letter read as follows:

A tempest is coming, dear friend. Prepare yourself. The Attorney General
of the Empire is going to have your New Testament examined by Catholics,
Lutherans, and Calvinists, and then leave the final judgment to His Imperial
Majesty. The Suffragan Bishop von Scheben, who is really a very nice man
told me yesterday, he would be compelled by his office [2] to sound the bell
because of it. I have not been able to learn who denounced you. But just be
nice and quiet. I am in correspondence with the Suffragan Bishop and will
advise you of everything in good time.

Bahrdt does not say anywhere who the friend was who thus
warned him of the tempest threatening him, but it is hard not to
speculate who it might have been. First of all, the friend's statement that he was in correspondence with the Bishop makes it seem

109

likely, although by no means certain, that he was a Catholic. Furthermore, he seems to have had a certain interest in the New Testament paraphrase, and one can deduce from the language ("Der Herr Weihbischoff von Scheben, ein sonst lieber Herr, sagte mir gestern, er müsse deswegen die Glocke läuten kraft seines Officii.") that the Suffragan Bishop himself was somewhat reluctant to proceed against Bahrdt, whether because he was aware of the friendship that existed between Bahrdt and the unknown correspondent or for some other reason. Certain questions therefore arise: did Bahrdt have a Catholic friend who was particularly interested in the New Testament paraphrase? and was there any reason why highly-placed Catholic clergy might be reluctant to proceed against the author of the paraphrase? To both questions the answer is Yes.

The Catholic friend was a certain Professor Herwig in Würzburg, who had once been a Lutheran minister. Bahrdt had, of course, heard about his conversion and decided that he might be able to make use of him to gain certain ends of his own. He had, as he says, the false belief that from the dedication of his books to notable personalities and people of wealth and influence some benefit might accrue to him. On previous occasions he had been disappointed, for the dignitaries thus flattered had responded with gracious expressions of sincere appreciation but nothing tangible. Then at the time he was finishing the first part of his New Testament he happened to learn that the Prince Bishop Adam Friedrich of Würzburg had the admirable wont to requite every dedication with a present of excellent wine.[3] Now, good wine was something which Bahrdt never despised and he decided that he would try his luck with another dedication. There was, however, one considerable difficulty: that the dedication of a New Testament translation made by a Protestant theologian to a Catholic prince and bishop might prove so sensational as to be offensive. How to get around this difficulty? To Bahrdt's fertile mind there occurred the thought that Professor Herwig was living in Würzburg and might be useful.

Bahrdt therefore wrote to Herwig and acquainted him with his wish, explaining that this cordial overture of a Lutheran theologian to a Catholic bishop, who was known and admired for his enlightened outlook, would be a brilliant and impressive example of religious tolerance. In support of his representations Bahrdt pointed to the preface he had written to the anonymously published defense of the Catholic religion by J. H. von Gerstenberg[4] and hinted that he was planning to take other important steps to promote universal toleration. Herwig seems to have understood this as an intimation that Bahrdt himself might become Catholic and thus presented the whole question to the Bishop's minister, who secured His Princely Grace's consent to accept the dedication. Complimentary copies of the New Testament with the respectfully worded dedication were sent to Würzburg, and in due course Bahrdt received a case of fifty bottles of the very finest old wine.

It can therefore very readily be understood that it might prove embarrassing to Herwig, to the Suffragan Bishop, and to the Prince Bishop himself, if it were determined that permission had been sought and granted to dedicate a heretical book to one of the most prominent dignitaries of the church. Furthermore, as will seem likely from subsequent developments in Bahrdt's career, it is possible that Bahrdt's hint that he might become converted to the Catholic faith was taken rather seriously, for it would surely have been a sensation if this Lutheran theologian who was gaining notoriety for his heretical views returned to the Catholic church.

In reply to Bahrdt's request for support Moser sent a long letter which began with the observation that Bahrdt should have expected trouble of the kind that he described, for various theologians had expressed their opinion that the author of such a work as the New Testament paraphrase could not be considered qualified to hold a professorship of theology at a Protestant university. As for the problem of what to do to withstand the predicted tempest, Moser said he had no suggestions, inasmuch as he, being a layman, could not judge whether Bahrdt was guilty of heresy or innocent. He added that he had read the New Testament paraphrase with great pleasure and had received enlightment on many formerly obscure passages but had been somewhat troubled by the paraphrases, modernization, and expansion of many other passages. He concluded by saying that he would be sorry if Bahrdt were found guilty, for such great talents as Bahrdt possessed should be devoted to the common good, and he promised to protect Bahrdt should he be innocent. It should be said that this very temperate and reservedly appreciative letter of Moser was not purely hypocritical, for even in the damning report he made to Ludwig a year earlier, in connection with Bahrdt's desire to become Court Chaplain, Moser acknowledged the remarkable charm which Bahrdt exerted in the pulpit and in society, as well as his great ability. His summary was:

Along with his great talents and splendid gifts, which could make him a man of the first rank, he has a black, villainous heart, insatiable pride, and lust for power, and wherever he has been he has set everything ablaze.

For some reason, perhaps because of the circumstances of the dedication just described, no action was taken by the Imperial government against Bahrdt for his heretical translation at this time. And for almost a year there was no open feuding in Giessen that could have given Moser the occasion to take action against Bahrdt. On the thirtieth of October 1774, however, a spark was struck which ignited the powder train leading to the great explosion, which ejected Bahrdt from Giessen to the apparent satisfaction of both Bahrdt and his enemies.

The spark was a letter written by a student of theology named Johann Michael Mehl to his former teacher, Rector Bast of Buchsweiler. In this letter Mehl confessed to certain doubts and scruples stemming from the lectures of Bahrdt and Schulz (Bahrdt's one-time friend), who agreed in denying the existence of fallen angels. Bahrdt seems to have been particularly effective in his exegetical demonstrations that there was no passage in Holy Writ that could be accepted as proof of such beings. Mehl went on to say that the arguments of the two professors impressed him so much that he felt he might be obliged to make it a principle to acknowledge as true only those articles of faith which he was compelled to accept by force of reasoning. He had, he said, thus far not had any reason to fear serious consequences of his new outlook, for he was still unable to accept the arguments against original sin and eternal damnation, and he saw no reason to doubt the Symbolic Books, for they were in harmony with the Bible.

We do not know whether Mehl wrote this letter on his own

initiative or whether, as Bahrdt and Schulz maintained, it had been inspired by their enemies. But we do know that the recipient of the letter, Rector Bast, became very excited and turned it over to the Consistory in Buchsweiler so that measures could be taken to protect local candidates for theological orders from the heresies of Giessen. The Consistory looked upon it as a duty to forward the letter to Professor Ouvrier with the request that he confer with Mehl and persuade him of the folly and error of his incipient enlightenment. Ouvrier complied with the request and succeeded in reconverting Mehl to his pristine orthodoxy. In his zeal for righteousness Ouvrier went still farther: on January 16, 1775, prefacing his remarks with a reference to two unnamed professors who had the reputation of being heterodox, he read Mehl's letter to his assembled students and admonished them to beware of such principles and to come to him, Ouvrier, with their doubts and questions should they have any. As for reasoned proof, he said, he was confident that anyone who heard his arguments for the existence of the devil would find them so cogent as to dispel all doubt.

This lecture caused a great sensation among the students, for, although no names had been mentioned, it was plain that Ouvrier had been hitting at Bahrdt and Schulz, and public attack upon one's colleagues was, as we have seen, strictly forbidden. Report of the attack made upon them came to the attention of the two heterodox professors, who took drastic actions on the very same day by sending a special messenger with a report and formal complaint to the Privy Council in Darmstadt. (They thus made themselves guilty of not going through the proper channels.) They asked that Ouvrier be given an official reprimand and that the students be authoritatively informed that they had complete freedom to choose their lectures; that is, Ouvrier had no right to make his students boycott Schulz and Bahrdt. After speedy deliberation the Privy Council decided that both parties were guilty of unsanctioned actions and instructed Chancellor Koch to reprimand them both.

At this point the students at the University took a hand in the affair: a group of twenty-four sent a humble petition to *Serenis-*

simus to order an investigation of the scandalous attacks upon the most able and popular professors of the University, Schulz and Bahrdt. In support of this petition they enclosed copies of two scurrilous pamphlets[5] which traduced these excellent scholars. One of the pamphlets, the so-called first *Toleranzbrief*, in distinction from the second, which was in favor of Bahrdt, made the especially damaging charge against Schulz that he had asserted in his lectures that Job's affliction was in reality the "French disease." Moser stated to the Privy Council that it was his opinion that the student petition had been inspired and perhaps even written by Bahrdt, whose involved and flowery style he believed he detected in it. Nonetheless the Privy Council decided that it really had to learn the authorship of the pamphlets and also that Professor Schulz must be questioned under oath as to whether he had made the statement about Job attributed to him.

While this investigation was being carried on, not only Bahrdt and Schulz but Ouvrier as well protested earnestly against the reprimand directed against them. Bahrdt and Schulz pressed for an investigation of Mehl, asserting that his letter to Rector Bast had undoubtedly been inspired by their enemies, and Ouvrier denied that he could be held responsible for his actions to any authority lower than that of *Serenissimus* himself. Ouvrier's defiance lasted only a few days: the threat of suspension from office caused him to realize that it would be discreet to comply with Chancellor Koch's instructions. In his report about the Mehl affair, however, he maintained that he had merely done his duty. As for Schulz, he indignantly rejected all responsibility for the defamatory diagnosis of Job's affliction but said he was merely reporting what certain others had said; he himself believed the disease to have been elephantiasis.

By the end of January some progress had been made toward discovering where the pamphlets in question had been printed and by whom they had been written, but the whole matter had been complicated by two other literary efforts: the second *Toleranzbrief*, which defended Bahrdt, and Benner's *Programma apologiam pro mysterio, quo verbum caro factum sit, sistens* (Giessen, 1774), which Benner was now proposing to publish in

German to confute Bahrdt. Of these two complicating factors the
second was more easily dealt with: Benner was informed that if
he went ahead with his plan he would be fined five hundred
Gulden for adding to the discord plaguing the University. By the
middle of February Benner had replied that he would suppress
his translation. As for the other pamphlet, Chancellor Koch suspected that Bahrdt's friend Deinet was the publisher and continued his investigations in order to fix responsibility for all these
writings where it belonged. By the sixth of March he was able to
report that Deinet was not responsible for the second
Toleranzbrief and that the author of the first one was Professor
Schwarz, whose outline of church history had been so unfavorably
reviewed by Bahrdt in the *Frankfurter Gelehrte Anzeigen.*
Furthermore, this same Schwarz had arranged also for the publication of the *Sendschreiben,* supposedly the work of a certain
theologian whom Schwarz would not name.

But even as it was thus being made clear that Bahrdt's old
enemies were keeping up the feud with him in various ways, an
abrupt shift of sentiment occurred in the Privy Council. The proceedings, which had for a while been concerned primarily with
the responsibility of Ouvrier and secondarily of Schulz and
Bahrdt for the scandalous discord within the University, were
now directed solely against Bahrdt, and Schulz and Ouvrier were
no longer involved.

It is not completely clear why this shift occurred. The direct
impetus came from a resolution by *Geheimrat* von Hesse, the man
who had done so much to bring Bahrdt to Giessen and who had
supported him so staunchly at first. As a result of his motion on
the twenty-seventh of January 1775, the Privy Council declared
that the investigation of the uproar occasioned by Professor
Ouvrier was secondary to the question:

Are there at Giessen professors of theology who publicly teach errors
which conflict with the system of doctrine of the Evangelical church and
its Symbolic Books?

On the same date the Privy Council sent to Ludwig a detailed
account of the entire matter, and to the theological faculty they
sent an order to make a report on the dissensions and agitation

caused by the publication of Bahrdt's New Testament and to make
a recommendation how to deal with him. The interesting questions, however, are why did von Hesse turn against Bahrdt at this
time? and why did the Privy Council suddenly cease to have any
interest in the case of Mehl and Ouvrier and in the authorship
of the four documents about which the whole investigation had
hitherto turned? Can it be that something had occurred to cause
Ludwig himself to change his opinion of Bahrdt? Such a change
could indeed explain a great deal, and it might even be surmised
that Moser would then be able to exert far more pressure on the
members of the Council, such as von Hesse, than he had before.
The answer to the question just posed is that it is at least possible
that something did occur which turned *Serenissimus* against
Bahrdt, namely that Bahrdt was denounced to Ludwig as a damned
low-life Socinian (*ein verdammter hundsföttischer Socinianer*) [6]
by his chief chaplain or *Feldprobst* Venator.

After considerable delay and repeated admonitions, the three
other members of the theological faculty, to whom various groups
of pastors throughout the Landgravate had sent complaints about
Bahrdt, made their recommendations. Bechtold recounted a long
list of Bahrdt's heresies but expressed his opinion that Bahrdt
should be given time to reform. Ouvrier's opinion was presumably completely negative, and Benner's advocated getting expert
opinions from other theological faculties, a proposal which was
made by the Giessen Consistory also. In presenting all the
material to the Privy Council, however, Moser declared that it
was unnecessary to solicit opinions from outside and that the
answers to two questions should be required of the Consistory
and the Definitory of Darmstadt: whether Dr. Bahrdt, considering
his translation of the New Testament, was loyal to the system of
doctrine of his church, to its confession of faith, and to his own
oaths as a doctor and professor of theology; and, second, if he
could not be declared loyal, whether he could any longer be tolerated as an academic instructor and Evangelical pastor without
reproach accruing to the church, disgrace to the university, and
harm to young people and to his congregation.

Thus the headsman's axe was poised and ready to fall, but the headsman had reckoned without the culprit. The Consistory and Definitory had not even received Moser's instructions before Ludwig IX himself received a direct communication from Dr. Bahrdt, in which he "placed his entire fate at the feet of His Princely Serene Highness," for he had received the offer of a responsible position which would bring him a salary of two thousand florins. He declared, however, that he would prefer to remain in Ludwig's services and would even guarantee to write nothing whatever that touched upon theological controversy if Ludwig would only grant him two petitions: first, to strike down the legal action now being taken against him and forbid all further attacks upon him and, second, to free him from the prospect of being kept subordinate in his ecclesiastical duties to some hostile authority by giving him formal assurance that he would succeed Benner in the position of *Superintendent* in Giessen. This step, he pointed out, would not entail advancing him over the heads of Bechtold and Ouvrier on the theological faculty and so should be offensive to no one.

Ludwig, however, was no longer interested in supporting Bahrdt and gave instructions that Bahrdt's request for dismissal of the charges should be granted, thus bringing the hostilities to an end that cannot have pleased Bahrdt's enemies too greatly. Moser, in referring Bahrdt's resignation to the Privy Council, wrote:

The attached material [Bahrdt's letters to Ludwig and to Moser himself] shows with what snakelike viciousness Dr. Bahrdt has tried to secure acceptance of his resignation from *Serenissimus* or rather, to force his continued stay in Giessen and triumph over his opponents.

After recommending that the necessary steps be taken to release Bahrdt from his duties, Moser went on to urge that Bahrdt not be allowed to escape like a mouse from a trap but that the legal action initiated against him be continued to the end and sentence passed. To Dr. Bahrdt, however, this last gesture must have seemed rather empty, for he was about to leave for Switzerland, where (so he hoped) honor, glory, and a comfortable living awaited him.

To his enemies, however, his departure was the signal for triumphant rejoicing. Götze proclaimed to all the world that

Bahrdt had been forced to quit Giessen without being allowed
to preach a farewell sermon. And Benner resorted to Latin, both
prose and verse, to celebrate the victory with due solemnity.
"Hoc mense," he wrote in May, 1775, in the records of the theological faculty, "divina nos clementia a Bahrdtio liberavit. Abiit,
excessit, evasit, erupit, virulenta semina et dedecoris haud parum
reliquit." [7]

XIII

⟨PROGRESSIVE EDUCATION⟩

O NE EVENING in the late autumn of 1774, Bahrdt tells us, he was taking a simple meal in the company of his wife, when the maid announced an unknown visitor, who was admitted and introduced himself as Salis of Marschlins. "Come, sir, and take pot luck with me," said Bahrdt, "you find me completely at your disposal." The visitor accepted Bahrdt's invitation with alacrity, saying that he was not one to stand on ceremony. This unaffected and direct manner as well as the man's large flashing eyes and kind and gentle mien made the very best impression upon Bahrdt as they sat down at table and began a most interesting conversation.

Bahrdt soon learned from this visitor, whose imposing and even intimidating appearance was tempered by an apparent frankness, a very simple and friendly bearing, that he was one of the wealthiest and most influential of the nobility of the Swiss republic of Graubünden or Grisons, which was at that time a bone of contention between France and Austria. Bahrdt felt himself immensely flattered to have this great statesman, who in his capacity of representative of the Court of Versailles in Graubünden had the title of Minister, so intimately sharing a simple ragout. When the great statesman augmented the flattery of his presence by offering Bahrdt an annual salary of two thousand *Gulden* to go with him to Graubünden and take over the directorship of a Philanthropinum or boys' school, Bahrdt's happiness must have been as keen as was his curiosity to learn how Salis happened to be interested in a boys' school and particularly how he had happened to come to Giessen to offer Bahrdt the directorship.

119

The origins of the school went back to 1761 when a group of friends began to meet informally to discuss matters of general interest and common welfare. A year later the group had named itself the *Helvetische Gesellschaft* and was beginning to direct its energies more and more to the problem of education. Prominent among those associated with the group were such men as Isaak Iselin, Franz Urs Balthasar, Johann Caspar Lavater, and Johann Jakob Bodmer. Ulysses von Salis himself was not attached to it until 1765. But the member who was most active in the educational work of the association was Martin von Planta, who was a pastor in Zizers near Chur. The idea of establishing a school seems to have suggested itself first to him, and he then discussed it with his particular friend Johann Peter Nesemann and with Ulysses von Salis. At length Planta and Nesemann began in a small way in the parsonage in Zizers and then obtained permission to set up their academy in *Schloss Haldenstein,* in which Salis had a half interest.

Planta defined the twofold purpose of the school as first, the imparting of a Christian education, by which he meant the employment of reason and philosophy in the service of Revelation and, second, the preparation of young people for political, economic, military, and business careers. In method Planta and Nesemann advocated teaching the children to use their intelligence rather than to rely on mere memory. In teaching Latin, for example, they required the memorization only of the nouns and verbs, leaving syntax and usage to be developed from the reading of standard authors. Instruction in the history of Graubünden and of Switzerland was given by Ulysses von Salis, whose participation in the work of the school, however, was not made generally known, because Salis was a most unpopular man in his own little country. In fact, it was his office as Minister of the Court of Versailles which protected him from attempts of the Graubündener on his personal safety. The Graubündener suspected with justice that Salis was trying to influence the political outlook of his native land in this rather long-range fashion, and it was not long before Planta and Nesemann won the reputation of being the henchmen of the greatly feared and hated Minister.

At the end of May 1770, Salis proposed to a meeting of the *Helvetische Gesellschaft* that the school be relocated in *Schloss Marschlins,* his own personal residence. *Schloss Haldenstein* was unable to accommodate the growing number of pupils, but *Schloss Marschlins* was much larger and could readily be altered to house a hundred children or so as well as the necessary staff. Whether Salis was motivated by pure philanthropy in making this suggestion has been questioned, chiefly by Bahrdt, who writes that Planta and Nesemann had made their academy very profitable and that Salis lured them into his own castle for the sake of gain. This is undoubtedly an exaggeration, for most reliable testimony is to the effect that the academy really had outgrown its quarters and that Salis offered Planta and Nesemann such favorable terms that they could not refuse his offer. Nonetheless, according to the testimony of Rector Keller of Aarau,[1] the tale was still abroad in Graubünden in the 1880s that the school had been transferred from Haldenstein to Marschlins because Salis owed money to the academy and hoped to be able to liquidate his debt much more easily by furnishing food and other tangibles directly from his estate in Marschlins.

In the spring of 1771 the school moved into the new quarters, but on March 29, 1772, the presiding genius of the school, Martin von Planta, died, leaving his friend Nesemann to carry on as best he could. Nesemann, however, felt himself unequal to the task and made it clear that a successor must be found for Planta. The first man to be invited to take up responsiblity for the school was Johann Bernhard Basedow, of whom more will be told presently, but Basedow refused, saying that he could spare no time from the task of completing his great *Elementarwerk*. For two and a half years Salis, Nesemann, and some other interested members of the Helvetic Society carried on the search for a director and issued a number of invitations to various more or less prominent people including the eminent mathematician and physicist, Johann Heinrich Lambert. Finally, Salis, who had been struck by the fact that Basedow had, by the mere process of excogitation, arrived at many of the pedagogical principles which Planta and Nesemann had worked out in practice, decided that he would consult with Basedow directly. So he set off to Dessau where this renowned personage resided and had finally established his highly touted academy or Philanthropinum under the patronage of Leopold Friedrich Franz, Duke and Prince of Anhalt-Dessau.

According to the story which Bahrdt says he had directly from Salis, the two educators spent several days together discussing the theory of philanthropinism and considering who might be a qualified candidate for the directorship of Marschlins. Many learned men had been passed in review but all were deemed unfit in some respect. Finally, Basedow had promised to take the problem to bed with him, where he did most of his creative thinking, and he felt sure that he would hit upon the right answer, for he knew that any difficulty whatever could be solved by the force of his nocturnal mental concentration. The two men retired for the night and at four o'clock in the morning the alarm went off in Basedow's mighty mind. He leaped out of bed and, clothed only in his nightgown, rushed into Salis's room, shouting, "I've got the man!" When Salis recovered sufficiently from shock to ask who it might be, Basedow replied, "It's Bahrdt! He is precisely the man you need."

Thus it came about that Salis knocked at Bahrdt's door on that fateful autumn evening and that Bahrdt received the opportunity to play a role in the philanthropinical movement, that now nearly forgotten eighteenth-century precursor of twentieth-century "progressive" education.

As is well known, the latter half of the eighteenth century was, among other things, a pedagogical age, a time when Rousseau's *Emile* inspired almost universal enthusiastic acceptance of the belief in the naturally good and unspoiled infant, who needed only to be allowed to unfold his innate virtues to attain to the perfection of his flowering. It goes without saying that the pedagogy of Rousseau was a corollary of the theology of Wolff, Reimarus, Ernesti, Fischer, Semler, and other "enlightened" critics, whose researches had undermined the authority of the church and challenged the doctrine of the natural sinfulness of man. The new pedagogy was therefore not in any exclusive sense Rousseau's creation, for Basedow had both evolved the practice and formulated his theories by 1752, ten years before the publication of *Emile*. What Rousseau did for Basedow was to stir up a storm of enthusiastic sympathy for the ideas which had already come to Basedow[2] and which he now advertised throughout Germany with fabulous energy and legendary success.

Basedow was the prototype of the modern stock-figure or caricature of the educational psychologist whose misunderstood children pay dearly for their parents' professional eminence.

Born in Hamburg on the eleventh of September 1723, he suffered much as a child from the brutality of his wigmaker father and the depressions of a mother who was melancholy to the point of madness. As a young boy he had no other occupation than picking up and delivering wigs for his father, who wished his son to take up the trade. One day Johann Bernhard ran away from home and found refuge with a country doctor, who took him on as a servant for a year but, recognizing the boy's exceptional intelligence, persuaded the father to allow him to attend the Johanneum, the Latin school of Hamburg, where Reimarus, the posthumous publication of whose heretical *Fragmente* by Lessing led to the well-known controversy with Götze, was a teacher. It is thus probable that Basedow imbibed the spirit of heterodoxy from Reimarus himself, and it is at least equally probable that the stiff and rigid system of instructional drill and memorization to which Basedow was subjected caused him to oppose orthodoxy in the schoolroom as well as in the pulpit. His unruly energies could be harnessed only with great difficulty to the systematic pedestrianism of school routine, so he was in a sense almost self-taught, even though he did later go to the University of Leipzig. By 1746 he had come to feel dedicated to the task of penetrating to the heart of all disciplines pertaining to morals, ethics, and religion, in order to make use of them not only in the pulpit but also in the schoolroom as they applied to the education of youth. Three years later, when he was twenty-six, he became a tutor in the home of *Hofrat* von Qualen in Borghorst, Holstein.

Here he had the opportunity to practice his theory of teaching, to instruct by amusing. Whatever the subject, he devised games that would illustrate and inculcate the principles involved and facilitate the mastery of the material. The teaching of Latin became one of his great specialties, although before he was faced with the necessity of teaching it, Basedow had forgotten almost all the Latin he had ever learned. The years with the Qualens laid the foundations for his career, for not only did he gain so much experience that he was able to compose a Latin thesis[3] on his method of pedagogy which earned him the degree of *Magister* from the University of Kiel, but he also earned the gratitude of his employers, who recommended him most highly to the Danish government.

As a result he was appointed professor of philosophy and eloquence at the Academy of Soroe, a post which he filled ably and with such popular success that when he was later authorized to teach a course of theology as well, his envious colleagues, who had already accused him of bad personal habits, received the opportunity they had wanted and got him convicted of heterodoxy. But the government kicked him upstairs by making him a professor of philosophy at the Gymnasium of Altona without discontinuing his salary from Soroe. The charge of heresy clung to him, however, and caused such furor that he was retired from lecturing on full pay. Basedow thus became an independent force, free to turn his energy to anything he pleased.

Now that he did not have to work for a livelihood he poured forth a torrent of theological writings, publishing eighteen works in four years. His theology, however, was merely an echo of the general "enlightened" position of such scholars as Michaelis, Ernesti, Reiske, and Reimarus and cannot be said to have gained him anything more positive than the bitter enmity of Pastor Götze and the orthodox camp, who attacked him with great vigor and succeeded in having him barred from the communion of the Lutheran church. Since Basedow had neither the training nor the tenacity to engage in sustained successful controversy with the theologians, his reputation was beginning to suffer seriously. Just at this point Rousseau published his *Emile,* which set off a wave of enthusiasm for matters of pedagogy. To Basedow, who was incapable of producing a philosophy and who was in danger of being overwhelmed by the churchmen, this was a godsend, for the one field of endeavor in which he had had real success, teaching, was now in the forefront of attention.

It was not long before Basedow produced a detailed plan[4] for reorganizing what would now be called elementary and secondary education. Some notion of the scope and spirit of the plan can be gained from the organization of the teaching staff of the Gymnasium as he set it up. Basedow envisioned four teaching categories: the educational supervisor, the professor of rhetoric, the professor of philosophy and mathematics, and the professor of Greek and antiquities. The educational supervisor would have no other duties than counselling the pupils on all matters, both academic and personal, and would receive a supplementary salary to enable him to entertain the pupils often in his home in the company of ladies and gentlemen of distinction and social elegance. In his dealings with the pupils the educator would speak only French and English. The professor of rhetoric would teach in Latin and German alternately, the professor of philosophy and mathematics would speak only German, and the professor of Greek and antiquities would teach in Latin. As for religion, the school would be strictly neutral, a feature which won for Basedow the active support of many Catholics and Jews as well as heads of state and other influential persons who were responsible for a mixed population.

It was plain to Basedow from the first that there were two conditions necessary to effect a true educational reform: a seminary for training teachers and an encyclopedia of instruction. He promised to write the encyclopedia himself, and to this end he waged a campaign of propaganda and advertising that might well be the envy of modern specialists in similar undertakings.

It was plain that such a work as Basedow proposed would cost a great deal of money to publish, so Basedow invited the nation to subscribe to it in advance. He sent announcements of his projected *Elementarwerk* to every person of wealth and influence he could think of, and enclosed a handwritten letter with every announcement. He travelled up and down the land enlisting the active support of such people as Sack, Spalding, Sulzer, Ramler, Büsching, and Moses Mendelssohn, and of Nicolai and his

Allgemeine deutsche Bibliothek, that extraordinarily powerful instrument of Enlightenment. At the end of five months of campaigning he had collected 1700 *Taler,* but he estimated that publication costs would run to more than 5000. He informed his correspondents of this estimate with the result that by 1770 he had taken in 7,413 *Taler* and by May 1771 he had 15,000 *Taler,* an enormous sum for that day. After the first of June he had to announce that he could accept no more subscriptions. It is some indication of the widespread interest in his plans that the Empress Catherine of Russia gave him a grant of one thousand rubles.

When Basedow settled down to work in earnest on his great *Elementarwerk* he engaged as his secretary and collaborator a certain C. H. Wolke, who stayed with him for many years and turned out to be the sober steadying force which gave tangible shape to Basedow's wild enthusiasms. To Wolke he assigned the sections of the *Elementarwerk* on mathematics, natural sciences, and the arts. Basedow also turned over to him responsibility for managing his correspondence, reading proofs, and educating his children according to the new system. Together Wolke and Basedow produced first a less elaborate preliminary version of their main work, the *Methodenbuch für Väter und Mütter der Familien und Völker* (Altona und Bremen, 1770), and, four years later, the monumental *Elementarwerk, ein Vorrath der besten Erkenntnisse zum Lernen, Lehren, Wiederholen und Nachdenken* (Dessau, 1774).[5]

This primer of human knowledge was published in four volumes and included an atlas containing one hundred engravings, some (the natural-sciences charts) by Wolke, but most by the celebrated engraver Chodowiecki. Basedow believed he had included everything useful for a young person to know except specific religious teachings. In general method Basedow is in agreement with John Locke and Amos Comenius, from whose illustrated book for children, *Orbis sensualium pictus* (1658), the *Elementarwerk* is in the direct line of descent. That is, he shared with them the assumption that languages and natural sciences were completely utilitarian and also the basic principles of instruction of acquainting children first with things through touch and sight and then with the words for the things. In Basedow's system education tends to be national and independent of any church, to be narrowly utilitarian as far as the individual is concerned, and to be intuitive and re-creative in the means employed.

Although even in the eyes of sympathetic modern critics and some sympathetic contemporary critics[6] the *Elementarwerk* has shortcomings, the book was very successful and influential in certain circles. Frederick the Great's minister of education, Baron von Zedlitz, was loud in its praises at a meeting of the Royal Academy in Berlin. Joseph II sent Basedow a letter of thanks for his great book and presented him with a medal bearing his own likeness, and many other German monarchs signified their approval. The orthodox, however, whether humanists or theologians, bitterly attacked Basedow and derided his newfangled methods. Prominent among the critics were such men as Rector Schlegel of Heilbronn, Rector Krebs of Grimma, and Professor Schlözer of Göttingen, who lashed out at Basedow in the preface to his translation of the *Essai sur l'éducation nationale* of La Chalotais, from whom Basedow himself had learned much. And the criticism took literary or semiliterary form in two works by Johann Gottlieb Schummel, *Fritzens Reise nach Dessau* (1776) and *Spitzbart, eine komitragische Geschichte für unser pädagogisches Jahrhundert* (1779), and in Laukhard's imitation of *Spitzbart* in his *Beyträge und Berichtigungen zu Herrn Karl Friedrich Bahrdts Lebensbeschreibung in Briefen eines Pfälzers* (1791), all of which will receive further mention in connection with Bahrdt's career as an educator. Criticism, however, whether fair or unfair, did not deter the Prince of Anhalt-Dessau from giving Basedow the means to translate his theories and plans into brick and stone, flesh and blood.

Scarcely had the *Methodenbuch* begun to appear, before Basedow announced that he was ready to begin with the second part of his gigantic task of school reform, the establishment of a seminary. He got out a special brochure, indicating that he needed 27,000 *Taler* for the purpose and that he would reserve for himself in this seminary the role of counsellor, collaborator, ideaman, and writer. But he would refuse to take up the duties of the directorship because his pedagogical writings had first claim upon the energy left him by his advancing age, poor health, and failing eyesight. No sooner had the brochure appeared than he flung himself into an advertising tour which took him all over northern Germany and brought him to the court of Leopold Friedrich Franz, who had resolved that he would reform the educational system of his principality of Anhalt-Dessau. Although the Prince's first impression of Basedow was not favorable, he gradually came to pin all his faith for the projected educational reform upon his ideas even if perhaps not upon his personal qualifications, and he invited Basedow to come to Dessau.

By 1774 Basedow was ready to commence operations, and he attacked the problem with all his old verve and impetuosity. It was during his well-known travels along the Rhine in the company of Goethe and Lavater (see footnote six) that he seems to have hit upon the name "Philanthropinum" for his model school. At any rate, in the same year he issued a bulletin[7] describing the projected school in detail and publishing its regulations even down to such trivial rules as one that the pupils, except for purposes of reading, drawing, and writing, would be required to be on their feet during the entire schoolday, presumably to keep them active and alert. Basedow promised to transform all the memory work usually required in such subjects as the languages, history, and geography into games. He would charge a maximum 250 *Taler* tuition fee for children of the wealthy and charge correspondingly less for the children of the less wealthy, and he appealed to rich people everywhere to donate funds to enable him to set up a system of scholarships which would allow children of poor parents to attend also. He announced that he had now consented to accept the directorship of the Philanthropinum but only for three years and without salary. (He was still receiving his regular allowance from the Danish government.) At the end of the three years he planned to turn over management of the school to a supervisory commission in which he, as *Fürsorger* or Curator, would have the deciding vote. He concluded his description with an appeal to the German nation for 22,000 *Taler* (rather than the earlier estimate of 27,000) , saying that he addressed himself only to good people everywhere. As for the others, let them keep what they had, spend it on banquets, luxury, voluptuous entertainment, operas, useless buildings, the increase of armies, the perfecting of methods of taking human life, and similar base pursuits.

On the twenty-seventh of December 1774, the sixth birthday of the young Prince of Anhalt-Dessau, who was not present, the Philanthropinum was opened amid appropriate ceremonies, chief of which was a long oration by the founder, who reiterated that there was an urgent need for 22,000 *Taler* to be donated by public-spirited people of means. Greatly to Basedow's surprise money did not come pouring in in support of his project. Apparently the public was not interested in making contributions to an institution that few of them would ever see or derive benefit from. Even Duke Leopold Friedrich Franz was at first rather indifferent to the school, for his main interest had been in Basedow's theoretical writings. The Philanthropinum therefore got off to a very modest start: three masters, Basedow, Wolke, and a certain Benzler, and three pupils, Basedow's children Emilie and Friedrich, and a little boy named Schwartz.

Emilie Basedow was the sensational proof of the effectiveness of Basedow's methods of teaching. Not that Basedow himself was ever directly occupied with her instruction, for he was much too busy telling other people how to teach to spare time for his own children. What concerned Basedow most about his little daughter was what she should be named. When his frantic wife thwarted his intention to call her Praenumerantia Elementaria Philanthropia he settled for Emilie and turned her over to Wolke, who, following his master's system, turned her into a child prodigy. At the age of eighteen months little Emilie could spell and at the end of her third year she learned to read in one month. Once when Basedow returned from a six-week propaganda tour he was pleasantly but perhaps only mildly surprised that Emilie had learned French, in which language she was able to express all her needs and interests after two and a half months of teaching. Domestic accomplishments such as sewing, cooking, and knitting she acquired in the same easy and happy fashion, for everything was learned through play. Wolke earned most admiration for the speed and ease with which he taught her Latin. On Michaelmas (Sep-

tember 29) 1773, when Emilie was four and a half, she knew no
Latin; by Christmas of the following year she could speak the
language with facility and correctness. If anyone ventured to suggest that Emilie was an exceptionally gifted child, Basedow and
Wolke could back their assertion that her rapid progress was due
to the method by pointing to the two other children, Friedrich
Basedow and young Schwartz. Friedrich had had a very bad start
in life, having been seriously ill for his first three years. Indeed,
at the age of two he had been able to say neither Yes nor No. But
when he got over his illness, thanks to the method, he arrived at
a fine understanding of things, and soon learned to converse with
intelligence and fluency in German, French, and Latin. And finally there was young Schwartz, who learned Latin in four months
and shared with Emilie the ability to identify more than fifty
trees and plants not only by sight but also by mere touch.

It was while Basedow was thus engaged in the very beginnings
of his school in Dessau that Ulysses von Salis, who had read
Basedow's publications with the greatest interest and enthusiastic
acceptance, came to consult him. When, therefore, the supreme
pedagogical oracle of Germany finally spoke at four o'clock on
that fateful morning and said "Bahrdt," Salis hurried off to
Giessen and laid his proposition before Bahrdt without inquiring
further into his qualifications or personality. He made only one
stipulation, that Bahrdt go to Dessau to steep himself in the philanthropinical spirit, and gave him thirty *louis d'or* to cover travel
expenses. Bahrdt accepted with joy and alacrity and set off for
Dessau with his friend and pupil, a man named Heres.

The philanthropinical spirit in which he was most liberally
steeped upon his arrival in Dessau proved to be Malaga wine,
for which Basedow had a notorious weakness. Master and pupil
did very little serious work but ate and drank heartily together,
frequented wine and coffee shops, smoked much tobacco, played
cards for hours on end, and enjoyed each other's company very
much. When they parted late in the evening, Basedow, it seems,
went to bed and dreamed up more and more pedagogical precepts, which Bahrdt, sleeping soundly, never got to hear, save for
some confused material on methods of language teaching which

Basedow dictated on one occasion.[8] Thus, instead of making careful studies and taking copious notes, Bahrdt merely skimmed through the *Elementarwerk,* caught the general idea, supplemented his knowledge by scraps of information picked up while talking informally with Basedow, and soon felt qualified as an expert. Basedow agreed with Bahrdt's estimate of himself and wrote to Salis that in the short space of twelve days he had initiated Bahrdt into the method and that this industrious, learned man who was also experienced in matters of education was now actually able to correct some of Basedow's own mistakes and improve the system. Basedow also sent Salis a bill for one hundred *louis d'or* to cover the cost of entertaining and instructing Bahrdt in Dessau.

Bahrdt and Heres returned to Giessen in order to make the trip from there to Marschlins in the company of Bahrdt's family. Certain difficulties arose in this connection, for Bahrdt owed money in Giessen, and his creditors were unwilling to let him leave town without settling his debts. According to Bahrdt he had borrowed 200 *Gulden* in order to buy a chaise and two horses to please his wife, who tormented him with her irrational jealousy. The man who had lent him the money knew that Bahrdt was going to leave and had said nothing about the matter, so Bahrdt thought he might save himself the embarrassment of asking for an extension of the time for repayment. He assumed, he says, that his creditor understood that the only reason he did not wish to repay the money at that time was that he wanted to have ample cash when he arrived in Marschlins. Accordingly, he set off in broad daylight but had gone only as far as Butzbach when he was overtaken and threatened with arrest unless he paid his debt. Fortunately, he had an acquaintance in Butzbach who was willing to guarantee payment and so the little company of travellers was allowed to proceed.

Another version of the story exists, however, as Deinet reported it in a letter to Salis, according to which Bahrdt had announced his intention of making formal calls of leave-taking on various notables of Giessen at four o'clock. As he was being awaited with interest in several households Frau Bahrdt drove out of one city gate with a certain Snell, who was also going to Marschlins to

teach, and Bahrdt and Heres walked out through another gate,
thus playing a sort of farewell prank on the citizens of Giessen,
one of whom did, however, catch up with him in Butzbach, as
Bahrdt himself recounts.

The trip to Marschlins could not have been very comfortable
even if the roads had been excellent, for the chaise, which Bahrdt
himself had equipped with an improvised top over the back seat,
was occupied by Bahrdt and his wife, two children, Heres, Snell,
and a young Frenchwoman who was going along to teach French
and be with Snell, who had to ride on the coachman's box. It was
Bahrdt's self-appointed task to get up at two o'clock every morning, rouse the coachman to get the horses ready, make coffee,
wake the passengers, and help feed and dress the children so that
they would all be able to depart promptly at four. When they
stopped at a post station at eight o'clock in the evening they
had covered about thirty or forty miles.

Bahrdt decided to go by way of Ulm in order to call on C. F. D.
Schubart, the well-known writer and musician, whose long and
arbitrary imprisonment by the typrannical Duke Karl Eugen of
Württemberg still lay two years in the future. This visit is of interest for two reasons. In the first place, it is one of the indications
that music meant a great deal to Bahrdt, and the whole picture
of Bahrdt's personality is given a rather different tinge by the
knowledge that he planned his travel route so that he might
have a chance to talk with Schubart and possibly enjoy his music,
as indeed he did. For he was granted the rare privilege of having
Schubart play the great organ in the cathedral for him, and he
records that he was completely spellbound by the power of
Schubart's artistry. In the second place, the visit to Ulm entailed
stopping over in Lindau, a place which Salis, so Bahrdt says, had
planned for him to avoid, because the innkeeper in Lindau was
the dismissed manager of the Philanthropinum from whom
Bahrdt could learn things it was not in Salis's interest for him
to know.

Whether Bahrdt's story is completely true is at least questionable, but it is not impossible that the tale he heard from the innkeeper represented something rather close to what was generally

told about Salis and his pedagogical enterprise in Graubünden. For Salis, as has been mentioned, was greatly feared and hated by the ordinary citizens and had to flee the country some years later when the French Revolution deposed the power that maintained him as its minister.

When Herr Rader, the innkeeper, engaged Bahrdt in conversation and learned that he was on the way to Marschlins to become the director of Salis's school, he turned away sadly and said, "You have my sympathy, dear Doctor." As soon as Bahrdt was able to speak privately with him he questioned the innkeeper closely, who supposedly told him that Nesemann and Planta had earned much money from their enterprise and that Salis had prevailed upon them, much to their regret, to transfer the school to Marschlins, for he was eager to share in the profits. When Planta died, so went the story, Salis took complete charge of all but purely educational matters, which remained in Nesemann's hands. The result was a deterioration in all household matters, for Salis dismissed the former manager, that is, Rader himself, and engaged a couple named Bawier or Baviere. This couple was employed, so it was charged and so Bahrdt affirms, because Mme Bawier, the daughter of *Superintendent* Karrer in Memmingen, was Salis's mistress.[9]

But the alleged scandalous liaison between Salis and Mme Bawier was not the only cause of the manifest decline of the Philanthropinum, according to Rader. The other two were the unwholesome location of Marschlins, which undermined the health of the pupils,[10] and the autocratic rule of Ulysses von Salis, who exercised rigid and arbitrary control over the entire institution down to the very last detail. And now, Bahrdt says, he realized that he had been duped into taking on a well-nigh impossible task to save Salis's investment under conditions that would cause even the stoutest heart to quail.

Now I saw into whose hands I had been placed. My wife moaned. My young friends cursed their fate. But I—remained calm nonetheless, for I had complete faith that by discretion in my behavior and by the exercise of my entire strength in restoring the institution, I would be able to soften the hardhearted man and compel him to give me his love and esteem.

And so, undaunted, Bahrdt resumed his journey to Marschlins to meet his fate and to add a lurid chapter to the history of "progressive" education.

XIV

⟨PREVIEW OF PURGATORY⟩

BAHRDT'S VEHEMENT denunciation of Salis as an inexorable greedy tyrant who compelled the teaching staff to take their payment in kind, charging exorbitant prices for food, lodging, and fuel, has been emphatically contradicted. Hunziker's article on Salis in the *Allgemeine deutsche Biographie* states that he had in him the stuff of which the best monarchs of the age of enlightened despotism were made and quotes Salis's own son to the effect that he was determined to unify and uplift the confused and riven political life of Graubünden, and that he saw in the Philanthropinum a means to achieve this end. When it is added that he had acquired his extensive stock of knowledge largely through his own efforts, we begin to see in him a man of strong will, opinionated, in a situation so incommensurate with his capability and talent that he had to give vent to his energies by personal supervision of every detail of the small-scale enterprises that occupied him.

Most illuminating is the estimate which is made of him in his relationship to Bahrdt by Heres, who was, during the Marschlins period, Bahrdt's intimate and devoted friend and who later came to see Bahrdt in a very different light, while never giving up his affection for him. Heres writes:[1]

Bahrdt has wronged Herr von Salis in his description. He is not an unfeeling tyrant and base miser and niggard. Salis was, of course, the master and did indeed regard Bahrdt as his employee. Had the latter adapted himself better to his position, had he possessed better knowledge of his special province, if he had, therefore, satisfied Salis better and been less insistent that Salis be his friend, and if he had likewise been more effective and persistent, then his situation in Marschlins would not have been so unpleasant. Besides, Bahrdt was not the man who could study a character

135

such as Salis and win him over. In all his actions Salis is a systematic man, who never loses sight of his goal and remains unalterably fixed in his principles. Bahrdt, on the other hand, was completely unsystematic, was determined by the impression of the moment, and swept off his feet. How could there be harmony between two minds which were at such odds with each other?

It seems clear, therefore, that Bahrdt and Salis could scarcely have worked well together under the most favorable conditions. But, to make matters worse, the seeds of discord had been planted long before Bahrdt set out from Giessen. This had happened when Salis, on his way back to Graubünden from his interview with Bahrdt, had stopped in Frankfurt and called on Deinet the publisher. Deinet had for some reason become irate with Bahrdt and described him to Salis in such unfavorable terms that Salis apparently felt some hesitation in fulfilling the agreement he had already made with Bahrdt. The latter, meanwhile, had been on tenterhooks until he received the firm offer which enabled him to request promotion or dismissal from Ludwig IX. Indeed, it is at least possible that Salis would never have gone through with the agreement if he had not been in well-nigh desperate straits, for he had quarreled so seriously with Nesemann that their difference had later to be settled in court. Meanwhile Deinet was sending letters to Salis denouncing Bahrdt for his frivolous mode of living and advising Salis to keep a very tight rein on his new Director. It is therefore scarcely to be wondered at that Bahrdt thought he detected a certain chilliness in Salis's manner when he welcomed the newly qualified pedagogue and his train to their home and duties in *Schloss Marschlins.*

As time passed the chilliness and aloofness grew ever more intense. Salis never took the Director into his confidence, severely limited his duties and authority to such matters as planning the courses of study and assigning the pupils to their proper classes, and refused to consult with him in any way whatever. Bahrdt says that during the first summer months he toiled like a workhorse with the patience of a lamb, and it is likely that he did keep himself busy at first, at least until after the public demonstration and examination which, it began to be rumored, would take place at Michaelmas.

When Bahrdt asked him for further particulars Salis informed him that he need not concern himself, for he, Salis, would manage the matter. Salis soon thereafter left Marschlins for a trip, informing the Bawiers and the Inspector (officer of pupil discipline) that after his return he expected many visitors from all over Switzerland to attend the ceremonies. After Salis left, the staff had many hours of anxious consultation on the subject of what would be required of them and their pupils, for Salis had said that he expected to find everything in good order upon his return.

In the circumstances, Bahrdt says, he felt he could do only one thing, namely, make the arrangements himself.

I made the assumption that the Minister wished to make sure that those attending would be pleased. I saw the impossibility of pleasing them by means of unadulterated truth. So I resolved to substitute illusion where truth was deficient. I arranged the schedule so that we had three days of ceremonies and that there was something new every day for the curious spectators to see, something that would make them well disposed to the Institute. In a word, I did as Basedow did. I occupied the eyes and imagination of the public as much as I could.

He had, he says, only eleven days to make his preparations and in that time he performed the labors of Hercules. He drilled his staff and the pupils in those lessons that were to be open to public view; he worked out a Philanthropinical Code or book of rules which described the duties of the entire staff and the regulations governing the conduct of the pupils; he composed several speeches, each one to take about an hour, for delivery on various significant occasions during the ceremonies; he sketched a comedy for presentation by the pupils and wrote songs to be sung during solemn processions; and he prepared a printed program for distribution to the guests.

Finally Salis returned and with him came a good many people of importance, among them Lavater himself. Bahrdt greeted him, bowed, and handed him a program saying,

You have given me no previous instructions. I have therefore had to undertake the provisional arrangements for the examination ceremonies. I flatter myself that by indefatigable industry I have made myself deserving of your approbation.

Salis glanced at the program and put it in his pocket saying coldly, "Very good, *Herr Direktor.*" No further notice was taken of Bahrdt, who was not presented to any of the guests but left entirely to his own devices, so that he retired to his room, where he remained until the formal ceremonies began on the following day.

When Bahrdt was out of the way, so Heres reported, Salis called the pupils together and presented them to Lavater, "the great seer of Zürich," who had won renown as the leading exponent of the modish "science" of physiognomy.

Lavater stood at Salis's side and had the entire Philanthropinum before him in a semicircle. Salis loudly requested him, in such a tone of voice as a saint might use in addressing a seraph, to designate the three best minds among them by virtue of the magic power of his physiognomy. Lavater was willing. He walked through the semicircle, looked at each one full-face and in profile and finally selected three, among whom one was really our brightest pupil but the other two were the dullest boys in the world. Salis was dismayed by the seraph's *faux pas* and quickly plucked at the flap of his garment. Lavater felt it. He turned around quickly. "Stop, let me just take them in profile." And now he assured everyone that they looked very different in profile and he absolved the stupid boys from the honor of being geniuses.

On the morning of the first day, which was a day of formal dedication, the forty pupils, led by the Inspector, escorted the Curator (Salis) from his apartment to the refectory, the walls of which were hung with pictures of famous men. Here a cantata was performed which had been written by the school physician Dr. Amstein[2] and set to music by J. C. Dözer, who gave the boys lessons in violin and piano. The title of the cantata was *Education, the only Remedy for the Moral Depravity of the World.* Then came the dedicatory oration by the Director (Bahrdt) followed by a sermon delivered in the chapel by Lavater.

After the midday meal Bahrdt read aloud from the Philanthropinical Code which he had drawn up, although it seems that Salis's perusal of it early that morning had roused his ire to a mighty pitch. And well it might have done so, for the Code prescribed rules of conduct not only for the pupils but for everyone else, including the Curator. In accepting the Code, Salis had to promise that his administrative regulations would never be dictated by self-interest, self-will, or by any base motive whatever, and that in judging the behavior of the fellow citizens of his school community, whether pupils or members of the staff, he would never be swayed by emotions that may have been aroused by abominable talebearing or by any other ignoble intention. The question arises, whether these faults of character and conduct against which the Curator was specifically admonished to guard, were merely invented by Bahrdt or whether Salis felt a certain sting of truth in the imputation. Whichever was the case, when Bahrdt finished reading, Salis offered his right hand to him and to all the teachers as a pledge to strive and surmount all obstacles.

Eventually [he said] our contemporaries, or surely a more just posterity, will recognize that we do not seek our own.

The ceremonies were concluded by a solemn oath, taken by everyone, including the Curator, to be loyal to Bahrdt's Philanthropinical Code. His hand on the book, Salis concluded with deep emotion,

I promise you, I swear by my love for you, I will work, toil, suffer, sacrifice with redoubled zeal and intensified resolve . . . will do everything, everything that is in the power of a man who acts from the impulse of his heart, from feeling. May the Lord our God bless our effort.[3]

The second day was devoted to the examinations proper, if such a name can be given to lessons which had been prepared in advance and were run off for the benefit of the visitors. The impression they made seems to have been not unfavorable, for one of the guests, N. A. Kirchberger, wrote to Iselin, who did not attend, that although the teachers were not perfect in Basedow's method, there was nonetheless ample evidence that young people who had been attending the school for only a short time had made considerable progress. The showpieces on this occasion were exercises in what was called the Socratic Method, by which Bahrdt meant a particular way of asking questions so that the pupils seemed to evolve the desired information or judgments by means of their own efforts. This method was felt to be sharply distinguished from the catechetical method according to which the child was required to memorize a set of answers to given questions. Bahrdt, in fundamental agreement with and dependence upon Basedow and empirical thinkers generally, maintained that the teacher could elicit from the pupils the appropriate theoretical insights by skillful manipulation and combination of data which they had already received in the course of daily experience.

By causing the child to put known facts into new and significant relation to each other the teacher can help him build up a whole theoretical structure that was previously unknown.

Thus, we can imagine that on the day of the public examinations the visitors were invited to witness how, for example, the Socratic Dr. Bahrdt would bring home to a little boy the understanding of what is meant by sin. Beginning with something that lies well within the range of the little boy's experience, the teacher commences his dialogue:

Teacher: Do you think it is good, my dear Fritz, if you eat too much?

Fritz: No!

Teacher: Why not?

Fritz: It isn't healthy.

Teacher: Is everything unhealthy bad? Then God must have made many things that are bad. Has the good Lord made anything bad?

Fritz: No. It says, "And behold, everything was very good."

Teacher: Right! Everything that God makes is good. But there are many things that hurt a man if he eats them.

Fritz: The good Lord can't help that.

Teacher: So God is not to blame? But who is?

Fritz: The man.

Teacher: But how is he to blame?

Fritz: If he eats them.

Teacher: You mean he doesn't have to eat them if he doesn't want to?

Fritz: Yes, of course, nobody forces him to do it.

Teacher: Well then, if I do something that hurts me or other people, something that nobody makes me do, then I am doing something bad?

Fritz: Yes, of course.

Teacher: Then what is meant by doing something bad?

Fritz: Doing something harmful that you weren't forced to do.

Teacher: Right. What you do of your own free will that hurts me or others is bad, morally evil. But what do you say? Is evil always hateful to the good Lord and therefore a sin?

Fritz: Yes.

The whole dialogue from which this example is taken is, as it stands in Bahrdt's description of the school in Marschlins, much longer and defines the idea of sin with greater refinement. But this short excerpt does give some idea of how Bahrdt used the aims and methods which he had learned from Basedow and Wolke. Indeed, the astonishing thing is with what facility and ease he grasped the principles of the philanthropinical method, with what fertility of invention he applied them to the specific needs of his classes. One must admit the justice of Lavater's judgment expressed in a letter to Herder (November 8, 1775):

I have just come back from Marschlins, where I found Bahrdt, infinitely clever but without any indwelling power, without any belief in himself.[4]

On the morning of the third day a French comedy was performed by the students, and in the afternoon an unintentional comedy was performed by Salis and all the school. At least, thus Bahrdt describes in retrospect the dedication of the four Philanthropinical Temples. The entire assembly, staff, students, and guests, departed from the courtyard of the castle and mounted the hill before it, Salis leading the procession and followed by a servant carrying four pointed stakes. Having arrived at a level spot in the ascent, Salis called a halt, pounded a stake into the ground and intoned, "Thus I dedicate the Temple of Wisdom," whereupon Dr. Bahrdt gave a speech on the beauties of wisdom. Three other sites were dedicated in like manner: one to the Great Men of History, one to Virtue, and one, the highest, to Christ. From that time on it was to be the responsibility of the teachers to address the student body in each of those places every Sunday and exhort them to dedicate their hearts to wisdom, noble deeds, and virtue, but especially to animate them with love for the religion of Jesus. Eventually, of course, these quasi-religious services were to take place within the temples that it was the plan to erect. But after the dedicatory ceremonies were over, the stakes, although they remained planted in the ground, were never again to witness philanthropinical assembly and the temples were never built.

At the conclusion of the exercises just described, Bahrdt says, he received no word of praise or recognition but had to hitch

himself to the plow again and go on with his work as though
nothing had happened. The truth seems to be, however, that he
went off to Lindau for what he no doubt considered a well-earned
rest and vacation.

Upon his return he was in rather poor health for a time and
was much less interested in the performance of his regular duties
than he had hitherto been. He was frequently to be seen in pursuit of conviviality in various inns about the countryside, he
went driving in his carriage, and in general seemed to be idling
away his time, although he did return to the school at the end of
the day for the pleasant and easy task of supervising the pupils'
recreation. Despite his seeming idleness, however, his always
active mind was occupied with two different kinds of concerns.
For one thing, he was filled with various projects to advance
his own interests, as he saw them; and for another, he had to compose a full description of the Philanthropinum, its staff, curricu-
lum, aims and methods.

One of his earliest projects had been to take over the stewardship of the school, the office from which Herr Rader, the innkeeper in Lindau, had been dismissed, and which was now the
responsibility of the Bawiers. According to Bahrdt, as we have
seen, Mme Bawier had great personal influence upon Salis, who
was ready to overlook the fact that her food was badly prepared
and ready to eat and even praise dishes which tasted as though
she had used tallow rather than butter in preparing them. One
of the teachers in the school, Johann Georg Philipp Thiele,[5]
wrote in a little book of his own that everything Bahrdt said
about Salis and the Bawiers was a fabrication and that Bahrdt really tried to stir up discontent with the fare that was offered so that
he could obtain the stewardship and increase his earnings. When
Salis refused to be swayed, Bahrdt made up the completely slanderous story.

Other money-making schemes which filled Bahrdt's head at
this time concerned a philanthropinical publishing house, which
he hinted to Basedow and others ought to bring in 20,000 *Taler*
a year. He also weighed the possibility of establishing a little
Philanthropinum of his own and, according to Thiele, when he

learned that a certain estate was to be offered for sale, he wrote to Deinet and requested him to make the purchase on behalf either of himself or of Salis! Deinet, however, suspected that there might be some irregularity about the proposed transaction and wrote to Salis, inquiring whether Salis had actually authorized such negotiations for a new school, and Bahrdt received a rebuke for a maneuver that seems so clumsy that it is hard to believe that anyone could have been guilty of attempting it. And yet, it somehow bears the stamp of Bahrdt's incredible naïveté, his astonishing implicit premise that his operations were exempted from the usual workings of cause and effect and not subject to common moral judgment. He seems to have had the feeling that so many things he did and said did not really "count," that they would involve no consequences to himself, and that somehow, because it was he who did them they were not truly reprehensible. And yet, as we shall see, he had despite all assertions to the contrary a hard core of integrity, if by integrity we can mean a simple and unreflecting inability to act otherwise than according to the dictates of inner necessity, regardless of loss or advantage.

There was, however, a noticeable lack of integrity in the Prospectus of Philanthropinical Education,[6] which he and Salis had prepared for publication by the end of the year 1775. Salis exercised general supervision and contributed the foreword and two chapters, one on student expenses and one on discipline; Bahrdt wrote the rest. But regardless of authorship and ultimate responsibility, it is completely unreliable as an account of what the school in Marschlins was really like. On this point even Thiele agrees with Bahrdt, for Thiele writes that the description of the Philanthropinum is actually a work of fiction and mentions arrangements that had either never been made or were impossible or else were quickly forgotten after a brief trial. And Bahrdt writes,

I frankly admit that at the high behest [7] of the Curator I lied in this book as no writer had ever lied before. Not one third of the fine pedagogical method, gymnastic drill, and the like was ever put into practice or even planned. The public was to see merely an ideal of philanthropinical education and imagine that this was made actual in Marschlins.

Hollow though it was, the prospectus was a fine business success and brought Bahrdt a bit of extra money. To be sure, the
Swiss were no longer greatly interested in supporting Salis's institution in this or any other way: only 333 copies were sold in
the entire country, two thirds of that number in Graubünden
itself. But more than 900 copies were sold in Germany, largely
through advance subscription. The list of subscribers is headed by
the name of the Margrave Karl Friedrich of Baden, who took 275
copies. The list of subscribers which was included in the printed
book, includes a good many other noble patrons, city councils,
various personages such as Goethe's father, and even a regiment
of hussars in Further Pomerania. Salis could write with satisfaction
to Iselin that in Germany there was scarcely a single small town
that had not subscribed for ten, fifteen, or twenty copies. And
with some bitterness he added that the indifference of the Swiss
injured him in the eyes of Basedow, the latter's enemies, and the
entire German nation.

The work was planned to appear in two volumes. In addition to
the one which did appear, there was to be one to which it was
hoped that great men of the age would make contributions, and
which was to consist of a collection of philanthropinical songs,
plays, Socratic dialogues, edifying prints, descriptions of the most
successful instructional games and experiments, and other samples
of the method. It was anticipated that Lavater would provide
the song texts to be set to music by Philipp Christoph Kayser of
Frankfurt, that Goethe would contribute a comedy for children,
and Chodowiecki would do the illustrations. Thus, the second
volume would be a demonstration manual which would provide
the concrete and specific illustrations of the theory explained in
the first volume. All this was announced in the rather pompously
pious foreword which Salis wrote for the first volume, declaring
that the philanthropinical experiment was so significant and that
public interest was so great that publication had become impera-
tive.

Salis's foreword is followed by a list of the thirteen members of
the staff, including a mechanic and a bookbinder, and then come
fifteen chapters of theory and description,[8] in the first of which

Bahrdt makes a threefold division of the special concerns of philanthropinical education: first, training of the body; second, instruction in the intellectual disciplines; third, the ennobling of the heart and the perfecting of it in virtue.

It is Bahrdt's boast in this first section that the philanthropinical schools first provided for physical education as a regular part of the course of instruction. The traditional schools confined themselves to drilling vocabulary, paradigms, arithmetic tables, and similar "facts" of all kinds into the memories of the pupils, but in the Philanthropinum the class periods devoted to instruction proper were alternated with periods of play or physical training.

We accustom our pupils [writes Bahrdt] to cold baths, which they take daily as soon as the weather permits. . . . In the summer we take them into the forests, where we live with them in tents for several days at a time and thus teach them to enjoy enduring cold and heat, uncomfortable beds, sparse fare, and all kinds of harmless inconveniences. We train them in racing, wrestling, balancing, fencing, dancing; in brief, in everything that makes the nerves vigorous, the limbs supple, the senses keen, and the whole body robust, agile and strong.[9]

The teaching of cultivated social deportment was another of the avowed aims of the philanthropinical method. Gait, bearing, speech, and gesture of the pupils were to be refined so as to be free of foolish timidity and unabashed impudence. Supervision of the pupils' social manners was the special province of the Inspector, whose duties were obviously most arduous, for he could not cease his vigilance as long as the pupils were awake, and the administration of philanthropinical corrective measures must have required no small degree of ingenuity. Thus, we learn that deep-seated bad habits were to be corrected by forcing the pupil to repeat the habitual act for fifteen minutes at a time so that it would become thoroughly distasteful. But elegant behavior was rewarded by admission to the society of the most distinguished personages in the castle. On these occasions the conduct of the pupil was observed and "graded." Permission to attend concerts, assemblies, and teas which the aristocratic families of the neighborhood frequented, was the supreme reward for excellence in etiquette.

As for instruction in school subjects in the more limited sense of the term, it was based upon a thoroughly empirical theory of knowledge and learning and followed where Comenius and Locke had led. From the major premise, *Nihil est in intellectu quod non antea fuerit in sensu,* it followed that the pupils must first be made familiar with the sight and touch and smell of things before being required to deal with them intellectually.

We start with the easiest things [wrote Bahrdt] and proceed by degrees with the more difficult. We show them meadows, gardens, fields, vineyards, houses, mills, etc. We take them to the craftsman's shop, to the anatomy laboratory, to the physics laboratory, etc.[10] With all the things that we have them observe, we first give them just an over-all view, tell them about the use and value of the things, and we also tell them about the misuse of the things as well as their true use. The second time (the first course lasts half a year) we have them look deeper, show them material, form, parts, structure, arrangement, art, beauty, etc. Everything which they have seen in nature we soon thereafter have them find again in engravings and models. And so that the impressions may be really vivid and permanent we make drawing exercises the very first exercises of the Philanthropinum. Before the child writes, it must draw. We have it sketch or copy the outlines of all the things they have already seen in the original.

After the child had thus been provided with sense impressions and corresponding concepts, it was to be given the task of studying exhibits independently, finding the exhibited objects in a state of nature on field trips, dissecting and observing things and so on. Thus the child was to be taught to formulate general principles on the basis of particular experiences.

To the modern reader all this sounds quite familiar and acceptable, even though reservations must be made about the absolute validity of the basic premise. The defect in the method itself is that the creative force of the imagination is not given its proper recognition, but it must be conceded that the general mode of procedure as here stated is good. And, of course, it is a matter of historical record that it recommended itself to Johann Heinrich Pestalozzi, who was in 1776 a still rather obscure member of the Helvetic Society of Schinznach. Pestalozzi was successful where Basedow, Salis, and Bahrdt failed,[11] so that thirty years later the philosopher Herbart, who was born at the time of which we are speaking, was able to say without a thought of Salis, Bahrdt, or

Basedow, that Pestalozzi's method of teaching tackled more boldly and eagerly than any previous method the duty of shaping the child's mind, of building up in it a definite and clearly seen structure of experience. That is, the great advantage of Pestalozzi's method was that it did not proceed as though the child already had accumulated experiences, but it provided them. The child was not engaged in conversation as though it already had a need to elaborate and communicate what it had taken in, but the child was given the material that was to be worked over and discussed. This succinct characterization would, of course, apply equally well to Bahrdt's *Philanthropinischer Erziehungsplan*.

Work on the prospectus had entailed for Bahrdt closer contact with Salis and had increased the friction between them. Bahrdt calls these weeks a real purgatory and his duties so hateful that he debated with himself whether he should not flee precipitately and return to Germany, even though he had no prospect of securing any sort of position there.

It was during this time that he received the unexpected news of his father's death, which, so he tells, did not affect him very deeply. One morning as he was about to give the signal for the first class period to begin, Salis handed him a letter bearing a black seal and addressed in his brother's hand. Although he realized at once what news the letter contained he went on with his classroom duties as usual and dismissed the matter from his mind until eleven o'clock, when he returned to his apartment for the midday meal, after which he composed a letter to his brother in which he gave up his rights of inheritance to his mother. Thus, he says, he shook off the oppressive thoughts of death and did his work as before with cheerfulness and vigor.

The anecdote is characteristic of Bahrdt but should not be interpreted to mean that he did not love and respect his father, for the opposite seems to have been true. As we shall see, he was capable of the same behavior at the end of his life when he lost his daughter, to whom he was deeply attached by the strongest bonds of mutual trust and affection. The significance of the anecdote seems to be that it helps to illustrate how he was able to slough off disagreeable and disturbing thoughts, to make himself numb to feelings that threatened to reach to the center of his being and disrupt it. Indeed, the anecdote seems to confirm what has been said earlier in this chapter about Bahrdt's sense that certain things he did could not really "count," to point to his capacity for self-induced moral anesthesia.

That the numbness of feeling was not due to anything like stoic apathy is made plain by another anecdote about a letter which caused

the second great ecstasy of my life. [As he describes the event] I sank to my knees half swooning and clasped my hands with a glance up toward heaven, "God, how wondrous are thy works!" My wife happened to enter the room. She was frightened when she first saw me in this attitude. "Mother! rejoice! God has saved us!" I told her of the contents of the letter. Our tears of joy were mingled.

The letter which occasioned this ecstasy had been written to him by *Diakonus* Schöll in Dürkheim an der Haardt to inquire whether Bahrdt might be interested in accepting the position of *Generalsuperintendent* in Dürkheim with a salary of one thousand *Gulden*. Bahrdt would probably have agreed to any proposition at all that would take him from Marschlins.

Just picture [he says] the hell in which I had been living. Picture the despot under whose cruelty I sighed, my slavish toil which gained me not so much as a friendly expression, the almost complete lack of my accustomed social life and of everything that produces true joyousness and thereby renews the elasticity of one's mental powers and stimulates activity.

And now came the chance to obtain the highest ecclesiastical position in the domains of Count (later Prince) Carl Friedrich Wilhelm of Leiningen-Dachsburg and all its associated offices and responsibilities such as membership in the Consistory, superintendency of schools, and senior pastorate in the city. Small wonder that Bahrdt felt the benevolent eye of Providence upon him.

Of all this, however, there was not a word in his reply to *Diakonus* Schöll, for he did not wish to seem too eager, as he felt he had been when Bechtold held out the possibility of a professorship in Giessen. Instead he wrote to Schöll on the eleventh of March 1776,[12] that his first thought upon receiving the inquiry was that he could not accept the position, because to do so would give him the reputation of being unable to persevere in his purposes, because he felt a deep and almost irresistible devotion to his pupils, his children, in Marschlins, because he had formed the intention eventually to establish an educational institution in Germany, and because his salary in Marschlins was somewhat more generous than the salary offered him in Dürkheim. But then, he went on, he discussed the matter with his most intimate friend, who pointed out certain considerations that outweighed Bahrdt's reasons for refusing the offer. First, the atmospheric conditions in Marschlins caused him a good deal of illness; second, there were certain peculiarities in the local situation that interfered with a completely satisfactory performance of his duties; third, he felt a patriotic attachment to Germany; fourth, he had obtained from a student in Giessen the most favorable impression of the Count's noble character, enlightened outlook, and sincere concern for the welfare of his subjects; and finally, it was plain that the new position would offer him greater scope and enlarge his sphere of action. He was therefore ready to accept the appointment under certain conditions. Indeed, when all things were considered it seemed very probable that he was being guided into the service of the Count by the very Hand of Providence and that Bahrdt's higher mission for the benefit of humanity and education could best be realized in the domains of the House of Leiningen-Dachsburg.

XV

⟦OUT OF THE FRYING PAN⟧

ALTHOUGH BAHRDT wished Schöll to believe that he had to turn the matter over in his mind for several days before coming to a decision, he lost no time in announcing to Salis that a German prince had offered him honors and responsibilities. Salis received the news in the Valtellina, where he had been spending several weeks engaged in party politics. What he did not learn until he returned to Marschlins was that Bahrdt was taking Heres with him to Dürkheim and attempting to enlist other teachers for his own projected school. Although he was not successful in this, the loss of two of the most important members of the faculty was a severe blow to the Philanthropinum. Salis found the operation of the school increasingly difficult until finally it collapsed.

Bahrdt meanwhile had been laying the groundwork for the establishment of his own Philanthropinum. In a second letter to Schöll written on the fifteenth of March he further explained what he had meant by the educational institution (*Erziehungshaus der Deutschen*) he had mentioned. It was his idea, he said, that the school would be his private concern until he should be able to offer the Count an opportunity to participate in the venture if he so desired. It would not, he went on, entail his withdrawing from any of his duties or obligations, for the school would run itself and would cost the Count nothing. Indeed, it could be expected to bring at least 100,000 florins into the Count's domains.

We can suspect that it was to secure more time to devote to his projects that Bahrdt requested of the Director of the Count's Chancery Gerauer that he should not be considered remiss in his duties if he should occasionally deputize a colleague to act for him in conducting funeral services and similar functions which might expose him to inclement weather or put too great a strain upon his constitution. For although he was able to perform prodigies of work, still he suffered from a certain delicacy of health which required him to take particular care of himself. The reply from the Chancery, although not giving formal assent, was favorable to the request.[1]

At the same time that he was feathering the nest he planned soon to occupy he had to make the necessary preparations to leave the old one. He had to settle his finances with Salis, who owed him a good deal of money. Somewhat to his surprise he was able to work this out rather smoothly by transferring his claim to a certain Dr. Bohner, who advanced him the required ready cash. Perhaps the ease with which this was done had something to do with Salis's apparent softening toward Bahrdt. If the latter can be believed, as the time for Bahrdt's departure drew near, Salis seemed to come to some understanding of how groundless his distrust of Bahrdt had been and that he really owed him a debt of gratitude. On the last day, as the horses were being hitched, he even admitted to Bahrdt that it was Deinet who had planted the seeds of suspicion and discord in his heart.

The task of hitching the horses to the carriage was the final and easiest step in a long series of preparations that had to be made for the journey. For the carriage in which Bahrdt and his family had made the trip from Giessen to Marschlins had proved to be unwieldy on the narrow rutted roads of Graubünden and had been adapted to the new conditions. This had meant providing it with new and shorter axles, a new boot, and a new fore-carriage. Now the carriage had to be remodeled for the journey back to Germany.

His most difficult problem resulted from the circumstance that the carriage had been reduced in width in order to make it usable on the narrow roads of Graubünden, and it would have to accommodate three adults, himself, his wife, and Heres, and three children, one of whom was an infant [2] born toward the end of 1775. Whereas the baby could be held by the three adult passengers in turn, the other children, four and five years old respectively, could not comfortably sit on the grown peoples' knees day after day as they bumped along the poorly kept roads. He solved the problem by setting up on the floor in front of the seat a detachable upright, to the upper end of which a strong crossmember was made fast. To the crossmember he secured an oval board which would seat the two girls back to back. He then provided a semicircular backrest for each seat and attached a strap to each one. By means of the strap the two girls could be buckled in so that they would not be thrown out as the carriage lurched along. He friezed the backrests and upholstered the seats so that the girls could sit in relative comfort as well as safety, each one looking out her side of the carriage. The whole thing was provided with a waterproof canvas top, which Bahrdt had made himself, so that everyone was sheltered from the elements, even though not from certain dangers incident to travel at that time.

As they were climbing a hilly road with the help of two post-horses in addition to the two Bahrdt owned, and had slowed down to a crawl because of the ascent, Bahrdt's coachman got down from the box to stretch his legs by walking alongside his team. Bahrdt, who knew the fiery temperament of the mare he used as a riding horse, warned the coachman to stay close. But the coachman, assuming that Bahrdt's horses, which were preceded by the two plodding post horses, could be trusted to cut no capers because of the uphill drag, put the reins up on the box and proceeded to light his pipe. At that very moment the mare gave a bound and began to run away. The near horse shied and broke into a run also. The coachman leaped for the reins but missed and came close to falling under the wheels. Now the post horses became terrified, and when the shaft began striking their legs they too broke into a run and, despite the best efforts of the postillion to control his team, the carriage was soon careening full tilt along an elevated roadbed, ready at any moment to tumble into the ditch below.

I saw the whole thing with complete self-possession [writes Bahrdt] and made ready to save the children and to hold tight so that I would not fall on them when the carriage tipped over. Then I saw the horses jump down to the right, and then the carriage plunged into the ditch. By a stroke of luck our lives were saved. As the carriage rolled over, the tholepin came out and the horses ran off with the front wheels into the underbrush where they were caught and finally stopped.

When everybody had crawled out from the wreck and it was ascertained that none had been seriously injured, Bahrdt inspected his carriage and found that the top he had made was badly bent.

I got out hammer, pliers, and axe (which I always took with me) and repaired the bird-cage as well as I could, so that we could take our places again. In the next town, where we took lodgings, I stayed up all night and sewed fresh canvas on so that we could continue our journey in excellent style the following morning.

The rest of the trip was uneventful, and the party reached Dürkheim in good condition. Their reception was cordial: Schöll, two deputies of the citizenry, and the tavernkeeper bade them welcome and had a tasty meal ready for them. The house in which they were to live was new and attractive and had a garden. Bahrdt was treated with deference and respect. As he looked back upon the situation he had just left, he felt he had emerged from Purgatory into Paradise. But, as he writes, the angel with the sword was not far away and was already brandishing his weapon to cut the thread of happiness which Bahrdt's tutelary genius had just begun to spin. But for a while life seemed good.

The day after his arrival he paid his respects to the Count, whom he found to be not a brilliant mind, but a warmhearted man of unpretentious good sense. He was kind and friendly towards everyone, respected merit and ability, and had a deep sense of justice. It was apparent from the way he received Bahrdt that he had already had favorable reports of him.

The ordinary citizens of the place had also had reports of Bahrdt, but they were not as favorably predisposed as was the Count. "The new preacher doesn't believe in God," said some. "No," said others, "he doesn't believe in the Father." "Oh no," said a third group, "it's the Son he doesn't believe in." And some added that he didn't believe in the Devil either. But for all that, both the Count and the city seemed proud, as Bahrdt observed with satisfaction, to have a Doctor of Theology and a famous onetime professor as their preacher.

Bahrdt's duties in Dürkheim were not arduous, even though his position brought with it a great many titles of office. He preached at the morning service every Sunday and at the midweek service once every three weeks. He was not concerned with

instruction of children in the catechism, and there were no con-
fessions to hear. He was under no obligation to be concerned with
individual spiritual counselling, to visit the sick, or to give private
communion. The only real burden which rested upon him was
confirmation. For a week just before Easter he had to examine the
candidates on the knowledge of the catechism which they had
acquired through previous instruction.

I really suffered [he writes] when I had to make the children recite ideas
and propositions which I considered to be in part utter nonsense and was
not allowed to set them right. And so I let them just rattle off their dogmatic
catechetical rubbish and memorized material and concerned myself only
with imparting good moral ideas and sentiments. It pained me most deeply
when finally I had to make these children lay down at the altar a confession
of faith which contained so many absurdities and was, so to speak, imposed
upon them. For it surely cannot be denied that a faith is imposed upon the
children when one drums into them as divine truth ideas which they do
not understand and the true or false ground of which they do not know. And
is it possible to conceive of anything more shocking than swearing to a belief
which is not within the province of our free will? Is swearing that one will
conceive of something thus and thus one's whole life long and will believe
in it as true not just as unreasonable as swearing that one will always love
a certain thing or will always have good powers of digestion?

Bahrdt thus had plenty of time to himself, to read, to reflect,
and to ponder new schemes for advancing his material welfare.
For his remuneration was not ample. Although his income was
estimated at 1000 *Gulden,* only 300 *Gulden* were received in cash
from the Count's treasury. The rest of it consisted in perquisites
of office such as lodging and fuel. That Bahrdt's statement that he
and his family lived very modestly in Dürkheim is true has been
confirmed by Albert Schreiber, who made a thorough study of
the official records pertaining to his affairs.[3] Leisure and modest
circumstances were things which Bahrdt could not well endure,
especially since his home life afforded him such little satisfaction.
Frau Bahrdt, of course, had not become any less simple or more
understanding of her husband's complications and vagaries but,
if his account can be believed, continued to torment him with her
jealousy and to bore him with her inadequacy. Despite Bahrdt's
assurances to the contrary, there is no reason to doubt that he did
give his wife grounds for jealousy, even though perhaps he was

innocent of amorous inclinations toward either *Frau Rätin* Sand-
herr, whose husband became his friend, or toward Count Carl's
mistress, about both of whom Frau Bahrdt harbored unhappy
suspicions.

Apart from the Sandherrs Bahrdt had few intimate friends in
Dürkheim. Heres had come with him, to be sure, but Heres had
an unhappy disposition and was not the companion with whom
he might enjoy life. Most of the clergymen were extremely limited
in their outlook, with two notable exceptions. One of these was
Schöll, the man who had first written Bahrdt about the possibility
of coming to Dürkheim. The other was Pastor Böhme, to whom
we owe some very illuminating anecdotes about Bahrdt. Böhme
was a Reformed clergyman who lived in Frankental, which was
far enough away so that the two saw each other only rather in-
frequently. According to Bahrdt, he was a man of intelligence and
knowledge, a jolly companion, in whose company Bahrdt could
spend three days at a time without boredom. He was inexhaustible
in learned conversation or the most entertaining and sidesplitting
jokes and anecdotes.

And besides, he had a heart so pure, loyal, and affectionate, a character
so steadfast, and judgment so sound, mature, and experienced that one
could wish for no better guide and adviser or repose one's confidence in
no one with greater justice than in him.

And it is well to record here that Böhme seems to have cherished
an equal regard for Bahrdt to the end of Bahrdt's life and beyond.

Bahrdt's situation in Dürkheim, therefore, although it left some
things to be desired, would have been quite tolerable and even
pleasant if it had not been for two things. One, of course, was his
own restless nature, the compulsion to devise schemes which he
hoped would advance him professionally or materially. The other
was the presence in Dürkheim of a powerfully placed man with
whom he inevitably came into conflict.

This man, who was born not far from Strassburg, is known to
history as Phillippe-Jacques Rühl, a minor figure in the French
Revolution. The son of a Lutheran minister, he had studied theology at the University of Strassburg and then become a tutor in
the household of a Count von Grumbach but was soon dismissed

for unseemly conduct. Nonetheless he quickly obtained a position as rector of a school in Dürkheim and thus came to the attention of the Count, who engaged him to sort and organize the family archives. Rühl had great aptitude for this kind of work, for he is credited with an extraordinary memory and a phenomenal range of knowledge. Indeed, the author of the article on Bahrdt in Schlichtegroll's *Nekrolog* for 1792 says that if Bahrdt had had in addition to his own lucid mind and sound judgment only half of Rühl's stock of information, his scholarship would have been truly sensational.[4] Rühl's most important task as archivist for Count Carl was to find records which would support the Count in his litigation with another branch of the House of Leiningen. Rühl went at this problem with zest and composed three refutations of the pretensions of the Count of Leiningen-Güntersblum to part of Count Carl's territory and won the case. Rühl also won the unreserved admiration and gratitude of his noble master, who conferred on him the title of *Hofrat,* put him in charge of his finances, and made him his chief adviser in all matters. Rühl was, in short, the petty prime minister of a petty state, whom the Count considered indispensable and, according to Bahrdt, even feared.

Bahrdt says, and there seems to be little reason to question this statement, that the core of Rühl's character was composed of pride and egotism which had no regard whatever for any other creature in the universe. He constantly strove to augment and enhance his own standing and sacrificed anyone and anything to the idol of his ambition without compunction and without questioning the wisdom and justice of his own decisions. To egotism was joined sadistic cruelty: "Human misery not only did not touch him but it actually gave him sensual pleasure," says Bahrdt. He relates a characteristic anecdote about a report made by *Hofrat* Michaelis, one of the Count's officials, concerning the inability of the peasants of a certain village to pay the taxes that had been levied upon them. The peasants, who had been visited by a series of misfortunes, which made them unable to meet their obligations, had first had their clothing and beds taken from them in lieu of payment, had then lost their household utensils, and were now, according to Rühl's orders, about to lose their cattle. *Hofrat*

Michaelis reminded Rühl of the desperate plight of the village and pleaded with him to relent, stating that the peasants would be forced to leave their homes and become beggars. During this recital, which Bahrdt says he heard with his own ears, Rühl sat at ease in his armchair, toying with the ruffle of his shirt and wearing an expression as though he were listening to the report of a disaster that had befallen his worst enemy.

And when the official finally shed a tear himself and implored the *Hofrat* for the sake of heaven to grant some indulgence to the poor whimpering subjects and to revoke the command to exact the final pledge, he laughed aloud and said: "Sir, you are an old woman. Let the *canaille* go to the Devil. Ha ha ha ha! I would like to see that rabble. Take extreme measures of enforcement. And when the dogs are completely destitute come back and entertain me again with your report and your tears. I really enjoy seeing people be so softhearted."

This anecdote cannot, of course, be accepted without reservation since it is told by Bahrdt in support of his contention that Rühl was a monster of iniquity. And yet it may very well be true, for what is known of the rest of his career does not make it seem improbable that he was truly driven by a monstrous ambition which made him, as Bahrdt says, "hate God and humanity, because they dealt unjustly with him and let him, a man who belonged on the pinnacle of honor and fortune, remain in the position of an unimportant councillor of an unimportant prince."

And he did remain the unimportant councillor of an unimportant prince until revolution had undermined the power of the King of France. He then abruptly forsook the service of Count Carl and maneuvered himself into the position of representative of the county of Saarwerden, from which post he advanced to the position of administrator of the *département du Bas-Rhin,* and then of deputy to the National Assembly. From the outset he advocated severe measures of expropriation, repression, and pillage, having apparently transferred his hatred to the princes from the rabble, whom he now joined and incited to ever greater excesses. In 1794, as a member of the *comité de sureté générale* on a visit to Reims, he assembled the elders of the city to deliver an inflammatory harangue. To emphasize his radicalism he seized the sacred vessel from which the kings of France had been anointed ever since it had been brought by a dove from heaven for the coronation of Clovis (496) and smashed it to bits at his feet. He joined the party of Robespierre, advocating even greater terror and brutality than his leader, and after the death of Robespierre, finding that the tide of events had set irrevocably against him, stabbed himself to death on the twenty-ninth of May 1795.

Rühl was at first well disposed towards Bahrdt. Indeed, he was probably largely instrumental in securing the appointment for Bahrdt, for, it will be recalled, he had studied theology himself and presumably approved of Bahrdt's "enlightened" position. As events took their course, however, Rühl's early friendship turned into reserve, distrust, and hatred. Perhaps this change was due merely to Rühl's despotic pride, which could brook no one of comparable stature and position near him. But there is another possibility, one which Bahrdt carefully does not mention: he conceived the scheme of undermining Rühl's position, of causing him to lose the Count's favor, of himself becoming the power behind the throne. Here, for once at least, the shrewd judge of character, Bahrdt, made a monumental blunder and apparently did not sense that he was about to take a bear by the tail.

XVI

⟨ PRACTICAL PHILANTHROPINICS ⟩

THE REMOVAL from Giessen and the professional concerns of a practicing scholar seem to have marked a turn in Bahrdt's inner development. During the year in Marschlins he had, of course, neither the time nor the opportunity to push deeper into the thicket of Old Testament philology, criticism, and exegesis. In fact, his reflections and his encounters with others caused him to lose faith in the value of this line of endeavor. Thus, his meeting with Lavater, he says, shook and almost toppled his deluded belief in the supernatural and miraculous.[1] With Heres he frequently conversed about the Old Testament, and together they found in this book many mythical elements which they could not take seriously. Thus it had come about, he writes, that he had gradually attained the insight that the Old Testament was a book of no consequence for religious instruction but which, on the contrary, because of being overburdened with miraculous and supernatural elements, turned the heads of the masses and nullified their power of reasoning. Thus he came to lose his former keen interest in the philological studies which he had once pursued in the interest of biblical exegesis, and he now turned increasingly to the field of religious ethics.

The new interest was not only natural but necessary if he was to find material for his sermons. He could no longer expound the doctrines of the Trinity, satisfaction theory, supernatural grace, original sin, or eternal punishment, for reason no longer allowed him to believe in them. All that was left of his original orthodox structure of faith was belief in the immediate mission of Jesus and the divine nature of Holy Writ, subjects which could not long

159

continue to furnish material for his preaching. His sermons became, therefore, disquisitions on Christian ethics and the practical conduct of life, and they derived their support not only from the Bible but, to a greater extent, from Bahrdt's own theory of the motives of human action,[2] which was, as we shall see, a practical hedonism.

Since Bahrdt was a very powerful pulpit orator, since he took care not to express views which were in direct conflict with established doctrine, and since the aristocratic and intellectual circles in Dürkheim were receptive to his message, he soon rose in popular esteem and was well on the way to becoming an established and respected public figure. In what peace and contentment he might have lived, he says, if he had had the happy thought of writing popular books in an ethical–theological–philosophical vein (as he later did in Halle) to augment his income by means of this very useful kind of work. But the idea did not occur to him, and he had no good friend who could point out to him where his real strength lay and say to him, "This is the talent you received to put out at interest." If he had understood the value of this talent, he says, he would not have been so strongly tempted to accept the Count's suggestion that he establish a new Philanthropinum. For the Count supposedly asked to see Bahrdt's printed description of the school in Marschlins and conceived a great admiration for it, causing Rühl to communicate to Bahrdt the information that the Count desired to have such an institution in his domains.

Now we know that this account of how Bahrdt came to set up his own school is fictitious and that the truth is that he had conceived the project in Marschlins and broached it to Pastor Schöll in the very first letters he wrote to him concerning the possibility of coming to Dürkheim. All the same, it is very probably true that the Count viewed the establishment of the school favorably, for he did grant Bahrdt the use of a vacant fifty-room palace in Heidesheim together with its splendid grounds and various outbuildings, including an inn. And it is also probably true that Rühl did at first give Bahrdt a good deal of assistance and encouragement, even though there is no reason to accept Bahrdt's statement that Rühl enticed him into the venture. On the contrary, Bahrdt had the greatest confidence in his own experience and ability to manage every detail of running such an institution as he planned to establish. He was familiar with the pedagogical theory, had observed the mistakes made in Dessau and Marschlins, was familiar with the practical details involved in housing and feeding a number of boys, and was himself a qualified chef. When he then calculated that he could accept fifty pupils at fifty *louis d'ors* each, furnish them with everything required, pay a staff, and make several thousand *Gulden* profit, his heart beat faster in anticipation of the comforts and luxuries which were to be his only for the application of a little time and energy on his part.

Another kind of expenditure was also required of him, however, namely money, for although he built his calculations on the rent-free use of the Count's palace together with its gardens, inn, and smaller buildings, he had to equip it throughout, including buying a new stove for the kitchen and horses for the riding school, as well as paying moving expenses for the teaching staff. The upshot was that his costs for the first six months of his operations amounted to some ten thousand *Gulden*.

To meet the obligations thus incurred he hit upon the idea of republishing his New Testament in a revised and cheaper edition. It is striking testimony to the keen and widespread interest in Bahrdt and his works that within a period of three to four months this publication had brought him a profit of five thousand *Gulden*, which he was able to invest immediately in his new school. Sizeable though this sum of money was, however, it amounted to only half of the amount that was needed, and so Bahrdt had to incur various debts which grew to be an ever greater burden upon him and contributed a great deal to the eventual collapse of the school. Bahrdt, who all along regarded his venture into pedagogy as a financial operation, attached to the school so many different enterprises which he hoped would make money that the Philanthropinum resembled nothing so much as a modern business which is in the process of diversifying itself out of its original identity.

Since Bahrdt was first and foremost a man of letters, he quite naturally thought of books as a means of augmenting his income. First of all, as soon as the announcement of the new school was published,[3] a book dealer from Heidelberg proposed that he be allowed to set up a branch of his publishing and retail business in the new school. Bahrdt agreed, and before long a wagonload of books was dropped off in the palace, and the new store was ready to do business on specified days when the dealer would be present to accept the customers' money.

Book publishing seemed like such a profitable business that Bahrdt, relying on his associate's promise to support their joint venture by risking his own capital, was persuaded to make an arrangement whereby a certain Gegel of Frankental agreed to transport two presses to Heidesheim and to put trained workmen at Bahrdt's disposal, supplying him with paper, printer's ink, and other necessary materials. Bahrdt was to keep the presses going and the workmen busy with the printing of his own books, school texts, editions of Greek and Latin authors, anthologies of edifying selections and so on. In no time at all he had prepared a new edition of his description of the Philanthropinum in Marschlins and launched a pedagogical journal, the *Literarisches Correspondenz- und Intelligenzblatt* (Heidesheim, 1776). This journal, as we shall see, eventually got him into serious trouble, even more serious than the unpleasantness caused by another serial publication, the *Kritische Sammlungen der theologischen Literatur aus der Allgemeinen Deutschen Bibliothek* (Heidesheim, 1777–1778).

The publication of the second of these two journals, so Bahrdt says, but not very convincingly, had been urged upon him by "innumerable" people, in order to bring the message of Enlightenment to those who were not able to afford to subscribe to the *Allgemeine deutsche Bibliothek* itself. To make excerpts from books and publish them seemed to him to be anything but unusual or illegitimate and, in this case, it seemed positively meritorious. For there was no denying that the *Allgemeine deutsche Bibliothek* was one of the main sources of enlightenment in Germany and contributed most to the growth of liberal thinking in the country. And Nicolai, the publisher, could certainly not lose anything by having abstracts and excerpts of the theological articles thus brought to the attention of a still wider circle of readers. Nicolai, however, did not view the matter in this light but accused Bahrdt of piracy, threatened him with legal action, and tried in every way to put a stop to Bahrdt's unauthorized reprinting.[4] This happened after Rühl and Bahrdt had fallen out, so that Rühl was happy to persuade Count Carl to order Bahrdt to desist from this bit of questionable business. Bahrdt, however, secretly continued reprinting the excerpts until he had rounded out the volumes as planned. He concludes his account of this episode by saying that in this way he succeeded in giving a few hundred orthodox pastors and pillars of the church sufficient cause to gasp, and he tore the scales of orthodoxy from their eyes so that they learned how to do a little independent thinking about religion.

It must not be overlooked that at the time of which we are speaking the nature of property rights to literary and artistic works was the subject of fierce debate. It was maintained by some that the very concept of property entails the possibility of the owner completely giving his property away or of completely taking it back, a condition which did not apply to thoughts and ideas. For this reason, it was maintained, exclusive rights to intellectual possession and exclusive rights of publication are impossible.[5]

In view of such a defense of a widespread practice, it must be conceded that the mere act of unauthorized republication was not *eo ipso* culpable, even though in other contexts Bahrdt himself advocated legal protection of an author's rights to his own work. But what was culpable was that in reproducing certain excerpts from the *Allgemeine deutsche Bibliothek,* he shortened the original articles by omitting material that did not favor his own point of view. Worse than that, he sometimes reversed the author's intent by altering the text. Thus, originally unfavorable reviews of one of his father's works were made to seem favorable. And, of course, negative criticism of his own books was also changed into praise.[6]

The philanthropinical publishing house was not the only business venture which Bahrdt attached to his school in order to support it and in the hope of making handsome profits, but there were several other ventures both sound and foolish. It was, for example, a good idea to grow as much food as possible in the extensive

palace grounds and barns, and, since an inn had already been established in connection with the palace, it could not unreasonably
be expected that the many visitors to the school would lodge there
and thus make some contribution to the material prosperity of
the Philanthropinum and its director. But it was certainly a risky
business to set up different kinds of manufactures at the suggestion
of a certain Sigmund, who offered his services as a teacher of religion and ethics as well as business manager. When Sigmund
vowed that he knew how to make magnificent tallow candles as
well as an unsurpassed green axle grease, Bahrdt's imagination was
inflamed, for he saw at once how much of the suet and tallow that
would be obtained from the philanthropinical slaughterhouse
could be utilized. Needless to say, the candles were not a whit
better than other candles and the axle grease, although it was
good, had to be sold at a loss. Even this experience did not cause
Bahrdt to lose hope of hitting upon some lucrative by-product
of education. When the custodian of buildings, a man who had
greatly impressed Bahrdt by his skill in various handicrafts, di-
vulged that he knew how to prepare a metallic alloy which so
closely resembled silver that it could be used in place of the
precious metal, Bahrdt's inexhaustible optimism caused him to invest in this scheme also. It was, of course, a failure, as was eventually the entire Philanthropinum.

What is perhaps most astonishing about this episode in Bahrdt's
life is that a man of so much undisputed practical ability should
have been so completely lacking in good sense when it came to the
essential matters in establishing and managing his school. Despite
his experiences at Marschlins, Giessen, and Erfurt, he seems to
have had no conception whatever of the fact that an educational
institution, be it university or preparatory school, *is* to all intents
and purposes, its faculty. Bahrdt proceeded to hire his teaching
staff haphazardly, without interviewing the candidates, without
taking even the most elementary precautions to make sure that
he was securing suitable people. This is all the more astonishing
in view of the fact that he is generally conceded to have been a
shrewd judge of character, a view which is substantiated by the
telling thumbnail sketches of eminent contemporaries which

Bahrdt published in his *Kirchen- und Ketzeralmanach*. But when it came to selecting able and trustworthy men to help him in what he hoped would be the most important and lucrative enterprise of his life, all sound sense deserted him, and he acted as though he were the favorite child of an indulgent Providence.

No sooner had the news spread abroad that Dr. Bahrdt planned to establish a new school in Heidesheim than he was bombarded by letters from aspirants to whatever positions he might have to offer.

The first such letter came from a certain Weinmann or Weidman (Bahrdt is uncertain about the name) who was rector of a small city school. The letter gave the impression of an able and deserving teacher, sincere and unaffected, clearheaded and enlightened, an indefatigable worker.

And [says Bahrdt] what affected me most deeply, an unhappy man, persecuted and impoverished, at the very edge of desperation. I trembled with joy when I read this letter. "How Providence is arranging things," I thought to myself. . . . "How grateful this man will be, devote himself to the institute with all his soul out of thankfulness for coming upon better days here."

The second letter came from the pastor in Bechtolsheim, Sigmund, the man who knew how to make candles and axle grease.

His language was that of an old experienced business manager, who knew all about agriculture, brewing, distilling and everything connected with those matters. He described his financial situation so that I should realize that he was motivated not by a desire to improve his position but by enthusiasm for my institution and myself.

Sigmund said he had money to invest in the school and, as we know, he offered Bahrdt his knowledge and skill as a chandler and grease maker.

The third man to offer his services was a private scholar in Heidelberg, named Junker, who wrote in an interesting style and assured Bahrdt that he was precisely that gentle, patient, loving type of philanthropinical man whom Bahrdt needed to instruct the pupils in elocution. "Aha!" as Bahrdt records his thought, "here we have our *bel esprit!*" and hired him.

In the same way Bahrdt engaged all the other instructors, of whom only two deserve special mention. The first of these was a native of Danzig who went by the name of Thomson although his name was really Ibbeken. The other was a Catholic priest named Weimar, who also volunteered his services in a very polite and almost obsequious letter, in which he explained that as the only Catholic clergyman in all the domains of the Count of Leiningen-Dachsburg, he hoped that any Catholic pupils who might attend Bahrdt's institute would receive their religious instruction from him. Since Bahrdt felt sure that no Catholic pupils would come to his school and thought that it would be diplomatic to stay on the good side of a man who might be able to damage the institution, he replied that he would employ him as a teacher as soon as any Catholic pupils should be enrolled.

Upon receiving this promise Weimar seemed to become Bahrdt's best friend: he came to call on him in Dürkheim and volunteered to secure subscribers for the new edition of Bahrdt's New Testament. To all his friends and acquaintances Weimar praised Bahrdt as a learned scholar and excellent man, even going so far as to introduce him to the Suffragan Bishop von Scheben, who, as we have seen, was already quite familiar with Bahrdt's New Testament from having considered the possibility that it might have to be suppressed. Bahrdt found the bishop a boon companion who liked good wine and fresh oysters as much as Bahrdt himself did and whose learning seemed to be more gastronomical than ecclesiastical.

Shortly before Bahrdt was ready to announce the formal dedication of the school, open enmity was declared between him and Rühl. Just what had led up to this declaration is not known, but it is not unlikely that Bahrdt had already challenged Rühl's authority in some way, and it is also very possible that Rühl, observing how Bahrdt went about securing his staff—all such appointments came under his official surveillance—decided that the Count and his government could not afford to be intimately connected with the new school. Bahrdt says that Rühl had been putting him off for a long time and had postponed presenting him with the document by which the Count conveyed to Bahrdt the privilege of using the palace in Heidesheim along with certain other substantial benefits. Finally, one day when Bahrdt was attending a meeting of the Consistory, Rühl appeared with the document and proceeded to read and comment upon it in language which plainly indicated his expectation that the Philanthropinum was bound to fail. Because the school seemed to have such little chance for success Bahrdt was ordered to state explicitly in all descriptions and bulletins that Count Carl was in no way associated with the Philanthropinum, which was to be a purely private undertaking of Dr. Bahrdt, and in no way supported by the government, although subject to its supervision. When Bahrdt protested, Rühl's outburst of fury was terrible to behold: he stormed and raged and foamed at the mouth so that all the councillors made ready to flee should physical violence occur. That is, all but Bahrdt, who stood his ground calmly and attempted to reason with a man seemingly gone mad.

Whatever may be the truth about this angry scene, there is no doubt that Bahrdt and Rühl quarreled openly and violently. A letter from Bahrdt to Rühl has been preserved [7] which gives plain expression to Bahrdt's anger.

I must tell you [it begins] that it cost me effort to speak with you yesterday and the day before in the tone of someone who despises you. It is not natural to my heart. It is not appropriate to the dignity of my position or of yours. Finally, it is painful to me in consideration of the favors you have done me. I therefore wish very much to be enabled to change this tone. . . . [But] if you continue to demand that I approach you as though you were a speaking godhead, as others do, cast down my eyes before you, nod in humility, say yes to everything, and swallow insensibly every manifestation of your anger, then you will compel me to show you that I have too keen a sense of my own worth to lower myself to crawling before you.

Rühl, of course, could not be brought to terms by this approach but instead denounced Bahrdt most vehemently to Count Carl and threatened to resign. This threat produced a panic at court and the general excitement rose to a fever pitch. On the following day Bahrdt obtained an audience with the Count and, if he can be believed, succeeded in impressing the Count with the justice of his case so that Rühl was commanded to draw up a more favorable instrument of conveyance, by which Bahrdt was granted the use of the palace and gardens in Heidesheim for ten years, full responsibility for managing the school, and permission to devote as much time to the project as he needed.

As much time as he needed was more time than Bahrdt had,

although he now took up residence in Heidesheim and made the three-hour trip back to Dürkheim only on Saturday evenings in order to preach the Sunday sermon and rush back to Heidesheim in the afternoon to get things ready for the grand opening. After performing prodigies of work he felt happy that he could count on having twenty pupils present for the ceremonies, and about twenty more had contracted to enroll the following summer. The teachers had been engaged and were asked to report for duty a week before the formal opening. The pupils, who had also arrived a few days early, were provided with a uniform of brown trousers, blue vest, brown jacket with steel buttons, and round white hats with blue plumes. The uniforms were to please the eye of the public, which, as Bahrdt observes, pays much more attention to such external details than to really important matters. And so finally the big show was ready to be staged, down to the large diagrammatic schedule of every pupil's activities for every hour of the day, which Bahrdt had devised himself and hung in a conspicuous place for the edification of the visitors who were expected from far and near.

And visitors did come from far and near: not only the parents and close relatives of the pupils who were to be entrusted to the pedagogical skill of Bahrdt and staff but many people who came merely to satisfy their curiosity. They came from Speyer, Heidelberg, Mannheim, Kreuznach and other more or less distant places and also from nearby towns and villages, and all had to be lodged or at least fed and provided with entertainment. Every day Bahrdt was kept busy running here and there, giving orders, supervising operations, writing letters, until his head swam and he was ready to drop. But in the evening he went to bed confident as a king looking forward to a proud and happy reign.

The high point of the dedication ceremonies, which took place May 1, 1777, was, of course, a speech by Bahrdt. In one corner of the palace courtyard he had had a great pulpit built from which to address the visitors, who were too numerous to be accommodated in any room indoors. At first there was a threat of rain but at ten o'clock when the courtyard was full of people and all the palace windows looking out into the courtyard could hold no more, the clouds broke and the sun shone down upon the assemblage.

I mounted the pulpit [says Bahrdt] and made a speech on the philanthropinical method of dealing with children in respect to physical and moral education, and I enchanted both aristocrats and commoners, so that they would all have gladly turned over their sons to me, if their purses had allowed it and if their sentiments had subsequently continued in accord with their first enthusiasm.

XVII

┤A SEA OF TROUBLES├

IN THE SPEECH which so inspired the guests, both high and low, who had gathered to see and hear the famous Dr. Bahrdt, the famous doctor explained his philosophy of education, which was a system of rewards and punishments. This system rested logically upon a basis of religious hedonism, the main tenets of which can be briefly described. As is evident, Bahrdt's philosophical position is eclectic: in what follows, the dominant elements are familiar from the better known views of Locke, Adam Smith, Rousseau, Basedow, Lessing, Goethe, and Kant.

It is the will of God, according to Bahrdt, that mankind be happy, but, of course, human actions which conform to the will of God must also be just and righteous. The true moral maxims are therefore: do that which makes you happy and content, advancing your own welfare and happiness in such a way that it contributes to the general happiness and welfare. This is the voice of Reason and the voice of the Universal Father; whoever fails to heed this voice brings down misery upon himself, for God so disposes that the unpleasant consequences of evil-doing tend to correct the disposition of man to selfish wickedness. God therefore leads his children to moral perfection by rewarding them for goodness and punishing them for evil. It must not be supposed that in this process God actually grows angry or that he is in any human sense to be propitiated, for in God there is no alteration. The only alteration possible is in man: if he leaves the path of virtue, unhappiness is the result; if he returns to the path of virtue, he once more enjoys happiness and the contented sense of being at one with the will of God. And it is not hard to know when one is travelling the right

170

road, for there is a certain sign: that action is contrary to the will
of God which destroys happiness or, if it were made universally
permissible, would destroy all happiness. The question to ask,
therefore, is: will this contemplated action destroy happiness, mine
or anyone's, if it is taken as a norm of behavior? It is possible to
understand what would impair the happiness of others by virtue
of the bond of sympathy which unites all God's creatures. In the
bond of sympathy is the basis of all noble impulses of mankind; it
is the material of which love and virtue are fashioned; it gives rise
to conscience, which drives man to seek the love and esteem of
sentient beings outside himself. Conscience, which warns man
when he is about to put his foot on the wrong path and spurs him
on along the right path, is the God-given sympathetic feeling of
right and wrong which is common to all men. But it is self-evident
that this moral sense is dull in the unenlightened: the road to
moral and religious perfection is therefore a kind of education of
the individual and of the human race.

This last thought, familiar to us from Lessing's *Erziehung des
Menschengeschlechts* (1780), Bahrdt makes the starting point of
his own systematic statement on the purpose of education.[1] Left to
his own resources, says Bahrdt, without education, man would require many centuries to become that which he ought to be. From
this it is evident that education is indispensable and that its purpose is to help the human being to come more quickly to the goal
of happinesss.

Happiness, however, must not be taken as a generally pleasant
sensual state, but rather as the pleasant feelings which come from
the exercise of the mental and imaginative powers. All gratification,
however, be it sensual gratification or true happiness, is the result
of activity, the free and proper exercise of one's true capacities.
Since the highest powers of man are of an intellectual and spiritual
nature, it follows that the highest happiness consists in the exercise
of these intellectual and spiritual powers and that the purpose of
education is to accustom the individual to activity, to the full use
of his faculties.

The educator has three classes of responsibilities, corresponding
to the three classes of human activities, the vegetative, the animal,

and the mental. On the first level (*e.g.*, sleep) the educator acts arbitrarily for the welfare of the child; on the second, he takes precautions to ensure that animal sensations do not make an unduly strong or lasting impression; and on the third, he tries to make sure that the pupil obtains correct sense impressions, enhances their value by reflection, and by contemplation works over the entire mass of ideas received.

Bahrdt attempts to answer the question of why certain ideas give pleasure by postulating that man has an innate need to have everything about him cheerful. The child enjoys light and color, and we are all drawn toward those beings in whose presence we feel a sense of satisfaction. This is the social urge. We try to gain for ourselves evidence of the happy approval of our fellows: the urge for honor. We acknowledge God, who regards our actions with approval or displeasure: conscience. We desire to give happiness to others: love. The pleasure of love is therefore the purest, sweetest, most lasting and most perfect. Love must therefore be the central point of religion and the first principle of hedonistic doctrine; training in this kind of love must be the highest purpose of the educator if he seeks the happiness of his pupils.

The educator has two means of achieving his purpose. The first is imitation or emulation. That is, the child learns to accept or reject certain ideas and modes of behavior from the example of the adults he sees around him. The educator must therefore keep the child from seeing and perchance admiring those who exemplify bad behavior. The second means is discipline, by which Bahrdt does not mean corporal punishment, but expressions of disapproval on the part of the teacher, refusal to associate with the child, verbal scolding, and so on. And always the teacher must be ready to capture the good will of the child by providing satisfactions of one sort or another.

Finally, something should be said about the more inclusive purpose of education, the relation to church and state. In Germany, says Bahrdt, the purpose of education should be to confirm the Germans in a sense of belonging together, to preserve them from the folly of imitating foreign traits, fashions, frivolities, and to give them confidence in their own worth and appreciation of their own language. As for religion, the school should teach the general truths of God, virtue, immortality with sincerity and warmth, but should deal with specific differences of dogma only historically. The great aim should be to inculcate in children tolerance and respect for every form of established religion, even if it were merely idolatry. Thus the product of the Bahrdtian system would be the loyal citizen of a nation but one who would transcend the purely local ties through a cosmopolitan outlook, for only through the combination of the national and the supernational can the human being become truly human in the full sense of the word.

Limitations of time, of course, did not permit Bahrdt to develop his educational theory in full in the speech with which he opened his school in Heidesheim. But he did explain his system of rewards and punishments as based upon the pleasure principle; he spoke of the pleasure principle itself as the master impulse governing human conduct; and he spoke of love as the sentiment which embodies the highest form of the pleasure principle. In conclusion he said,

If, O fathers and mothers here assembled, I am ever forgetful of the duty devolving upon me, to be both father and friend of your children, then may God be forgetful of me and of my children also.

After this address the guests were invited to partake of the pleasures of the table, for the philanthropinical tavern stood ready to serve, and tables had been set up in four great rooms of the palace to accommodate one hundred and twenty diners. Bahrdt the restaurateur had his share of pleasure also, for on the first day of the three-day celebration which now ensued he took in five hundred *Gulden*. And there were still other pleasures, for there was the opportunity to inspect the entire school and admire the philanthropinical timetable and then, in the evening, there was the great ball which was opened by Sabinchen Michaelis, *Hofrat* Michaelis's very beautiful daughter, the rays of whose hedonistic charms reportedly fell upon the just and the unjust. And the taverns and inns of outlying villages were likewise full of seekers after pleasure and devotees of love, whose activities, according to the estimate of *Geheimrat* Koch in Alzey, added at least fifty to the number of illegitimate children in his district.

Bahrdt himself seems to have partaken rather liberally of the less spiritual pleasures during his years as church dignitary in Dürkheim and guide of youth in Heidesheim. It was in Dürkheim, for instance, in his capacity of *Superintendent* that he made the acquaintance of Dorothea Eberwein of Grossbockenheim, whose pastor had excluded her from the communion of the church because of her illegitimate child. She appealed to the highest ecclesiastical authority in the land, namely Dr. Bahrdt, for absolution, which he accorded her in a way that may be literally called paternal. His name was inscribed in the church records of Grossbockenheim as that of the father of a second illegitimate child of Dorothea.

If Dorothea's child was the product of a sort of universal human sympathy, the twin girls of Anna Barbara Stählin may be said to have been the result of Dr. Bahrdt's devotion to philanthropinical hedonism. For these twins, who were born in Neuhof near Fischbach the first of the year 1778, may very well have been conceived during the festivities attendant upon the solemn opening of the school in Heidesheim. Their mother, who was a maidservant in the palace, was unwilling or unable to care for them, so Bahrdt arranged through a certain Herr Graf to have them brought up by a cobbler named Schüler in Hochspeyer. After about two years payment for their care was no longer forthcoming, so Schüler informed Herr Graf that he could not continue to feed and clothe them without compensation. Thereupon Herr Graf put the girls in the care of another foster-family. Payment became irregular and ceased almost at once. Then came the most shocking part of this story of callousness and indifference. The girls were stealthily taken from their new home and simply thrown upon the mercy of fate. One was left at the door of a shoemaker in Ufstein, who heard her crying and took her in, and the other was left near the gates of Worms where two little girls found her. They would both have died of exposure to the cold of winter if they had not been found in time. Eventually the mother claimed them and took them with her to Neustadt where she was in domestic service.

The actual extent of Bahrdt's direct culpability in this horrifying story is not known.[2] It is positive that he did not expose the children, for he was in Halle when this was done. Presumably the exposure was the work of his agent Graf, who resorted to this extreme measure when Bahrdt came on evil days and seemed to have been ruined forever. But however indirect may have been Bahrdt's responsibility for this part of the affair, the flagrant sexual promiscuity which seems to have been accepted conduct even for clergy in that part of Germany at the time may help to explain his behavior as what may be called part of a culture-pattern,[3] but it does not exculpate him either as a professor of Christian ethics or as a human being. There is no gainsaying the fact that Bahrdt could not stand prosperity, or what he believed to be prosperity, and that when he felt that things were going his way he was strengthened in the illusory belief in himself as excepted from the general principles of moral behavior. This very ugly aspect of Bahrdt's personality is clearly reflected in another bit of un-savory business connected with the unfortunate twin girls. It was apparently this affair, together with other reprehensible conduct of which Bahrdt was guilty, that affected Heres so deeply that an almost intolerable strain was put upon the relations between the two men.

The cause of the dissension is best revealed in Heres's own words in a letter[4] written to Bahrdt in May 1780, after Bahrdt had gone to Halle.

I have another matter to write you about [says Heres]. Since you wish never again to defend yourself against me and since I have promised never again to reproach you, I wish merely to tell you, without any bitterness and without reproaches, that I have incontrovertible evidence in my hands that you have shown various people a document in which I am supposed to have declared myself to be the father of the children who were born in Fischbach. *Herr Hofrat* Rühl is in possession of this document; whether a copy or the original (which you are said to have left behind) I do not know. It is enough that he is in possession of it. Since this matter can sooner or later do me harm, I believe that in consideration of my honor and my pos-sible future happiness I am justified in demanding of you that you send me a statement exonerating me of this false accusation. I promise that I will make no use of it. But I must have such a statement in my possession.

This astonishing letter is, of course, testimony to the basest as-pects of Dr. Bahrdt's character, touching, as it does, not only on the affair of the twins but upon certain other matters which will be discussed in their proper context. But the picture of Bahrdt which it helps to paint is still not the simple black and white portrayal which is accepted by most writers who have occasion to mention him, for it is evident that even at the time of writing the letter Heres was still genuinely attached to him, even though bitterly disillusioned. And a year later, in June 1781,[5] we find Heres once again trying to help Bahrdt to extricate himself from the difficulties which continued to beset him as a result of his enmity with Rühl and of the bankruptcy of his school. Thus, the continuing devotion to Bahrdt of such people as Heres, *Bergrat* Baumer, Pastor Böhme, and Chancellor Koch strengthens the impression of a cetrain naïveté in Bahrdt, the puckishness of a willful child who needs to be protected against himself.

That Bahrdt's was a poor temperament for the director of a boys' school goes without saying. Everything was bound to go wrong and soon did so; it might possibly have done so even if the teaching staff had been composed of able and devoted men. Since this is so and since the rest of the story of the school in Heidesheim is the chronicle of a collapse, it will be well to say now whatever good things can be said about Bahrdt as a schoolman, and there is, surprisingly enough, testimony to his having exerted a good influence upon his pupils.

This testimony is to be found in the very full article on Bahrdt in Schlichtegroll's *Nekrolog auf das Jahr 1792,* the author of which consulted a good many people who knew Bahrdt intimately. Among them were Heres, Schöll, and Böhme, all of whom were personally acquainted with the school in Heidesheim.

According to Schlichtegroll the Philanthropinum was almost certain to fail because the teachers whom Bahrdt engaged were so eminently unfitted and because Bahrdt, who was mainly interested in making a profit, felt it necessary to admit pupils who were already grownup and confirmed in their vices. That is, most of the pupils must have been what would now be termed "problem children."

Nonetheless [the article goes on] it cannot be denied that Bahrdt himself worked at the moral betterment of his pupils and that he succeeded in freeing some of them of certain youthful sins to which they were prone before they came to the institution. A dissolute man whom Bahrdt had engaged as a music teacher corrupted some of the pupils, but upon being discovered he was locked up and then dismissed in disgrace. Bahrdt mentions among his pupils the illegitimate son of Prince von S. who had already seen military service in Corsica. Even in the case of this young man, who had suffered both physical and spiritual neglect, Bahrdt's training seems not to have been completely wasted. Several of his grateful former pupils praise his treatment of them and his teaching, and the author of this article was acquainted with a talented young man among others who owed a part of his cultivation to the institution in Heidesheim and his correct and excellent power of elocution to Bahrdt in particular. One is strongly predisposed in Bahrdt's favor when one has the assurance that all the pupils held him in high esteem and love and exerted themselves to attain his approval and praise. It was, of course, natural that a man who in his behavior towards younger people combined seriousness with kindness and affection in due proportion would gain the love and respect of pupils who had their hearts in the right place, especially if he dealt with young men who were in a position to form some idea of the superiority of his mind.

When that has been said, however, the sum of the good things it is possible to say about Dr. Bahrdt as a school director has been exhausted, and everything else that can be recorded about his Philanthropinum in Heidesheim bears the stamp of the grotesque, the bizarre, and the indecent. The fact that it continued to operate as long as it did seems to suggest that if Bahrdt had chanced to secure the services of two or three able assistants, it might have functioned for some time as the Philanthropinum in Dessau did after Basedow had elevated himself to the status of a presiding genius. But the men whom he had engaged to perform the most important duties proved to be less than worthless, and the four or five who took their duties seriously were not able forever to offset the mischief done by the others.

The trouble broke out almost at once, for only four weeks after the opening ceremonies, on the thirtieth of May 1777, Bahrdt felt impelled to make another statement of philanthropinical policy. This statement was in writing and was in the nature of a series of severe admonitions addressed to the staff to mend their ways, for, said Bahrdt in his introduction, the school had already gained a very doubtful reputation. He felt it necessary to warn them in all seriousness that only a few more weeks of such misconduct as had hitherto characterized them would mean the end.

No supervision of the children, [he wrote] no kind of order at all, either in the class hours or between. No apparent excellence in teaching. No cleanliness. No character building. No association between pupils and teachers. No proper models of behavior among the teachers themselves. In short, nothing that we promised the public with great fanfare, and everybody is calling us empty braggarts and hypocrites.

The rest of the document is composed of specific rules too numerous to summarize, but some idea can be gained of conditions in the Philanthropinum from the fact that Bahrdt found it necessary to instruct the teachers to come to dinner neat and clean in dress and appearance, never to give the impression of being drunk, never to indulge in coarse language, and always to speak politely and respectfully to each other in the presence of the pupils.

The men to whom this solemn warning was addressed did indeed constitute a true rogues' gallery which Bahrdt vividly describes in his autobiography.

Weidmann, the former school director who had given the impression of being so experienced, devoted, able, and diligent, turned out to be a liability in every respect. Immensely tall, gaunt and ashen, the very picture of hunger personified, dull of eye, low-browed and wide-mouthed, in appearance alone he would have immediately filled with dismay the heart of any physiognomist. Bahrdt, however, who did not have faith in Lavater's views, was not completely disillusioned until he had attempted to converse with him about pedagogy or the Greek and Latin classics, the man's special field, and had found him to be an ignoramus, incapable of even working out a class schedule. Moreover, the man turned out to be a sot, who kept brandy in his room and who was frequently seen walking with an unsteady gait. And besides, the drink and the good food of which he partook so stimulated his appetite for other sensual pleasures that his indiscretions became public, and the Philanthropinum had to pay off a wench whose child he had fathered.

Junker, the *bel esprit,* was a kindly soul and a fine upstanding young man but excessively sentimental, his head filled with literary rubbish instead of sound information. The children liked him, but if a child showed any sign of finer feelings Junker was sure to make a "softy" of him.

As for Sigmund, the businessman-preacher who had money to invest in the school, he was Bahrdt's greatest disappointment, for all his possessions turned out to be a marriage bed, half a dozen chairs and tables, a clothes press or two, and several kegs of brandy. We already know of his failure as a chandler and grease maker. He had a bleating high-pitched voice that so grated on the ear that everyone who heard it tried to get away from him. In manner he was coarse, aggressive, and impertinent, and he "possessed a degree of ignorance that made him unfit for anything except functioning as an assistant steward." But even this arrangement proved costly to Bahrdt, for Sigmund and his wife made free with the food and the other goods that came under their administration.[6]

Aside from a French candidate for ordination in the Reformed Church with the instincts of a faun, whom Bahrdt discharged for grossly immoral conduct, the two most troublesome teachers were Thomson and the Catholic priest named Weimar. As for Ibbeken alias Thomson, he was a man of impeccable outward behavior which served as a cloak for intrigue and scheming. He constantly flattered Bahrdt in order to gain his confidence and trust and thus be able to undermine his position. He even went so far as to form an out-and-out conspiracy against Bahrdt into which he drew several of the staff, including Sigmund. This group held secret nocturnal meetings and planned to get the entire faculty to resign simultaneously. Bahrdt would thus be ruined, and Ibbeken could then step forward and assume the responsibility for managing the institute and giving proper guidance to the children whom Bahrdt had so shamefully neglected. One of Bahrdt's loyal teachers, a certain Reinhold, got wind of the plot, gained the confidence of the conspirators by pretending to join in their plans and reported all the details to Bahrdt. When the conspirators learned that Bahrdt was accurately informed of their doings they all, even Ibbeken, professed sincere repentance and things continued as before.

Continuing as before meant, of course, a frenzy of activity of which we can form some notion from the various projects which we already know that Bahrdt had undertaken to earn money. But, of course, it was impossible for Bahrdt to hope for any kind of support from such a gang of incompetents and ne'er-do-wells as he had gathered. Therefore he was obliged to attend personally to a multitude of tasks that must have strained even his energies and capabilities. He had, for one thing, to keep an eye on the stockroom, for there were so many visitors to the school that scarcely a day passed when sales of books and pamphlets were not made. In the printing shop Bahrdt had to act as foreman, tell each employee what to do, and make sure that there was no loafing on the job. He had to produce a steady stream of manuscripts for his journals and even do all the proofreading and correcting himself, for not one of the teachers possessed enough ability to do this accurately, to say nothing of writing essays and criticisms.

It was enough to drive me to distraction [writes Bahrdt] when one typesetter after the other called for work, or there was not enough manuscript for the journal, or disagreements and quarrels in the print shop had to be straightened out, or customers who wanted a book from the bookstore called for me, or Gegel pressed me for an advance, etc.

The lack of collaborators who could furnish Bahrdt with material to print was probably the greatest difficulty he had to contend with: it forced him to publish worthless trifles and finally to give up his publishing altogether, leaving him indebted to Gegel for a considerable sum.

Thus overwhelmed by a sea of troubles, Bahrdt quite naturally from time to time yearned for a respite, for the secluded life of an unspoiled child of nature who lived on the fruits of his toil— a rationalist's romantic dream. Yearning for an idyllic existence was a constantly recurring feeling in Bahrdt, best described in a very suggestive and somehow touching story told by his good friend Pastor Böhme.[7]

In the year 1779, some weeks before the final collapse of the school, Bahrdt and a certain Pastor R., whom he also liked, were the guests of Pastor Böhme. At the midday meal, during which nobody mentioned the Philanthropinum, Bahrdt expressed the wish to get away completely from the "madding crowd" and to live quietly by himself.

If I only knew of some island in the Rhine [he said] that I could lease and that had enough land to support me and my family in a modest way,

then I would lead a patriarchal life, would build myself a very simple low-
ly cottage, get as much livestock as I needed, dress myself and my family
in simple linen smocks, set a table just as simple, modest, and quite according to nature, cultivate my plot of ground myself and train my children to do the same, and thus divide my time between household and literary
tasks. Our greatest delicacy would be fresh May butter on rich nutritious
rye bread.

Bahrdt's lively imagination seized on this picture of an island
utopia and filled in so many delectable details that he not only
believed completely in the possibility of realizing this dream, but
fevered with the desire to find the island and commence his rural
labors. Now, as it happened, Böhme and his friend knew about
the existence of an island in the Rhine only about an hour's walk
from Frankental. They explained to Bahrdt that they had played
on this island as children, that it was just the right size and could
probably be leased. Bahrdt caught fire at once and insisted that
they hurry through dinner and rush off to the island, where in
his imagination he was already spreading fresh May butter on
thick slabs of good rye bread, while he composed popular sermons
and kept off all visitors except a few choice friends.

Thus, about one o'clock on a hot and humid afternoon the
three men set off to find Bahrdt's future paradise, Bahrdt meanwhile planning furiously how he would set up his farm buildings,
furnish his house, arrange his fields, plant his vegetable garden,
set out his fruit trees, plan his menus, budget his time, choose his
literary subjects, and select the friends whom he would allow
to pass the gates. After an hour's walk filled with this onesided
conversation the three, dripping with sweat, came to the bank of
the Rhine. But no island! Perplexed, Böhme asked a group of in-
quisitive peasants what had happened and they explained that
the river had changed its course and that the former island was
now part of the farther riverbank, the trees had been felled, and
the land was under cultivation.

I watched our doctor from the corner of my eyes [Böhme is reported as
saying]. There he stood, leaning forward on his walking stick. His wig got out
of plumb. It rose up in back, and in front it settled down at least an inch
toward his nose. His brow was furrowed. He blinked as though the wind
had blown dust in his eyes. Then he made a face like a man who has bitten
into a green apple or has a toothache but is determined to laugh it off. He

had a sort of lugubrious expression, as though the fresh May butter had fallen off his bread. At that moment he got control of himself, straightened up, looked around cheerfully, leaned back and began to roar with laughter that echoed from bank to bank. But during this whole scene he didn't say a word. Then he straightened his wig, made an about-face and set off on the way back so fast that we had trouble keeping up with him. Thus he rapidly strode away from a place where one of his most beautiful projects had melted like snow in the sun. From that moment on there was never another mention of the island or the May butter and, as was only decent, we never spoke of the matter to him again. On the road back, to be sure, the conversation was very sparse and forced, many long pauses interrupted our clumsy efforts to talk. But as soon as we had gotten back to my house, where other matters engaged our attention, the whole unsuccessful venture was put aside once and for all. Bahrdt was once again as cheerful and happy as before, took a little more refreshment and drove home to Heidesheim in good spirits.

The home to which he returned, however, was full of the sighing, complaining, and nagging of an unhappy wife, who saw in every woman who visited the school or attended the weekly dances an actual or potential rival. Well founded as her jealousy and suspicions were, whatever she did to recover her husband's affection was wrong and bound to make her seem even more tedious or stupid in his eyes than she already was. For the most part she seems to have upbraided him for his philandering, both privately and publicly, and to have demanded his amorous attentions as her conjugal right, a proceeding that was bound to estrange him still more. At other times the foolish woman seems to have gotten it into her head that she might regain her husband's love through wanton behavior, for on one occasion, while the young philanthropinists gathered at the palace moat to watch, she and Bahrdt disported themselves naked in the water. Bahrdt's thoughts on this occasion can only be surmised, but it is not unlikely that he was filled with cynical amusement and contempt: he was confirmed in his conviction that he had married a goose.

XVIII

⟦ INTREPID VOYAGER ⟧

ANOTHER GRAVE threat to the Philanthropinum which has hitherto been merely mentioned in our narrative came from the Catholic priest Weimar, who, as the time for the festive opening drew near, began to assert his rights to the position which Bahrdt had provisionally assured him would be his. Weimar now insisted that he must enter upon his duties at once, regardless of whether there should be any Catholic pupils in the school, and he demanded a salary of 500 *Gulden* instead of a normal 150. Bahrdt did not dare to make a flat refusal but put him off with a promise to use his services if he could, firmly intending, of course, to call upon him only if Catholic pupils were enrolled.

But on the Monday after the opening of the school, when all the classes were to begin, Weimar appeared, ready to take up his duties. Bahrdt was unfortunately not present, as he says without offering any explanation of why the Director of the school was obliged to be away on that morning of all mornings. Thus, when Weimar strode in and demanded to see the schedule of classes so that he could begin teaching, it fell to the lot of one of the teachers to take him to the master list, asking modestly whether Father Weimar was to be one of the teachers. Weimar angrily replied that he was indeed and proceeded to study the great bulletin board, where he found no mention of himself. He therefore had to be content with inquiring into every detail of the conduct of the school, stayed uninvited for dinner, ate heartily in ominous silence, and at length departed, vowing to repay Dr. Bahrdt well for the insults which he had suffered.

According to Bahrdt, Weimar betook himself to Worms to his friend, the Suffragan Bishop von Scheben, to whom he had previously introduced Bahrdt and with whom they had both dined well on various occasions. Weimar, says Bahrdt, proceeded to fill the Bishop's ear with poisonous tales about Bahrdt's heretical New Testament, which Weimar himself had helped to sell and make popular. It was therefore supposedly at Weimar's instigation that Scheben, as *Bücherkommissarius,* once again took up the case of the New Testament translation, not this time, however, in the edition which was dedicated to the Bishop of Würzburg, but in the revised cheaper edition which Bahrdt had put out to raise money for his school. The first result was that the book was confiscated wherever the authority of the Church to take such action was recognized. Bahrdt took notice of this by publishing in his *Correspondenz- und Intelligenzblatt* an announcement of the fact followed by the punctuation!!!!!!?????? What Bahrdt does not tell us is that he had also published in this same journal some disparaging remarks about Scheben's erudition as compared with his epicureanism—this, even though Bahrdt himself had been a guest at the Bishop's lucullan banquets. Infuriated and goaded by Weimar, the Bishop made a formal denunciation of Bahrdt as a dangerous heretic to the Imperial Aulic Council [*Reichshofrat*], the institution of the Holy Roman Empire which had general supervision of legal matters within the various Imperial domains. It was notorious for its tardy and ineffectual functioning: when F. K. von Moser, for instance, appealed to it for protection against the persecution of Ludwig IX, the proceedings lasted for eight years and in no way inhibited that monarch in the exercise of his will. What finally terminated the affair was Ludwig's death. Thus, even if Bahrdt knew of Scheben's action, he was probably not overworried and was able to dismiss this somewhat unreal threat from his mind.

Meanwhile, as we have seen, his troubles with the school and its various associated projects were mounting, as was also his indebtedness—at the end of a year he was not taking in enough money from tuition fees to make satisfactory payments to his creditors. The specter of bankruptcy threatened to put an end to the school even before it had properly begun to function.

I saw now [says Bahrdt] that all my hopes and expectations were deceived. The duties which overwhelmed me, the cares which oppressed me,
the vexations which consumed me, the ailing and impoverished condition of
the institution which distressed me, all became unendurable. The loss of my
peace of mind, of my health, of my life was inevitable. I pondered ways to
save myeslf. The Philanthropinum must be brought to the height of prosperity, this was my resolve, or it must perish entirely. This halfway condition
is intolerable. Either something real or nothing at all.

These considerations produced the, I would say, desperate resolution to
undertake a trip to Holland and England and there to enlist pupils who
would pay better than the *Pfälzer*. The idea shone forth upon me like a
rising sun. The trip was speedily decided upon and speedily undertaken.

With these words Bahrdt leads his narrative over to an episode
which in retrospect obviously gave him great satisfaction and
which he embellished with a great deal of fictional material. And
indeed, the very first part of the story, as he tells it, is so effective
and amusing in a way he did not intend that it is well worth repeating here in condensed form.

Who among his readers, Bahrdt would like to know, might
possess so much resolution and resourcefulness as he displayed in
undertaking this perilous journey? Everybody advised against the
trip. His children implored him not to go and pictured to him
the angry storms at sea which could overwhelm his ship. His wife
implored him not to go because she dreaded the prospect of pri-
vation and helplessness in the absence of *paterfamilias;* she also
feared the wiles and snares of some British beauty to whose charms
her husband might be susceptible. But Bahrdt resisted all this
piteous pleading and remained firm in his determination to surmount all difficulties.

And there were difficulties almost too great to surmount. The
greatest was the lack of money, for he could not, of course, draw
upon the scanty resources of the school for this venture. No cash,
no credit, no source of help in prospect. Besides, Bahrdt could
speak neither Dutch nor English, and his Latin could not help
him in England, because in that country the pronunciation of
Latin was English. Moreover, he had no acquaintances or connections in either England or Holland save for a certain Triest [1]
in Amsterdam. In addition, he was not in good health, and because he was poor he would be unable to travel by comfortable

conveyance. And if one considers the precarious situation in which he would have to leave his school and his family, it is plain that it was only his iron will which enabled him to surmount all these obstacles. But surmount them he did and set off on his perilous mission with only two *Gulden* and fifty *Kreuzer* in his pocket.

His own horses took him as far as Frankfurt, where he planned to lodge with Herr von Reineck, an associate of his friend Schellenberg, a local businessman. When he stopped off at this man's house his capital was reduced to a mere twenty-five *Kreuzer,* for he had spent one *Gulden* and twenty-five *Kreuzer* on the road and had given his groom the remaining *Gulden* for the return trip. Herr von Reineck was not at home, but his servants provided the visitor with a good meal and a bottle of fine wine and made his room ready for him. Then, although it was about eight o'clock in the evening, Bahrdt decided not to retire for the night but to go for a stroll in the expectation that after returning he would enjoy an even sounder sleep than usual. But this evening stroll had far greater consequences than Bahrdt could possibly have anticipated, for, as it turned out, the chain of seemingly trivial circumstances which set him to walking the streets of Frankfurt at that particular time on that particular evening was quite plainly the work of the Hand of Providence.

As Bahrdt was walking along in good spirits, his cares momentarily put aside, he observed a man not far away who seemed to be looking at him attentively. When he turned around to get a better view of the supposed stranger this man came up to him and cordially shook his hand, expressing his pleasure at the unexpected encounter. He was, as it happened, someone with whom Bahrdt had already had some dealings, the nature of which we may only speculate about. Bahrdt, recognizing him at last, responded with a hearty, *"Ach, guten Abend, mein liebster Herr Löw Bär Isak. I am happy to see you looking so well,"* and then, in answer to questions, went on to explain that he was merely passing through Frankfurt on his way to England on important business.

Löw Bär Isak was greatly perturbed by this information and tried to dissuade Bahrdt from his purpose, urging him to remain in Heidesheim for the sake of his school, which was sure to suffer

The frontispiece from Volume I of Dr. Bahrdt's autobiography.

Vignettes from the title pages of Volumes II
and III of Dr. Bahrdt's autobiography.

from the absence of its director. But when Bahrdt told him of his purpose in making the trip, he insisted that Bahrdt go home with him to share a bottle or two of old Rhine wine and explain the whole affair.

With these words, [says Bahrdt] old Löw Bär Isak pressed my hand so cordially and fraternally that a strange feeling stole over my heart. "This is the man," I thought at once, "whom the good Lord has sent you." I accepted the invitation, although I had never been intimately acquainted with the man. I had seen him at Schellenberg's house and bought some light cotton material from him on two or three occasions. And once I had been in his home and complimented his lovely daughter on her musical talents. That was the extent of our friendship. I entered the room and spoke to the lovely girl with my usual amiability and was received with such truehearted cordiality as though I had been among my very best friends. The old man called for rolls with caraway seeds and salt, and went himself to draw a bottle of wine from the barrel. His daughter soon seated herself at her grand piano because I had previously told her that music was one of my greatest consolations, and she played with such charm that I gave her a kiss and her father handed me a fine goblet and seated me beside himself on the sofa.

Then ensued a most remarkable conversation, in the course of which Löw Bär Isak learned from Bahrdt that his entire wardrobe consisted of the rather shabby suit he was wearing, that his entire capital consisted of twenty-six [sic] Kreuzer, his trust in Providence, and the hope of finding friends who would help him on his way. Löw Bär Isak was sure that he would find the friends, for nobody was so deserving of rich and helpful friends as Bahrdt, but he felt also that Providence should be aided somewhat, for in Holland it simply would not do to seem to be poor, and the semblance of wealth was all that was necessary to establish credit. Löw Bär Isak therefore sent forthwith for a tailor who arrived promptly. Isak withdrew with the tailor and Bahrdt could half hear them discussing terms in an adjoining room while he remained seated, drinking in the sweetness of both music and Rhine wine. After a while his host returned with the tailor, who took Bahrdt's measurements and departed. Isak then requested Bahrdt to come back for breakfast at a certain time the following day, by which time he promised that he would have arranged for Bahrdt's passage on a river boat as far as Mainz, from which city boats departed for Cologne every hour or so.

The following morning at the appointed time Bahrdt returned to find Löw Bär Isak waiting for him with every mark of pleasure.

"Well, *lieber Herr Superintendent,*" said he, pointing to a table, "I have done what I can. May God give you friends who will do something for you too."

On the table lay a fine new costume of purple velvet. On top of the new suit lay a money bag with a hundred *Gulden,* and underneath the table was a leather portmanteau in which Bahrdt could store his effects. But even this was not all, for the magnanimous Jewish merchant put a ring worth at least four or five hundred *Gulden* on Bahrdt's finger, saying that it was for show.

"Return the ring to me when you are back safe and sound, and repay the money when you have become a rich man," said he. Deeply touched by so much kindness and overjoyed by one more instance of help unsought and unexpected I grasped his hand. "May God requite you, excellent friend of my heart." The lovely maiden was sitting at her piano and hot tears rolled down her cheeks. "Now play your song of farewell," said her father. She played, sang, and sobbed. The scene was touching in the extreme. I embraced now the father and now the daughter and was beside myself with joy. But infinitely greater was the happiness of father and daughter. If all men only knew how blessed it is to give!

That this account is for the most part a bit of fiction done in the spirit of enlightened philosemitism goes without saying. Reviewers of Bahrdt's autobiography immediately pointed to it as an example of his mendacity and maintained that Löw Bär Isak was merely a figment of Bahrdt's imagination. Or, they said, a Jew did actually accost Bahrdt in Frankfurt at this time but only to demand payment of a debt which Bahrdt satisfied by pawning or selling a collection of old coins which he had with him. The truth of the matter seems to have been that Bahrdt's friend Schellenberg was associated with Löw Bär Isak, who was an agent for the courts of Hessen-Darmstadt and Hessen-Homburg and had extensive and important business connections. Bahrdt therefore went out of his way to go to Frankfurt in order to present to Löw Bär Isak a letter of credit which he had received from Schellenberg. Löw Bär Isak was in actuality a well-meaning, honest, and even magnanimous man, who, in addition to his serious business dealings, amused himself by making highly speculative loans of moderate size with little or no security. Since he conducted his little game systematically, having set aside a certain sum for this express purpose, he was prepared to lose his investments now and then, for in the long run his speculations gained him some profit. These doubtful loans were usually not made entirely in cash but partly in the form of jewelry on which he set a high price, so that he realized a good return when and if the loan was repaid. Such was the material of which Bahrdt built up his dream picture of religious toleration and human generosity.[2]

After equipping himself for the journey, Bahrdt set off down the Main on a swift little fishing vessel which offered him scant protection against the cold rain and wintry blasts. By the time he reached Mainz he had developed a feverish cold with digestive complications and had to seek lodgings and take to his bed. In order to draw profit from his enforced idleness he made known his presence in the city and received visitors.

Among the people who came to see Bahrdt was a certain *Kanonikus* Rediger, who, so Bahrdt says, attempted to persuade him to turn Catholic. Although this story has been disputed, it is actually quite plausible when it is considered that Bahrdt had made misleading overtures to the convert Herwig in connection with the dedication of his New Testament to the Prince Bishop of Würzburg. It is therefore not impossible or perhaps even not improbable that certain dignitaries of the Catholic church were keeping their eye upon Bahrdt with a view to making a convert of so notorious a freethinker. And the probability is increased by the circumstance that a very few years later Bahrdt was the object of much solicitous interest on the part of the crypto-Catholic Johann August Starck.

In outward appearance and manner, so Bahrdt says, Rediger was very pleasant and attractive. He spoke well, mixing wit with philosophy, and acted the part of a freethinker. He flattered Bahrdt greatly and told him that this spectacular step would bring him a very substantial material reward. Bahrdt says that he attempted to break off the conversation at this point but that Rediger pressed on, pointing out that the externals of religion were of little consequence and that a philosopher could very well adopt a principle that might be described as *Ubi bene ibi ecclesia*. Finally, he offered Bahrdt a benefice of a thousand *Gulden* a year from the Elector of Mainz and at the same time hinted that Scheben was marshalling powerful forces against him. Bahrdt then put a stop to the interview, and resolving to resume his trip earlier than planned, made arrangements to hire a private boat. But before he could leave, a messenger came with a letter from Rediger offering him five thousand *Gulden* a year to enter the services of the Elector. Bahrdt, however, would not be tempted and continued his journey down the river to Holland and England.[3]

Bahrdt's long description of his experiences in these two countries, although interesting and vivid, is so plainly tendentious that it must be considered untrustworthy. The Catholic Rhineland, especially Cologne, he found to be full of superstition and vice, and the Hollanders he ridicules for their worship of money. But the English, exclusive of the nobility, who were depraved and outdid the French in luxury, intrigue, and vice, were almost wholly admirable.

The central trait of English character is a sense of freedom and virtue. The genuine Englishman is noble, loyal, and absolutely incapable of committing a base act which might offend against the laws of decency or make him ridiculous in the eyes of the right-thinking majority or be in any way deleterious to liberty. In friendship he is firm, unchanging, and magnanimous. When one first makes his acquaintance he is cold, indifferent, and reserved. He first studies the outsider for several weeks. But when his confidence is won, when once he has said, "I am your friend," then he becomes confiding and candid, and one can count with certainty upon his friendship. In association with others he is natural. He is an enemy of stiffness, pedantry, and empty ceremoniousness.

How Bahrdt, not knowing the language,[4] could have made these observations at first hand during the two months he was in England is not easy to understand, even though he did make very useful acquaintances, among them Johann Reinhold Forster and his famous son Georg, and a Pastor Wendeborn, who had a small German church on Ludgate Hill.

The elder Forster, a former clergyman who had turned from pastoral duties to the study of natural science, especially botany, had been invited to go with the illustrious Captain Cook on his

second voyage of exploration and discovery. His son Georg, then
only seventeen, went with him. When they returned three years
later it was the son to whose lot it fell to write up the story of
their journey; the result was the masterpiece[5] which so powerfully gripped the imagination of the European reading public
that the name Otaheiti became and remained for a long time the
symbol of the blessed isle.

To the Forsters Bahrdt owed his first foothold in his undertaking
and almost literally his life. Not only did they translate the prospectus of his school into English and suggest changes and improvements that would appeal to the English, but they gave him a
standing invitation to dinner and were vexed when he did not
avail himself of it. Even though he did dine with the Forsters
as often as he felt he could, he was brought to the very edge of
starvation until, again as though by the direct intervention of
Providence, a servant brought him the first installment of the
tuition of his first English pupil.

Bahrdt's relationship with Pastor Wendeborn seems to have
been particularly cordial and fruitful. He writes of him in the
warmest terms, saying that all the pupils he recruited in London
he owed to Wendeborn's recommendations. He was, says Bahrdt,
extraordinarily talented, was well informed, had good taste, and
was versed in the ways of men and the world. He had a truly enlightened congregation, to whom he preached a religion of pure
naturalism, representing Jesus as a human teacher of the truth
which leads to blessedness. He invited Bahrdt to deliver a sermon
in his church and helped him to find other opportunities to preach
before congregations which might better be described as lecture
audiences, people whom curiosity concerning the notorious German theologian brought together in one or another of the approximately thirty privately owned church buildings which were
for hire in London at that time. To Wendeborn he says that he
owed some personal acquaintance with the seamier side of life in
London, an allegation that Wendeborn himself denied.[6]

Bahrdt made some other noteworthy acquaintances in London,
including Rudolf Erich Raspe, the author of the Münchhausen
tales which were later translated into German by Gottfried August

Bürger, and a certain Hesseltein, as Bahrdt spells the name, who was grand secretary of the Great Masonic Lodge in London. To the latter Bahrdt brought letters of recommendation from Prince Louis of Hessen-Darmstadt, the son of Ludwig IX, and as a result was speedily initiated into the order. He was given three degrees and a certificate in one evening at a cost of only five or six guineas but felt that he had not penetrated to the true arcana. Somewhat later he met a fellow Mason who was able to enlighten him as to the true esoteric purpose and nature of the society, and he professes to have been delighted and edified by the experience and to have profited greatly from it. To anyone who has some acquaintance with Bahrdt's lively and enterprising turn of mind it will come as no surprise that he later attempted to establish a kind of Masonic order of his own.

After two busy months in London, toward the end of January 1778, Bahrdt sailed for Amsterdam with the four pupils he had recruited. In Holland he picked up the other new pupils along the way: he left Amsterdam with two full coaches, and by the time he reached Krefeld he had thirteen pupils filling three coaches. Old friends and acquaintances on whom he called along the route congratulated him in joyous amazement, and his progress through the country resembled a triumphal procession. As he drew nearer home he made arrangements to reach Mainz about midnight, get fresh horses, and proceed immediately to Oppenheim, where he expected to arrive in time for breakfast. From there it would be easy to reach Bechtheim by noon for a midday meal, which Frau Bahrdt, who had come to meet her husband and his pupils, had ordered for them all.

But in Oppenheim, where all my soul was bathed in the peaceful joy which was occasioned by the thought of my wife, my children, my institution, and the happy future—even now I feel a cold shudder when I think of it— I came to the end of my happiness. My pupils were hopping joyfully about their breakfast table and were jubilantly looking forward to wonderful Heidesheim, as I, in deep contentment, was walking back and forth in the room and happened to catch sight of the Frankfurt *ristretto* on a table and read: "On the ——— of this month sentence was passed against Dr. Bahrdt by the Imperial Aulic Council suspending him from all his offices and . . ." At this point my arm fell powerless and I felt as though a bolt of lightning had struck me.

XIX

⟨CONFESSIO FIDEI⟩

THE *Reichshofratsconclusum* which had just struck Bahrdt like a bolt of lightning did not, however, put him out of action. Although he was provisionally suspended from the performance of his ecclesiastical functions, Count Carl not only continued to allow him that part of his salary that was contributed by payments in kind until the publication of a final decree, but made some attempt to have the preliminary decree reversed. And for a while the thirteen new pupils plus the nicely filled money bags which Bahrdt brought home from abroad raised the credit of the school. But then news of his suspension from office reached some of the parents, and difficulties set in again, which Bahrdt attempted to counter by a new financial maneuver.

Bahrdt's plan was to turn his school into a kind of privately owned stock company, of which the shareholders would constitute the board of directors. At first about twenty people signified their interest in such an investment, but eventually the board of directors (*ökonomische Gesellschaft*) consisted of Bahrdt himself, his friend Philipp Christian Schellenberg, the Frankfurt merchant and business associate of Löw Bär Isak, Johann Adam Specht, an innkeeper in Dürkheim, and Johann Heinrich Koch, the town clerk. A formal agreement was drawn up and given government approval on the condition that the board take full responsibility for all Bahrdt's debts. According to the agreement Bahrdt was given five shares in the enterprise and put on a salary of 500 florins. The board as a whole was to manage all matters pertaining to finances, purchasing, and hiring of employees, but Bahrdt continued to exercise sole authority over academic matters. When

193

the agreement had been drawn up to everyone's satisfaction, signed by the interested parties, and countersigned by the Count, the news was given the widest possible publicity in order to revive public confidence in the institution.

Creation of the board, however, did not greatly help matters. True, Bahrdt got some relief from the overwhelming mass of duties which devolved upon him, but this advantage was offset by the fact that he had no authority to make any expenditure whatever without consulting the other three, so that eventually a small fund had to be established for his independent use. The worst conditions, of course, the deficiencies of the teaching staff, were not altered in any way save, perhaps, for the worse. The teachers were unhappy because of the economies that had been decreed and felt that they now had four superiors rather than one. And the unpleasant tales about hygienic conditions in the school continued to circulate among the populace. Indeed, it was at this time (summer of 1778) that the Amsterdam merchant Triest visited the school and was so disillusioned that he withdrew his son and wrote a pamphlet describing the neglect and disorder that he had observed in Heidesheim.

All this time, however, Bahrdt was making his school go through the motions of an active, healthy institution. From the eleventh to the thirteenth of May 1778, in the presence of several hundred visitors, he conducted the first public examinations and later published an account of this event, which he hoped would bring him more pupils. On the twelfth of July, even though he had been suspended from the performance of his ecclesiastical duties, he officiated at a solemn service of communion, which was also described in his pedagogical journal.[1] On the twenty-fifth of August there was held what would be called in modern parlance an honors convocation, and Dr. Bahrdt delivered the main address. Thus Bahrdt continued on the round of frenzied activity already described until the very last, although after March 27, 1779, when the *Finalconclusum* of the Imperial Aulic Council was published, everyone knew that the school was doomed and that Bahrdt had lost everything.

The final decree came at the end of about a year of actions and counteractions which involved even Pope Pius VI, who in a special

message to his Suffragan Bishop von Scheben assured him of his
particular approval, esteem, and affection (April 1778). Bahrdt,
of course, defended his New Testament translation and his right
to make it, but the decision of the Council to have the book
confiscated throughout the domains of the Empire and to submit
the translation to the theological faculties of Würzburg (Catholic)
and Göttingen (Protestant) for their expert opinion remained
in effect.

The question asked of the two faculties was whether, and to
what degree, Dr. Bahrdt's translation deviated from the doctrines
of the three religions established in the Empire. The faculty of
Würzburg, assuming that Bahrdt's New Testament was to be
compared with the principles of the faith as codified in the Symbolic Books, found that Bahrdt's phraseology deviated from traditional and accepted standards whenever there was mention of
certain cardinal points of doctrine, such as proof of the divinity
of Christ, the personal divine character of the Holy Spirit, or
Adam's original sin and its fateful consequences. In other words,
Bahrdt's translation was spreading the heresies of Arianism and
Socinianism. The faculty of Göttingen disagreed, stating that the
chief teachings of Christianity and of the faith accepted by the
three established religions were contained in Bahrdt's translation.[2]
Despite the conflicting opinions the Aulic Council published its
final decree on the twenty-seventh of March 1779, confirming
Bahrdt's suspension from office, and adjured him to recant and
make plain confession of the divinity of Christ as well as of the
Holy Trinity on pain of banishment from the Imperial domains.

The ecclesiastical, political, and cultural implications of this
decree were sweeping, for the Protestant subject and highest
church official of a Protestant prince was to be forced to leave his
country against the will of his sovereign and without being given
a chance to be heard personally at any sort of trial. In the Protestant states this action was looked upon as Imperial and Catholic
intervention in purely internal affairs that might become a very
dangerous precedent.[3] Emphatic protests were made not only by
the Protestant clergy but also by distinguished jurists and professors of law. They denied the authority of a secular body, the
Reichshofrat, to pass judgment on ecclesiastical matters and upon

persons who were directly subject to the bishops, the church, and
the state authorities. They contended that no one save the church
or its authorized representatives had the right to make decisions
concerning doctrine, internal regulations, and discipline.[4] There
were, of course, those who defended the action of the *Reichshofrat*
on the theory that it was the duty of the Emperor as defender of
the faith to guard his subjects against the infection not only of
other religions than the three established faiths but also of heretical deviations within any one of them.[5] But enlightened opinion
generally sided with Lessing, who, without judging the quality
of Dr. Bahrdt's New Testament, pointed out that denying his right
to make and publish his own translation was tantamount to an
attack on the very basis of Protestantism, since Dr. Bahrdt had
no less a right to make his translation than had Dr. Luther to
make his.

And if Bahrdt had his defenders throughout the length and
breadth of German-speaking territories he also had defenders as
well as enemies in his own small land. His congregation petitioned
on his behalf without success. And Count Carl, who had all along
favored Bahrdt but who had not dared to intervene very vigorously for fear of jeopardizing his chances to win some delicate
legal matters then being examined by the Imperial courts, sent
a protest to Vienna against this infringement of his sovereign
powers. Or rather, he gave instructions to his minister to lodge
such a protest. But Rühl seems to have been bent on destroying
Bahrdt and to have disregarded the orders of his prince: the
protest was not forwarded to Joseph II.[6] So much for the one implacable enemy of Dr. Bahrdt. The other was the notorious doctor himself.

Bahrdt's detractors have never wearied of repeating that he was
completely unprincipled and would do anything for the sake of
gain or the gratification of his senses, that he believed in nothing, but professed to believe in whatever promised to bring him
some advantage. The falsity of this view is apparent from what
he now did when called upon to recant, when a little pretense
would have saved him from ruin, for he flung the challenge back
into the teeth of his enemies and published a confession of faith.[7]

When it was clear that Count Carl would eventually be forced to expel him from his lands or imprison him, Bahrdt decided to seek asylum in the domains of the freethinking King of Prussia, Frederick the Great, who was powerful enough to protect him against molestation by the Empire or the Church. At the same time he wrote his confession of faith and sent it to *Consistorialrat* Teller in Berlin asking him to submit it to theologians and jurists for their opinion as to whether it could pass Prussian censorship. Teller let it pass,[8] and Bahrdt was thereby precipitated into the most violent storm of controversy of his career thus far. It was at this time that publishers and scribblers first learned to exploit the fact that any book bearing Bahrdt's name as author or in the title was sure to become a best seller. Since he could be attacked with great sensational effect, many of the publications dating from this time are little more than collections of coarse epithets and abuse.[9] Thus it came about that an act of resolution, courage, and even a certain nobility set the indelible stamp of "notorious and base" upon Dr. Bahrdt's reputation, a stamp which literary, cultural, and church historians have been prone to reimpress upon it despite the more balanced judgments of a few investigators who have found in him a mixture of many contradictory elements.[10] The confession proper was prefaced by an address to Emperor Joseph II which first briefly summarizes the actions already taken by the Council and their effect upon Bahrdt and his family. Bahrdt then goes on to say that if, as his opponents maintain, he has hitherto failed to state his position with complete clarity, he will now set forth his beliefs with utmost candor, convinced that His Imperial Majesty will look with greater clemency upon an honest and resolute man than upon a hypocrite. He will therefore confess that for some time he has been convinced that in the Protestant religious structure there are dogmas founded neither upon scripture nor upon reason. Some of these jeopardize the attainment of happiness in God and others, being contrary to reason, are the source of skepticism and scorn of religion among thousands. Examples of such dogmas are: original sin, imputation of the sin of Adam, salvation through the workings of the Holy Spirit upon the passive human being, justification of the sinner by faith alone without regard to moral improvement, the divinity of Christ and the Holy Spirit in the Athanasian sense, eternal punishment and so on. Then Bahrdt goes on to say that in the exercise of his pastoral functions he has never attacked these points of doctrine, feeling that the pulpit is not the place to expound technical theology. However, he stoutly defends his position that the dogmas he rejects are positively harmful, pointing out, for example, that the dogma of salvation by mere faith does nothing to counteract moral deterioration and a drift into sinfulness.

The *confessio fidei* proper follows these introductory remarks and states Bahrdt's position in clear and temperate language under the heading "What I do and do not believe."

1. I believe that I and all men are sinners who stand in need of God's mercy and compassion. However, that this condition (that we are sinners) is inborn and that all men come into the world with the propensity for all evil, this I doubt. Rather it seems to me that men are to blame for their own corruption. For I see in them so many splendid predispositions to virtue, so many innate noble feelings and inclinations that perhaps the only thing necessary to restore to humanity its original goodness might be a different system of education and a mode of life farther removed from tyranny and luxury.

2. I believe that just as man is indebted to God for everything good, just so does he owe whatever moral goodness he has to the grace of God. However, that God himself effects man's regeneration and that man does nothing but hold still for God is contrary to scripture, and this error depends for the most part upon the term grace [*Gnade*], which most teachers of the church have misinterpreted.

3. I believe that God forgives us our sins as an act of pure grace and that our virtue and zeal for the good, since it is basically an act of God's charity and is so imperfect and faulty, is not worthy of a whole eternity of reward and bliss. I believe, however, that our regeneration and virtue constitute, on the one hand, the condition under which God bestows upon us forgiveness of sin and eternal bliss for the sake of Christ (*i.e.*, because through Jesus Christ He has promised and sealed this gift of grace to all the virtuous) and that, on the other hand, they are the natural source of the highest bliss, which proceeds from them naturally and of itself. However, that God should forgive me my sins merely because of a human sacrifice and because of another's virtue overlook the imperfections in my own virtue, that is contrary to my reason and I have never found anything about it in scripture.

4. I believe that God endowed the apostles with his spirit, but that this spirit is a Third Person in the Godhead I am not convinced. Rather, I find

in scripture no other meaning of πνεῦμα ἅγιον than these two: that it signified either God-granted gifts, talents, and abilities, or else the *nomen Dei*, who imparts these gifts.

5. I believe that God was in and with Christ and that we are consequently bound to venerate the Son as we venerate the Father. However, the way in which God was in Christ, whether according to the conception of Athanasius (which I consider to be the very worst) or the opinion of Arius or Sabellius or of someone else, this is for the purposes of religion, that is, for the improvement and ease of mind of men, very unimportant and should never be decided by ecclesiastical authority, but it should be left to each one to decide how he wants to think of it. Meanwhile this much seems to be completely evident to me from reason and scripture, that Christ and the one God Jehovah whom he calls his father are very different and that at the least Christ is not called God in the same sense in which the one God Jehovah is so called, as he himself has declared plainly and frankly enough in John 10, when he says to those who accuse him of blasphemy: "If scripture calls all those people gods, πρὸς οὕς ὁ λόγος θεοῦ ἐγένετο, that is, who have received divine enlightenment for the instruction of men, how could I reproach myself for this name (ὅν ὁ πατὴρ ἡγίασεν) since the Father has distinguished me so particularly?" [11]

6. That for Christians belief in Jesus Christ is the indispensable condition of salvation is undeniable. However, that this obligation extends to non-Christians also I consider unreasonable, inhuman, and contrary to scripture. And that this belief consists in laying hold of and appropriating the merit of Christ I consider just as false. At least there is in the New Testament so little about this conception of belief that it is a puzzle to me how teachers of the church were ever able to hit upon it. Belief in Christ is acceptance of and obedience to Christ's teachings and firm faith in the promise which he sealed with his death in future blessedness of the virtuous.

7. That God will make all the virtuous blessed in another life I believe. But that He is equally disposed to torture the wicked for all eternity and turn them over to the devil I do not believe. For He says himself: "I am a jealous God, visiting the iniquity of the fathers upon the children, upon the third and upon the fourth generation of them that hate me, and showing loving kindness unto a thousand generations of them that love me and keep my commandments." From this I conclude in opposition to those who would make God out to be just as vengeful as merciful: as four is to one thousand so is God's disposition to punish in relation to his disposition to show kindness.

8. That there are angels and devils may be true. However, that they are what the teachings of the church say they are, that they take physical possession of human beings, that they show themselves in the shape of ghosts, that they affect the souls of human beings and are able to produce evil thoughts and intentions, I have never found a sufficient reason to believe.

9. That the sacred scriptures of the New Testament contain certain divine teachings for man's attainment of bliss to which we owe complete trust and obedience, I am certain. But that God has inspired all the words contained in these scriptures, of this I have never yet read a satisfactory proof.

10. It is certain that all Christians are bound to believe and obey the religious teachings which are to be found in scripture without forced interpretation, but that it is within the just province of the church (by which I really understand nothing else than the mass [*plurima vota*] of the clergy, who, as has already been said above, at no time have had the most valid claim to profound insight, erudition, and impartial judgment) to impose upon me doctrines and concepts which have been cunningly derived from statements of Scripture, I do not believe. At the least this would be completely contrary to the basic principles of Protestantism, which claims equal rights and dominion with Catholicism within the German Empire. For according to these principles I am, so far as my faith is concerned, bound by no man's authority, but I have the right to test all things and to hold fast only to that of which I feel convinced by the word of God. And in the case of Protestant teachers this right extends even further than in the case of Protestant laymen. For as a teacher I am a part of the church in its representative function and I have therefore the obligation not only to examine the teachings of my church but to present to my co-religionists the results of my examination if they are of any consequence, as I have already done in some of my writings and shall continue to do, and as I am now for the first time honored to do in this my public confession before the highest of all tribunals.

As Bahrdt pointed out in his conclusion, there was nothing startlingly new and original in this creed. Indeed, it rather fairly represented the convictions of a very considerable fraction of the people, both clergy and laity, upon whom the reasonableness of the main propositions had exerted a compelling influence. But what did cause a tremendous stir was the boldness, the outspokenness of Bahrdt's declaration. For stating openly, candidly, and with impressive earnestness what "everybody" had really long felt to be true, Dr. Bahrdt became in a certain sense a martyr for the Enlightenment.

XX

{A NARROW SQUEAK}

WHEN BAHRDT decided that he would have to flee to Prussian lands he wrote to the illustrious Johann Salomo Semler in Halle, who had once so warmly recommended him for the position in Giessen and requested Semler's assistance in gaining a foothold in Halle. Semler, however, became alarmed by the thought that his name would be linked with that of the notorious doctor and urged him to go to Duisburg or anywhere, only not to Halle. He informed Bahrdt that if he did come to Halle and try to establish himself at the University even in an unofficial capacity, he would feel compelled to oppose him in every way he could. Nonetheless, Bahrdt remained resolved to go to Halle and began to make preparations for his trip.

Preparing for the trip, however, was no easy matter, for he had no money and no prospect of obtaining any, but was deeply in debt to a number of people who kept close watch upon him and his movements, lest he try to get away and leave them in the lurch. Bahrdt's situation was therefore well-nigh hopeless: his school was collapsing and putting him deeper into debt, with the result that his creditors pressed him even harder for their money. He was, by a decree of March 27, 1779, finally and completely dismissed from all offices and deprived of all salary in whatever form. He was therefore unable to leave the country, and yet he was commanded to do so or face imprisonment unless he recanted. Little wonder that he yearned for the life of a recluse on an island in the Rhine.

At this point Rühl seemed to have had a change of heart, for he came to see Bahrdt privately and offered to pay him the sum of four hundred *Gulden* which the Count had granted him from his private purse in lieu of the payment in kind to which Bahrdt made claim as a church official. Bahrdt was to receive the money at Dienheim, a very small town not far from Oppenheim, as he passed through on his way out of the country. The sum was thus intended to help him make his way to Halle. The entire affair was to be kept secret, especially from Bahrdt's creditors. Since Rühl had a statement from the Count's own hand that the money had actually been granted, Bahrdt, amazed and puzzled though he was by the magnanimity of his great enemy, had no other recourse than to accept the offer of apparent kindness. As for the Philanthropinum, so Rühl informed him, it would be taken over and managed by Rühl himself, who had begun his career as a schoolman.[1]

Now that Bahrdt seemed to have the means of getting to Halle, there remained the problem of eluding his creditors and getting out of the country. Announcement was therefore made of another three-day series of public examinations to be held in the middle of May. On the fifteenth, while the usual ceremonies and demonstrations were in full swing, Frau Bahrdt and the children left in an open carriage in the direction of Dürkheim, but once away from town she took the road to Monsheim, where she was awaited by the family of a friend of Bahrdt's, one La Roche, who was himself in Heidesheim attending the examinations. When Koch, one of the board of directors, saw Frau Bahrdt setting off for Dürkheim and came to inquire of her husband why she was to be absent from the school on a day when there were so many visitors, Bahrdt replied that she had urgent domestic duties in Dürkheim, and he continued to play his role as host and examiner with his usual aplomb and affability, proposing a game of cards as relaxation after the formalities were over. As it grew towards evening the guests began to leave, and La Roche also said that he would have to go since he was expecting guests at his home in Monsheim.

How would it be [he said to Bahrdt] if you came with me? You have nothing more to do today and Herr von ———— who is coming over from Worms has long wanted to make your acquaintance. I should think you might ride with me. I'll see that you get back in my carriage.

Bahrdt pretended to reflect for a while and then seemed to accept the invitation on the spur of the moment. Still dressed in light indoor garb, he called for his hat and walking stick, gave the servants a few instructions, and told the doorman to wait for him at the gate with a light, since he expected to be back by eleven o'clock at the latest. With that he mounted his friend's carriage and they set off for Monsheim on the first leg of Bahrdt's flight for freedom and a new life.

In Monsheim he was reunited with his wife and children, save for an infant girl named Dorchen, who was so ill that she had to be left behind. The Court Chaplain Wolf in Grünstadt, whose wife was the child's godmother, had promised to take care of the little girl in his own household. For some reason, however, perhaps because the child took a sudden grave turn for the worse, Wolf did not take her home, and she died in the Philanthropinum on the eighteenth of May, three days after her parents had fled.

Ignorant of the baby's condition, the parents took a last meal with their host and shortly after midnight continued their journey. At four in the morning they were in Dienheim, where one of the Count's secretaries was awaiting them at the inn and posthouse, which was also a customs station. Bahrdt received the money, signed a receipt, and the secretary set off for Dürkheim. Bahrdt urged the innkeeper and customs inspector to hurry and give him fresh horses to replace La Roche's team which had brought him thus far. Hesitating and embarrassed, the inspector gradually broke the news to Bahrdt that he had been placed under arrest at the instance of his creditors. Rühl had induced him to flee by the promise of money merely in order to betray him and ruin him forever.[2]

In this desperate situation Bahrdt recalled that in Oppenheim there was a preacher who had studied under him in Giessen and was his warm friend and admirer. He therefore asked the innkeeper, whom he knew well, to get word to this preacher. The innkeeper gladly complied with the request, and soon the preacher arrived with another clergyman. The three sat down to devise some means of setting Bahrdt and his family at liberty. The upshot of their deliberations was that Bahrdt would have to use one-fourth of the money he had just received to bribe the local authorities. This stratagem worked, and after much excitement the carriage was again in headlong flight along the Oppenheim road and headed for the ferry which Bahrdt's former student had paid to wait for them. Only when they were all aboard the ferry did Frau Bahrdt and the children cease to moan and cry and Bahrdt himself to tremble in a cold sweat. But once the Rhine flowed between them and their pursuers, Bahrdt regained his customary composure, he says, and devoted himself coolly to the task of slipping through the Catholic territories that lay between them and the domains of the King of Prussia, whose subject he now became. Finally, on the twenty-eighth of May 1779, they arrived in Halle with the barest minimum of possessions [3] and dependent upon the charitable contributions of Bahrdt's friends and acquaintances in Germany and Courland to keep alive and make a fresh start.

XXI

⟮HELPING HANDS⟯

O NCE AGAIN a whole town was agog over the imminent arrival of the notorious Doctor Bahrdt. In Giessen, it will be recalled, he had won over the populace by delivering an affecting sermon, but in Halle there would be no opportunity of this sort. All pulpits were closed to him and, if the theological faculty and Doctor Semler, who prodded the University Senate into petitioning the ministry to this effect, had had their way, all academic lecture platforms would have been closed to him also. But under Frederick the Great the affairs of the ecclesiastical department, which had the responsibility for educational and academic matters also, were administered by Karl Abraham *Freiherr* von Zedlitz (1731–1793), a man who fully shared his illustrious master's well-known indifference to denominational and sectarian interests. The protests of Bahrdt's enemies were therefore rejected, and Bahrdt in due course received from Zedlitz a letter[1] bidding him a cordial welcome to Halle and expressing the minister's gratification that Bahrdt had found asylum in Prussian lands. He went on to say that he held a high opinion of Bahrdt's learning and abilities, but at the same time he would warn him against giving way to quarrelsomeness.

You have spoken and suffered [he wrote] for what you considered the truth. Now take a respite and deem it beneath your dignity ever to initiate a controversy to which you are not summoned by truth, duty, and conscience.

Thus the voice which spoke for the highest authority in Berlin, the citadel of the *Aufklärung*. And the lesser champions within that citadel also did as much to give aid and comfort to their troublesome ally, whom they could not in conscience allow to perish for confessing to a belief they knew to be their own. *Consistorialrat* Teller, who had allowed Bahrdt's confession of faith

205

to pass censorship, wrote in the same vein as Zedlitz and sent him a letter of introduction to his friend Johann August Eberhard. Nicolai, whom, it will be recalled, Bahrdt had injured by reprinting articles from the *Allgemeine deutsche Bibliothek,* wrote to him on the eighth of June 1779,[2] that he considered it the duty of everyone who loved truth and liberty to come to the aid of a man so unjustly persecuted and that the injury done him by Bahrdt had no bearing upon his conviction. He went on to advise Bahrdt to remain in Halle, where the opportunities to earn money by lecturing were bound to increase and urged him in all future writing to employ the moderate tone of his *Glaubensbekenntnis,* which he, Nicolai, completely approved. But the Berliners did not limit their help to advice and friendly exhortations. They also collected money which was forwarded to him by Biester, editor of the *Berlinische Monatsschrift.*

But Berlin was not the only source of material aid and spiritual comfort, for money came to Bahrdt from Mitau, the capital of far-off Courland, through his connection with one of the mysterious figures of the age, Johann August Starck (1741–1816).

Born in Mecklenburg, the son of a pastor, Starck became a student of theology and Oriental languages in Göttingen, and then in 1763 he went to St. Petersburg as a teacher. In 1765 he went to England and then on to Paris, where in 1766 he received the degree of *Magister,* not from the University of Paris, however, but from the University of Göttingen. In the same year he returned to Mecklenburg to become for a time *Konrektor* of the Gymnasium in Wismar. In 1768, however, he was back in Russia on some mysterious errand, but in 1769 he had become *Professor extraordinarius* of Oriental languages in Königsberg. Here he remained and prospered until his growing reputation as a neologist[3] and a Freemason brought him into a conflict with his colleagues and university authorities so sharp that Professor Bock denied him the right to study certain rare manuscripts in the library. In 1777, therefore, he resigned from his various posts and dignities in Königsberg and went to Courland, where he became a professor of philosophy in the academic Gymnasium of Mitau. In 1781 he succeeded to a post to which Bahrdt had once aspired, that of court chaplain in Darmstadt. This was his final position and both Ludwig IX and his successor must have been pleased with him, for his influence grew and he increased in honor, being awarded the grand cross of the *Ludwigsorden* in 1807 and being ennobled with the title of *Freiherr* in 1811. And this in spite of truly startling accusations made against him by Nicolai and by Gedike and Biester in their journal, *Berlinische Monatsschrift.*

At first the accusations were merely whispers and rumors, but from 1786 on it was publicly charged that this Protestant theologian and court chaplain, this apologist of Masonry, this champion of neologism, was in reality a Catholic priest. Starck, of course, denied the allegations, but he was never able to shake off the suspicion. And after his death the truth of the accusations was confirmed, when in his apartment there was found a room which had been set up for celebration of the Mass. Starck had apparently been converted to Catholicism in the Church of St. Sulpice in Paris in 1766 and from then on pursued the secret purposes of a double life.[4]

One can only speculate how Bahrdt may have fitted into the designs of this prominent crypto-Catholic. Perhaps among some servants of the Catholic church there was still a hope that the notorious Dr. Bahrdt might eventually go over to Catholicism, for it will be remembered that Bahrdt had hinted at his readiness to entertain the idea of conversion when he sought permission to dedicate his New Testament to the Prince Bishop of Würzburg. And it will also be remembered that Bahrdt professes in his autobiography that in Mainz, when he was on his way to England, a certain *Kanonikus* Rediger tried to persuade him of the advantages to be obtained by joining the Catholic church. It may therefore be possible that Starck's mission or aim was to influence Bahrdt in this sense. Or if his aim was not to make an active convert of Bahrdt it may have been that he saw in Bahrdt an unwitting agent in the spread of denominational indifferentism, which, by sapping the fiber of the Protestants, would make them the less significant element in an amalgamation or union of the Catholic and Protestant branches of European Christendom. It was precisely this kind of indifferentism that Starck was accused of preaching in his book *Theoduls Gastmahl*.[5] And it must be acknowledged that the end of Bahrdt's brand of *Aufklärung* was to loosen the hold of the Protestant churches upon their communicants. Thus, even though Bahrdt might consider the Catholic faith to be the most absurd of positive religions, he could in one sense be said to have aided this faith by undermining the Protestant heresies.

Among all the uncertainties as to Starck's aims and motives one thing, however, is certain and that is that it was he who approached Bahrdt with friendly advice and words of comfort. For on the fourth of August 1779, he addressed to Bahrdt a letter[6] which began,

Your Reverence will pardon me for taking the liberty of thus paying my respects, even though I do not have the good fortune to be personally known to you.

Starck then went on to say that he had learned of the unhappy situation in which Bahrdt now found himself and had the most profound sympathy with him, even though he could not agree with all the principles expressed in Bahrdt's confession of faith. Nonetheless he deplored the fact that the spiritual descendants of Luther and Melanchthon were now beginning to indulge in those practices of intolerance and persecution for which the Roman church was censured. Bahrdt was, he continued, to be congratulated upon having found asylum in a place where he was allowed freedom of thought, research, and publication. In this connection Starck mentioned a rumor that had come to his ears to the effect that Bahrdt was about to receive an appointment to the University of Königsberg. Whether the rumor was well founded or not, Starck wrote, he felt compelled to put Bahrdt in possession of certain valuable information, that salaries in Königsberg were very low and that the possibilities of taking in any sizable sum from lecture fees were not great. He also warned Bahrdt that he might expect to be persecuted as a heretic by some of his possible future colleagues, specifically Professor Bock, as he himself had been. And in conclusion, he suggested that Bahrdt might learn more about his, Starck's, own troubles in Königsberg from Professor Eberhard in Halle and from Dr. Büsching, Starck's old and intimate friend.

This very warm and friendly letter was the prelude to a rather extensive correspondence, for Starck enlisted on Bahrdt's behalf the sympathies of a considerable number of personalities in Courland, such as *Superintendent* Hube, the latter's son-in-law Dr. Besecke, professor of law at the academy, and the Duke of Courland himself. These people collected the sum of about 450 *Taler,* of which the Duke personally contributed ninety. This money was sent to Bahrdt to use either to help defray his living expenses in Halle or to pay the cost of transportation to Mitau and to help him establish himself there. For Starck soon urged Bahrdt to petition the Duke to call him to Mitau in some official and learned capacity, and he wrote in great detail about living conditions in the Duchy of Courland. Although left in no doubt about the extremely provincial character of Mitau and the intellectual isolation in which he might expect to find himself, Bahrdt was interested enough to address a petition to the Duke. Starck intercepted this letter and explained to Bahrdt that it had not been framed just right to get the favorable attention of the Duke. Consequently, after some exchanges, Starck, having given the petition the proper form and content, let it reach the addressee and endeavored at the same time to influence the Duke in Bahrdt's favor by other means. The Duke, although favorably impressed, saw no specific way in which Bahrdt could then be employed, and the whole plan came to nothing.

It would be interesting to know why Starck exerted himself so vigorously on behalf of a man whom he had never met. Perhaps his own experiences in Königsberg had made him very sensitive to such intolerance and persecution as he now felt Bahrdt endured. In response to some question or remark by Bahrdt, Starck wrote that it was true that they were associated through membership in the Masonic Order, and he went on to discuss how he might try to tap the resources of various lodges, for example, in Stettin and Königsberg, if Bahrdt should need more money. At the same time he impressed upon Bahrdt the importance of not letting anyone know of their connection, for, he said, he could be of greater use to Bahrdt as a secret than as a declared ally.[7]

One of the men whom Starck mentioned as knowing about his

unpleasant experiences in Königsberg had also been the target of orthodox intolerance. This was Johann August Eberhard (1739–1808), who was also in close connection with Nicolai and the "enlightened" men in Berlin who actively supported Bahrdt. He had incurred the displeasure of church circles when he was still a very young man because of his almost daily association with Moses Mendelssohn. But it was his book *Neue Apologie des Sokrates oder Untersuchung der Lehre von der Seligkeit der Heiden* (1772) which provoked the orthodox party to take action against him when he was a candidate for a pastorate in Charlottenburg. Although he received the appointment through the personal intercession of Frederick the Great, who observed that the election of the Pope of Rome could not have caused a greater stir than the filling of this vacancy, his enemies made him so uncomfortable in his post that he was relieved to receive a call to the University of Halle as a professor of philosophy. Here he was able to devote himself to his researches in theology, metaphysics, synonymy, and aesthetics.

Eberhard became for Bahrdt a kind of mentor and friend, who forwarded to him the money that Nicolai, Gedike, Biester, and other *Aufklärer* collected for him. Bahrdt speaks very appreciatively of him but complains that Eberhard never permitted himself to get on a footing of real intimacy with him. Nonetheless Eberhard was one of the three men from whom Bahrdt received the impetus to shed every remaining vestige of allegiance to the doctrines of Christianity or belief in its supernatural origin.

The other two men who, so to speak, pushed Bahrdt into the final phase of his development were Johann Salomo Semler and Ernst Christian Trapp, one of the freethinking theologians at Halle. Bahrdt's relations with Semler will have to be discussed at some length later on. As for Trapp, who became an associate of Bahrdt, he merely spoke the right word at the right time. In the course of a conversation, when Bahrdt protested that something said was contrary to the word of God, Trapp burst out laughing and exclaimed, "Bahrdt, with all his reason, still believes in revelation!" This laughter proved to be the death knell of any such belief. Trapp, however, was a much less significant figure than

Eberhard, whose influence upon Bahrdt was in some respects parallel to the influence which Johann Wilhelm Baumer had exerted upon him in Giessen. Both Baumer and Eberhard were men of solid attainments who impressed Bahrdt by the persuasiveness of their learning.

The already mentioned *Neue Apologie des Sokrates* is the book by which Eberhard's reputation was established, and the ideas developed in it naturally formed the subject of his conversations with Bahrdt, who was not only convinced by them but embodied them with embellishments in some of his own books such as *Briefe über die Bibel im Volkston* and *Ausführung des Plans und Zwecks Jesu*. For this reason and because the book created a great stir in its own day, dealing as it did with a burning issue between the orthodox and enlightened points of view, it will be of interest to consider it a bit more closely.

In 1767 there appeared a novel entitled *Bélisaire*, written by Jean François Marmontel, member of the French Academy, contributor to the *Encyclopédie*, critic, dramatist, and story writer. The hero of the book is Belisarius, one of the generals of the Byzantine Emperor Justinian I. Falsely denounced to his master as a traitor, blinded and imprisoned, the aged Belisarius forgives his enemies and endures his fate with stoic fortitude, while discoursing of his ethical, political and religious convictions. He cannot believe otherwise, he says, than that when he has attained the Christian heaven he will there see and converse with virtuous pagans such as Marcus Aurelius and Cato, for it is no part of true religion to attribute to the merciful God the cruel desire to inflict eternal damnation upon anyone.

The shocking softness of this view aroused a storm of indignation among the defenders of the faith, who showered Marmontel with pamphlets proving the contrary. And the Sorbonne fulminated against the thirty-seven *impiétés de Bélisaire*. In the nearby Netherlands also holy wrath flared up, and Pastor Peter Hofstede of Rotterdam undertook to survey the sins and vices of all the famous men of pagan Greece and Rome to prove that none of them could see salvation. He directed much of his fury against that presumed pederast, Socrates, whose honor was in turn defended by the Remonstrant preacher C. Nozeman. Hofstede returned to the attack, and Nozeman replied; others joined the fray on both sides as the controversy spread to Switzerland and to Germany, where Eberhard wrote his carefully reasoned book on the subject.

Eberhard attacks the problem by asking two questions: Is a pagan necessarily damned because of his religion? and is a pagan incapable of moral goodness?

In answer to the first question he points out that it is necessary to distinguish among pagans: the concept of God held by some groups and individuals is more or less adequate than that held by others. The primeval religious experience, Eberhard feels, must have been the worship of a single divine being and upon this followed veneration of various minor and tributary forces, although even among some polytheists the consciousness of a supreme and single godhead was not lost. The true error of paganism is in idolatry, for idolatry, even though it shrouds the truly religious sense that the world is dependent upon something beyond itself, mistakenly elevates finite things to the status of divinities. Paganism, even in its crudest form, is therefore seen to be a form of error, and an error is not punishable in and for itself. A pagan is therefore not necessarily damned because of his religion.

In answer to the second question Eberhard points to the good and noble men of whom we have a record from Greek and Roman history. Their virtues are known to all lovers of classical literature and civilization, and St. Augustine is not merely wrong but deliberately misanthropic in his insistence that these pagan virtues are invalid because their wellspring was impure. Love of the gods was indeed the source of the nobility of such a man as Cato, for example, and even if in the case of other noble pagans the impetus to virtue sprang from the desire for fame, this certainly does not indicate a state of damnable sinfulness. Moderation, justice, magnanimity, self-respect are positive qualities, no matter in whom they are manifest.

But even those pagans (as well as Christians), Eberhard maintains, whose wickedness deserves divine chastisement are certainly not condemned to eternal torment. Eberhard is led to this conclusion by the consideration that the notion of never-ending suffering inflicted upon sentient beings is so contrary to every reasonable concept of divine governance of the world as to be completely inacceptable,[8] for divine punishment may not be equated with vengeance. It is God's purpose to cleanse men of their sins and to eradicate their will to do evil. God punishes us out of love and not to secure satisfaction for offended honor.

All of this was, of course, immediately acceptable to Bahrdt, and some of it was already familiar to him, but two ideas were perhaps of especial significance. One was a favorite idea of his that man's redemption through Christ and his punishment for sin were evidence of God's love. The second was new to him and made a great impression: that Jesus' ethical teachings may have been learned directly or indirectly from Plato's writings. Bahrdt asserts that Eberhard demonstrated this to him in the course of their conversations, an assertion which has been disputed (e.g., in Neueste Religionsbegebenheiten of 1791, page 364) on the ground that it was a misrepresentation of Eberhard's belief. It may therefore be pointed out here that Bahrdt was probably telling the truth in this matter, for on page 33 of the Neue Apologie [9] is a passage which points out that some of the earliest fathers such as Justin Martyr, Clement of Alexandria, and Origen were such enthusiastic students of Plato that they dared, according to St. Augustine, to maintain that Jesus had learned from the writings of Plato all the ideas that compelled their admiration.[10]

The tendency of this line of thinking is plainly to make Socrates out to be a kind of enlightened man's Jesus and Plato his St. Paul, if not actually to make of Jesus a poor man's Socrates, and the question concerning the salvation of pagans hinges upon the matter of implicit faith. Implicit faith, says Eberhard, is a concept which was designed to solve the difficulty of admitting such pagans as Socrates to salvation. St. Jerome, for instance, imputed to noble heathens a fides implicita, by which is meant the readiness and worthiness to accept Christian doctrine had such doctrine ever come to their attention. This, Eberhard contends, boils down to honesty and conscientiousness, and if these qualities constitute a key to heaven, then certainly Socrates as well as many other non-Christians will be there.

All this was, of course, grist for Bahrdt's mill, and he proceeded to grind away, turning out volume after volume and lecturing to such large numbers of students that the theologians of the University were greatly alarmed, and Semler's worst fears were fully realized. That Semler himself had furnished Bahrdt with much of the grist he undoubtedly knew in the depths of his conscience, and the thought was very disquieting, especially since Bahrdt was not reluctant to acknowledge his indebtedness. Thus Semler, who had already felt compelled to take a conservative stand against the famous *Wolfenbüttler Fragmente* which Lessing had published, was now stirred into such bitter opposition to Bahrdt that he seemed to have become untrue to himself. He, no less than Bahrdt, was driven to an extreme position in the heat of controversy and by the pressure of outside forces, one of which was the mere presence in Halle of the notorious Dr. Bahrdt, the popularizer of Semlerian ideas.

XXII

⟨DISSENSION AMONG ALLIES⟩

SEMLER, WHOSE immense erudition gave invincible force to the arguments and considerations which led eventually to the downfall of naïve orthodox theology, had never been noted for logic of thought or clarity of expression. Indeed, it had become customary for anyone reviewing his books or writing about him to make some allusion to the prolixity and obscurity of his style. But it was only through his controversies with Lessing and Bahrdt that the basic ambiguity of his position became obvious to everyone.

The ambiguity seems to have had its roots in Semler's own rather timid, overly conscientious, submissive nature, which was coupled with a fervent personal devoutness, a need to know God in his own way. These traits had been confirmed in him by his boyhood experience with Pietism, for his father had become a chaplain to Duke Christian Ernst of Saalfeld, who had fallen under the spell of Count Zinzendorf. Semler's father gradually found it expedient and politic to lean more and more in the direction of Pietism, and his brother adored the sweet wounds of Jesus with a fervor that bordered on the hysterical. All this combined to draw Semler himself rather closer to Pietism, and he responded to the deeply personal aspect of religious experience as it was felt and understood by the truly devout. At the same time, however, he saw that professions of piety allowed hypocrites to gain preferment and that knowledge and learning could safely be derided by the stupid and lazy who claimed to have the faith. For this reason he never became really affiliated with the movement, however sympathetic to some aspects of it he might have been.

The Pietists, on the other hand, with their literal and spiritual,

215

their grammatical, logical, and mystical modes of interpreting the Bible and their dread of reason and objective standards, found no more to admire and accept in Semler's work than did the orthodox, who bent their understanding of the Bible texts to conformity with dogma. For Semler, who read everything he could lay his hands on and remembered it all, had come to recognize the stamp of particular times and places upon all the Bible texts, including his own specialty, the New Testament. It therefore became his passion to read and understand every document of consequence for the history of the church as informed contemporary opponents as well as partisans of each document must have read and understood it.

His method presupposed, of course, the principles and achievements of that other acknowledged founder of modern biblical science, Ernesti, whose work extended to sacred texts the philological methods established for classical secular texts. But if Ernesti saw the language of the Bible as subject to the natural conditions of speaking, writing, and copying, Semler saw the content, the message, as subject to the natural conditions of living in the particular place at the particular time when the document was composed.[1] This insight became the negative pole of Semler's theological world, whereas his personal Christian devoutness remained the positive pole. In the one hemisphere of his world where objectivity ruled, the biblical canon, church history, and dogma were subjected to the acid test of historical and psychological method; in the other, the Bible was venerated as the only true source of religious knowledge. To be sure, it had been written for particular readers in particular circumstances and was not literally inspired, but nonetheless it was the ultimate revelation, and its truths, though diversely garbed, were transcendent. Semler himself, far from feeling that his schizoid system of hermeneutics involved him in insoluble contradictions, applied the principle of reference to the exoteric and the esoteric, the public and the private, planes of meaning to everything from theopneusty to alchemy, in which he was also deeply interested.[2]

Semler did, to be sure, see that the idea of revelation would have to be adjusted if his basic hermeneutical principle was valid.

It was unthinkable, he felt, that God had communicated with the writers of the various Bible texts in any but their own language in terms intelligible to the reason of each one. Revelation, therefore, cannot be contrary to reason and can have neither the purpose nor the effect of undermining or cancelling the forms or the results of natural cognition. To the universal rational faculty of cognition, therefore, there corresponds in Semler's system natural revelation, by which knowledge of God is made universally possible, even though specific revelation or revelation of particulars had to be accommodated to the mental and cultural state of the inspired men who received it. Apparently no impression was made upon Semler by the consideration that if revelation in the New Testament, for example, had been thus accommodated to the particular needs of those people who first heard the message, it would follow that it would have ever diminishing applicability as time and space intervened to an ever greater degree between living men and the biblical ages. Or at the very least, it would seem that mankind would have need of an ever renewed revelation.

To do Semler justice, it must be pointed out that he did attain to the idea of a progressive revelation in history (in his *Abhandlung von der freien Untersuchung des Kanons* II (1772), according to which the whole Bible is the record of and witness to an ever widening and deepening human experience of God. This, of course, is an idea which is basic to Lessing's *Die Erziehung des Menschengeschlechts,* and indeed Semler even makes use of the comparison of the Bible to school texts, which is such a striking feature of Lessing's exposition of the education of the human race. For Semler points out that sophisticated readers of the Bible will inevitably feel that certain portions of it contain very childish notions of God and morality, and that they are in fact an A-B-C book, which is not suitable for teaching children who have already learned to read ["στοιχεῖα nenne es auch Paulus"]. But Semler was unable or unwilling to pursue this line of thinking to a consistent conclusion, and Lessing and Bahrdt offended him, the one by his rejection of Christ as the unique and universal savior, a logical consequence of Semler's position, and the other by his accommodation (in a Semlerian sense) of the New Testament to what he conceived to be the needs of his contemporaries. Thus, for Semler, the devout believer, the New Testament was not only the earliest but also the immutable source of Christian belief. How serious the split between the temporal and eternal was in his view of the Gospels may better be appreciated if we consider a little further some of the specific conclusions to which Semler, the erudite and objective scholar, came in the course of his investigations.

It is interesting to recall that one of the earliest indications that Semler's work was to prove truly epoch-making came in a book that dealt not with sacred texts but with a matter of contemporary interest. This was the case of a young woman of twenty-one, named Anna Elisabeth Lohmann, who fell into trance states during which angelic and demonic voices spoke through her. Her spiritual counsellor, *Propst* Gottlieb Müller, had some success in calming her but failed in his attempts to exorcise the spirits by a ritual of his own devising. He remained convinced, however, that he was attempting to deal with a genuine case of demonic possession and so described it in his *Gründliche Nachricht von einer begeisterten Weibsperson.* In the following year, 1760, Semler published a refutation of Müller's theory in a work entitled *Abfertigung der neuen Geister und alten Irrtümer in der Lohmannischen Begeisterung zu Kemberg nebst theologischem Unterricht von dem Ungrunde der gemeinen Meinung von leiblichen Besitzungen des Teufels und Bezauberung der Christen.* With a show of great erudition Semler demonstrated that only a reasonable explanation of the case, which of course precluded demonic possession, was acceptable. But this was only a skirmish preliminary to the real attack on all belief in demonic possession whatever, specifically in biblical times. This attack came in a Latin *Dissertatio de daemoniacis, quorum in Evangeliis fit mentio* (Halle, 1760), the argument of which was mainly philological but the effect and purpose of which was to demonstrate the validity of natural and rational interpretation of the apparently supernatural events reported in the New Testament. Characteristically, however, Semler provided himself with certain escape clauses, namely his disavowal of intention to dispute the existence of the devil, which was for him a fact of biblical revelation, and his admission of the possibility that in New Testament times miracles and cases of physical possession might have occurred by special divine dispensation.

But if Jesus and, to a lesser degree, the Apostles understood the true natural causes of things, the question arises as to why these irrational ideas about the supernatural are to be found in the Gospels. Semler's answer to the question follows his usual dual mode of interpretation: the true, privately known explanation by natural causes was "accommodated" to the knowledge, needs, circumstances, and language of the people at the particular time and place. Thus, when speaking before conservative Jews, Jesus employed a narrow, timid mode of teaching, but before a group with a broader Hellenistic background he showed himself to be superior to Jewish prejudices. The two lines of thought, timid Jewish and liberal Hellenistic, however, continued to be manifest in early Christendom for some time, the former being represented by St. Peter and the latter by St. Paul. Only toward the end of the second century of the Christian era did a Catholic church arise from the union of the two parties. To contemporary scholarship, therefore, Semler assigned the task of establishing a geography as well as a history of Christian theology, ethics, and language, and he himself made noteworthy contributions to that end.

To accomplish the task of charting such a geography, of course, there was required for competent scholars the most perfect freedom of investigation and thought, and Semler simply assumed that he, as a Lutheran professor of theology, had such freedom and exercised it to the full. Later he denied Bahrdt the same right on the formal grounds that Bahrdt had ceased to be a professor. His position on the canonical books of the Bible, which he developed in his *Abhandlung von der freien Untersuchung des Kanons* (4 vols., 1771–1774), illustrates how completely he had freed himself from the fetters of orthodoxy.

The biblical canon, so he maintained, can in no sense be said to owe its existence to special divine decree, nor can it lay claim to holiness in any unique sense, for canon means merely a list, and canonical books are those which appear in the canon, that is, on the list. This list is not the work of a single person composing it by divine inspiration and is no more divine than a corresponding list of books which have been excluded from the canon. Furthermore, there were great differences among the church fathers as to exactly which books were and which were not canonical, some books which were otherwise excluded being tolerated in certain localities because they had come to have special meaning for the congregation. The canon therefore came into being over a long period of time and was compiled by human agents using natural powers of reason for the sake of establishing doctrinal norms. This is, of course, radical rejection of any belief in the immediate verbal inspiration of the Bible.

On this last point Semler is explicit. The traditional view that all the books of the Bible were inspired either literally or in substance is without foundation. As far as substance or content is concerned, the Pharisees and the pagans knew the same historical facts and chronicled them in their own normal language. And even if there at one time had been an act of verbal inspiration, it can no longer be said to be effective, for such great changes have crept into the text in the course of copying. The various writers of the Bible texts, to be sure, experienced a personal inspiration which awakened in them the insight into moral law and divine purpose and thus provided Christian believers with a trustworthy guide to moral perfection and salvation. The Christian need only obey the precepts and have faith in the insights in order to test their truth and become persuaded of it. But God has made known various salutary moral truths among the heathens also, and even by means of heathen philosophers, poets, and lawgivers, he has revealed truths which must be called divinely inspired. But if inspiration in the proper sense is not limited to the canonical books of the Bible, some new criterion of inspiration is needed, since inspiration has been shown not to be an externally limited historical event.

Semler tries to formulate such a criterion by saying that only those Scriptures or portions of the Scriptures are divine that are demonstrated to have a divine effect upon the moral, inner spiritual life of men. This means that only that biblical book or portion of it is divine which confirms, extends, or improves natural moral and spiritual insight. Where this effect cannot be ascribed to a

Bible text, divine inspiration is lacking, and the text is demonstrably limited in its significance to the purely temporal and local conditions under which it was written, has no universal meaning, and does not apply to modern times. The Old Testament is particularly full of such merely local matter, for the Jews cultivated their sense of isolation, and their thinking became particular and exclusive to an extreme degree. But the New Testament also contains such limited material as, for example, what Paul writes about women's garb, or improved arrangements for public meetings, or what will happen to those who are living on the last day. There are also a good many specifically Jewish ideas in the New Testament, like the notion that the dead will be awakened by the sound of a trumpet. As a logical outgrowth of this view Semler recommends that a condensation of the Old Testament be prepared which would leave out the irrelevant and the particular. In the story of the fall of man, for example, the important part is that sin and evil must not be attributed to God. And, of course, many of the prophecies are unintelligible and inapplicable, and it is doubtful whether any moral lesson can be drawn from the Song of Solomon.

It will not escape the reader how vague Semler's idea of personal inspiration is and how subjective is his criterion of what is and what is not divine in the Bible. It is, moreover, no far move from Semler's idea of an abridged Old Testament to Bahrdt's modernization of the New, a fact of which Semler was probably peripherally and uneasily aware. It is also plain that Semler's view of inspiration is one more instance of his method of interpretation by the principle of the exoteric and the esoteric, for basically it rests upon a distinction between Scripture and the Word of God, the former being public and the latter private, audible to the individual in the depths of his religious consciousness.

Perhaps the most striking instance of this principle of analysis lies in Semler's distinction between theology and religion. From his vast knowledge of the history of the Church and of Christian dogma he had become convinced that the different creeds and systems of doctrine had come into being exactly as had the canon; that is, they had been evolved by human beings using natural reason for the sake of establishing norms and effecting a community of public worship. Thus the distinctions made by theologians concerning the specific modes of being of the three Persons of the Trinity and the relation of one to another are of little moment in the true intimate religious experience. Religion is a private, inner, practical experience of divine truth; theology is the conceptual codification of this truth, its exposition by the means available to human reason operating according to the rules and categories of logic to meet the specific needs of a particular occasion. However acceptable the conception of religion which is defined by this distinction may now seem, it has certain far-reaching consequences for theology which became most apparent in Semler's position as a result of his controversies with Lessing and Bahrdt and which will be discussed later in that connection. But even Semler's idea of religion brought him very close to the position of the naturalists, who replaced revelation by the natural light of reason to which all men had a right and which would reveal the universal religious truths. For such naturalists the truth of Christianity was measured by the degree to which it restored natural religion. In defending his subjective idea of religion Semler then unwittingly involved himself in a logical circle: Christianity can be true only if it restores natural religion, and unquestionably it restores natural religion because, after all, it is true, as we know on faith. Lessing of course avoided this circle by his restoration and radical reinterpretation of divine revelation.

That his general position would not be acceptable to traditionalists of any stamp Semler well knew, for he experienced much personal hostility in that old stronghold of Pietism, the University of Halle, which had once spewed forth Christian Wolff. In principle, moreover, he freely acknowledged the right of those who differed with him to attack his work. As he wrote in his *Einleitung in die dogmatische Gottesgelehrsamkeit:*

As for dogma itself, we cannot, by the most serious exhortations, prevent other people situated differently in life, from summoning up all their knowledge and therewith attacking our own knowledge, to which we are wholeheartedly committed but which is not recognized by them as valid.[3]

From this just and temperate view of how to debate differences among scholars and thus extend the boundaries of established truths, we would expect Semler to be compelled to acknowledge that the unknown Fragmentist and Bahrdt himself must be answered in the same moderate and good-tempered way. That he could not do this may be explained by his sense that his own ideas were proving to be a vehicle for carrying him far beyond the point he cared to go. When Bahrdt wrote in his confession of faith that there were thousands who agreed with him, Semler felt that he would be generally regarded as being in the forefront of these multitudes, a position which he dreaded to occupy. It was one thing, and a seemingly indifferent one, to defend old heresies and deviant sects, but it was something else to be tolerant of the modern heresies of a Bahrdt or a Fragmentist.

Neither Semler nor any other theologian paid much attention to the first of the so-called "Wolfenbüttel Fragments" which Lessing began to publish in 1774, attributing them to some anonymous personage and fictitiously asserting that they had been discovered in the ducal library of Wolfenbüttel. As is now, of course, well known, they were excerpts from a manuscript entitled *Apologie oder Schutzschrift für die vernünftigen Verehrer Gottes,* which had been written by Hermann Samuel Reimarus (1696–1768), the widely esteemed professor of Eastern languages at the academic Gymnasium of Hamburg. Reimarus had written, among other things, a treatise on natural religion containing a rationalistic demonstration of the existence of God that had received favorable comment from Immanuel Kant and a book on the behavior or drives of animals, particularly such patterned activities as nest-building, web-making, courtship, etc. The *Apologie,* however, he had felt to be too radical to publish, and when his children, Elise and Hinrich, gave Lessing permission to make use of the manuscript, concern for the reputation of their late father, as well as the desire not to embroil the survivors in the bitter theological controversy which was bound to ensue, dictated anonymous publication.

The excerpt published in 1774, *Von Duldung der Deisten,* was inoffensive enough to attract only a little attention, and Lessing waited until 1777 to proceed with the publication of five additional Fragments. These were called (1) *Von Verschreiung der Vernunft auf den Kanzeln,* (2) *Unmöglichkeit einer Offenbarung, die alle Menschen auf eine gegründete Art glauben können,* (3) *Durchgang der Israeliten durchs Rote Meer,* (4) *Dass die Bücher des Alten Testaments nicht geschrieben worden, eine Religion zu offenbaren,* (5) *Über die Auferstehungsgeschichte.* To make it clear that he did not share the viewpoints of the Fragmentist Lessing appended to each excerpt certain reservations or rejoinders. For example, he seeks to correct the thesis of the fourth of the fragments of 1777 by suggesting that even though, or perhaps just because, the writings of the Old Testament reveal inconsistent concepts of God and none at all of immortality, they do contain in the record of the progressive religious development of a rude and savage people testimony to the revelation of himself by God to these people in and through their history. This rejoinder constitutes, of course, the provisional form and leading idea of Lessing's later work, *Die Erziehung des Menschengeschlechts* (1780), an idea which had already presented itself to Semler in his work on the canon. And in his rejoinder to the fifth fragment of 1777 Lessing points out that all the conflicting and contradictory reports concerning the Resurrection which the unnamed author lays bare do not justify his conclusion that there never had been any such event and that the disciples had stolen the dead body of Jesus in order to perpetrate a great deception. For, says Lessing, contradictions in various accounts of an event do not signify that the accounts are all false in their entirety, particularly in respect to the one thing that they agree did take place.

After the publication of these excerpts Lessing did not have to wait long for the expected storm of indignant protest to break. In reply he published one more fragment before entering the lists in his own person. This was the excerpt entitled *Vom Zwecke Jesu und seiner Jünger,* which appeared separately in 1778 and which had as its thesis the contention that it was the purpose of Jesus and his disciples to establish a messianic kingdom, to overthrow the existing order, and become the rulers of a new one. In his preface Lessing contents himself with justifying his publication of all the fragments by comparing the unpublished manuscript to a hidden smoldering fire, which may creep through a building and destroy it undetected. By bringing the Fragmentist's attack upon the Christian religion to the attention of everyone, Lessing says he has made it possible for the defenders of the religion to refute the arguments publicly and put out the fire. In the often quoted words, *Dem Feuer muss Luft gemacht werden, wenn es gelöscht werden soll.* And Lessing added the assurance that if the Christian religion is truly divine, and the gates of hell cannot prevail against it, then the attacks which he was publishing could only reveal the imperviousness of the religion to such assault.

As Semler followed the course of Lessing's controversy with the various champions of orthodoxy who stepped forward to accept the challenge, from Johann Daniel Schumann and Heinrich Ress to Johann Melchior Götze, the most extreme and most renowned of them all, he must have had much opportunity to reflect upon what use the librarian of Wolfenbüttel was making of his, Semler's, researches and achievements, for it was patent that Lessing had studied and assimilated much of what Semler had written. The most notable correspondences are to be found in Lessing's *Axiomata,* which he published in the course of his controversy with Götze. In ten pregnant propositions or "axioms" Lessing sums up his position on the question of the literal inspiration of the Bible.

(1) The Bible patently contains more than what is pertinent to religion. (2) It is a mere hypothesis that the Bible is equally infallible in this additional material. (3) The letter is not the spirit, and the Bible is not religion. (4) Consequently exceptions taken to the letter and the Bible are not also exceptions taken to the spirit and religion. (5) Besides, there was a religion before there was a Bible. (6) Christianity was before the evangelists and apostles had written. Some time passed before the first of them wrote, and a very considerable time before the whole canon came into being. (7) Therefore ever so much may depend upon these writings and still the whole truth of the Christian religion cannot depend upon them. (8) If there was a time in which the Christian religion was already so widespread, in which it had already claimed so many souls, and in which nonetheless not a letter had been written down about the material concerning it which has come down to us, then it must be possible that everything written by the evangelists and apostles might be lost again and that the religion which they taught might nonetheless continue to exist. (9) Religion is not true because

evangelists and apostles taught it, but they taught it because it is true. (10) The written traditions must be interpreted in the light of the inner truth of religion, and all the written traditions are unable to give it inner truth if it has none.

To much of this Semler had to assent because he and the learned world knew that it was in essence what he himself had taught. The eighth axiom, of course, and the further conclusions which followed from it made Semler very uncomfortable, and he felt the need to dissociate himself from Lessing as well as the unnamed Fragmentist, while exhibiting all outward signs of respect for Lessing himself.

The burden of Semler's reply[4] is a repetition of his general position with which we are already familiar, and we need not therefore consider it in any detail. He quite readily concedes that Lessing is right in pointing out that the Christian faith is older than the books of the New Testament and not identical with them. In fact, he says, the idea of literally inspired Gospels originated with Luther and Melanchthon.[5] As for the theological doctrines, they arose only slowly in human ways, and there is nothing supernal about them. Actually, a person's concept of the Trinity is indifferent to his being a Christian, for the doctrinal distinctions in this regard served and serve only to distinguish among Christian sects,[6] and the true personal religion is untouched by an attack upon doctrine. At the same time Semler was himself deeply attached to the church differences and rituals which he wished to preserve and defend, even though this involved making statements about the Absolute which, in Semler's view, must be merely formal and have merely practical value, being by any standards of truth meaningless. Here it can be pointed out that whereas Semler might have been quite ready to subscribe to meaningless statements about the Absolute for the sake of tradition and practical management, this was a shocking idea to many others who saw such statements as meaningful. And, of course, meaningful statements about the Absolute, when they differ, lead to absolute differences among those who hold to them and justify intolerance and persecution, or at least seem to do so.

Here, as will be seen later, was a main point of difference with

Bahrdt as well as with Lessing, who in the year 1774 had already published an essay in his *Wolfenbütteler Beiträge,* which served as a reminder, if any were needed, that doctrinal disagreements may be fatal. This was an account of Adam Neuser, a religious enthusiast of the sixteenth century who had forsaken the Lutheran for the Reformed church and had come to entertain serious doubts about the doctrine of the Trinity and the divinity of Christ. Neuser managed to elude the attempts of church and state to have him broken on the rack for his heresies and escaped to Constantinople and became a Moslem. But Neuser's associate, Johannes Sylvanus, who had similar beliefs and doubts, paid for them with his life in 1572. Lessing's essay is a posthumous defense of Neuser and an impassioned attack upon the heresy-hunting theologians' thirst for blood. It is a disgrace, he says, that for two hundred years no one has come forward to make out a case for Neuser, who was driven by his orthodox persecutors to take an indefensible step, the acceptance of Islam. The established church-men were at least as much to blame for Neuser's defection as he was himself. Thus Lessing. Now, another two hundred years later, it is possible to see a certain parallel between Neuser's being driven to Mohammedanism and Bahrdt's being driven to naturalism by intolerant orthodoxy. That such a parallel could never have oc-curred to Semler is understandable, but it is far less understandable that he could fail to take seriously the historical evidence that doctrinal differences are a good deal more than mere badges of membership in one or another religious society.

But such considerations were apparently of no significance for Semler, who had become thoroughly alarmed that the weapons he had forged could be wielded by hands other than his own to strike to the heart of his faith. How deeply troubled Semler was by the reasoning in the Wolfenbüttel Fragments may be judged by the vehemence and intemperance of his reply to the unknown author, the invective against his scholarship, his logic, and his intentions. Especially his intentions, for Semler felt that it was his own be-loved religion that was being undermined by the attack upon theology, and he feared with reason that it could be said that his own theological position was not far removed from that of the

Fragmentist. Upon the head of the anonymous writer he therefore poured all sorts of abuse, scorn, and vituperation, declaring
him incompetent on all counts. And, although he took pains to
observe the amenities when he had occasion to mention Lessing
himself, there can be little doubt that he felt Lessing had acted
irresponsibly. This he made abundantly clear by appending to his
reply two so-called "fragments" by an anonymous writer of his
own. The second of them is an extensive examination and refutation of the calculations by which the Fragmentist justified his
conclusions that the story of the passage through the Red Sea was
absurd on the basis of logistics. But the first one was the more
telling of the two. It attracted more attention and occasioned great
amazement because of its wit, a quality which had been con-
spicuously absent from anything that had hitherto been associated
with the name of Semler. And it is, indeed, sufficiently amusing
to be summarized here.

In this fragment of a conversation one Sir John Bowling appears
before the Lord Mayor of London, accused of having set fire to a
house and thus of having endangered the entire city. Sir Bowling,
as the title is given, admits the charge and says that he feels he deserves a reward for his deed, explaining that he discovered a lighted
candle at four o'clock one afternoon in his neighbor's attic and
realized at once that if the candle were allowed to burn unnoticed
for three or four hours it could very well cause a great nocturnal
conflagration. But since help is more readily available in the daylight hours he threw the candle onto a few bundles of straw and
opened the roof-vents to give the fire some air. The flames and
smoke poured out through the openings and were seen, so the
pumps and hoses were rushed up, and the fire that could have
been very dangerous at night was quickly extinguished. Besides,
in this way a good occasion was provided to demonstrate that the
neighbor's house was fireproof and could not be burned up entirely, that the neighbor himself was a man of great equanimity,
and that the fire brigades were very effective. At this point the
secretary interjected that the man was palpably guilty and should
go to prison. "No," rejoined the Lord Mayor, "he is really not a
wicked man, just touched in the head. Take him to Bedlam."

Lessing, himself a master of biting wit, was enraged by the comparison of himself to a madman. To Elise Reimarus he denounced Semler as a base rogue, an impertinent goose of a professor and had the intention to flay him publicly in a "Letter from Bedlam." This plan was not carried out, however, but among the papers and notes Lessing left behind after his death there is one item which indicates how serious would have been Semler's difficulties if the controversy had gone on. For it was Lessing's intention to call upon Semler to make a frank, clear, and exact explanation of three things: (1) in what the universal Christian religion consists, (2) what are the local elements of the Christian religion which could be excised in any particular place without detriment to the universal religion, and (3) in precisely what can ethical conduct and Christian edification which is not impeded by the local elements be said to consist. Failure to make a specific answer would, in Lessing's eyes, justify identifying Semler's views with those of the Fragmentist, at least in a general way.

From all this it is evident that Semler had been thoroughly aroused and alarmed by Lessing's publications and that in his irritable mood he no doubt longed for some way to put an end to the acrimonious debate which was growing so distasteful to him. Indeed, it was suspected that he had made representations to the Queen and the Ministerium in Berlin, as a consequence of which Lessing was forbidden to continue publishing controversial writings to the detriment of revealed religion.[7] When, therefore, in the midst of these vexations[8] Bahrdt made an open confession of faith and sought refuge in Halle under the aegis of Minister von Zedlitz, Semler's bitterness and apprehension knew no bounds. As the newly elected dean of the theological faculty he was the moving spirit behind the letters of protest which this faculty sent to Zedlitz, urging that Bahrdt be kept as far as possible away from Halle. But he went much further than this and incited churchmen in Westphalia to protest directly to the King against Bahrdt's being accorded a refuge in Halle, and he threatened to exclude from the pedagogical seminar students who had anything to do with Bahrdt or Trapp.[9]

Ernst Christian Trapp, it will be recalled, was the man whose mocking laughter had crystallized Bahrdt's still amorphous disbelief in revelation. His presence in Halle was as odious to Semler as that of Bahrdt, for the two were associated in a way that was extremely painful and humiliating to him and that may have had something to do with Semler's later sensational defense of the notorious Edict on Religion promulgated under Frederick William II by Minister Wöllner in the period of reaction which followed the "enlightened" reign of Frederick the Great.

The apple of contention was the theological seminary, of which Semler had long been the director, and the pedagogical institute which had become attached to it. Semler had taken over the seminary from his venerated teacher, Baumgarten, and in 1769 had secured the assistance of one Christian Gottfied Schütz, who took a great interest in the pedagogical activities of the seminary and prepared the ground for expanding the work to include the preparation of schoolteachers. This idea appealed to Zedlitz, who was greatly interested in education and who encouraged Schütz to go to Dessau to study Basedow's philanthropinical system. At length, in the year 1778, the pedagogical institute was established, with Schütz as "inspector" under the directorship of Semler, but Schütz did not long retain responsibility for the institute. In December of the same year he reported to Zedlitz in an unofficial letter that he had received a call to the University of Jena, and he inquired what increase in salary he might count upon as an inducement to stay in Halle. Zedlitz's reply was to take the unofficial communication as a letter of resignation and to congratulate him on his new appointment, no doubt partly because the funds budgeted for the institute were so meager, but perhaps also because Schütz and Semler were not as enthusiastic about philanthropinical ideas as Zedlitz would have liked. Schütz then had no recourse but to make formal application for dismissal, which he did in April 1779, and he left Halle in July of that year. Zedlitz, seeking a successor to Schütz and hoping to find a man in sympathy with Basedow's philanthropinical principles, now had his attention drawn to Dr. Bahrdt, who was in "enlightened" eyes not only a martyr to orthodox machinations behind the cloak of Catholic tyranny but also one of the true fountainheads of philanthropinical

wisdom. Zedlitz seems to have calculated that if he could provide a
haven for Bahrdt, and if Bahrdt could prove himself reliable, the
pedagogical institute would be provided with a master educator at
small expense. But Semler, anxious to avoid being lumped with
the Fragmentist, Basedow, and Bahrdt, and offended that his
friend Schütz had been so unceremoniously allowed to leave, not
only resolved to publish a refutation of Bahrdt's confession of
faith but made his abhorrence of Bahrdt's notorious unfitness as a
guide of youth so strongly felt that Zedlitz had to drop this project.
Thus it came about that Trapp was made head of the pedagogical
institute under Semler's direction.[10] This was obviously an arrangement that could produce nothing but friction and bitterness
that persisted even beyond and was aggravated by Zedlitz's removal
of Semler from the directorship of the seminary on the grounds
that he no longer possessed public trust and confidence. And
Zedlitz was right in saying that Semler had lost much public trust
and confidence, for his bitter and vehement denunciation of
Bahrdt's confession of faith seemed to a large segment of liberal
thinkers an unsportsmanlike attack upon someone who refused to
knuckle under even at the risk of his entire future. Besides, they
felt, in attacking Bahrdt's creed Semler was really tearing down his
own achievements.

In all Semler's reply to Bahrdt's confession of faith [11] there is
very little that is new or unfamiliar to us. After a preface in
which he denies that he is one of the thousands who Bahrdt maintained were in agreement with the confession, Semler briefly reviews his relations with Bahrdt and makes a few remarks about
his position in general before proceeding to the detailed discussion. In the early part of this section, "Über das Bekäntnis
[sic] selbst," he readily grants that it is not only the right but the
obligation of every thinking Christian to make a thorough and
searching examination of his faith, for it is the inestimable privilege of his contemporaries to be secure in freedom of conscience.
But, says Semler, in preparation for what he plans as a major
argument, whoever asserts his right to think as he please must
respect his neighbor's equal right to follow his own conscience too.
If, therefore, a seeker after truth finds that he is better satisfied by

the teachings of a religious sect other than his own, he should by
all means go over to the sect he prefers. But if he tries to persuade
a recognized sect or church of the greater validity of his own convictions, he is inviting civil authority to take action, for it is the
function of civil authority to determine the external forms of
worship of its subjects in the interest of maintaining law and order.
And anyone who, convinced of the error of established doctrines,
publicly seeks to cause all or some of them to be abandoned in
favor of his own ideas is not just a heretic but a usurper and a
tyrant. Semler therefore bitterly accuses Bahrdt of intolerance
and attempted suppression of religious liberty!

Even more disingenuous is Semler's point by point discussion
of the cardinal items in Bahrdt's confession, as Karl Aner has
plainly stated.[12] As we have already seen, Bahrdt professed a belief in the possibility of moral betterment and responsibility rather
than in inherited sinfulness. He maintained that the striving for
moral improvement must be present in order for divine grace
to be effective, and he denied the forgiveness of sins merely by
virtue of the atonement on the cross. He disbelieved in the
tripartite Person of the Trinity and maintained that belief in
Athanasian, Arian, Sabellian, or other doctrine was of no consequence for personal salvation. All of these and many others were
ideas that Semler himself had put forth in his books on investigation of the canon and elsewhere. Semler's attempt to dissociate
himself from Bahrdt's theology, says Aner, rested upon the very
worst kind of hair-splitting sophistry.

What is perhaps the most astonishing thing about Semler's whole
position is the naive skepticism, even cynicism, with regard to
doctrinal differences. In his *Versuch einer freien theologischen
Lehrart* of 1777, for instance, he had taken the position, completely
in agreement with Bahrdt, that personal salvation was not dependent upon understanding and acceptance of any specific doctrine. As he writes in this book (pp. 204–5), political and social
differences existed between, for example, the Lutherans and the
Zwinglians, and such differences entailed differences in how certain teachings of the church were to be interpreted. Lutheran
interpretation of the sacraments and of communion, for example,

could not be made binding upon any except Lutherans. Such differences are therefore merely outward signs of partisanship and do not admit to or exclude from salvation. Indeed, such doctrinal differences are of concern only to professional theologians. This did not mean for Semler, however, that sectarian differences could or should be abolished in favor of a united Christian (or at least Protestant) church. He was too keenly aware of the importance of the particular, the local, the temporal in human and even superhuman affairs to believe in this possibility. Moreover, differences in outward forms of worship had been fixed by church and state authorities, said Semler, and it was the good right of such authorities to maintain the differences. The last point was one that Semler strongly emphasized in his controversy with Bahrdt. The state and the ruler, he writes on pages 108 and 109 of his answer to Bahrdt's creed, maintain universities where future teachers are trained and have the obligation to convince themselves of the correctness of the doctrines that distinguish one religious group from another. If they are so persuaded and are qualified in other respects also, they become ministers of the gospel and servants of the state. If they wish to eliminate doctrinal differences for the sake of a union of various churches, they must do so from outside the church and not as servants of the state.

In all this is evident that curious mixture of innocent cynicism, kowtowing to authority, timidity, and insistence upon freedom of conscience and research which was so characteristic of Semler, especially in his latter days. He apparently had no idea or wish to consider whether Bahrdt had been injured by the doctrinal differences which to his historian's eye had only the validity of badges of party membership. It is even probable that he actually failed to see that the dogmas, especially those dealing with the nature of the Trinity, profess to describe attributes of the Absolute and that intolerance is the inevitable corollary of dogma. One who knows absolute truth must reject all other views, and among societies with differing absolutes there can be no tolerance. But to Semler, the radical, although perhaps innocent, cynic, dogma was nothing but a fictitious structure which said nothing about the truth and the Absolute but to which authority justly required public submission and obedience, private religion being a matter between the individual and his conscience. In his view the sole importance attaching to doctrinal affirmations concerning the Absolute was that they help support the status quo. To Bahrdt, who was also naive in his own way, this was an impossible, if not actually hypocritical, position. Bahrdt saw the force of Semler's revelation of human illogic in dogma, accepted the consequences, and preached the conclusions which inevitably followed unless refuge were sought in mystic symbolism.

As can readily be anticipated, Bahrdt lost little time in replying to Semler's *Antwort*. He immediately published a *Kurze Erklärung über Herrn Doktor Semlers Antwort auf das Bahrdtsche Glaubensbekenntnis*.[13] A better contrast to the tedious prolixity and peevish casuistry of Semler's *Antwort* can scarcely be imagined than this simple, straightforward, eight-page pamphlet. On the point of Semler's feeling himself to be meant as one of the thousands whom Bahrdt had declared to be in essential agreement with him, Bahrdt says:

Since I did not name him as one of the thousands, he could be one of the other thousands who are not of the opinion I have confessed to be mine. In the introduction he says himself that he had warned me in a letter, before my confession of faith had appeared, that he would write against it, that is, before he knew that I would say anything about those thousands. An obvious contradiction!

In reply to Semler's statement that Bahrdt wished to arrogate despotic powers to himself Bahrdt says:

Herr Doktor Semler accuses me of having wished to force a new universal religion upon the world and to abrogate the laws of the state. Answer. I hereby declare and it is self-evident in my published confession that I have never wished to impose any such thing on anyone. Making representations to the law-giving authority or a part of it concerning a law is not the same as abrogating the laws of the state. In England the law-making body is frequently petitioned to abolish subscription [to the Thirty-nine Articles of 1588], and never have the petitioners been accused of committing a crime or intending to abrogate the laws of the state.

And he points to the example of Archdeacon Blackburne of York, who had called some of the propositions of the Thirty-nine Articles immoral and absurd without being forced to resign his church offices. Small wonder that the *Allgemeine deutsche Bibliothek*, re-viewing Semler's *Antwort*, questioned whether Semler could really suppose Bahrdt to be so stupid as to believe it possible to impose his new universal religion upon the world.[14]

Lessing was perhaps the least affected both outwardly and inwardly by these dissensions among allies in the cause of religious enlightenment, great as was his debt to Semler for the historical and philological materials which he used with such effectiveness. Semler himself may be said to have fared the worst of the three since his inconsistency and timidity had plainly put him in a false position. As for Bahrdt, his course had been set, and Semler's angry blasts served to fill his sails and speed him on as he was going, not, to be sure, into any snug harbor but through the stormy seas of controversy and popularization.

XXIII

⟨A BUSY MAN⟩

THE EIGHT years following Bahrdt's establishment in Halle up to July 1787, when he gave up his official connection with the University, were filled with a multitude of academic duties, literary activities, money-making projects, and schemes of downright rascality. In outward respects these years brought little change: there is no sequence of events to chronicle, no struggle leading to a certain or uncertain outcome. And in respect to Bahrdt's inner development these years saw his final confirmation in his own very popular and influential brand of natural religion. In Albert Schweitzer's *Geschichte der Leben-Jesu-Forschung*, for example, Bahrdt's works from this period are recorded and discussed as the earliest fictionalized life of Jesus, a pioneer work which pointed the way to the strict research and scholarship of the nineteenth and twentieth centuries.[1]

As one reads through the various documents stemming from this epoch in Bahrdt's life and later ones pertaining to it, the strongest impression is of wonder that so many contradictory and random activities were crammed into the life of a single person. But to Bahrdt himself this period in his life undoubtedly seemed no more random and aimless than the earlier ones. It is just that we, having no thread leading from here to there on which to string the events, become a little bewildered contemplating a life as it was led.

In the last two chapters we have gained some idea of how much of Bahrdt's time and energy must have been consumed in merely trying to obtain a foothold in his new environment. But in order to feel our way into his situation we must not forget that the connections with Heidesheim had by no means been severed. From

236

the very beginning, Heres showered him with letters[2] upbraiding him for his thoughtless conduct which had plunged so many friends and associates into financial embarrassment and for his callous behavior toward his wife, for whom Heres seems to have had a very high regard.[3] Heres also kept Bahrdt informed of events in Heidesheim, particularly about the auctioning of his effects and, as we have seen, the part which Rühl had played in bringing about Bahrdt's total ruin.

Among the effects that Bahrdt most wanted to reclaim were, of course, his books, and he wrote many letters to many people, including Biester and Rühl himself, as well as Heres, to attain that end. Heres agreed to buy them at the auction as though for his own use and then to let Bahrdt have them. But Heres took the opportunity to urge and implore Bahrdt to return to Thiele a manuscript which it was now revealed Bahrdt had actually taken with him upon his departure from Marschlins, although he had steadfastly denied it. Another manuscript that caused Bahrdt much concern was the copy he had made in Leipzig of *Fausts Höllenzwang*. In fact, he even induced Zedlitz to intervene on his behalf to secure the return of this precious text, in which he had apparently not lost faith as completely as he would lead us to believe. And this is not the only evidence that, although he might have lost faith in the supernatural aspect of Christianity, he had retained a good deal of gross superstition. For example he still believed in sympathetic healing, which he wanted to learn from an old and simpleminded shepherd as well as from an old woman whom he consulted for the purpose of having his erysipelas cured by means of charms. And he no less than Semler was interested in alchemy and tried to learn some of the secrets of making gold from the so-called "Paracelsus of the Enlightenment," Beireis in Helmstedt.

Among the letters from Bahrdt's former associates in Heidesheim, there is one that is particularly interesting for the light it sheds upon the Löw Bär Isak episode in Frankfurt. As will be remembered, Bahrdt represented the Jewish moneylender as a man of extraordinary magnanimity, although some of Bahrdt's biographers and critics have maintained that the whole story

was a fabrication and that Löw Bär Isak never existed. The letter
is ample evidence that he did indeed exist but also that he was
not the paragon of munificence we know from Bahrdt's account.
It also, of course, gives us an insight into the troubles which beset
not only Bahrdt but his creditors and friends as well. It is dated
the fifteenth of May 1781, and was written by Johann Adam
Specht. It runs in part:

> You know and are assured by me that I have done more for you than
> my fortune allowed. If you do not now help me in turn, then I will be
> ruined forever, together with my wife and children. I can never in my life
> by dint of toil and work earn as much as I am to pay out for you. I ask and
> implore you for God's sake to come to my aid with some money as you have
> promised to do. We still owe 2600 florins on your account to Bär Isak in
> Frankfurt, and I am not able to secure five florins from my household ex-
> penses for this payment. For I have borrowed from Herr Frohn in Mann-
> heim to pay the interest on the 1500 florins which I as well as every other
> one of us have had to pay to Bär Isak.

But such letters of justified complaint were not the only ones
Bahrdt received from old friends and acquaintances in the
Palatinate. On the tenth of January 1780, for example, Court
Chaplain Wolf of Grünstadt, to whom Bahrdt had entrusted
his infant daughter who was too ill to be taken on the flight
from Heidesheim, wrote a letter which began:

> One hundred *louis d'or* will be yours if you can find a spouse with a few
> hundred thousand *Gulden* for our Hereditary Count or else a young lady
> of good ancient nobility.

Bahrdt, of course, responded very positively to this proposition,
wrote to his friends in Courland, and was soon able to make certain
not wholly acceptable suggestions. About the same time he became
involved in a somewhat similar affair in which he had ample scope
for his propensity to play the part of an Eulenspiegel. This was
the case of a certain Herr von W. who had eloped with a young
lady from Frankfurt and wished to marry her despite her family's
opposition. Since the family was influential it was difficult to find
a minister who would perform the ceremony, but Bahrdt agreed
to make the arrangements for the consideration of 500 *Taler*.
His victim was a certain Pastor Blumenthal in Micheln, whom
he persuaded to marry the couple for a trifling sum, while he him-

self pocketed most of the money which had been paid out as a bribe. Furthermore, when the news of the affair leaked out, Pastor Blumenthal was involved in painful legal consequences.[4]

During these years Bahrdt's immensely fertile and active mind generated and executed plan upon project upon scheme, anything that seemed to promise a chance of making a profit or giving greater scope to the exercise of his talents. Thus, for example, he conceived the idea of establishing public bathing-houses on the river Saale and petitioned the King for the exclusive right to manage such an establishment. To this petition he received the reply that such exclusive privilege would be in contravention of the natural right of everyone to bathe in a river and the assurance that if his projected bathing-houses were sufficiently comfortable and convenient and if the price charged for their use was reasonable, then he might expect that his business would prosper.

That the banks of the Saale did not confine his ambitions, however, has recently been demonstrated by the discovery in Philadelphia of a letter which he wrote in 1783 to George Washington.[5] In this letter he offers his services to Washington and the recently independent United States, saying that America's good fortune is all his joy and Washington's name his pride. He anticipates that the new nation will have to expand its functions and multiply its activities in many fields, including those of education, culture, and the arts in general. Bahrdt says that he would like to have a share in propagating the arts and sciences in America, being a specialist in philosophy, mathematics, the theory of education, history, and languages, and he describes himself as a theologian who regards enlightened reason as the purest source of religious knowledge. He is thus, he feels, qualified to assist in making plans for the establishment of a university as well as various other educational and religious institutions. It is not recorded that Washington ever answered the letter.

Most of Bahrdt's efforts of ambition, however, were directed towards securing power, position, and income within Prussian domains. How importunate he was can be judged from an impatient letter addressed to him by Zedlitz, on the fifth of November 1782, in which Zedlitz writes,

How you plague me cannot be conceived. In addition to the demands of
G. R. Lamprecht, who intends through my intervention to have you made
an army chaplain and heaven knows what else, you beleaguer me through
Minister Münchhausen and Director Hoffman . . . I feel that I am compelled
to repulse you by a serious declaration of my views. For it is scarcely possible
for any vacancy whatever to occur, from master of the horse to full professor
of mathematics or of anatomy, which you do not demand for yourself and
for which you do not get yourself recommended by G. R. Lamprecht and
all my acquaintances.

In the narrower sphere of his professional activities also, his
mind threw off plans and projects as a pinwheel showers sparks.
Some of these can be described as very successful academic achievements, others less so.

There was, for example, the matter of his university lectures,
which, because of the opposition voiced by Semler and his colleagues, all lay outside the purely professional interests of the
students. The students who elected Bahrdt's courses, therefore,
were motivated entirely by interest in the man himself and his subjects. Since he was forbidden to lecture on theology, he offered
courses on Tacitus and Juvenal, Hebrew grammar, logic, metaphysics, rhetoric or homiletics, and popular ethics. The last subject was intended to attract not only regularly matriculated
students of the university but also any and all who might be interested: burghers, officers, professors, and state officials, and also
their wives and daughters.

These public lectures occasioned one of the scandals of the
day. When the lectures were announced, great interest in them
was immediately aroused both because of their novelty and because of Dr. Bahrdt's notoriety, as well as his gifts of oratory. A
great number of auditors, both men and women, registered for
the lectures. Bahrdt had set the time on Sunday from eleven to
twelve in the morning at the conclusion of divine services. Bahrdt's
enemies protested against this hour to higher authorities, apparently on the grounds that the lectures would disturb the peaceful
Sunday routine, but Minister von Zedlitz had indicated that he
was little impressed by these representations. Bahrdt therefore
proceeded with his plans but found the auditorium locked and
sealed, and thus he was forced to change the hour to Wednesdays

at five and Saturdays at two.[6] But, as might have been foreseen, the altercation probably increased the general interest, and Bahrdt profited from his augmented notoriety, for he lectured to about three hundred regular students and one hundred interested townspeople, who followed him so intently that, as he says, he was able to speak in extreme pianissimo without a syllable being lost. And, indeed, his gift of eloquence must have been extraordinarily compelling, as is attested by an anecdote concerning his lectures on homiletics, which instructed as much by demonstration as by precept. On one occasion, for example, he opened the hour with a prayer that impressed and enraptured everyone by the force of its disposition and the nobility of its delivery. At the conclusion, while the audience was still under the spell of reverence, Bahrdt burst into laughter and said that his purpose had been to show them that in public speaking dramatic performance was everything and that a consummate actor could produce any feeling in the audience whatever without sharing in it in any way.

At first glance it might seem that the lectures on Juvenal and Tacitus constituted a new departure for Bahrdt, but in reality they served the basic purposes which animated him.

There is some dispute, of course, as to his attitude toward the passages of Juvenal which cite the immoral practices of the Romans, some saying that in his lectures he dwelt with relish on the salacious details, but others, including students who heard the lectures, insisting that he showed real distaste for them. It is a fact, however, that his published translation of Juvenal toned these passages down in such a way as to diminish the value of the translation as a whole. But whatever his feeling about certain aspects of his subject matter, Bahrdt, in translating and lecturing on Juvenal and Tacitus, was pursuing his by-now fixed goal of rationalizing and humanizing Christianity, in this instance by demonstrating the possibility of a conception and code of ethical conduct among heathens.

But beyond this polemic intent there was also the hope and purpose of making a profit, for he had conceived the idea of putting out a series of classical authors in translation. To this end he sought to enlist the help and interest of everyone he thought could exert some influence in his behalf, from his old friend Meusel to Samuel Friedrich Nathanael Morus, Ernesti's faithful pupil and professor at the University of Leipzig, to King Frederick himself. Morus, a capable exegete, was greatly interested in the project, offered suggestions and constructive criticism, and exerted himself to find subscribers for the published book. Meusel was no less interested, reporting to Bahrdt that the reviews of the Tacitus volume were generally favorable, except for that by Schütz, the former director of the theological seminary in Halle. No one, however, seemed able to stir up enough public interest in the project to ensure a good sale of the books. Bahrdt therefore devised a scheme which he hoped would secure just this effect.

On the second of June 1781, he dispatched a presentation copy of his *Tacitus* to King Frederick and addressed to him a letter of dedication and the outline of a plan, "a most submissive proposal for the increased dissemination of Roman and Greek literature among students." This proposal is interesting in two ways, first, for Bahrdt's very intelligent analysis of the reasons why study of the classics was not more popular, and second, for the suggestions he makes to remedy the situation and, not so incidentally, to line his own pockets.

Bahrdt attributes the relative unpopularity of the classical literatures to a number of causes, the most important of which he considers methods of instruction.

The school teacher [he says] crams analysis, phraseology, and grammar into his pupils, and the professor makes a great to-do with variant readings and interpretations, so that the learner gets nowhere, takes much time to read little, never gets a general view of the author, never becomes familiar with the spirit of the Ancients, and consequently never develops any interest in reading them but considers the whole study burdensome and boring.

Other causes of indifference to classical literature he finds in the lack of good translations and the high price of satisfactory editions. For all these ills he feels he has the remedy, namely the publication of the classical authors in a cheap critical pocket edition and companion volumes of translations. If His Majesty would graciously deign to charge Bahrdt with this business, he, Bahrdt, would wish to stipulate certain conditions. First, he would request for himself the continuing exclusive right to print and sell these editions. Second, he would urge the preparation of a uniform syllabus of studies for all schools and universities in Prussian domains, which would make the use of the texts and translations mandatory. He also would expect that all rectors and school superintendents would be accountable to him for the money realized on the sale of the books to their students. In conclusion Bahrdt assured His Majesty that these humble suggestions had been inspired by nothing save his love of work and the desire to be of use to his Fatherland.

In due time Bahrdt received a reply dated Potsdam, June 19, 1781, and signed by Frederick, which expressed grateful acknowledgment for Doctor Bahrdt's meritorious efforts in translating Tacitus "whose powerful ideas and concentrated style make him the most difficult of all Latin authors." The same memorandum contained the information that Bahrdt's proposals had been sent on for study and evaluation.

A week after this memorandum had been dispatched, Zedlitz, into whose province the proposals just outlined fell, sent Bahrdt a letter on the subject. First, he demanded of Bahrdt what he meant by a continuing exclusive right of publication, pointing out that nothing could be done about pirated editions and that the texts of the classical authors were in the public domain. He further pointed out the absurdity of compelling the schoolmen to base their examinations on the subject matter of the books edited and translated by Bahrdt or of insisting that all the pupils studying Greek and Latin buy new copies of the texts in Bahrdt's edition. Having declared that he would never attempt to dictate to any rector or teacher what books to use, Zedlitz went on to say that he nonetheless was convinced that Bahrdt's translation of Tacitus was the best one in German.[7]

Another useful and valued publication from about the same time was a journal containing subjects and outlines for sermons which many a poor preacher found to be a veritable gold mine.[8] Before withdrawing from full responsibility—the first four volumes were almost entirely his work—Bahrdt had given the journal such a good start that under a continuation by W. A. Teller and other subsequent collaborators it survived its founder by half a century. It should be added that Bahrdt very wisely did not permit his name to be associated with the magazine for fear that devout pastors in search of a sermon would never seek aid from so notorious a heretic.

Less valuable was a curious New Testament lexicon[9] in which each Greek entry was followed by a transliteration in German type, the avowed purpose being to enable an unschooled reader to understand the New Testament from the Greek.

The money-making and educational projects which have just been described, however, still left Bahrdt with enough time and energy to continue his controversial writings also, and during these years he repeatedly took up the cudgels against various outsiders as well as maintaining a major running feud with the theological faculty of Halle. Let us turn first to the controversies with the outsiders.

In 1778 and 1779 Georg Friedrich Seiler of Erlangen had written a two-volume work on the concept of atonement,[10] attacking Eberhard and Gotthilf Samuel Steinbart, who had propounded an ethical eudaemonism. Bahrdt, who admired the work of both Eberhard and Steinbart, published a so-called "apology for reason." [11] The book has seventeen chapters beginning with an historical introduction and also an appendix which outlines the history of Bahrdt's convictions. The basic ideas are already familiar to us: punishment is a natural result of sinfulness, a blessing in disguise, and cannot therefore be endured vicariously, and, indeed, vicarious punishment would be unjust. However correct Bahrdt's reasoning may have seemed to the rationalists, it made, as might be expected, no impression upon Seiler, who continued to believe in supernatural punishment. And it made no impression, that is, no convincing impression, upon other heretic-hunters such as *Konrektor* Karl Christian Voigt in Quedlinburg, who, apparently at the behest of Court Chaplain Boysen, had written an attack upon *Consistorialrat* Hermes. A friend of Hermes in turn asked Bahrdt to defend him, and Bahrdt did so in an abusive book which of course provoked the inevitable replies.

A much more important and still highly interesting bit of satire was Bahrdt's famous *Kirchen- und Ketzeralmanach*,[12] in which he gave characterizations of various figures both in and out of the church. In format it was like the popular farmer's almanacs in which each day has its saint, and there are weather predictions and rules for planting and so on. But in Bahrdt's almanac the saints are replaced by well-known contemporaries such as Basedow, Lessing, and Bahrdt himself. Basedow's day is put down as good for drinking Malaga, and Lessing's and Bahrdt's days are predicted to have beautiful and lovely sunshine. The body of the book consists of satirical sketches which enraged Bahrdt's enemies but which have always been admitted by everyone familiar with the period to be shrewd and penetrating in very many instances. For Lessing he has high praise and warm words of appreciation for his learning and acumen.

Your Fragments [he exclaims] are the true Carthage of the Christian Church on which the champions of Zion will long exercise their strength and never emerge from a skirmish without having learned something new.

About Semler he says that if he had only left the stage at the height of his achievement, before his attack upon the Fragments, he would have been the pride and joy of all Germans, but instead of this his fame had been dimmed and he had injured himself by his controversy with Bahrdt. Of Goethe he writes,

As every genius does, he goes his own way even in theology, too clever to defend the religion of a Götze or a Seiler, and too proud to join the reformers. Therefore, together with Herder and a few others, he has taken a middle course and dealt out slaps to both the orthodox and the heretics, and actually he has been laughing at the public.

Bahrdt's own prejudices, of course, show through everywhere, and his own name appears wherever an occasion to mention it occurs, appropriate or not. Most amusing is the article on his father and himself, especially his self-characterization as one of the best minds and hardest workers of the age.

Every right-thinking person [he writes] must regret that a man of such rare powers has been made useless to the world partly by misfortune and partly by his own heedlessness. . . . Only posterity will be able to form a just opinion of this man, who is so remarkable in every respect.

Obviously, any moderately attentive reader was able to guess that it was Bahrdt who had written the Almanac. Meusel wrote him late in January 1781, that the book was creating a great stir: everybody owned it, and nobody admitted owning it. And Bahrdt's old friend Heres suffered one more disillusionment, for Bahrdt had taken a few digs at various former associates in the Palatinate, notably Pastor Wolf in Grünstadt. But all this stir merely helped to make the book better known and increase the sales, so that it was brought up to date and enlarged in 1787, and replies, imitations, and copies kept appearing until as late as 1800.

Not long after the initial excitement caused by publication of the Almanac began to die down, Bahrdt seems to have decided to stir things up again by a publication of a different kind. This was a compilation of lecture notes from his student days in Leipzig. The purpose of the compilation was to focus attention once more upon the system of orthodox belief in order not to let its absurdities be forgotten. Even though the purpose was polemic, the treatment of the subject was historical and objective, as was accurately set forth in the title, *Systema Theologiae Lutheranae orthodoxum cum brevi adnotatione dissensionum recentiorum.* At first no objections were raised to the publication, but as rumors about the book began to circulate, the theologians of Halle grew uneasy, and the censor, Schulz, who was dean of the theological faculty, suddenly refused to allow the printing to continue. The grounds for refusal were that the divine nature of Christ and of the Holy Spirit was denied in the footnotes, that is, the dispute was mentioned as an historical fact. Bahrdt countered this move by securing permission to resume publication from Berlin. Now it was the turn of the theological faculty to strike a blow, and they did so in an article in the *Hallesche Gelehrte Zeitung* of December 11, 1784. They disavowed responsibility for giving Bahrdt the imprimatur and discredited the as-yet unpublished book as a wretched compilation of out-of-date notes and sarcastic attacks upon Christianity. Here the faculty was at fault in two ways: first, for publishing a devastating notice of a book that had not appeared in print largely because of their opposition, and second, for asserting an untruth about the book, namely that it contained blasphemies directed against Christianity. Bahrdt, of course, lost no time in putting his case before a public forum,[13] in which he pointed out that his book contained no blasphemies that could not be found in any impartial church history which merely gave an account of beliefs that had been declared heretical. The faculty replied with an attack upon Bahrdt's character, and Bahrdt counterattacked with an invitation to the faculty to attend his lectures on ethics in order to learn the meaning of moral conduct theoretically and practically.

At this point there was published a satire against the theological faculty so sharp and in certain passages so witty that the theological world buzzed with shock and curiosity. For a while it was supposed that it was Bahrdt himself who had composed the work, but eventually Bahrdt let it be known that not he but his friend Trapp was the author. Trapp's satire was a "theological demonstration" that Dr. Bahrdt was to blame for the earthquake in Calabria,[14] a demonstration that rested upon an analysis of the various kinds of reason. Nine varieties of reason are enumerated, beginning with pure reason, of which Kant has written a critique but which is not for ordinary mortals. Other varieties are sound reason, with the motto *ne quid nimis* (which is usually bestowed at birth), political reason, mercantile reason, philosophical reason (which is concerned with things which are not things and often declassifies things which are things into non-things), pedagogical reason, medical reason (the mistakes of which are underground), legal reason, and theological reason. The last variety, the queen of all varieties of reason, is responsible for a great many remarkable things such as the creation of the sulphurous pit of hell with its horse-hoofed ruler and original sin, which produces the population of the pit. Theological reason has various subdivisions such as pagan theological reason. Turkish theological reason, Jewish theological reason, which transforms rods into serpents and Nile water into blood, and Christian theological reason, which in its turn may be still further subdivided. These subdivisions are: (1) Catholic Christian theological reason, which can transform bread into flesh which does not become flesh; (2) Reformed Christian theological reason, according to which a sinner such as Cesare

Borgia may, if fate so decrees, become a guest at the celestial banquet tables and even a St. Paul may go to hell; (3) Lutheran Christian theological reason with its various Göttingian, Wittenbergian, Hallensian, and other branches.

The satire had it that theological disputes must be debated in terms of theological rather than sound or legal reason and that the Hallensian branch proceeded on its own principles in every controversy. In the present instance the five persons of the Hallensian faculty submerged their differences in certain quinitarian principles such as: (1) they attribute their own sins to Bahrdt, attack and say that Bahrdt attacked; (2) what according to sound reason is a contradiction is none according to theological reason; (3) the opponent must be made out to be as black as possible; (4) all evils in the world are to be attributed to Bahrdt. In this way it will be possible to prove by theological reason that Dr. Bahrdt is to blame for the earthquake in Calabria. The starting point of the demonstration is a strong feeling on the part of the Hallensian quinity that Dr. Bahrdt really is to blame. This is equivalent to dreaming vividly that he is, and it is not susceptible of being disproved. Positive reasons in support of this feeling can be adduced in the following way: What other cause can there be of the persistent earthquakes in Calabria than the persistent wrath of God? What other cause of the persistent wrath of God can there be than the persistent heresies of the notorious Bahrdt? Theological reason knows that nothing is so hateful to the good Lord as heresies, and of heresies those are the most hateful that have the greatest resemblance to sound reason, and this description fits Bahrdt's heresies perfectly. Furthermore, either the theological faculty of Halle or else Dr. Bahrdt must be to blame for the persistent earthquakes. Since the former alternative cannot be true, the second must be. And again, the fact that Bahrdt's heresies and the earthquake are contemporaneous points to a causal connection, though surely the earthquakes are not the cause of Bahrdt's heresies. Therefore it is plain that the heresies must be the cause of the earthquakes. And so on.

Meanwhile Bahrdt's book on orthodox theology had appeared, but it had little success. It was therefore in order to write something in the hope of earning a little money, and so now he turned out a book on the study of theology,[15] and at the same time he submitted to Berlin a student welfare plan. The book on theological studies is eminently practical in its approach. Since most students of theology are preparing themselves to minister to simple congregations, the course of study should be shaped to that end. Church history, Eastern languages, dogmatics, polemics, and all these technical things, says Bahrdt, are of little use to a man who is to be a teacher and a model of proper conduct. What he needs is philosophy, natural religion, New Testament, natural science, physics, anatomy, arithmetic and geometry, the Greek and Roman classics (as an antidote to supernaturalism), history and literature, a bit of medicine, pedagogy, Socratics, rhetoric, stylistics, public speaking, and, in the last semester, a brief survey of technical theology. It will be seen that the modern divinity school has not caught up with Dr. Bahrdt even now.

All these suggestions, of course, were predicated upon a completely naturalistic and rationalistic conception of religion and of the mission and person of Jesus. And it was in the Halle period of his life that Bahrdt worked out and set down in detail his system of natural Christianity, the high point of which is his fictional life of Jesus. As Schweitzer says, this was the first attempt at a consistent natural and historical presentation of the supernatural story of the Gospels, that is, the first to offer a rationally conceivable and coherent explanation of the causal forces and connections in the events of Jesus' life and inner experiences from birth to death.

XXIV

⟦JESUS' LIFE STORY⟧

THE IMPULSE to work out a rationally conceivable and coherent explanation of the events and sayings recorded in the Gospels had, of course, already been manifest in Bahrdt's New Testament paraphrase. As we know, the germ of this idea was not original with Bahrdt: Reimarus had offered an explanation of the purpose and plan of Jesus and the disciples, and even earlier a lengthy work by Johann Jakob Hess had appeared on the history of the last three years of Jesus' life.[1] But in Bahrdt himself the idea developed by organic growth in response to his personal experiences and also by assimilation of certain key ideas of the "enlightened" theologians and philosophers whose works he studied. The fictional life of Jesus was Bahrdt's great achievement: in writing it he accomplished something which had not been done before and which was destined to be done again and again after him down to the present inheritors of the tradition, the Hollywood scenarists and the syndicated comic strip writers.

It happened to be Basedow who gave Bahrdt the encouragement to continue with his attempts to adapt the Bible to the needs of the age as they conceived them. Basedow had come to Halle to confer with Bahrdt on the propagation of the philanthropinical method, for these were still the days when Bahrdt hoped to be entrusted with the directorship of the pedagogical seminary. Basedow, whose habits were nocturnal, kept Bahrdt up night after night hinting in long harangues that he might be persuaded to

250

make Bahrdt the recipient of his favor, his wisdom, and his financial
aid, if Bahrdt could prove himself to be worthy of such magnanimous condescension. Finally, after four to six weeks of such
visitation, one evening after dinner Basedow seemed ready to reveal to Bahrdt the great plan he had which would lead to fame
and fortune. He declaimed steadily, except to puff at his pipe,
from nine o'clock to one in the morning. At this point Bahrdt
could stand it no longer and implored him to break off for the
sake of sleep, for it had become plain that if Basedow had any
concrete idea in mind it necessarily involved such complete submission to him as to be totally impossible. This marked a turning
point of their relationship; after a few more weeks Basedow returned to Dessau without having revealed his great scheme.

Bahrdt did, however, profit from Basedow's stay, for one of the
latter's favorite topics of one-sided conversation was the unsuita-
bility of the unabridged and unaltered Bible for the general
reader. He suggested that Bahrdt prepare an abbreviated adaptation, and this idea Bahrdt seized upon: in 1780 he published a so-
called Little Bible.[2] The original purpose was to make a compilation of excerpts from the Old Testament suitable for children
and uneducated people, but the task so fascinated Bahrdt that he
finally included much more than he had originally intended. The
characteristic and important thing in the present context is, of
course, the way in which certain material was altered and omitted.
Thus, for example, the Old Testament passages which seem to
prophesy the birth of Jesus are omitted or given a more historical
explanation. The miracles are omitted. The extreme longevity of
Methuselah and other patriarchs is a matter of hearsay. The children of Israel did not pass through the Red Sea but only marched
along the shores where the water level had fallen. And so on. As for
the New Testament, Jesus is made to seem a man of the
Aufklärung, who was animated by indignation at the despicable
attempts of the priesthood to enslave reason by pretended oracles
and sacrificial worship. Jesus made it his mission to bring religious enlightenment to the world, by teaching purer conceptions
of God in order to free the human mind to pursue truth and
virtue.

Up to this time Bahrdt's inner development had consisted mainly in discarding beliefs and attitudes that he felt could not endure the acid test of rational examination. No radical synthesis had taken place. Nothing new had formed in his mind. But at this point in his life he rather unexpectedly and by chance saw various ideas and miscellaneous bits of information in vital and significant relationship to one another. By a creative act he fused the separate elements into a new conception.

Actually, Bahrdt's final confirmation in the new stage of his religious outlook was the result of embarking upon another of his schemes to popularize the rationalist view of Christianity and to earn a little money for himself.

My first idea [he writes] was merely to read through the New Testament and make the effort with the help of exegesis and logic to have some reasonable idea about every passage and to so instruct my readers.

The form which he chose to carry out this purpose was that of a series of weekly letters about the Bible in a popular vein,[3] for the intimate tone of a letter-writer seemed to him the most convenient to speculate and philosophize about the supernatural aspect of the Gospel accounts. It was, therefore, in the course of writing and publishing this weekly series that Bahrdt arrived at the final form of his new synthesis.

The elements which had entered into Bahrdt's subconscious as well as conscious mind and there caused the ferment out of which this synthesis was produced are for the most part already more or less well known to us. First, perhaps, should be mentioned the principle established by C. G. Heyne of the aesthetic interpretation of a classical text from a knowledge of the historical, cultural, and real background of that text, a further development of Ernesti's philological method. This principle, as expounded and practiced by Semler, became one of the cornerstones of modern biblical research. For Semler, understanding of the New Testament came to be absolutely dependent upon knowledge of the local and temporal conditions out of which the various texts had sprung. Then, of course, there were the truly epoch-making Fragments of Reimarus, which offered an explanation of the life and death of

Christ in terms of the mental background of the historical Jesus. Bahrdt decisively rejected Reimarus's contention that it was Jesus' purpose to establish a temporal Jewish kingdom, and the rejection forced him to come forward with his own hypothesis. Another impulse came late in his career ("I confess it to my own disgrace") in the reading of Semler's works on the canon. Bahrdt was shaken, for here he found that Semler resolved the conflict between reason and revelation by the principle that reason and ethics became the touchstones of divine authenticity, for only those portions of scripture are truly inspired that are edifying in their effect upon man. And as for Semler's refutation of Reimarus, it was based so solidly upon natural premises that Bahrdt professed to have been completely taken aback, his faith in the supernatural undermined. Bahrdt was therefore left with a Jesus who was a product of his place and time, whose seemingly miraculous deeds and talk of the supernatural must be explained by Semler's principle of prudent accommodation to the benighted mentality of his contemporaries. Or perhaps some of the supernatural elements in the Gospels were accretions due to a mythologizing process similar to that which Bahrdt at this time learned about in a book by Gedike on Greek and Roman philosophy. Here he read that a demon had appeared to Plato's father announcing the birth of this more-than-natural child and that the parents had made sacrifice on Mount Hymettus and placed a bit of honeycomb on the infant's lips so that, as tradition has it, the prophecy of Homer might be fulfilled: From his mouth speech flowed sweeter than honey.

By this chance [says Bahrdt] I came upon further traces of the miraculous, which love of the marvelous produced in the old story, and I immediately went at my Matthew from this point of view, in order to show my readers how possible it was that out of enthusiasm for Christ, this most sublime teacher of humanity, similar conditions of birth and supernatural origin had been fictitiously imputed to him also.[4]

But if the supernatural elements of the Gospel stories are attributable to a mythologizing process, and if Jesus was also the most sublime religious teacher, the question must arise: in what natural way did Jesus obtain his amazing wisdom? To this question Eberhard, as we have seen, provided the answer in his book on Socrates. In Bahrdt's words, he once had a conversation with Eberhard concerning Socrates,

about whom Eberhard spoke with such extraordinary enthusiasm that I felt it a challenge to refute the extravagant praise of this man. On this occasion I asserted that Socrates' ethical wisdom was not comparable with the system of Christian teaching. And Eberhard convinced me that Christ had not preached a single essential principle which Socrates might not also have taught. In our debate I did not give in to him . . . but when I got home, I felt the force of his assertions and felt that I was beaten. And now the main consideration which had hitherto kept me from disbelief [in revelation], namely that Christ had taught things which he could not possibly know except through revelation, vanished. I saw the plain possibility that Christ could have learned and built up his wonderful teachings from the writings of Greek sages, which Providence could have played into his hands through his association with Hellenistic Jews.

Small wonder, after this, that, as we have seen, no more was required to annihilate Bahrdt's faith in revelation than Trapp's mocking laughter.

All that was lacking to give Bahrdt's letters in a popular vein a unified purport was a central hypothesis to account for the way in which Christ and his disciples carried out their mission. This hypothesis came to Bahrdt through his chance reading of Starck's book on the ancient mysteries and contemporary Freemasonry.[5] Two-thirds of this book are devoted to a description of the Mithraic, Orphic, and Pythagorean mysteries and the last third, to Masonry, which, as the modern inheritor of the mysteries, taught monotheism and immortality of the soul and was organized through a series of initiatory ceremonies into a peripheral and central membership.

And behold, [says Bahrdt] this gave my thinking a direction. This awakened in me my own spirit of Masonry with which I had been suffused in England and fanned into flame the idea that Christ must have had the plan to establish a secret society in order to preserve and transmit to mankind the truth which had been thrust aside by clerics and temple priests.

Bahrdt was very well aware that he had passed a significant milestone in his religious progress. He now considered his earlier years a time of testing and growth and came to feel that the writings of these years contained, mixed up with many valuable truths and insights, so many concessions to an ingrained acceptance of supernaturalism, that he publicly repudiated everything he had written before his confession of faith. He declared that only the writings that followed were a true representation of his mature convictions. He had found the means to understand and explain away the supernatural elements in the New Testament and hoped that by doing so he could present the sublime founder of Christianity in a light acceptable to all honest and rational men.

My Christ was no longer to affront reason as a god and a miracle man, but neither was he, as an ambitious hypocrite, to estrange from himself the hearts of the virtuous. I resolved to guide him and his story past both reefs which were so menacing to his honor and represent him as a man who, as the most benevolent instrument of Providence, had sacrificed himself for the enlightenment and happiness of mankind, and thus to make him the object of love and veneration for all people of noble mind.

The only vestige of the supernatural in this view is the notion of Providence, which Bahrdt felt had so often directly intervened in his own life when he was unexpectedly rescued from a desperate situation. Providence, of course, worked only in natural historical and causal ways, reason was its chief instrument, and Bahrdt himself one of its agents.

I now regarded revelation as a normal and natural arrangement of Divine Providence. I looked upon Moses and Jesus, as well as Confucius, Socrates, Luther, Semler, and—myself, as instruments of Providence by means of which it works for the good of humanity according to its pleasure. I was convinced that all these and similar men had drawn solely upon the fountain of reason. And only the external circumstances under which they had lived and acted and through which they had been led to their rational certainties and the manner of propagating these certainties I regarded as the means which Providence had used to teach them these certainties and, so to speak, to force them into these modes of action.

The account of Jesus' life that resulted from the ferment just described was, as Bahrdt was well aware, a fiction, a supposition or hypothesis, which could provide a natural and consistent frame for the episodic material of the Gospels. Bahrdt was under no illusion that he had somehow divined the literally true facts of Jesus' life. He knew very well that in the dialogues in his account, for example, he was putting words into the mouths of the speakers. But he did feel that the actual events in Jesus' life, his encounters with friends and strangers, must have been of the kind which he supposed, for on no other basis could he make sense of what he read in the New Testament. The modern reader of Bahrdt, from the perspective afforded by nearly two hundred more years of biblical scholarship, is impressed by the inadequacy of Bahrdt's answers to his own questions, as well as by his naïve, although not innocent, reading of himself and the cultural presuppositions which made up his mentality into the figure of Jesus, "the greatest naturalist of them all." Bahrdt referred to his letters on the New Testament as a Christodicy. In fact they are a Bahrdtodicy, and Goethe's lines from the "Prolog zu den neuesten Offenbarungen Gottes" remain the sharpest and truest criticism of Bahrdt: "Da kam mir ein Einfall von ungefähr, So redt ich, wenn ich der Jesus wär."

But if, as we shall see, the answers to the historical and biographical questions concerning Jesus are to a modern eye more than just a bit ludicrous, the questions themselves are keen and pertinent to the subject. Indeed, they are necessary and inevitable questions if one is in quest of the historical Jesus, and the subsequent writers of lives of Christ have had to seek answers to them in their turn, whether or not they knew they were following in the footsteps of the notorious Dr. Bahrdt.

A really complete account of Jesus' boyhood [writes Bahrdt in the fourteenth of his letters in a popular vein] would necessarily be the most informative book ever written. For I assume that it would contain not merely separate anecdotes about events and actions of Jesus but that it would reveal to us in its entirety the nature of his upbringing and the gradual unfolding of his mental and spiritual powers, so that we could see very plainly how his ideas and his insights gradually arose within him: what conditions were effective in producing them, what sort of influence was exerted upon his heart and mind by schooling, example, home life, associations, reading of contemporary writings and so on; how he gradually freed himself from Jewish prejudices, how he gained his more mature insights, how his heart came to glow for the truth he had attained, and how he resolved upon the formulation and execution of his plan. In a word, I conceive of such a story of his boyhood as would answer for us all these questions: What purpose did

Jesus really have in mind in all his undertakings? What sort of plan had he developed before the so-called entrance upon his ministry, according to which he intended to realize this purpose? How did he gradually hit upon this purpose and this plan? How did he himself come to understand the divine nature of his calling? How did he gradually become convinced that God had appointed him to carry out this plan?

Nothing, maintains Bahrdt, could be of greater interest and moment to someone who truly venerates Jesus than the answers to these questions, if it is assumed that Jesus worked and suffered for men freely and out of love for them and not as the mere tool of a Godhead acting immediately and arbitrarily, a conception to which Bahrdt himself could never subscribe.

In the fifteenth letter Bahrdt begins to answer his questions by trying to demonstrate that a great many circumstances had to be conjoined in order to make Jesus' ministry possible, and the fact that these particular circumstances were thus conjoined was, of course, the work of Providence. In explanation of what he means, Bahrdt says that God could have selected no more suitable time to let the light of the Gospels shine forth upon the world than the age of Jesus. Pre-Mosaic times, for example, were the infancy of mankind, in which human reason was too feeble and the power of the senses too great to permit the purer concepts of God and his principles of morality to be comprehended. The earliest man was what Heyne had called a *homo mythicus* and therefore

in the earliest times you will find only sensuous notions of God, who was not so much intellectually conceived as he was seen and heard, approaching in the rustling of the evening wind, showing his benevolence in the rain or his wrath in the thunder.

In Mosaic times contact with heathen peoples had so favored idolatrous notions that religious enlightenment would have been still more difficult in that age. But in the age of Jesus civilization and religious history had progressed in such a way as to create a favorable social climate. The Jews had in a sense been prepared for Jesus by their messianic hope, and Oriental philosophy had pointed the way to nonsensuous religious concepts. The dispersal of the Jews had, so to speak, prepared seedbeds of the rational knowledge of God throughout the world. Moreover, the arts and sciences had come to flower among the Greeks and Romans, with Greek as a common language. In a general atmosphere of religious tolerance (or at least indifferentism) as well as universal peace in the Roman Empire, idolatry had lost ground to such an amazing degree that Lucian, Juvenal, and other writers scoffed at the fictitious gods.

Socrates especially, whose principles and vicissitudes bear an uncommon resemblance to the teachings and vicissitudes of Jesus, had already shed light upon the noblest conceptions of God and of worshipping him. His writings [*sic*] contain an almost pure although not entirely complete system of ethics. He discoursed about God, Providence, immortality of the soul, prayer and the love of mankind more truly and warmly than any sage up to that time.

And finally, the widespread immorality of the age made it natural that every man of conscience should be ready to accept the right teaching when it came.

Without these circumstances, [Bahrdt concludes] Jesus would never have become that which he became. Without them he would not only not have performed the great work of bringing bliss to the world, but he would never even have thought of it.

Bahrdt then goes on to explain his notion of how Jesus came by his remarkable knowledge and powers and devises a number of imaginary episodes from Jesus' boyhood in order to give dramatic impact and specific substance to his ideas.

In the eighteenth letter he paints for his readers a sentimental idyllic scene.

As you [dear readers] can readily imagine, the conversations of Jesus' parents were concerned most frequently with their own fortunes and prospects. So I picture these lovers on a summer evening in a shaded bower after finishing the day's work, in the company of their child enjoying the sweetness of rest.

Joseph and Mary express their gratitude that God has not forsaken them but granted them peace and happiness at last after their sojourn in Egypt. The child Jesus asks whether the new king of Judea might not be as hostile to them as his father was if he should hear of their presence in the kingdom and expresses his readiness to return to Egypt if need should be. Mary's gentle heart

flinches at the thought of her boy among the heathen, but little
Jesus consoles her with the observation that God's sun shines everywhere and that when he is a grown man he will be glad to go to
Egypt to tell them about the good dear Lord whom his parents
have taught him to love. This tender and tearful conversation is
interrupted by the approach of two beggarwomen, one Jewish
and the other Phoenician. As the parents are about to give alms
to the Jewess, the child wonders why the Phoenician woman, who
seems so kind and friendly, should not also receive from them, since
God's gifts of grain and oil are not withheld from the Phoenicians
any more than from the Jews. Joseph not only admits the force
of this observation but takes the opportunity to confirm his son in
the knowledge that God's goodness is not withheld from anyone
and that loving and aiding God's creatures makes man like unto
him.

After this a caravan from Persia stops in Nazareth outside the
home of the Holy Family. The traders ask for water for their
animals. This request is freely granted. The child Jesus watches the
proceedings with interest and sees how one of the Persians, whose
hand had been injured in a fall, is speedily helped by the application of a few drops from a vial. Jesus asks the old man with the
medicine for some of it so that he can help the Nazarenes who
receive injuries while working. The wise old man gives the boy
not only a vial of medicine but also recipes for two other medicines, one for the nerves and one which often "very quickly opens
the membrane covering the eye of a blind man, so that he learns
to see again." In the ensuing conversation the old Persian expresses an idea which noticeably affects the child:

God is everywhere, visible nowhere, but everywhere knowable, everywhere
benevolent, everywhere active through the thousandfold goodness which he
shows his people whom he loves and makes happy, all without exception.

In the twentieth letter Bahrdt advances the theory that the
young Jesus must have made more than one trip to Jerusalem, for
sojourns in that city were surely the easiest way in which Providence could perfect the knowledge of this remarkable boy. In
Jerusalem he would meet and talk with the Hellenistic Jews who

had cast aside innumerable prejudices of their Palestinian confreres.

Let us try to imagine an encounter such as would be in accord with the character of the times and the personages.

A group of Alexandrian Jews, chief among them Schalem, Selim,
and Haram, are struck by the boy's remarkable appearance and
bearing, and they engage him in a conversation, in the course of
which they learn that Jesus had once lived in Alexandria and
been permitted to listen, at the age of four and a half, to the
teachings of the old sage Nathan of Tachpanches. The child expresses wonder that the Alexandrian Jews continue to live among
the heathen, so far from the Holy Land. But the three visitors
point out that Palestine can have no monopoly on holiness, that
Alexandrian Jews are not sinful because of where they live, that
God dwells not only in the temple in Jerusalem but everywhere,
and that the priests are not in sole communication with God's
spirit, which is present wherever God's power is manifest. The
boy Jesus understands this reasoning so readily and so ardently
expresses his wish that all men might come to have the true conception of God, that Schalem and Haram feel convinced at the end
of this interview that, as they say to his father, a great fire glows
within him which may even consume him.

In the twenty-second letter Bahrdt traces still further the
progress of Jesus' religious enlightenment. Haram assures the
boy Jesus that there are many wise and virtuous people among
the heathen. One of the wisest was Socrates, who was a paragon of
virtue and a beacon of religious and philosophical enlightenment.
But, as with every productive person (Bahrdt is here alluding to
himself) there were those who envied and slandered him. False
charges were trumped up against him, but he, too lofty to humble
himself before corrupt judges and too full of longing for a better
life hereafter, took upon himself a martyr's death, pardoning his
enemies, secure in his belief in God and immortality.

Toward the conclusion of this narrative the boy's expression grows more
and more troubled. Soon tears come into his eyes, and finally he bursts
into unrestrained weeping and sobbing, so that the three friends them-

selves have no idea what is wrong with him, since they receive no answer to all their questions.

After a while it develops that the cause of this outburst is little Jesus' despair that a heathen has won the highest prize attainable by a human being, the prize upon which Jesus himself had already set his heart. The three Alexandrians console him with the prediction that he will exceed Socrates in greatness, that is, in doing good and bringing happiness to mankind. The child shows them that he already possesses some means of alleviating mankind's woes in the various elixirs given him by the Persian. To Haram this is a clear sign from Providence and he gives him another elixir, this one a specific against madness, that is, demonic possession, as well as copies of various dialogues of Socrates. With this he departs, saying as he turns away, "You will become much, much greater than Socrates. Comprehend this and become greater."

In the remaining letters in a popular vein Bahrdt goes on to describe how Jesus, together with John, studies the dialogues he has received and makes use of his various medicines to effect cures which seem miraculous—rousing people from a deathlike coma and so on. As for the other miracles, since they were impossible in Bahrdt's system, he had to invent various fictions to account for them. For example, the feeding of the five thousand was made possible by having one basket of sliced bread after the other brought out of a cave where they had previously been concealed. Jesus only seemed to be walking on the water; in reality he just balanced himself on a great cedar beam one hundred ells in length. And of course it was an easy matter for an experienced weather watcher to seem to calm the storm by merely predicting its end from infallible indications.

Between the years 1783 and 1785 Bahrdt published in Berlin a ten-volume continuation of these letters (two additional volumes appeared in 1791) entitled *Ausführung des Plans und Zweckes Jesu. In Briefen an Wahrheit suchende Leser.* As is apparent from the title, Bahrdt here attempted to answer the Fragmentist's thesis that the purpose of Jesus and his disciples was to establish a temporal mundane kingdom,

Basing his thought upon his own experiences in Freemasonry and upon Starck's book about the mysteries, Bahrdt put forward the theory that Jesus founded a secret society to aid him in his purpose to destroy superstition, eliminate all positive religion, restore reason to its rightful rule, unite people in a rational faith in God, Providence, and immortality, and thus establish universal brotherly love. The entire membership, according to the thirty-third letter, had the general designation of the Baptized, but Bahrdt professes to have learned from a comparison of various scattered passages that there were three ranks or degrees among the followers of Jesus: first, those called merely the Baptized, second, the Disciples, and, third, the Chosen.

He speaks of dwelling places of the Chosen, which he calls his Father's mansions and, on the analogy of Jewish terminology, Heaven or the Heavens. (The degree of the few Chosen apparently ceased to exist in the third century.) He speaks of a kingdom, a community, a flock, whose king, head, shepherd he is. He speaks about the goods and treasures of this kingdom and its secrets. He talks with the Disciples, the second-degree brothers, in a metaphorical language which the first-degree brothers do not understand, and his discourses with them are noticeably different in content from the discourses with the people of the lowest rank. Finally, he conducts the brothers who have the wish and the capacity to be elevated to the second degree to a certain place where they are alone with him for a few hours, but we do not discover where he was and what went on there. It is therefore undeniable that we must infer that there were arcana and a ritual of initiation in Jesus' fraternal order.

With evident relish Bahrdt then proceeds to give a hypothetical description of such a hypothetical initiation.

Two disciples of John who have been found worthy of elevation are led by Jesus and three assisting brothers to a cavern (there are many caverns in the Holy Land), where they discourse of truth and then walk on. At the end of a dark passage they stop in front of an opening in a rock wall. The opening has been closed by stones which have been laid up in such a way that all will collapse when one is removed. Jesus, seizing a hammer, strikes the stone wall and cries "Hephata!" The rocks crash to the ground with an appalling noise, the two neophytes fall to their knees in terror, for it seems to them that the whole mountain is collapsing upon them.

The assistants, however, support them, and Jesus turns to them and says,

Be not afraid. God is love, and whoever believes in this God has love and not fear, for perfect love casts out fear.

Still trembling, they get up, see at the rear of the cave before which they are now standing a bright light like the rising sun, and religious dread shakes their limbs once more. The light comes from a number of lamps of polished crystal arranged in a circle in such a way that from a distance they seem to be a single light. Then Jesus says,

Behold the light of God which shall in the future illumine the world. Whoever learns to walk in this light will find life and bliss. You do not know this as yet, because your eyes cannot endure it. What this light will sometime be to all, I will be now to you. Whoever believes in me believes in the light and will attain to the life which will teach him to walk in the light without me.

Hereupon he steps between them, takes each by the hand, and walks with them toward the light. The three assistants fall back. But now as they walk over the rocks which are lying about Jesus says,

The way to light and life is at first hard and toilsome. Well for him who surmounts the toil and perseveres unto the end.

Soon thereafter it becomes less difficult to walk, and they come to soft ground strewn with green leaves where they can move on toward the light without trouble. "Behold," says Jesus, "how the road to life becomes ever more pleasant the farther one advances." As they draw near the light, and the disciples' hearts beat higher with every step, Jesus directs their attention to the floor, which five paces away from the goal is covered with flowers that fill the air with fragrance.

Thus [he says] will be the end of the path which I am opening up to you. Lift up your eyes and look beyond the first goal [this was a small stone altar on which a weak light burned] to which I lead you. Hail to you when once you completely attain to that full light where you will no longer have need of my guidance!

With these words he lets go their hands and disappears by

stepping back through an opening in a portable black curtain
which the three assistants, unnoticed, have been carrying along
behind him. The neophytes now gaze into a brilliantly lighted
scene designed to enchant the Oriental imagination: about thirty
paces away a circle of radiance like the sun, the whole floor covered with flowers, on each side of the circle twelve men in white
robes. In the center of the circle of light in large letters is the
symbol of the fraternal order of Jesus:

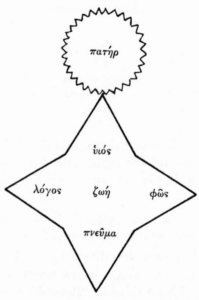

Round about the circle of light are the words which now comprise
the first five or perhaps fourteen verses of the Gospel according to
St. John. For a while the disciples are completely lost in the vision.
Finally, the curtain behind the sea of light is parted, and Jesus
steps forth and walks down the path of flowers to them. When the
twenty-four elders rise, Jesus delivers a Bahrdtian sermon on the
subject of faith and truth and the scheme of salvation. Among other
things he says that he is not such a Messiah as the populace awaits
but a Messiah who has come to free mankind from the bondage of
the priesthood and superstition. At the end of his sermon he conse-
crates the two new disciples by the ritual of bread and wine and
concludes the emotionally exhausting ceremony with a prayer.

In the tenth volume of the work on Jesus' plan and purpose Bahrdt records some "Private Thoughts of a Philosopher concerning the Death of Jesus." Beginning with the assumption that actual death and bodily resurrection could have no meaning for Jesus' real plan and purpose, *i.e.*, to found a secret ethical society, Bahrdt summarizes his views as follows:

Jesus was executed; he endured all the sufferings of a criminal, all the pangs of death, but he also survived them, he struggled through death back to life. From the burial cave in which, not dead but close to death and extremely feeble, he was kept alive and nursed by his intimates, he emerged fully restored on the third day after the execution and showed himself to his disciples as one who had just been revived. He then withdrew into the wilderness, where (I do not know for how long) he was secretly active, living in the Grand Lodge (in Heaven), that is, in the quiet circle of his intimates, and from there he directed the fraternal order and worked for his purpose, until it pleased God to call him.

Then follows a narrative in which Bahrdt reconstructs the story of the crucifixion and resurrection by harmonizing various traditional materials and supplying lengthy fictional connections and explanations. One of these is that the burial cave had a secret entrance, so that the members of the inner circle were able to nurse Jesus back to health and dislodge the stone at the regular entrance from the inside.

The Ascension is explained as follows:

Finally Jesus summoned the Disciples to the Mount of Olives near Bethany where he bade them farewell. . . . I imagine that this mountain, like all high mountains, was shrouded in clouds at the summit. On the west side I imagine a cave in which Jesus had his secret meetings with his intimates, the third-degree brothers, and which was unknown to the Disciples. In this cave must have been the Grand Lodge (if I may use this name from the present stage of the fraternity for the holy place) from which the fraternity was governed. On the east side of the mountain (which the Oriental always selected for his prayers) I imagine a beautiful terrace, where the view of a very beautiful region lifted up the glowing heart to the Creator of nature and where Jesus now gathered with his Disciples. He seated himself at the top, his friends all about him, and began to speak.

In his farewell sermon Jesus recapitulated his spiritualized and rationalized teachings about the universal God [*Allvaterlehre*] and sought to inspire the Disciples with the courage to endure their future tribulations. At the end of the sermon,

He sank to his knees and prayed so ardently to God . . . that everyone wept
aloud. . . . In this ecstasy of feeling he embraced each one, wept with him,
suddenly tore himself away and ascended the mountain. The poor people stood
there, dazed, beside themselves with grief, following him with their gaze as
long as they could. But the higher he climbed, the farther he penetrated
into the clouds which lay upon the mountain. And finally he could no longer
be seen. "The clouds removed him from their eyes." (Acts 1:9)

From this time on Jesus no longer showed himself in public but
carried on his work among the very few Chosen in the Grand
Lodge, to which St. Paul was in due time admitted to receive
direct instructions from him.

To the present-day reader these earliest answers to the abiding
questions of the biographical study of Jesus may seem shallow,
superficial, and amusingly inadequate. To multitudes of Bahrdt's
readers they were anything but that. Pastor Böhme in Frankental
was so enthusiastic about Bahrdt's weekly letters that he felt that
if only there were a mail delivery service the very angels in heaven
would subscribe. Some thought that Bahrdt had not gone far
enough in his rationalization, and others felt that these letters
were more dangerous than the anonymous Fragments. In Greifs-
wald they were made the object of critical university lectures, and
in Erlangen it was debated whether the University should not
revoke Bahrdt's doctorate. But very few, if any, of Bahrdt's contemporaries seem to have had the impulse simply to laugh him
out of court: his grasp of the vital issues was too sure and painful
for that. As for the absurdly operatic conception of Christ's mission
as a Masonic enterprise, it must not be forgotten that, as we know
from *Wilhelm Meister,* this was in accordance with the taste of
large segments of the contemporary population. Or rather, acceptance of "naturalist" ethical preachments, garbed in the robes
of human mystery and excogitated symbols, can be seen as the
compensation demanded by the imaginative faculty which had
been forbidden by reason to feed upon the supernatural. What
powerful needs and transcendent emotions are involved here it is
possible for us in some measure to understand, if, as we read about
the white-robed elders in the circle of light and the radiant figure
solemnly elevating the neophytes into a higher order of being, we

picture in our mind's eye the great temple scenes of the *Magic Flute* and hear the celestial singing of Sarastro. For the *Magic Flute* is, to be sure, the overwhelming artistic embodiment of the noblest and the best aspirations of the *Aufklärung,* as well as its joys, foibles, and frivolities.

Although Bahrdt, it need hardly be said, was no Mozart, he had great theatrical gifts and instincts. He had a strong impulse to externalize ideas which were vividly present to his mind, to unfold them in dialogue, to act them out in the pulpit, to make a production of them. He had now in his fictionalized life of Jesus hit upon the most dramatic idea of all: the great religious leader directing the faith and fate of multitudes through a secret organization. What a role for Dr. Bahrdt! And what a fine opportunity to pick up a little cash while enlightening the world. The house was full, the stage was set: On with the play! It was called "Die deutsche Union."

XXV

{MYSTERIOUS DOINGS}

THE IDEA OF producing his fictional account of Jesus' mission Bahrdt seems to have owed to an attack of gout. During a sleepless night in 1784 or 1785, spurred on by the twinges of an aching toe, he conceived the scheme to make himself the producer, manager, director, and star of an "enlightened" mystery play of his own devising. Best of all, the Bahrdt mystery would be just as closely interwoven with the cultural life of his time as the medieval mysteries were with theirs, for Bahrdt saw no limit to the possibilities of his scheme and actually hoped to supply his age and countrymen with all the religious and intellectual nourishment they could digest. Two or three years were to pass, however, before all circumstances seemed just right to permit him to begin to realize his personal messianic hope.

We are already familiar with some of the activities and controversies that at first prevented Bahrdt from doing much more than broaching the subject of the "Deutsche Union" to a few intimates, but a brief account of two additional matters which concerned Bahrdt at this time will help to round out the picture of him which we are trying to achieve.

The one had to do with Johann Melchior Götze, the indomitable champion of orthodoxy. When news came to Bahrdt that Götze had died on the nineteenth of May 1786, it seemed to him like an irresistible opportunity to let fly with a few satirical barbs against his enemies. The result was a mock funeral oration supposedly delivered at Götze's bier by Canon Ziegra, Götze's old companion-in-arms.[1] Since Ziegra had died in 1778 the satiric intent was announced in the title. In the oration which is put in Ziegra's mouth

Götze's sorrows and joys are described, the former caused by the spread of Enlightenment and the latter, to a large extent, by the misfortunes of Dr. Bahrdt, the thought of which brought solace to his last hours. Götze's last act was to call for a copy of Lessing's *Nathan der Weise* and with his remaining strength to fling it into the flames. Bahrdt writes about this satire that he did not regard it as a defamation of Götze, for Götze's sentiments and actions were actually as Bahrdt represented them but that it was designed to expose the orthodox party to ridicule. In his autobiography Bahrdt explains that he felt that Götze was in his way a truly learned man, one who was in many aspects of his character worthy of esteem. Even his seemingly malicious attack upon himself Bahrdt attributed to Götze's honestly mistaken judgment and not his heart. However that might have been, of course, Götze's friends and Bahrdt's enemies did not forgive him, and very speedily he had the doubtful pleasure of being able to read a "Funeral Oration Delivered at the Bier of the Late and Learned Doctor Bahrdt." [2]

The second affair with which we are here concerned is one in which Bahrdt became, for once, innocently involved.

Bahrdt's failure to make his position at the University of Halle completely secure undoubtedly caused him real concern, a concern which was augmented by the realization that it would not be too much longer before Prussian lands would be ruled by a new and very different sort of king. It therefore probably seemed prudent to Bahrdt to develop new possibilities of earning a living. He was, to be sure, doing pretty well with his pen, but, as can be imagined, the work was arduous in the extreme, his health was suffering from it, and it did not provide him with the security he needed. It may have been because of such considerations that he began to study medicine privately and had the half-formed purpose to take the medical degree at Jena. He did not carry out this purpose because he felt it due his dignity as a scholar that he be allowed to be examined for his degree privately by each of the professors concerned. The medical men would not agree to this, and so Bahrdt never did become a double doctor. But his interest in medicine was, of course, widely known and caused him to be suspected of being the author of a satirical pamphlet attacking Professor C. G. Gruner.

Gruner, professor of medicine at Jena, had made himself unpopular by his hotheadedness and his eccentricities. Among the latter was reckoned his marriage to a servant girl. Besides, he had given offense to a good many colleagues in his profession by the publication of an "Almanac for Physicians and Non-Physicians," which was anything but flattering in its appraisal of their competence. Among the numerous counterattacks upon Gruner one particularly aroused his wrath. It bore the long title "What Must a Professor of Medicine Do to Become Famous in a Short Time with Little Knowledge of Language and Literature and without Real Work and to Pass as a Competent Authority in Matters which he Understands Either Not at All or Only Superficially? A Prize Essay which Will Presumably be Awarded Neither a Gold Nor a Silver Medal. Submissively Dedicated to Court Councillor C. G. Gruner in Jena by Clemens Blasius." This appeared in 1786. The following year Gruner lashed out at Bahrdt, whom he believed to be the author, in an "Epilogue to Dr. Bahrdt" in his Almanac. He accused Bahrdt of having betrayed God, Christ, religion, virtue, and true honor, and of having defamed Pastor Götze after the latter's death. But Bahrdt declared upon oath that he was not Clemens Blasius, but that he had learned that the real Blasius was a certain *Bergrat* Müller in Halle. Thus the affair was settled: Gruner publicly proclaimed that Bahrdt was an honorable man and proceeded to lambaste Müller in a fresh publication.

Bahrdt was apparently so preoccupied with these concerns and other multifarious projects and activities with which we are already familiar that he had little time to devote to his newly conceived German Union. Besides, as long as Frederick the Great was living there was no need of a secret society for the preservation and transmission of the ideas and ideals of religious enlightenment. But on August 17, 1786, the great King died and was succeeded by his nephew Frederick William II, in whose book *Aufklärung* was a bad word. It was the old King's will to be buried in the garden of Sans Souci not far from his dogs. Instead, by command of the new King he was laid to rest in, of all places repugnant to

him, a church. Thus did Frederick William symbolize the spirit
of his reign.

Frederick William II was by nature and conviction in almost
all respects, save love of music, the opposite of his illustrious
uncle: large in stature, small in mind; personally licentious, officially devout; amiable in manner, weak of will, gullible, super-
stitious, pliable in the hands of a group of intimates who had
gained nearly unlimited sway over him, and through him, the
nation. It is not surprising that twenty years after he came to the
throne there was no Prussian power to resist the expansion of
Germany's neighbor to the west.

The story of the intrigue surrounding Frederick William is no
less sensational and operatic than Dr. Bahrdt's scheme for the
salvation of humanity and is a kind of actualized parallel to it. A
secret society, mysterious rituals, synthetic manifestations of the
supernatural, a long course of ethical and practical indoctrination,
all controlled by a mastermind bent upon carrying out certain
purposes—the basic elements are essentially the same. The difference lay in the hope cherished by some of the members that the
German Union would keep the spirit of the Enlightenment alive
during the benighted reign of Frederick William.

The mummery which threatened to put out the light of reason
in Prussia seems to have begun in an encampment where the forces
led by the then Prince Frederick William were recuperating from
the summer campaign of 1778 in Bohemia (during the War of
the Bavarian Succession). One day as the Prince was sitting in
his tent he felt himself touched by an invisible hand and heard a
voice pronounce the one word "Jesus." To the Prince it seemed as
though the Savior had actually thus introduced himself, but to
warier minds the more attractive hypothesis is that one of the
Prince's recent acquaintances, a Colonel J. R. von Bischoffwerder
(or Bischofswerder), having discovered the Prince's inclination to
mysticism and superstition, had resolved to exploit this trait. What
is certain is that after the experience in the tent the Prince was a
changed man, and from then on he was subject to supernatural
visitations wherever he went and was accompanied by Bischoffwerder.

Bischoffwerder soon managed another introduction, completely natural this time, even though fateful: he presented to the Prince his friend Johann Christoph Woellner and thereby substantially affected the lives of multitudes, including Dr. Bahrdt, who went to prison because of it.

Woellner (1732–1800), the son of a clergyman, had at the age of twenty-two been ordained and had accepted a call to the rustic pulpit of Gross-Behnitz, which was under the patronage of General Count von Itzenplitz, who engaged Woellner as a tutor for his children. Woellner so distinguished himself in the performance of his duties that when the General soon afterwards died, the Dowager Countess Charlotte Sophie came to rely more and more upon him for advice, not only in spiritual but also in secular matters and before long turned over to him the management of her estates. Woellner resigned his pulpit in favor of his father and plunged wholeheartedly and with great success into the practice and theory of agronomy. He wrote several books on management of land and rural economy, and for a number of years he was nearly the sole reviewer of books on agriculture for the *Allgemeine deutsche Bibliothek*. He was, in other words, a proponent of "enlightened" ideas as they applied to farm life. On January 14, 1766, he took a momentous step: he married his former pupil, the young Countess Amalie von Itzenplitz. In doing this he had the full approval of his bride's mother and brother but not of her other kinsmen, who informed King Frederick of what was afoot. The King, fearing that Woellner might be forcing the misalliance through some sinister influence, dispatched an official to prevent the marriage by placing the young Countess in protective custody. The official arrived twenty-four hours late, however, and the King was able to do no more than (quite arbitrarily) sequester Frau Woellner's inheritance. This in spite of the fact that an investigation revealed nothing to Woellner's discredit. As long as he lived the King did not lose his distrust of Woellner: when some time later an Itzenplitz connection sponsored Woellner's petition for ennoblement, Frederick rejected the request with the comment, "Woellner is a deceitful and intriguing parson." ("Der Woellner ist ein betriegerischer und Intriganter Pfafe.") Even some ten years later in 1777, when efforts were made to restore full legal rights to Frau Woellner and her mother, the King would not hear of it but insisted that the women who had voluntarily agreed to such a mismatch must be feebleminded and incompetent to manage a fortune. That Woellner found in his heart no love and admiration for the King goes without saying.

About the same time that Woellner was contemplating marriage (1765) he took another fateful step: he joined the Freemasons, becoming a member of the Lodge of the Three Spheres which stood for a moderate degree of enlightenment. Driven by a great passion to penetrate deeper into the mysteries of the Order, he rose from rank to rank and soon became the deputy of the Grand Master. But he then found that the Masons had no arcana that could appease his craving for mystic knowledge, and on January 12, 1779, he resigned from the Order. He had become acquainted with Colonel von Bischoffwerder and learned from him about the possibilities offered by an organization that specialized in esoteric lore, the Rosicrucians, who were blooming anew under the sun of Duke Frederick August of Brunswick. Woellner bloomed also: with the duke's blessing he established in Berlin, where he was now employed by Prince Heinrich, the King's brother, the lodge called Frederick of the Golden Lion, which Bischoffwerder joined when he took up residence there. The two conspirators were now ready to proceed with their plot to educate a future King.

It took some little time after Frederick William's great spiritual awakening in the tent to prepare him and make him worthy of initiation into the Order of the Rosicrucians. But finally a day, the eighth of August 1781, was appointed for the ceremony. In the presence of his three mystic brothers, Rufus (Duke Frederick), Farferus (Bischoffwerder), and Heliconus, or, as he was sometimes called, Chrysophiron (Woellner), the Prince shed the old Adam and put on the new, called Ormesus. He also listened to two long addresses mixed with prayers in which he was reminded of the signal mark of divine favor which he had received in the tent, and the solemn necessity of remaining loyal to the Order, the chosen instrument of God's purpose, was impressed upon him. It was further revealed that the Prince was to benefit by the especial attention and prayerful intercession of one of the wisest and holiest members of the Order, whose counsel was in effect the counsel of the Lord. Thus did the wise and holy man (Woellner) prepare for the course of lectures that he was planning for his royal protégé. He also took the precaution of providing the Prince with these addresses in black and white to be taken home for further reference. (Frederick William did take them home and preserved them until the day of his death.) A little later he augmented their number by two additional documents, both by the same wise and holy Heliconus or Chrysophiron, which he received on the occasion of his initiation into higher mysteries. The second two documents came to grips with the practical problems that would confront the Prince upon coming to power, encouraged him to believe that his decisions would be inspired by divine wisdom, and adjured him to re-establish in his realm the oldfashioned religious faith of his grandfather Frederick William I.

Having thus gotten the Prince into their hands, Bischoffwerder and Woellner proceeded with the brainwashing. To the former fell the task of managing apparitions and keeping open the lines of communication with the spirit-world. He seemed to find it quite easy to establish contact with one or the other of the many ghostly guardians who were ever hovering about, eager to bring a message from the Holy Spirit. And the Prince himself became able to hear their voices when the wind whistled in the chimney or the furniture snapped and cracked. To Woellner fell the task of tutoring the Prince (a man of about forty) in the various branches of knowledge of which he would have need as king. Of especial importance was the subject of religion. Woellner explained to Frederick William that religious tolerance of the "enlightened" sort led to lack of faith and indifference towards the sacred institution of the family and parenthood. In order to save his country from demoralization and depopulation, the future King would have to replace "enlightened" officials such as Zedlitz by men of the opposite persuasion, which meant in this case by Woellner himself, and he would have to present to his people the spectacle of a sovereign who was the very model of churchly deportment. (Frederick William's personal morality will receive some mention later in another connection.) But religion was not the only subject in which the Prince received instruction: in the course of three years Woellner lectured to him on forestry, population policy, finances and taxation, serfdom, and other pertinent matters. The new King's head was to be completely filled with Woellner's ideas.

Naturally, these activities could not be kept secret, and the "enlightened" circles in Berlin and throughout Prussian lands viewed the approaching transfer of power with apprehension. Frederick was urged by some to transform Prussia into a kind of republic with a hereditary presidency. It was, therefore, not such a farfetched idea to think of establishing an underground of the *Aufklärung* to preserve the spirit of independent thinking for a more auspicious future. Apprehensive watchfulness increased when the old King died, and Woellner was ennobled sixteen days later, after he had already (August 26, 1786) been given the office of *Oberfinanzrat*. He did not become Minister of Finance as he wished, but he did receive various other dignities to appease him while he plotted the downfall of Zedlitz, which he encompassed slowly but surely, maneuvering his way into Zedlitz's post by July 3, 1788. Zedlitz, powerless to act, found himself in the unrelenting coils of his enemy, who proceeded to dismember and devour him with deliberate speed. Dr. Bahrdt, estimating his chances of survival in the altered academic atmosphere as poor, took a bold and dramatic step: in July 1787, he resigned his lectureship at the University and bought a tavern with a vineyard a comfortable distance away from Halle. Here he settled down with his family to commence a mode of living that would permit him the free exercise of his scholarly, culinary, literary, and social gifts.

Now that he had an extensive establishment and was relieved of his academic obligations—his public ministry—Bahrdt saw the possibility of simulating an ascension such as he had described in his book on the plan and purpose of Jesus: he would retreat into Heaven or the Grand Lodge of the German Union in the tavern on the summit of his own vine-clad slopes. None but the Chosen Few should know who toiled there for the salvation through enlightenment of the multitudes still in darkness.

Bahrdt began his operations by sending out a message to

"Friends of Reason, Truth, and Virtue" [3] in which he disclosed that a group of Twenty-two had been formed a year and a half earlier and had devised a plan to accomplish two things. First, they wished to promote the enlightenment and education of mankind and gradually to destroy everything that had stood in the way. Second, they had in mind to establish a "benevolent institution," which would bring the most secure and agreeable situation within the reach of every deserving man. All those interested were invited to send their names and addresses to the persons from whom they had received the communication. There were seven men of professional standing to whom prospective members could write, the most notable of whom was a certain Inspector Müller in Calbe, who was Bahrdt's right-hand man in this venture.

The response to this invitation seems to modern eyes simply astounding, but it is evident that very many responsible men of the time shared the sentiments expressed in a letter from one Schumann in Hirschberg, who wrote:

The more the atmospheric indications in this part of the world seem to signify a fog which might perhaps not completely blot out the dawn of enlightenment but might at least impede and delay its breaking through to daylight, the more delighted I was by the hint of a hope for something better which came to me through news of your plan. . . .

And Professor Johann Gottfried Eichhorn, who opened up the Bible to mythological research, wrote:

Your communication, Noble Friends of the Good and of Enlightenment surprised me very agreeably, since, convinced by history that there is no sovereign help against the enemies of human welfare other than the one proposed by you, I have for a considerable time been occupying myself with a similar idea. I therefore extend to you the hand of brotherhood.

To the very considerable number of people who had expressed interest in the purpose of the Twenty-two and who promised to maintain silence concerning it there was now sent a "Preliminary Plan of the German Union." In this it was stated that the primary purpose of the Union was to work for the welfare of humanity, which is furthered by "true enlightenment and by the dethronement of fanaticism and moral despotism." In order to achieve this purpose the following principal means were to be used.

(1) "The Union has a secret plan of operation which will make it possible to bring the book trade into its sphere of action, and to this end, in order not to injure established book dealers, it will endeavor to gain them for its purposes. By winning over the book trade it will gain the possibility of multiplying the number of writings in favor of enlightenment and diminishing the number of those opposed, since the authors of the latter will gradually lose their publishers and readers." (2) The Union was to publish a literary-political magazine which, through its extraordinary excellence and the influence of the members of the Union, was intended to supplant all similar journals and thus gain an enormous influence upon the reading public. (3) By means of reading clubs the Union was to create the taste and demand for literature of the enlightened variety exclusively. (4) The Union was to establish a system of rapid communication among its members, so that each one would be kept informed at all times of how the campaign was progressing.

The preliminary plan had the desired effect: more and more people signified their interest in the Union, among them a few book dealers, including Georg Philipp Wucherer in Vienna, who alone recruited 111 new members, and Degenhardt Pott, who was first a partner and then the owner of a book business (Walther) in Leipzig. Neither of these firms was particularly distinguished or successful, hence the temptation offered by the monopolistic arrangement of the Union. A few more book dealers joined for the same reason, but the bulk of the membership was constituted by professors, jurists, physicians, and clergymen, many of them such as August Ludwig Schlözer, author of a long series of letters on historical and political conditions at home and abroad, and Baron Adolf von Knigge, the German Emily Post, men of considerable reputation. And then, of course, there were the mere associates in the reading circles which boasted up to 180 participants in just one town, and there were many such groups throughout German-speaking lands. It is therefore easy to understand that there was a great deal of excited speculation about the identity of the Twenty-two and the real nature of the Union. Some suspected that it was a recrudescence of the Illuminati, a similar society which had been established by Professor Adam Weishaupt of Ingolstadt as a counterforce to the Jesuits. The Illuminati had been suppressed through the efforts of the Jesuits, who represented them to Elector Karl Theodor of Bavaria as a threat to his reign and person. Therefore it was natural that those who suspected Bahrdt of having a hand in the business also thought that behind Bahrdt was the figure of Weishaupt. Others suspected Knigge, a former member of the Illuminati, of reviving the society for his own purposes.

Bahrdt, realizing that both of these presumptions, if widely accepted, would be damaging to the cause, persuaded a certain *Oberamtmann* Bartels to sign and send out to the members of the Union a statement to the effect that the Twenty-two had entrusted him with the post of executive secretary. Furthermore, they had commissioned him, he wrote, to propose to all associates of the Union to give it the form of a free republic composed of dioceses, each one headed by an elected diocesan who would transact all business and keep in touch with the center in Halle. The proposition won approval, dioceses were formed, and the correspondence was channeled through an office in the tavern where Bahrdt retained a secretary named Röper to help him manage the affairs of the Union. Bahrdt, working behind the scenes, now prepared and submitted for approval a new plan of organization, this one called "Geheimer Plan der Deutschen Union zur gemeinsamen Berathung für Diöcesane und Vorsteher." The preamble described the Union as an unobtrusive association of readers and writers, the ultimate purpose of which was to remain a secret from the brothers of the lowest degree. After some other generalizations the document proceeded to a more detailed discussion of the membership and functions of the Union. There were three degrees of membership: aldermen, men, and youths, the aldermen being, of course, the oldest, the most distinguished, and the most privileged group, from among whom the officials were democratically selected. All members were obliged to subscribe to the official magazine or *Intelligenzblatt,* to promote the sale of all books which contribute to the spread of enlightenment, and to publish their own books through the Union, provided it was to their advantage to do so. In connection with the reading circles, provision was to be made for Union libraries—Bahrdt estimates that their number would soon reach 400—which of course had an obligation to buy books written by the aldermen. A special section of this proposal is devoted to the *Intelligenzblatt,* published three times a week, original in regard to style and quality of contents, and the "most respectable newspaper in the world." In addition to extracts from the writings of the aldermen, whose books were above criticism, to critical reviews of books by men and youths and by foreign authors, to various notices and brief anecdotes, the magazine was to contain

political news from all parts of the world, for which the office of the central archives must maintain such an extensive correspondence that no other newspaper can be found so complete, so up-to-date, and so entertaining. But we will never show bias.

It was also foreseen that the Union would perform benevolent and philanthropic functions by helping to support the ill and aged and also by subvening the production of books, musical compositions, scholarly work of all kinds, scientific, commercial, and military achievements, and so on without end. Finally, Bahrdt proposed a whole series of distinctions and awards for men of merit culminating in a statue to be erected in the portico of the Union building. In conclusion he wrote:

What an important influence for the welfare of humanity! That an abundance of joys will come to you, men of the Union, from bringing recognition to the deserving and from providing for so many a valuable person, to say nothing of the certain hope of receiving support and aid in old age and misfortune. Advantages to mankind are the rise of the sciences, general interest in arts and literature, tolerance, freedom, diminution of scribbling, training of children, hospitality, saving of many an unfortunate, more brotherly concord of scholars, general promotion of love, and finally, perhaps . . . Amen!

The vista from Bahrdt's tavern was truly unlimited.

And now that the Union had been organized, and the machinery described had begun to function, Bahrdt sent out a new communication to the diocesans. It was entitled "Most Secret Plan of Operations, which the diocesans must for the time being keep to themselves and must not divulge even orally." Recognizing that the multitude needs mystification and symbolistic ritual to occupy the imagination, but maintaining that the elect can stand the pure light of reason, Bahrdt proposes to the diocesans to incorporate the Union into the Masonic Order and to make use of Masonic rites. He describes the ritual he wishes to see used:

(1) On the wall behind the Master J. H. S. in the most beautiful radiance produced by small lighted lamps. (2) Before the Master a table with a skull on it, out of which roses or other flowers bloom as a symbol of immortality. (3) Before the skull, wine and a plate of bread. It is the very ancient ritual.

Bahrdt probably hoped to achieve two results from this move: one was to give greater permanence to the society which he had called into being, and the other, to gain actual control of the Masonic Order through massive infiltration.

For a while the prospects of the German Union seemed fairly good. We have seen that the idea aroused much interest, that the membership grew, that the administrative organization functioned, and that the reading circles were formed. There was even some independent publication and printing business which was given to the publisher, Wucherer, as a just reward for his zeal in carrying forward the work in the German-speaking South and East. Most important of these publications was one by Bahrdt on enlightenment and the means of promoting it.[4] Although it was to a large extent a recapitulation of Bahrdt's earlier *System der moralischen Religion* (Berlin, 1787) it went through several printings very speedily, probably because it was a succinct definition of enlightenment similar to the now more famous one of Immanuel Kant.[5]

"What is enlightenment?" asks Bahrdt, "an enlightened man? enlightened times?" And he replies that it is not a matter of the magnitude of intellect any more than it is of the mass of information. What is essential to enlightenment is that a person learn to think for himself, have clear concepts of his own about things which he has selected in the world of the senses, which he has abstracted, compared, developed, tested. He must know the sources and criteria of truth and have made independent use of them so that he can pass judgment on the true, the untrue, the good, and the bad, on the basis of his own principles or experience.

It is necessary that he have thought through and tested the grounds of the truth he accepts, that everywhere he have seen with his own eyes, not been misled by appearances, have formed no belief or judgment on the basis of desire, of inclination or disinclination. He must not have blindly followed any authority, but before assenting to a belief, made an examination with his own plain common sense, and thus have seen truth in the light of God, in the light of reason, in brief, have striven for the most perfect knowledge and the highest degree of certainty possible. It is essential to the conception of enlightenment that it be the common possession of all men, and whoever honestly pursues the truth is a freethinker in the noblest sense of the word. His reason has been set free; he is an enlightened human being.

The German Union, however, like all Bahrdt's great projects, failed, perhaps largely because Bahrdt was unable to take any realistic account of the practical and human factors involved in realizing his plans. With his quick and superficial grasp of things, like a child he imagined himself at his goal before he had taken more than two consecutive steps in the right direction, and the obstacles, the hard facts, did not enter into his calculations. Baron von Knigge, in his reply to the invitation to become associated with the Twenty-two, writing out of his experience with the Illuminati, remarked upon the absolute necessity of making sure of the reliability and trustworthiness of every candidate for membership in the association, and in a later letter he expressed his consternation at the loose and incautious procedure. Just by chance at a friend's home he had heard the words "German Union" and "The Twenty-two," and when, pretending ignorance, he made further inquiries, to his great dismay he found that a matter which he had treated as a holy secret was here discussed aloud in irresponsible terms *inter pocula et coram mulieribus.* Knigge therefore urgently requested the Twenty-two never to mention that he was associated with them, for, he said, giving force to his request, his well-known earlier association with the Illuminati could only damage the cause of the Union. He then went on to point out that it would be impossible to gag the opposition, that truth can be brought to light only by free discussion, that Masonry was losing its hold on the imagination and its influence on public affairs, and that the book dealers would never abandon the profitable status quo and submit to the dictates of the Union. Nonetheless Knigge expressed his continued interest in an association of friends of enlightenment who would assist and support each other in the contest with obscurantism.

How right Knigge was about the book dealers soon became evident with the publication of something called "More Notes than Text." [6] *Geheimrat* Bode in Weimar had turned over to Göschen the publisher some documents issued by the Twenty-two. Göschen printed them together with a mass of biting commentary in the footnotes. Shortly afterward there followed the publication of a further inquiry into the German Union by Johann Gottlob Schulz.[7] Schulz had become acquainted with Bahrdt's confidential secretary Röper, who betrayed his employer by turning over to Schulz confidential documents, coded messages, and lists of members. When it was thus established that Bahrdt was the moving spirit of the organization, the whole thing blew up. Knigge, for example, with a fine disregard for the truth, denied that he had ever been associated with the Union, and others such as Bartels publicly announced their withdrawal. Only the sense of amazement was left that an association had really existed to capture the book business. Bahrdt probably gained nothing from the venture except greater notoriety; he always maintained that it had cost him a thousand *Taler*.

But all the while that Dr. Bahrdt, with varying success, and ultimate failure, was staging his great religious mystery play, another actor-manager, playing to his limited royal audience, was having considerable success. On the third of July 1788, Woellner was appointed Minister of State and Chief of the Ecclesiastical Department, with direct responsibility for all Lutheran church and school affairs. Six days later, on the ninth of July, was promulgated the notorious Edict on Religion. The Scribes and Pharisees were in control.

XXVI

⊰ PUBLICAN AND SINNER ⊱

M AKING THE world safe for the Enlightenment was, of course,
not the only matter that engaged Dr. Bahrdt's attention during these years: on one side of a certain door in his establishment
he was the man whom nobody knew, providing spiritual nourishment for all his people; when he stepped through the door he became the man whom everybody knew, owner of a public house,
purveyor of food and drink to paying guests.

He says himself, and there seems little reason to doubt this,
that the resolution to set himself up as a tavernkeeper was largely the result of the chance discovery that a maid in his employ, who
had already demonstrated her skill in domestic duties, had at
one time worked in a large country inn, milking cows, making
butter and cheese, drawing beer and wine, waiting on table, in
short, performing all the tasks that go with such an establishment.
And since Bahrdt himself had had practical experience along
similar lines, he suddenly saw the possibility of making himself
independent. So much is probably true. The rest of the story as
Bahrdt tells it is probably a mixture of fact and fiction, and it is
certainly an attempt at self-justification which cannot be accepted
at face value. Nonetheless, what Bahrdt says about the tensions that
developed between himself and his wife has a certain authentic
ring and is consistent with what is reported about Frau Bahrdt in
Schlichtegroll's *Nekrolog. Nachträge und Berichtigungen 1790,
1791, 1792, 1793,* which contains the most balanced contemporary
estimate of Bahrdt himself. Schlichtegroll says:

All who knew this woman are unanimous in their testimony that she was
an extremely bitter [*grämlich*], jealous, and vain creature, demanding and

moody, who had no idea of how to manage a household properly or to bring up her children well or to make her husband happy by her intellect, heart, and cheerful disposition. She greatly prided herself upon the unshakable devotion with which she clung to her husband. . . . Although this irresponsible man was much more unfaithful to his wife than she suspected, nevertheless, up to the last period of his life he had affection for her in his own way, treated her with courtesy, forebearance, and patience, and took her follies philosophically.

With this last point even Frau Bahrdt's brother, Pastor Georg Gottfried Volland, agrees in the book [1] which he wrote to vindicate his sister's honor. It was only after the purchase of the tavern and vineyard that Bahrdt ceased to be an affectionate and agreeable husband.

To a reader of Bahrdt's autobiography this statement of Volland seems to be somewhat exaggerated, for it is abundantly clear that Frau Bahrdt tried her husband's patience on many occasions before the purchase of the tavern. But it seems also clear that until this time Bahrdt felt somehow detached from his wife; his marriage was one of those things in his life we have mentioned earlier which somehow did not touch the center of his being. In an odd and thoroughly irresponsible way he felt that they did not count. Therefore he could put up with idiosyncrasies of his wife that would have completely alienated a man to whom marriage was not a peripheral affair. He could even feel contempt for the silly woman who would disport herself with him in the pond in Heidesheim, but he was not deeply affected by such a feeling. He merely withdrew himself from her society more and more, burying himself in his study, immersed in his countless schemes and plans.

Frau Bahrdt, of course, was offended by her husband's growing indifference. As Bahrdt tells it, she was hurt by their having so little to do with each other and deeply wounded by every expression of displeasure or mere indifference which she detected upon his face.

She had an ideal of love and enjoyment which, partly because of my industrious mode of life and partly because of her own incapacity, could not be realized. She wanted me to be about her constantly, constantly wearing a pleasant and affectionate expression. When she would often enter my study and interrupt my work twenty times a morning and for the sake of the most trifling things—if she had bought a fine piece of meat I had to look at, if she scolded the children and I was supposed to whip them, if the maid was impertinent and I had to correct her, if she was uncertain about how to prepare a certain sauce and I was supposed to tell her how I would like it—and when I then became angry because my train of thought had been broken off so inopportunely, then the idea took fresh hold of her each time that her husband did not love her any more, and with tearful eyes she returned to her children, whom she now made to suffer for her bad mood by constant nagging and scolding.

Usually there was not a single sound of happiness in my house from morning until evening. Every lost key, misplaced ribbon or similar trifle caused hour-long screaming and quarreling with the maid or the children, and every time it was later discovered that she had lost or misplaced the article herself. And such quarreling, which, because of her sharp and penetrating voice, often caused the people in the street to stand still, alternated with the quiet sighing and complaining which she poured out over me.

Love is no more an act of human free will than faith. It was therefore not in my power to fulfill her expectation. Everything I did and was able to do was no longer love but kindness, which owed its origin to reflection and its continuance to discretion. I valued her good heart, but I could not prevent her everlasting self-pity from having its effect upon me. As a matter of fact, the burden which her ill humor put upon me was made the heavier, more painful and unendurable, the more impetuously she seemed to insist upon my love and forced the ardor of her own love upon me. And my never-ending work, but especially my noticeably declining vigor and health, increased the impossibility of being the affectionate husband she wished.

At this point Bahrdt tells an anecdote about a violent quarrel with his brother-in-law which affected him so profoundly that his health was undermined and his digestion so badly impaired that from the years 1786 to 1790 he had to resort to enemas. He goes on:

From now on I myself became extremely hypochrondriac (although the malady was only in my body, and my mind never lost its naturally cheerful bent) and thereby, through no fault of mine, multiplied the number of instances that gave my wife occasion to conclude from my cold or irritated behavior that I no longer loved her and—the only thing for which she can be criticized—to complain about it to outsiders.

To this was added a circumstance that had even more serious consequences. My delicate health and—even more effectively—certain changes in my wife's physical condition which now occurred rendered impossible that which is natural to the married state and from which had sprung eight children already born by my wife. Now lamentation was really everlasting. Everywhere the old song of mourning was heard: "My husband does not love me any longer." So even if it had been in my power to love her, I would inevitably have ceased at this time for being so tormented.

Probably no one suspected in the fall of 1786 when Frau Bahrdt hired a new maid that this was the first step leading to a decisive change in her husband's feelings towards her. Christine (this was the maid's name) was not only an excellent cook who took pains to prepare Dr. Bahrdt's food well, but she seemed possessed of all the desirable qualities which Frau Bahrdt needed in a servant. For a time mistress and maid worked together in concord, but then the nagging temperament of the former led to Christine's giving notice of her intent to seek other employment. But Frau Bahrdt, fearing that her husband would be vexed at the loss of such a good cook, had a change of heart and succeeded in persuading Christine to remain in the household. The former confidence and intimacy returned: "My wife and Christine were a single heart and soul." If Bahrdt's account is reliable, Christine became so much a part of the household that during the winter she spent the evenings in the same room with the family in order to save fuel, and thus it was that Bahrdt learned that she had had much practical experience in managing a country inn. Once more it was possible for Dr. Bahrdt to feel that Providence was taking a hand in the disposition of his affairs; he bought the tavern and vineyard, severed his connection with the University, and moved with his family and Christine into the enlarged and re-modeled inn.

Bahrdt allowed his wife and children to have nothing to do with the tavern itself. The family lived in a separate wing, and Frau Bahrdt's only duties concerned the upbringing of the three daughters and the supervision of the household laundry and linen supply. Everything else, business management and financial accounts, supervision of cellar, kitchen, and livestock, and entertainment of guests, was the exclusive concern of Dr. Bahrdt himself and of Christine. Whether Frau Bahrdt ever agreed to this arrangement, as Bahrdt says she did at first, is uncertain. What is certain, however, is that she soon tried to terminate it. Bahrdt maintains that certain meddlesome people who had profited from Frau Bahrdt's poor management of the household in Halle began whis-

pering to her how degrading it was that she did not have charge of
things. They asserted that Christine could naturally not be trusted
either with money or with Dr. Bahrdt. In the first respect they
were probably wrong, but in the second, they were surely right,
for Christine did become Dr. Bahrdt's mistress and the only woman
to whom he ever felt a deep and abiding attachment. What a fine
ironic twist of fate that in the very last years of his life the inveter-
ate *bon amant*, who had always seemingly felt that he was in some
way exempted from moral obligations toward others and that his
betrayal of a person who loved him did not count—perhaps because he could not really believe in the possibility that he or anyone else could be totally committed to anything—should now com-
mit himself totally, irrevocably, and without regard for self-interest,
to this one woman.

When Frau Bahrdt insisted, for excellent reasons, that Christine
be dismissed, Dr. Bahrdt pointed out that Christine was absolutely indispensable to the management of the place. This consideration made, of course, no impression upon Frau Bahrdt, who now
complained of the situation to all who would listen, apparently on
the theory that she could shame her husband into doing as she
wished.

I did everything [says Bahrdt] to calm her heart, which really did seem to
love me, although it had gone astray to my disgrace and the ruin of my children. I pictured to her the comfortable situation in which I had put her. I
showed her the impossibility of maintaining my establishment without such
a person. I asked her to consider what dishonor her wailing brought upon
herself and our whole family.

It was all in vain: Frau Bahrdt continued to pour out her complaints to all and sundry, and her husband absolutely refused to
yield an inch.

There is, of course, no denying the egotism of the passages
quoted above from Bahrdt's autobiography or the transparent
attempt at self-justification through suppressing everything that
would be injurious to his own story. By the time he wrote this the
estrangement and bitterness had grown so great that he simply
could not live in the atmosphere of the silly woman who insisted
upon recalling him to her embraces. The fine philosophical de-

tachment of earlier days had gone: he could no more surrender to
the demands of his wife than he could to the demands of Benner,
Götze, or the Imperial Aulic Council. Marriage was no longer
peripheral, and the point had been reached when he had to say
No regardless of what it might cost him, and from then on each
contestant was determined to force the other to knuckle under,
and each one resorted to whatever weapons were ready to hand to
wound and injure and subdue the other. There is no denying,
either, that Bahrdt was both ruthless and shameless in the use he
made of the weapons available to him. If his wife rehearsed her
grievances by word of mouth and pen to every willing ear and
eye, he, as one of the sensational writers of the day, was able to
put the story of her weaknesses and his supposed innocence into
the hands of multitudes, and so he did, not only in his autobiography but also in a novel, *Ala Lama*.[2]

Quite obviously, in the struggle to win sympathy and gain
allies Frau Bahrdt had a great advantage: she was the injured
party and her will to power appeared in the guise of a wish to save
her marriage, uphold the sanctity of the home, and conform to
the demands of conventional morality. As a consequence, of course,
everyone pitied her, and everyone condemned Bahrdt and Christine and professed to find it incomprehensible that the learned
doctor could prefer the charms of an unlettered servant, who was
far from beautiful, to those of his cultivated wife. Everyone, that
is, with the significant exception of his children, particularly the
oldest daughter, Mariane, who, according to the grudging testimony of Pastor Volland, remained loyal to her father. She even
kept on good terms with Christine, a circumstance which needs
to be carefully considered in view of contemporary testimony to
the decent behavior and apparent good breeding of the children.[3]

Much of the unpleasant story was related at length in the book
published by Bahrdt's brother-in-law in order to contradict what
Bahrdt had written in his autobiography. Pastor Volland would
really have done better if he had not attempted the vindication of
Frau Bahrdt's honor, for in it he left such a monument to his
own stupidity as to make it seem likely that his sister was fully
as empty-headed as Bahrdt makes her out to be. Volland, as we

have seen, would persuade his readers of the superior moral and spiritual qualities of the lady by quoting Bahrdt verbatim and at length, and then merely saying, "This is not true." And he would also have us believe that the purchase of the tavern somehow made the erstwhile Doctor of Theology, Professor, Consistorial Councillor, and Superintendent so *déclassé* that a kind of galloping moral degeneration set in, which metamorphosed him from the kind and dutiful husband he had once been into a creature of the lowest sort.

At the same time Volland takes his readers through the complicated story of the business and domestic arrangements of the Bahrdts. The erstwhile professor needed his wife's signature as co-guarantor of a loan. She refused but indicated that she would comply if he dismissed Christine. He furiously rejected this proposition and told his wife never to let him lay eyes on her again, saying that he would rather let everything go to ruin than agree. Everyone was so impressed by his rage that Frau Bahrdt was persuaded that he was quite capable of carrying out his desperate threats, and she gave him the needed signature, hoping that she could thus obtain a hold on him. When he continued to be as cold and hostile to her as ever before, she went to live with her brother, but, let it be noted, the children, at least Mariane, remained behind. The struggle then continued at a distance. Volland printed a good many letters, from which it is plain that each one was trying to get the other at a disadvantage. Bahrdt tried to make it seem that his wife was guilty of desertion by going to her brother's house, and he kept repeating that he wanted her to return to him but that he must have full power to run the business as he saw fit. Frau Bahrdt insisted that she wished to return but that she would not do so until Christine had been dismissed and that as mistress of the establishment she must have the undisputed right to engage and dismiss servants, a condition to which Bahrdt would not agree. Finally the wife felt constrained to yield in order to be near her children and returned to the same situation as before.

The recriminations and quarrels continued, the oldest daughter openly siding with Bahrdt and Christine. Sometimes there were scenes of violence, as on the occasion when Frau Bahrdt tricked her husband into reading a letter written to him by her legal counsellor. Far from being brought to heel by the letter, Bahrdt flew into a fit of terrible fury and threatened Frau Bahrdt with a knife. As Volland records it,

She fell at his feet and begged him with tears for the sake of his honor and the welfare of his children to put the slut out of the house. "If you wish to murder me," she added, "I am ready. Thus I will be freed from my torment and I will even thank you for it as though it were the last good deed." What was accomplished by this self-abasement? I am almost ashamed to write it down; she was boxed on the ears and told to get out of his sight at once. She got up and sat down once again at her spinning wheel as though nothing had happened. He continued to rage: "If you do not go at once I will have you tied and dragged to your room." "That I will wait to see," she replied coolly.

Bahrdt stormed out but soon came back and succeeded in driving her out and to her own room, where she remained for several days.

Matters between them were at this stage when Bahrdt was arrested and taken to await trial on charges of having lampooned Woellner's Edict on Religion, an act of temerity that will occupy us at length in the next chapter. According to Volland, Frau Bahrdt made repeated efforts to cheer up her husband in his confinement and supplied him with all personal requirements and luxuries, even visiting him privately in his place of detention. Bahrdt, however, remained unfriendly and refused to give her the authorization she sought to dismiss Christine, who also privately visited Bahrdt in jail and with considerably more success: in nine months she produced a child.[4] When Bahrdt was sentenced to two years of arrest in Magdeburg he asked his wife to borrow money to pay Christine the two years' wages owing her, and he promised that he would allow her to be dismissed. Frau Bahrdt was overjoyed at this triumph and procured the money, but she insisted that Bahrdt give her a promissory note for the amount. And so Christine finally left the tavern, but only to go to Magdeburg in order to be near Dr. Bahrdt. Moreover, Christine did not go alone; Bahrdt's oldest daughter, Mariane, went with her.[5] Frau Bahrdt was therefore left to manage the business with the help of one maid and a younger daughter. The result was unfortunate: they ran into difficulties and contracted debts, which Bahrdt in his wrath refused to honor. Meanwhile time was passing, and in

due season Christine bore her child in Magdeburg and was attended by her own mother, whom Bahrdt had sent for, and by
Bahrdt's daughter. Now, according to Volland, Bahrdt planned
to bring Christine's parents back with him to the tavern and have
the help of his illegitimate family in running the business. Frau
Bahrdt, who had managed, or rather mismanaged, things during
her husband's absence, was to be excluded once again. When
Bahrdt finally did return, his wife realized that she had lost, and
she agreed to go and live with her brother on condition that Bahrdt
pay her a weekly sum for her support and give binding assurance
of her continued financial interest in the hostelry.

In the foregoing summary of the struggles behind the scenes in
Bahrdtsruhe (Bahrdt's own name for his establishment) we have
followed this one thread of the story to its conclusion and perhaps given the impression that domestic strife must have occupied
Bahrdt's attention and claimed his energies almost to the exclusion
of everything else. Indeed it is hard to understand how in the
midst of this bitterness he could have played the role of affable
and genial host at all. And yet there is ample testimony that he
did so and that the role suited him very well and freed time and
energy for literary labors and the business of the German Union
which we know about. To these matters he devoted his mornings.
Afternoons and evenings he gave up to the supervision of the hostelry and to conversation with his guests. Since he was, of course,
at least as much a household word in his day as Billy Graham is
in ours, it can readily be understood that sheer curiosity brought
him guests in great numbers. But once they had made the trip to
the inn, had shared in the excellent food and drink he provided
at reasonable prices, and listened to his witty and learned discourse, they returned again and again, and the business prospered
under his and Christine's management. Bahrdt's tavern became
a favorite resort of the students of the University, especially of
the theologians, who found Bahrdt's unofficial lectures rather
more stimulating than the official ones they had registered for.
And if there seemed to be some diminution in the number of
guests, the ingenious doctor, who in our day might have become
an advertising executive, quickly hit upon ways to stimulate trade,

such as announcing a grape harvest, a shooting match, fireworks, brand new pastries. It is reported that on one occasion he gave a few *Groschen* to a peasant woman who was on her way to market in Halle to spread the rumor that he had drowned himself: business was exceptionally brisk that day. Bahrdt probably congratulated himself upon his shrewd stroke and pondered ways to assure continuing prosperity. If only Frau Bahrdt could be brought to see the light of reason and be content to remain in her own quarters and ask no questions! What a pity that honest concubinage did not, so far as the middle classes were concerned, have ecclesiastical sanction!

Ecclesiastical sanction for felicity *à trois* was withheld or granted in the realm at this time according to the ancient principle *Quod licet Iovi non licet bovi*. The Prussian Jove, alias Ormesus, alias Frederick William, twice attained the state of triple blessedness, first in May 1787, just about the time Dr. Bahrdt had come to see how he could make full use of Christine's talents.

In our previous observations on the mainsprings of Frederick William's thoughts and actions we have considered only two, superstition and devoutness, and made mere passing mention of the third, sensuality, which was manifest in him at an early age. The hope which was entertained that his marriage at the age of twenty-two to Elisabeth of Brunswick would help him to lead a less licentious life was soon shattered. Instead of elevating her consort Elisabeth herself became debauched and was divorced in 1769 after three years of marriage. Frederick William was immediately married to a new bride, Princess Friederike Luise, daughter of Ludwig IX of Hessen-Darmstadt, whose influence upon him proved to be no more uplifting than that of Elisabeth, and Frederick William went his merry way as before, led on by servile courtiers who did not scruple to use their daughters and sisters as pawns in the game to win his favor. The chief mistress, however, was not of noble birth but the daughter of a court musician named Enke. This woman was provided with a fresh title, Countess Lichtenau, and a husband in name only, the Court Chamberlain Rietz, and the two of them became a formidable third power behind the throne alongside Woellner and Bischoffwerder.

Most of Frederick William's mistresses had to content themselves with a brief ascendancy over him; after a while he tired of them all except Madame Rietz, who avoided every appearance of jealousy and to whom he always returned. But one of the auxiliary mistresses, a Countess Julie Voss, sought a way to give permanent status to her position and insisted upon a form of church wedding, an astonishing suggestion in view of the fact that Queen Friederike Luise had not departed this life. Frederick William was apparently so enamored of this ambitious lady that he agreed to the suggestion, and it now became a matter of securing ecclesiastical approval and the services of a suitable clergyman.

Both were easy to obtain. The Supreme Consistory with Zedlitz at its head had been composed largely of men with "enlightened" views and, besides, there was a good precedent in the left-hand marriage of Landgrave Philip of Hesse at the time of the Reformation. The complaisant clergyman was right at hand in the Marienkirche of Berlin in the person of the freethinking J. F. Zöllner, a noted pulpit orator with an interest in natural science and history, who performed the church ceremony in May 1787.

It may very well be asked what attitude Woellner took toward this sanctified bigamy, which seems so much at odds with the churchliness he avowed. One does not have to look far for an answer: in 1788 Woellner replaced Zedlitz as head of the Ecclesiastical Department and presiding officer of the Supreme Consistory, which was transformed into a mere advisory body. In March 1789, Frederick William's supernumerary consort died, leaving vacant a position which he made haste to fill by contracting in April 1790 a second left-hand marriage, this time with a Countess Sophie Dönhoff; Zöllner again performed the ceremony. The King was apparently to be put under ever-growing obligation to his spiritual and political mentor, whose most burning ambition it was to spite the memory of Frederick the Great and force the "enlightened" servants of the state, clergy and scholars, to dance like trained bears to a tune of his piping. That tune was called the Edict on Religion, which, although it bore the signature of Frederick William, had been composed by Woellner or, perhaps, by Pastor Blumenthal.

If it was Woellner's expectation that publication of the Edict would be followed by the silence of enforced acquiescence, he was disappointed. Within a few years the list of writings on the subject, most of them opposed, had grown so great that in 1793 the *Allgemeine deutsche Bibliothek* devoted an entire volume (CXIV [2]) to them, and in the succeeding volume a large section was concerned exclusively with the closely allied topic of writings on the Symbolic Books.

The wave of protest received early impetus in the highest government circles: within three months after publication of the Edict the members of the Supreme Consistorial Council showed that although they had been subordinated to Woellner they had not been cowed by him. They submitted a formal statement affirming that doubt concerning individual points of doctrine was by no means evidence of irreligious sentiment and proposing that the clergy be instructed, among other things, to avoid all discussion of the Symbolic Books and to preach only the undisputed teachings of Jesus. The reply to this was that those Protestant preachers who had doubts about the Symbolic Books could, so to speak, merely report the contents without taking a stand.

Outside the government the surge of protest and discussion had begun to mount even earlier. In August 1788 two documents appeared, one by A. Riem, an editor of the *Berlinische Journal für Aufklärung,* and one by P. Villaume, a professor at the Joachimsthal Gymnasium.[6] The first one, full of thunderous denunciation but short on reasoned argument, went out of print immediately and had to be republished three times. Riem, however, received an official reproof and resigned from his post as preacher at the *Reformierten-Waisenhaus.* Villaume's book, in a reasoned and dispassionate discussion, demonstrated that the state had neither the right nor the possibility to control and police the faith of its citizens. This denial of the principle of *Cuius regio eius religio* laid down in 1555 in the Peace of Augsburg received peculiar force from the fact that Frederick William's ancestors had consistently ignored the principle ever since 1613, when the Elector Johann Sigismund went over to the Reformed faith and gave the House of Hohenzollern its legacy of religious tolerance. And

Villaume's thesis received added support in the year of its publication from Gottlieb Hufeland, a professor of law in Jena, who wrote a book [7] in which, on the basis of reason and natural law, he denied the right of sovereigns (or of anyone else) to impose religious belief upon their subjects and asserted the right of the congregation to modify its faith according to its needs and judgment. Protests against the Edict were even made directly to the King. A citizen of Hamburg living in Berlin, Dr. H. Würtzer, published some observations on the subject and sent a copy to Frederick William, who caused Würtzer to be arrested and brought to trial. And Frederick William's permanent mistress, Mme Rietz, seems to have tried to persuade him that attempts to restrict religious liberty had done great harm.

Although there was opposition to the Edict from all quarters, it received some support, notably from Semler,[8] a development which was scarcely a legitimate cause for surprise in view of Semler's earlier quarrels with Lessing and Bahrdt. In his defense of the Edict Semler merely made one further step in the direction we have seen him take. Invoking his principle of the clear separation of religion and theology, he asserted that the Edict could in no way affect private and personal belief and that its sole purpose was to protect the established churches and their congregations from attack by heretical-minded preachers and writers. In this judgment, Semler completely ignored the fact that the Edict specifically proclaimed the truth of the Symbolic Books, that is, attempted to put religion as well as theology into a permanent freeze. The Edict was undoubtedly a denial of the principle of religious liberty which had come to be so completely taken for granted in the reign of Frederick the Great that Semler was generally considered to have become a traitor to his own cause, and the government found it necessary to devise a method of effectively enforcing the terms of the Edict. Within a few months (December 19, 1788) of the publication of the Edict on Religion there was promulgated an additional edict, one on censorship.

The new edict required that all prospective publications of any kind be subjected to examination by censor in order to receive the Prussian imprimatur. Every kind and variety of writing ex-

cept for purely scientific investigations that had no religious or
political significance fell under provisions of the edict, even occasional poems and, of course, novels and plays. Procedures to be
observed, the competencies of various administrative bodies, punishments to be meted out, and many other details were all outlined. Even though it would have required a vastly augmented
staff of censors to put the edict into full effect, it was a measure
that gave the authorities ample power to suppress any book and
punish any writer who aroused the wrath of Woellner or offended
the majesty of the King, and the gentlemen of the Enlightenment
were put on notice that their activities might very well result in
getting their fingers burned.

It had, of course, become well known that one of the torch-
bearers of the Enlightenment, Semler, was in no danger of getting
his fingers burned, but what of Bahrdt? Would he cower in silence
under these threats, or would he defy authority and continue to
assert the human right to freedom of thought and the scholar's
right to freedom of research and publication? The answer was a
little long in coming, but when it did come it proved to be sensational. Because of it Bahrdt the publican, who had long been
a sinner, became also Bahrdt the jailbird.

XXVII

⟨ ENFORCED LEISURE ⟩

Among the hundred or so writings which attacked the Edict on Religion there was one which attracted especially much attention, a satire in semidramatic form. On the title page it was labeled a comedy, and the author's name was given as Nicolai the Younger.[1] It was in reality the work of Dr. Bahrdt, the most brazen product of his pen, and can scarcely deserve the name of comedy, for it has almost no semblance of dramatic structure, the third and fourth acts existing only as mere sketches of possible action which anyone can fill out in his imagination.[2] In the other three acts real personages of the time are portrayed as performing certain actions and expressing certain sentiments, but there the similarity to a play, in any proper sense of the term, ceases.

The first act is set in Micheln, a village not far from Köthen, in the parsonage of Pastor Blumenthal, the man whom Bahrdt had persuaded to marry an eloped couple. Blumenthal's wife and daughter, a preacher named Kinderling, and a candidate for the theological degree named Kluge are awaiting the return of Pastor Blumenthal. Presently Blumenthal arrives, escorted, or rather dragged in, by two peasants who had met him near the tavern, too sick and drunk to make it home alone. After a stormy scene Frau Blumenthal reminds her husband of certain letters he has received from Berlin. The reminder causes the haze of drunkenness to lift a bit, and Blumenthal remembers that he is supposed to

make up a new edict on religion for Brother Woellner,[3] an edict which will uphold the pure faith, curb the new Enlighteners and yet be so expressed as to make a show of tolerance.

297

In the ensuing discussion Blumenthal expresses the view that
God has given man reason in order for him to combat it, just as
he must combat his evil impulses. The proof of this, he points
out to Pastor Kinderling, is the fact of Divine Revelation,

for if men were to heed reason and learn the truth from reason, to what
purpose would Revelation be? And to what purpose precisely *this* Revelation
which contains teachings that can neither be understood nor proven by
means of reason?

Kinderling seems to be of one mind with Blumenthal, but
Kluge views things in a different light and points to Frederick the
Great, whose religious tolerance was an example to all Europe. He
also points out that the assertion that the increasing general licentiousness and immorality are due to the corruption of orthodox
faith, as Blumenthal maintains in the edict, is meant only to dupe
the simpleminded and ignorant.

Theoretical religion in general and positive religion especially has absolutely
no influence upon morality. Daily experience shows us that. There are large
numbers of naturalists who reject the supposed basic truths of your Christianity and nonetheless are decent and virtuous people. And on the other hand,
there are among those who firmly believe those basic truths a great many
rascals, cheaters, blockheads, and swinish drunkards.

Thereupon Blumenthal orders Kluge to leave and never hope for
advancement. He then proceeds with his composition of the edict
and reads it aloud as he goes along. In the absence of Kluge,
Blumenthal's wife and daughter point out inconsistencies, irration-
alities, and fundamental contradictions. For example, Frau
Blumenthal says, "Everybody knows that no naturalist has yet been
refuted and that none can be really refuted." To this Blumenthal
replies, "Mother, you and I know that, but the people have not
yet looked into the matter," and proceeds with his reading until
he comes to the end. Then, finding that all his listeners have gone
to sleep he nods off too, and the act closes.

In the second act Blumenthal has gone to Berlin and taken
lodgings in a hotel. Taking a meal in his room he pretends to eat
very little, but on the sly he devours vast quantities of food and
drink. He is visited by Rietz, the pseudo-husband of Frederick
William's mistress, who says that the King's powers are declining

and describes how he and Woellner keep the King in ignorance: they read all the documents and petitions addressed to the King and destroy what does not please them. If critical and satirical books or pamphlets are published which might come to Frederick William's attention, Woellner forestalls the intended effect by taking a copy to the King for him to read. But since the King never has time and patience to read anything, he asks Woellner to report on the book himself, and Woellner reads and comments upon selected and distorted passages in such a way that the desired effect is produced. If one or another of the old ministers of state should recommend such and such a document to the King's attention, Frederick William can then reply that he is already familiar with the wretched thing. After Rietz leaves, Friedrich Nicolai, the publisher of the *Allgemeine deutsche Bibliothek,* in which Bahrdt's books were not always favorably reviewed, appears and asks Blumenthal to put in a good word for him with Woellner. Blumenthal points out that Nicolai's reputation as a freethinker has not ingratiated him with court circles, but he acknowledges that the reviews in the *Allgemeine deutsche Bibliothek* have recently been tending a little more towards orthodoxy, and promises to see what can be done if Nicolai gives his word to favor the orthodox side more and more. Nicolai is overjoyed and exclaims, "Why, then I could probably have the *Bibliothek* approved for use in schools and churches!"

Blumenthal and Nicolai are now joined by a number of others, including G. F. Wach, the devout public prosecutor in Halle, and S. L. Apitsch, a businessman who led the movement to retain the old hymnal unchanged. Blumenthal delivers to them a sermon, explaining that their prayers and the prayers of all the devout believers in Brandenburg domains have not been answered because, under the freethinking reign of Frederick II, the naturalist vermin had been allowed such license. Pure doctrine had been corrupted by the accursed Enlightenment, the servants of God had come to be despised, and the land had been overwhelmed by a dreadful multitude of sins and vices. But Blumenthal consoles his listeners with the assurance that those defenders of the teachings of Jesus, Rietz, Bischoffwerder, and Woellner, have persuaded His Majesty that God will not appear in response to the prayers of holy men until the Enlighteners shall have been exterminated. Apitsch and Wach fall upon their knees, intoning "Now thank we all our God," Nicolai is so terrified of these madmen that he loses bladder control and leaves, muttering, "How could I know that I would get into the company of maniacs?"

The third and fourth acts, as we know, are only sketches of what is supposed to exist in manuscript, but the fifth is written out in the manner of the first two. The scene is the Tiergarten in Berlin, and the stage is filled with four groups of people all discussing the Edict. The first group consists of cobblers, tailors, and the like. They express a variety of opinions, some for and some against, but they end up agreeing that the Edict expressly says that the clergy may have any private belief they like as long as they take the prescribed line in their public preaching.

By God, the King would need only to have some machines with clerical robes made which could prate according to rule, like the machines that play chess according to rule; then we wouldn't need to pay preachers any more.

The second group is composed of people who were elevated to the nobility upon Frederick William's accession to the throne. They find it amusing that the Edict forbids people to fall into error, that is, to deviate from doctrine. How, they would like to know, can error be eliminated by decree? The third group consists of people whom Bahrdt calls philosophers, Steinbart, Zöllner, Teller, Spalding. They discuss the Edict more professionally and are soon joined by Pastor Schulz from Gielsdorf, widely known as *Zopfschulz* for appearing everywhere with his own hair done in a queue rather than wearing the regulation clerical wig.[4] Schulz says among other things that the Edict, at least at the present time, is producing a great many base hypocrites.

And I fear that even good people, especially when they are moved by love of wife and children and the drive to maintain earthly prosperity, will gradually grow accustomed to hypocrisy and become debased in character.

In the fourth group are the Crown Prince, the later Frederick William III, and gentlemen of his suite. The Crown Prince from his concealment implores the spirit of his uncle, Frederick II, to be near him and guide him until he shall become King.

Then all the Grand Inquisitors, visionaries, and Rosicrucians shall receive their reward for the disgrace which they have brought upon the Prussian state and throne.

And the act closes with angelic voices from heaven crying "Amen! Amen!"

Bahrdt's satire, published anonymously, was obviously a violation of the Edict on Censorship. But more than this, it made its author liable to the charge of lese majesty because of such expressions as "Der König schlenderte seinen Weg mit der Dicken [Mme Rietz] fort." Bahrdt was very soon (April 7, 1789) arrested and charged with being the author; his secretary for affairs of the German Union, Röper, had denounced him. He was brought to trial by none other than the public prosecutor G. F. Wach, whom he had satirized in the play, on the charge of having written "all sorts of unwarrantable things against religion and, particularly, indecent things against the Edict on Religion," including a so-called *Commentary*,[5] and also on the charge of carrying on "secret and highly questionable correspondence," namely for the German Union.

At the trial Bahrdt was absolved of authorship of the *Commentary*, and he was held to be innocent of any subversive intent in the matter of the German Union. There remained the question of the so-called "comedy." On this point, Röper's testimony proved convincing, and Bahrdt was declared to be the author and sentenced to two years in prison. Bahrdt steadfastly denied that he had had any other connection with the satire than to forward the manuscript to Vienna for publication. Apparently he felt that denial would get him off with a lighter sentence as long as some doubt remained, and he was ready to play any kind of game that would reduce his term.

As part of this game he sought help from the most unexpected sources, Semler and Woellner. In reply to his letter asking for help, Semler not only promised to intercede for him but sent him money as well, and Woellner also sent him money and tried to play a game of his own. This game was to exploit Bahrdt's predicament by making it worth his while to write a book against the Enlighteners. Woellner wrote to the King that he believed

Bahrdt had genuinely repented and was convinced that such a book would aid the good cause much more than severe punishment, and therefore he requested His Majesty to pardon Bahrdt.[6] Frederick William was at first unwilling to mitigate the sentence but did finally commute the two-year term to one year. On November 3, 1789, Bahrdt was taken to the fortress of Magdeburg, which he was permitted to leave July 1, 1790, without having written the promised book against the Enlighteners. Not that he was idle during this time, for he produced a good number of polemical novels, essays, and satires, but they were all directed against his old enemies, including Woellner, and against one noteworthy new enemy, Johann Georg Zimmermann, of whom more later.

Bahrdt's arrest and imprisonment cannot have been a terribly painful experience for him. To be sure, in his account of the affair [7] Bahrdt tells a dramatic tale of how he was unexpectedly seized by minions of the law and bundled off to a filthy place of detention in Halle to await trial. But even he has to admit that the imprisonment in Magdeburg was quite pleasant. He had private quarters with kitchen and cellar and was allowed to take the air as he wished. His daughter moved in with him and so did Christine, and all circumstances were so agreeable that his health improved greatly, and he was able to speed up his literary output.

At the time of his arrest he was just about to make a public attack upon an old benefactor, Johann August Starck. Starck, who had become Court Chaplain in Darmstadt, had published a defense against charges of crypo-Catholicism [8] made by Gedike and Biester. Starck's apology, which was to be published by Walther in Leipzig, contained passages which disparaged the religion of reason, and the publisher, who was connected with Bahrdt's German Union, saw an opportunity to increase the sale of the book by publishing with it a refutation of these passages. Bahrdt, of course, was the man to write such a refutation, because anything bearing his name became a best-seller. Starck got wind of the idea and prevented publication of the two writings as a single book, but he could not prevent them from appearing separately. Only a part of the *Beleuchtung des Starck'schen Apologismos* was by Bahrdt, however; Bahrdt was having other worries at the time.

Nonetheless there is no blinking the fact that Bahrdt betrayed a man who had done his best to help him. And Bahrdt's self-justification on the grounds that he had been compelled to make the attack by his veneration of the truth—the "truth" being in this case that the free use of reason and the right to be independent of priests, oracles, and the commands of a monarch, was the most sacred of human possessions—is far from convincing.

When he once more had the leisure and the energy to wield a pen, that is, during his confinement, he turned to the writing of a number of polemical and satirical novels as well as his autobiography.

It had never been his intention to put out an autobiography under his own name, for he was wise enough to know that anything he wrote about himself would be widely viewed as untrustworthy. For this reason he had turned over documents and sketches to Degenhardt Pott, one of his associates in the German Union. When Bahrdt was arrested, Pott wished to proceed with the venture by himself, and he received additional documents from Bahrdt's family. But Pott and Bahrdt were unable to come to terms, and Bahrdt decided to write up and publish his own life story. For this purpose he sought by diplomatic channels to regain possession of the papers then in Pott's hands. Pott was thus accused of having illegally acquired the documents through the use of sinister influence upon Bahrdt's daughter and was imprisoned. The latter accusation was false and had never been made by Bahrdt, so that Pott was really imprisoned by mistake, a circumstance that made him no less bitter and determined to have revenge by publishing his own version of Bahrdt's biography,[9] a book in which he violently assailed and denounced every aspect of Bahrdt's character. A reconciliation was effected between the two men, however: Bahrdt wrote in his book about his trial and imprisonment that Pott had been wrongly accused, and Pott regretted the publication of his biography of Bahrdt.

The modern reader can scarcely regret the misunderstanding which determined Bahrdt to write his own life story. As a mixture of fact and fiction or poetry and truth, it cannot, of course, be put in the same class with Goethe's autobiography, but it is highly readable, entertaining, and informative, and many cuts above comparable books by such contemporaries as Laukhard and Ulrich Bräker. And despite the uncertainty about many matters of fact and assertions of motive it is a wonderfully revealing self-portrait in spite of, or just because of, Bahrdt's various attempts to present himself in a favorable light.

The tendency to cast his ideas in the form of fiction, which we have seen in Bahrdt's New Testament studies and which found expression in the autobiography as well, was given free rein in the months of imprisonment. In the year 1790 Bahrdt published no less than four so-called "novels," [10] two of which may be allowed to claim some passing notice.

Both the *Geschichte des Prinzen Yhakanpol* and *Ala Lama* are in the utopian tradition which had been revitalized in Montesquieu's *Persian Letters* and in which Bahrdt's former associate Wieland had written his *Goldener Spiegel, oder die Geschichte der Könige von Scheschian* (1772). In form a fantastic Oriental romance, Wieland's book was in substance a book of precepts for rulers who would govern according to "enlightened" principles. That Bahrdt conceived of his *Ala Lama* as a companionpiece to Wieland's very successful book—Wieland owed his position in Weimar to it—is evident from the subtitle, *Der König unter den Schäfern, auch ein Goldener Spiegel,* but it was in truth little more than a vehicle for satirical attacks upon objects of Bahrdt's displeasure ranging from his wife[11] to the Edict on Religion. Under the name Ala Pogona (Greek πώγων, beard) Bahrdt portrayed himself as the wise minister of state under the benevolent ruler Ala Morade, who set out to reform his tiny kingdom. The chief reform concerned the power of the priests (*Brunzer*) who had corrupted the original simple belief in an impersonal numinous force. This had come about through the invention of a god, Bohama, by a man who became the priest of his own creature. This example was not lost upon other seekers after special privileges and powers, whether they were *Brunzer* or *Ramler,* a kind of inspired prophets. Finally, through the proliferation of oracles and temples, the people had completely lost the idea of an invisible deity and now worshipped Bohama under various carnal guises. Thus there was one sect which ascribed three noses to him, with which he smelled out the three classes of the virtuous, namely the industrious, the peaceloving, and the courageous. But another sect ascribed a fourth nose to him, with which he did *not* smell, in order to account for misfortunes happening to the virtuous. Basically, *Ala Lama* contained nothing new, and its success—after the original publication in 1790 it was republished in Görlitz in 1795—was due to the impertinence with which authorities were attacked and to the pleasure of seeing dignified and powerful personalities exposed to ridicule in transparent disguises.

The idea which underlies the *Geschichte des Prinzen Yhakanpol* is to present certain features of contemporary Europe as seen through the eyes of (supposed) heathens. Yhakanpol, heir presumptive to the throne of Quakanna, a remote and secluded land governed by a wise king and four equally wise and noble priests, is consumed by desire to see for himself what the best form of government might be and to discover an elixir of youth. By good fortune he is joined by another young prince named Amatophy, who wishes to discover the best religion. The irony of the situation is that the two young men try to find in foreign lands, that is, in Europe, what they already possessed. Quakanna, for example, was a limited monarchy, in which civic responsibilities and privileges were in proportion to the number of children of each citizen. Laws governing marriage were liberal: the women proposed marriage and everyone was allowed to be married three times but no more and not to more than one person at a time. The people believed in a god called Negatampo the Invisible, but he was worshipped through the cultivation of the ethical qualities of industry, temperance, justice, and concord. There were only four priests in the land, and they worked closely with the King for the welfare of the people. Belief in miracles and superstitions of all kinds had long since vanished, but the priests continued to maintain one illusion: because the people were unable to follow the philosophical proofs of the existence of God, of immortality, and certain other religious teachings, the priests considered it prudent to profess that the Invisible One had revealed all their knowledge and continued to make revelations. Quakanna had therefore the purest religion of reason supported by the idea which removed all doubts, the idea namely that Negatampo had said it himself.

And in reality, [Bahrdt comments] this deception had a certain truth, inasmuch as that which God teaches men through nature and reason can really be called divine instruction, and it can be said about every such truth that the Invisible One has made it known or revealed it!

The two princes go first to England, where they have disastrous experiences with prostitutes, gamblers, rakes, and quacks. Leaving London they go to Holland, where money rules and where they pay twelve ducats for a copy of the *Dortrecht Synod* with a commentary, both in Latin and both supposedly indispensable to the soul in search of salvation. They proceed up the Rhine and stop over in Cologne and are overwhelmed by the absurdities of Catholic worship. They feel that the deeper they penetrate into Europe the more abominable does religion become. Whey they arrive in Basel the innkeeper gives them Lavater's *Physiognomik* and *Aussichten in die Ewigkeit* to read. They are greatly impressed but equally dismayed when each one sees a resemblance in the other to one of Lavater's criminal types. They go on to Zürich in the company of a family which is close to being broken up for the same reason. In Zürich the great sage is consulted and found to be a deluded visionary. The princes go back to Germany and end up in Hamburg where one of Götze's sermons finally cures Amatophy of his foolish hope of finding the perfect religion in Europe.

The long voyage proves not to have been entirely fruitless, however, for in Hamburg the two princes meet a Dr. Ypsisch,[12] who invites them to his home and discourses with them about truth and the nearby source of truth, nature.

We are all agreed [he says] that there is a God, that is, a Being different from the world but which has given the world its form, if not its absolute existence, and has combined everything into a purposeful whole.

All present agree and Ypsisch goes on,

Then you must necessarily conceive of him as a wise and loving God who finds his own bliss in making his creatures blissful. And it seems to me that all creation confirms this conception of God—and I do not require to know more about him. For everything, everything that you see bears the mark of his love. Everything, everything is for man, for his pleasure. Everything is good and enjoyable.

The upshot of these remarks, which so delight the princes that they buy a house and garden as a present for the wise doctor, is that nature is the only real source of truth and happiness and that nature enjoins us to strive for the highest degree of pleasure through regularity, temperance, and personal hygiene. And, moreover, the attainment of one's own happiness depends upon the effort to increase the general happiness of our fellow men. "This," says Ypsisch, "is the essence of genuine Christianity."

Although, as we have seen, the stream of words flowed even more profusely from Bahrdt's pen during his imprisonment, it cannot be said that any of these works marked an advance in his development and thinking beyond the point attained in his fictional treatment of Jesus' life story. The autobiography, entertaining though it be and still vital for its sense of life as it was lived, is a retrospective work, and the others we have noticed are crudely satirical and repetitive. But even though Bahrdt had reached the end of his intellectual growth, his capacity to speak out with convincing eloquence had not left him, as was seen in his controversy with the distinguished physician, Johann Georg Zimmermann.

XXVIII

⟨THE DOCTOR AND THE CHURL⟩

To ZIMMERMANN (1728–1795) the epithet "distinguished" would probably have seemed altogether inadequate: "famous" or "renowned" would undoubtedly have been much more to his liking, for he was vain beyond the point of absurdity. At the same time it is generally admitted that his contributions to the theory and practice of medicine were very substantial, and his semiphilosophical essays, written in an easily intelligible and urbane style, were widely admired and did bring him some measure of the fame he so ardently craved.

A native of Brugg in the Swiss canton of Aargau, he went to Göttingen to study medicine under the guidance of his illustrious compatriot, Albrecht von Haller. Because of his extraordinary talent Zimmermann became Haller's favorite disciple but not, as Haller had hoped, the successor to take up his researches and push them further. Zimmermann felt that he had to enter practice, and with Haller's recommendation he found a good berth in Bern, which he kept for a short time until, again with Haller's help, he was appointed to a post in his native Brugg. At one time Haller secured for him the offer of a professorship of practical medicine at Göttingen which, for some reason, he refused. He did not, however, refuse the appointment as personal physician of His Majesty the King of Great Britain and Elector of Hanover, George III, but quickly cut his ties with Bern and Brugg in order to pursue the will o' the wisp of fame in Hanover. And the pursuit turned out to be, after a while, quite rewarding: the successful treatment of the young grandson of the Duke of Brunswick focussed attention upon Zimmermann, and his practice grew, along with his social status. But Fortune's smile was brief: in the summer of 1770 Zimmermann's wife died, and she was followed very soon by her mother, who had helped to manage the household. As a result Zimmermann was cut off from court life, for social entertainments were not compatible with mourning. But more than this, he was also obliged to go to Berlin to undergo a difficult and painful operation for hernia. During his enforced solitude Zimmermann busied himself once again with literary work, some medical writings in a popular vein, a revision of his *Betrachtungen über die Einsamkeit* of 1756, and miscellaneous essays, including some propagandistic material for Lavater's physiognomical works, which embroiled him with the satirical professor of physics, G. C. Lichtenberg. But very soon after he had come to the defense of Lavater he offended him by publicly attacking a bizarre figure of the Storm and Stress group named Christoph Kaufmann, whom Lavater had praised as a towering force. Kaufmann, let it be said parenthetically, was a Tarzan-like charlatan whom Zimmermann took to be a leading figure among the apostles of power and revolt clustered about Goethe but who in reality contributed nothing but the name *Sturm und Drang,* which he applied to a play of Klinger originally called *Wirrwarr.* By his attacks upon the Storm and Stress group Zimmermann alienated Herder also, who had thitherto been his friend, and from then on he conducted literary feuds with parties of both the left and the right. Although, as Werner Milch points out,[1] he was an *Aufklärer* of the purest sort, Zimmermann in his indiscriminate attacks drew no fine distinctions among those who aroused his ire, and finally he arrived at the violently self-contradictory position of expressing adulation of Frederick the Great, hatred of the Berlin Enlightenment, and flattery of Woellner and Frederick William in one and the same breath. This growing inconsistency, although apparent to everyone near at hand, was apparently not visible to the exalted occupant of a remote throne. The Empress Catherine of Russia was so impressed by Zimmermann's book on solitude that she showered him with marks of favor and esteem: personally written letters, invitations to come to Russia, medals and certificates, and above all the Order of St. Vladimir, which brought with it elevation into the nobility, so that the former Swiss republican now could and did sign himself Ritter von Zimmermann.

But even this mark of Imperial favor, which it may be supposed afforded Zimmermann as much satisfaction as the title of personal physician of His Majesty George III, was outweighed by the overwhelming distinction of being summoned in 1786 to the bedside of the ailing Frederick II of Prussia. This experience Zimmermann felt to be so shattering and so exalting that he was compelled to share it with the astonished world in a book[2] that led to his becoming the butt of every man's ridicule, not least of all Bahrdt's.

Although his mission was supposed to be entirely confidential, Zimmermann felt that the eyes of the world were upon him as he journeyed to Berlin to begin his treatment of the greatest of monarchs. Even the man who escorted him into the awesome presence for the first time had in his pocket an ode written by Anna Luise Karsch, in which the Prussian Sappho celebrated his arrival.

How terrible [he reflected] will now be the envy felt for me in all lands by physicians of the lower class, by the learned gentlemen, the schoolmasters, who do not like me! But oh, if only the poor envious rabble knew how I feel at this moment, what anguish, what depression, what dangers and what terrors surround me, then certainly they would confess, "We have no wish for such fortune!"

And then he took courage from the thought that if he could only survive the experience and win over this supreme and terrible man, then certainly nothing else could ever embarrass him,

then I can step with the greatest fearlessness into the presence of every great personage in the world and boldly and calmly look all men in the eye.

The strongest impression the reader receives from Zimmermann's history of the case is that he was much more concerned with himself and with his personal relations with the King than he was in trying to cure or even alleviate his royal patient's illness, which seems to have been a digestive trouble of some sort. He conversed with the King and prescribed a decoction of dandelions and conversed some more. He once feebly suggested, "The only dangerous enemies Your Majesty has are Your Majesty's cooks."

But the King would not listen to this suggestion; no sooner did he feel more comfortable than he ordered outrageously spiced food, which, of course, was a primary cause of his distress. As Zimmermann reports, when the daily bill of fare was brought to him for his approval,

with his own hand he crossed out what he did not wish (an office which I often desired for myself) and with his own hand he added the dishes which he wanted, [like] that polenta which I so often cursed in the silence of my soul.

In defense of Zimmermann it can be said, of course, that the King would probably have disregarded any and all attempts to regulate his diet and that there was no way to enforce a doctor's recommendations. But to this it can be replied that Zimmermann's only honest recourse would have been to present the King with the alternative of following his instructions or doing without his services. Instead of this Zimmermann tried to prolong his attendance upon the King in order to bask another day and another day in the light of his presence, perhaps with the already formed purpose of publishing an account of his brief association and rather limited conversations with the King.

Zimmermann apparently felt that the mere account of his attempted treatment and conversations would be too thin, and in the second half of the book added a good deal of material such as anecdotes and his own estimate of the King's personality and accomplishments. He gave an apologetic explanation of Frederick's low estimate of German literature and deplored his religious skepticism. With almost every additional sentence he wrote, Zimmermann involved himself in further difficulties and self-contradictions, for he now went on to a general condemnation of the Enlightenment, particularly the Berlin and Potsdam variety, disregarding the fact that he was actually allied with them and had had items published in the *Berlinische Monatsschrift* of Gedike and Biester. Even more embarrassing were his attempts to reconcile his attacks upon the Enlightenment with his worship of Frederick:

The King wanted moderate liberty, but the Enlighteners of morality and faith pushed everything to the most unrestrained shamelessness. . . . The men of the Enlightenment resisted any restriction whatever upon freedom of thought, the women of the Enlightenment resisted any restriction upon their hearts. In the sight of their wives the former in the broad light of the morning summoned *filles de joie* to their homes, just as matter of factly as the rabble sends for wine or snuff. The women then put antlers on their husband's heads not only for the love and pleasure of it, but from sheer joy and enthusiasm for the light of the general Berlin *Aufklärung*. . . . [But] one must not hold the King responsible for this gross misconduct of the Berlin and Potsdam sort, for what his subjects insisted upon, and he was unable to change, he simply indulged. . . . [But] it was necessary for King Frederick William to come and say to the Enlighteners of Berlin: Thus far and no farther.

The book was concluded by an appendix in which Zimmermann described an earlier encounter with the King on the occasion when he was in Berlin and so heroically endured his famous operation for hernia.

Small wonder that Zimmermann's book called forth a shower of replies and protests, the very titles of which punctured the balloon of the learned doctor's pomposity. Hippel wrote one called *Zimmermann I. und Friedrich II. von J. H. F. Quitenbaum;* Bahrdt's erstwhile friend Trapp produced a *Doktor Luther an den Ritter von Zimmermann;* and Knigge described the palpitations of a tailor concerning the fit of royal breeches in his *Über Friedrich Wilhelm den Liebreichen und meine Unterhaltungen mit ihm von J. C. Meywerk, Churhannöverschem Hosenmacher.* Zimmermann, of course, replied, and the quarrel grew as Zimmermann gathered his forces to annihilate the *Aufklärer* at one stroke by the publication in 1790 of a massive book·in three volumes (1100 pages) entitled *Fragmente über Friedrich den Grossen zur Geschichte seines Lebens, seiner Regierung und seines Charakters.* This was a jumble of anecdotes and opinions, including previously published material, in which Zimmermann bitterly assailed his former friends Gedike, Biester, and Nicolai, as well as a number of other *Aufklärer* such as Campe and Trapp. Bahrdt too was among the victims of Zimmermann's wrath, not because Bahrdt had in any way offended him, for on this occasion Bahrdt was only an innocent bystander, but merely because he was, as Zimmermann put it, an *Aufklärungs-dragoner,* and thus by definition worthy of chastisement.

It can readily be understood that Bahrdt was not reluctant to enter the fray; his reply was prompt and devastating, and bore the long and involved title, itself nearly a whole pamphlet: *Mit dem Herrn [von] Zimmermann Ritter des St. Wladimir-Ordens von der dritten Klasse, Königlichem Leibarzt und Hofrath in Hannover, der Akademien der Wissenschaften in Petersburg und Berlin, der Gesellschaften der Ärzte in Paris, London, Edinburgh und Copenhagen, und der Societät der Wissenschaften in Göttingen Mitgliede deutschgesprochen von D. Carl Friedrich Bahrdt, auf keiner der Deutschen Universitäten weder ordentlichem noch ausserordentlichem Professor, keines Hofes Rath, keines Ordens Ritter, weder der ersten noch dritten Klasse, keiner Akademie der Wissenschaften, wie auch keiner einzigen gelehrten noch ungelehrten Societät Mitgliede, etc.*

In this book Bahrdt, writing in a style reminiscent of Lessing's polemics against Lange and Klotz, selects Zimmermann's title of *Ritter* as a point of attack and challenges him to knightly combat, even though his own attack upon Bahrdt had been that of a varlet. And so throughout the book Bahrdt plays with his opponent like a swordsman who has his enemy completely at his mercy, taunting and lashing him for the base churl he is despite his title of knight. It was, of course, well known to Bahrdt that in his book on solitude Zimmermann had, like any true man of the *Aufklärung*, heaped scorn upon hermits and anchorites of all sorts, upon all who sought solitude for the sake of mystical religious knowledge. It was therefore particularly appropriate for Bahrdt to question Zimmermann's newfound devoutness and hold him up to scorn as being still of the same basic religious outlook as the *Aufklärer* whom he reviled.

What do you mean by Christianity? [he asks]. Do you perchance reckon miracles, original sin, the Trinity, eternal punishment in hell, justification by faith alone, and supernatural grace, and such superfluous curlicues of church dogma as part of Christianity? Impossible. You yourself make mock of Haller's hyperorthodox Christianity. Vol. I, p. 195 [of the *Fragmente über Friedrich den Grossen*]. You yourself attribute the greatest role in the taming of the passions and temper (the most difficult part in conversion) to strength of will and not to the supernatural grace of the Holy Ghost. Vol. III, p. 2. . . . You yourself say, "I believe in no miracles." Vol. III, p. 60. You yourself therefore confess to the said deviations from Lutheran, Calvinistic, and papistic Christianity. Consequently it seems that you too have taken up the

Berlin Enlightenment and have taught conceiving of Christianity as moral religion. If now it is well known that I and all proponents of Enlightenment do not attack Christianity insofar as it is identical with the teachings of Jesus but that we cry out against church teachings and superstition insofar as they have been used to disfigure his teachings, then how can you say of us that we mislead the people and undermine Christianity?

Bahrdt made two other points that must have been particularly galling to Zimmermann. One was his derision of Zimmermann's so-called treatment of the King: no attempt whatever was made to regulate Frederick's diet, and the decoction of dandelion was positively harmful; on the contrary, the prescription should have been increasing doses of squill mixed with a small amount of poppy juice.[3] The other was his mockery of Zimmermann's servile dread of the monarch: he asked Zimmermann to imagine that he had a young son in his first year at the university, who described in a letter to his father a visit to the rector in the same terms in which Zimmermann had described his conversation with the King.

Terrible and grand was the entire scene at the armchair of His Magnificence. In a kind of enthusiasm I said to myself: "If I survive this and get through things here pretty well, then nothing else in the world can make me uneasy." And I thought, "Now all my comrades in school know that I am here; they are bursting with envy because I am now standing here by the armchair of His Magnificence." But I prostrated myself before God and by means of prayer I surmounted the greatest and most dreadful perils.

In the second paragraph of this book Bahrdt, comparing himself with Zimmermann, had written that it was well known that he was a man who had been equipped by Mother Nature with an unusual degree of fire and boldness.

I am accustomed [he said] to charge with iron front [*mit eiserner Stirn*] at everything that gets in my way and to attack the follies as well as the knaveries of the believers with unsparing heat.

In the words *mit eiserner Stirn* Bahrdt had used a phrase which an anonymous enemy almost immediately sought to turn against him.

In 1790, the year of the publication of Bahrdt's book against Zimmermann, there appeared what purported to be a play in four acts entitled *Doctor Bahrdt mit der eisernen Stirn oder Die deutsche Union gegen Zimmermann*. The name of the author appeared as *Freyherr* [*sic*] von Knigge, an attribution which infuriated Knigge, for the book was little more than a string of the most crude indecencies imaginable, and he had in reality had nothing to do with it, as was indeed plain from a few hints here and there. But it took some time before the question of the authorship was finally answered.

For a while the general suspicion was directed against Zimmermann himself, for the play was not only a specific counterattack upon Bahrdt's *Mit dem Herrn* [*von*] *Zimmermann deutschgesprochen*, but it was an assault upon Zimmermann's enemies, the *Aufklärer*, and was written entirely from Zimmermann's point of view. The first scene opens in Doctor Bahrdt's room in the notorious vineyard. In the background are Bahrdt's lares and penates, specifically a lingam. Bahrdt, seated at a table, indulges in a long soliloquy in which he bewails the splendor of the days in Erfurt which he had spent in riotous living and reviews the main episodes in his life as well as his writings. A servant enters to announce a visitor:

There is something outside that seems to belong to the class of marine crabs. It has the humped back of a cat, a monkey-face, a lot of arms and legs with claws attached, and a set of false teeth in its maw.

This turns out to be the "little lustful moon correspondent" Lichtenberg, who is followed by a number of characters such as Nicolai, Mauvillon, Biester, Gedike, Kästner, Campe, Trapp, and others. They have a Seven Minutes' War which Bahrdt ends by uniting them against Zimmermann. When Lichtenberg discovers that they are in danger of being suffocated by their own noxious vapors, they adjourn to the garden, the scene of the second act, where a foul orgy takes place. Eventually Bahrdt summons the crew to order by exhorting them to undertake the campaign against Zimmermann, saying that he will do his part by accusing Zimmermann of being not a knight but a varlet. They all confirm the conspiracy by an oath on the lingam. The third act also is set in the garden and shows the members of the Union in various stages of exhaustion and catharsis. Bahrdt picks up a hammer and with it pounds his iron front to rouse his band. They begin to make speeches on what they intend to do. The spirit of Doctor Luther appears and admonishes each one with an appropriately adapted citation from the Bible. Bahrdt makes speeches quoting his polemic against Zimmermann so that the speeches constitute an anthology of abusive language from that book. He is boxed on the ears by the spirit of Dr. Goldhagen, whom he had quoted to the effect that Zimmermann was a poor physician. The fourth act takes place in Zimmermann's home. A servant brings him Bahrdt's pamphlet, which he examines with serene composure and with a smile decrees that it be taken to the privy. The scene changes to the privy, where various journals, such as *Die Berliner Monatsschrift, Das deutsche Museum, Der hamburger Correspondent,* and others, have already been installed. These journals, however, find Bahrdt's pamphlet too disgusting to tolerate, and they tear it up and even pursue it into the depths. With this all the actors have left the stage.

But what did poor Zimmermann do when he went to the privy and found no paper? He resolved to compose a notice requesting the countless people who envied him to make haste to write another pamphlet against him. Smiling, he casts a glance down into the privy where all the gentlemen are brawling in their element.

Thus is a purified outline of the sketch, which, of course, can give no idea of its indecency.

For some time literary and theological Germany was agog over this incredible production. Many felt that Bahrdt deserved this treatment, many others did not, but all were bursting with curiosity to learn who had written it. Eventually the author was smoked out and revealed as the young but already well known and influential playwright August von Kotzebue (1761–1819).

Kotzebue and Zimmermann had begun corresponding with each other as a result of the former's admiration of Zimmermann's essay on solitude, to which he alluded in his remarkably popular play *Menschenhass und Reue* (1789). Through his influence with the Empress Catherine, Zimmermann secured sick leave for Kotzebue, who was *Präsident* of the Russian province of Estonia. Kotzebue, back in Germany on leave, called on Zimmermann in order to express his thanks and regards; the two men liked each other and their friendship grew. Zimmermann, who greatly admired the talent of the German Aristophanes, as he referred to Kotzebue, had already had the idea that Kotzebue was just the man to write a telling comedy against the modern sophists, the *Aufklärer,* and had so written in a letter to a young friend named Stapfer.[4] Although Zimmermann informed Stapfer that he had dropped all thought of making such a suggestion to Kotzebue, the latter did in fact very promptly produce the sketch we have just briefly considered.

It is rather surprising that so many people at this time seem to have believed in the possibility of concealing their part in the production of a sensational book. Time after time the mask of anonymity was flung aside by official investigators and the true author revealed to all the interested world. The same thing happened to Kotzebue, although he desperately denied that he had produced so foul a work. Official investigation into the authorship began at the instance of a former friend of Zimmermann named Klockenbring, who had been infamously treated in Kotzebue's sketch. The investigators called upon all people who had been maligned in the play to come forward with their surmises as to the authorship. One of these was a certain Mauvillon, who wrote a book in which he developed a chain of suspicions pointing to Zimmermann and declared himself ready to take an oath that he felt that the distinguished physician was in truth the author. But Mauvillon was not alone in this belief; a general trend of opinion developed to the same effect. Zimmermann found it necessary to advertise in various newspapers that he was ready to take the most fearful oath that he had no share, either direct or indirect, in this work and that he had known nothing of the contents until he had the printed text in his hands. At this the epigrammatist and mathematician at Göttingen, Kästner, expressed his view that Zimmermann undoubtedly knew who the author was and that the taking of any such oath would make him guilty of perjury. This threatened exposure of possible dishonor on Zimmermann's part drove Kotzebue to take action to keep the matter hushed up. A certain Schulz had been helpful in having the manuscript of the sketch copied and in having an engraving made for the title page. Kotzebue feared that Schulz would, upon being questioned, give the secret away, and he wrote him a letter to persuade him to keep silence. Schulz, however, fearing that he might be held to be the anonymous author, showed Kotzebue's letter to various friends and acquaintances. Now Kotzebue actually did persuade a certain Schlegel in Reval to admit in a published declaration[5] that he was the author. But all these dodges led finally to the unmasking of Kotzebue, who was forced to publish a declaration in the newspapers that he really was the man.

It can readily be imagined that Bahrdt was not a mere disinterested spectator during this search. Assuming that Zimmermann was in some way involved, Bahrdt wrote an anonymous counterpart to Kotzebue's sketch which he called *Zimmermanns Auferstehung von den Toten, ein Lustspiel vom Verfasser im strengsten Incognito. Ein Gegenstück zu Dr. Bahrdt mit der eisernen Stirn.* In this sketch Zimmermann reads Bahrdt's *Mit dem Herrn [von] Zimmermann deutschgesprochen* and falls into a faint. When he recovers, the spirit of Dr. Goldhagen appears and reproves him for asserting that Bahrdt had falsely quoted him, the late Goldhagen, to the effect that Zimmermann was a poor physician. The doctor and the ghost come to blows, and the former dies from being struck on the nose. But he is resurrected by his youngest daughter, who praises *Dr. Bahrdt mit der eisernen Stirn* in his presence. As the inquiry into the authorship of Kotzebue's play progressed, and a considerable segment of the interested public began to suspect the true author, Bahrdt published a second augmented edition of this satire. He added another act with the title *Das öffentliche Gericht auf dem grossen Richterischen Koffeehause zu Leipzig über den Verfasser des Lustspiels Dr. Bahrdt mit der eisernen Stirn.* The actors in this part of the play, including Bahrdt himself, propose various conjectures about the author, and the theory is advanced on the basis of Mauvillon's book that it was actually Zimmermann, but the argumentation is rejected as false. Then a young man in uniform slips into an adjoining room, and Bahrdt, after going into this room himself, returns and says he has seen the author, namely Kotzebue, the young man in uniform. However, Zimmermann is accused of having furnished Kotzebue with necessary information, an accusation that is not entirely correct, for Kotzebue seems to

have obtained his knowledge of certain facts from a close friend
of Zimmermann named Markard.

Thus, it cannot be said that time really hung heavy on Bahrdt's
hands during his imprisonment, and when Frederick William
shortened his term to one year, and he emerged from the fortress
of Magdeburg to return to Bahrdtsruhe, he had not lost touch
with the outer world, and his controversy with Zimmermann had,
if anything, enhanced his reputation. Seemingly he was not to be
silenced, and there was every reason to expect the flow of writings
to continue indefinitely from his pen. But little time was left
him: in less than two years from his release he had been silenced
forever.

XXIX

⟦DEATH OF AN INNKEEPER⟧

IN THE BRIEF time that was left to him after his release from prison Bahrdt attempted to go on writing as before, but the publications from this period mark no advance in his development. There was, for example, a *Catechism of Natural Religion*[1] which was intended to impart Bahrdtian principles to the very young. In line with this attempt to affect the broader masses was a *Journal for Wives, Mothers, and Daughters*,[2] by means of which he proposed to raise the intellectual niveau of an important part of the population. A selection from Martin Luther's *Table Conversations*[3] was aimed at making a little money as was also a collection of largely salacious anecdotes.[4] This was the last book on which Bahrdt worked, apparently in the expectation of death.

My end [he writes in one place] is drawing near. I await it full of courage without priests and Bible. It is well with him who by means of independent thinking has come so far that he has no need of them.[5]

The final phase of Bahrdt's work was not entirely dismal and mediocre, however: in the last controversy of his life he once more showed himself at his best and took his stand on his convictions, even though it meant once more offending the majesty of Frederick William. This was the controversy with Professor J. F. Roennberg of Rostock.

Roennberg undertook to produce a justification of the Symbolic Books and the Edict on Religion based on a theory of constitutional law.[6] In this theory he identified the church and the nation and reasoned that the church, which has constituted itself in free conscience and organized itself for worship according to self-imposed doctrine, has the right to demand of all its members

320

respect, loyalty, and devotion to its dogmas. Therefore anyone who doubts the Symbolic Books cannot remain a member of the church. But the existence of a body of devout believers organized as a church is of paramount importance to the nation, because irreligion produces lawlessness. *Q.e.d.*, it is in the interest of the state to support the Symbolic Books, as Frederick William did in his Edict on Religion.

Roennberg's book was widely admired and praised by the orthodox, and the King himself decreed that it be distributed to the consistories throughout Prussian domains. People of different persuasion had nothing but scorn for Roennberg's loose reasoning. Such a one was Professor Villaume, who produced a book[7] that examined Roennberg's reasoning. This book, since there was no law which could be used to forbid its publication, was banned by a cabinet order of the King himself and had to be published outside Prussia.

There was therefore no doubt that Roennberg's book had official sanction and royal protection and that anyone who attacked it might very well incur the wrath of Frederick William himself. And Bahrdt was, of course, keenly aware of the possible consequences when he published his refutation,[8] the gist of which is that whereas the Symbolic Books can, to be sure, be authorized by the power of the ruler, in and of themselves they are not legally binding, and they are not essential to the church, the state, or the nation, since it is the Bible which is the eternal norm of Christian faith. Any attempt to enforce faith in the Symbolic Books is Catholicism in disguise, which interposes doctrine between the faithful and the Word of God. Thus did Bahrdt defy all his enemies, whether churchmen, statesmen, or King, and at the risk of once more being removed from his comfortable home and being cut off from the only occupation he ever found which gave him real pleasure without admixture of bitterness.

Imprisonment had not harmed his business. On the contrary, more people than ever were eager to come to see the famous innkeeper who had once been a professor and had served a term in prison. Since they found good food and drink, fine fresh fruit, a beautiful view, learned and witty conversation with the host, they returned again and again. And since Bahrdt had convinced his wife that she would do better to let him support her away from the tavern at her brother's home, the days passed for him in relative serenity.

Testimony to this is to be found in an essay by C. F. Benkowitz,[9] who was one of Bahrdt's frequent guests. According to Benkowitz, he was really in his element here. Here he was removed from all activities to which strict uprightness and an inviolable word of honor were essential, here he could not launch any cabals, nor could he be the object of them. Here he could practice farm and household management, which he loved so dearly, and make a living without having to write books, and here he could really show off his social talents and have use of his great reputation without being a writer. For who was not eager to become acquainted with the famous Bahrdt? What traveller passing through Halle did not wish to see the great doctor in his capacity of innkeeper? He was himself the great magnet who pulled everything to him, and he had furnished his abode with many kinds of attractions which just by themselves would have been sufficient to bring in guests.

The man's conversation gave his tavern its greatest charm, and this the guests enjoyed especially in the evening. In the afternoon the people played cards, and he usually joined in. Towards evening he would walk around among the players and make a note of those who intended to stay for the evening meal, so that Christine could make her preparations accordingly. They dined at seven. He always sat at the head of a long table, and everybody moved up close in order to share in the conversation. And this with good justice, for he usually opened up his heart at this time, especially concerning literary matters. Long before the publication of *Mit dem Herrn [von] Zimmermann deutschgesprochen,* the most biting passages in it were known, for Bahrdt regaled his guests with them at table. Benkowitz felt that the choice passage was the one in which Bahrdt compared Zimmermann in the presence of Frederick with a university freshman in the presence of the rector; on Bahrdt's lips it became a bit of vivid and dramatic comedy. He could not forgive Zimmermann, writes Benkowitz, for saying that his punishment was not severe enough, when he had, after all had to suffer so much during his detention in Halle while awaiting trial. But he did not deny that he had written against Zimmermann with malice and even once confessed that he really did not understand the effect of the decoction of dandelion and that he knew very well that the King was beyond help, but he wanted to take a slap at Zimmermann by ridiculing his medical treatment. When on this occasion someone asked him whether he was not afraid of a reply to this bitter attack, he answered that he no longer feared any scurrilous writings whatsoever. He had been abused with a violence that it was not possible to exceed and had long ago become indifferent to literary outrage.

Thus [says Benkowitz] this remarkable scholar, who in earlier years had made such a sensation as a theologian and had held so many offices, lived in the last years of his life as a tavernkeeper. Thus was his place of abode into which, after so many a storm and shipwreck, he had run as though into a safe harbor. What has often been said about it, both orally and in writing, and as it has been represented in the licentious *Dr. Bahrdt mit der eisernen Stirn*, namely that women of ill fame were maintained there, this is all a base defamation, and there was not a trace of indecency to be found there. The clientele consisted of honorable people who were seeking legitimate entertainment. The majority were students, who were often joined by professors and officers with their wives, and on Sundays and holidays one encountered people from all classes, since everyone was admitted. One rarely saw the doctor's daughters, whose mode of life was extremely decorous and quiet. And the notorious Christine never mingled with the guests but was almost always in the kitchen. Incidentally, she seemed like a goodnatured girl, but certainly could make no claim to beauty, and in this case the doctor's taste was cause for wonderment.

This almost idyllic life, as Benkowitz describes it, was not destined to last long. In January 1791, Bahrdt's daughter Mariane fell seriously ill. This was the daughter who, as it will be remembered, was her father's favorite and who had sided with him in his separation from his wife. She had also some local reputation as a singer, and Bahrdt was not only devoted to her but proud of her as well. He therefore undoubtedly thought he was acting in her best interest when he undertook to treat her himself, for, as we remember, he had dabbled in medicine and had once thought of taking it up professionally. But she did not improve, so Bahrdt was forced to consult Professor J. C. W. Juncker. Unfortunately,

it was too late: Juncker had to inform Bahrdt that there was no
hope. Bahrdt accepted the inevitable with stoicism: when death
was drawing near he gave her opium in order to let her die without pain. Then he joined his guests to await the end.

Benkowitz writes that he happened to be present in the tavern
when she was dying and was able to observe Bahrdt carefully. He
sat among his guests, apparently composed but serious, playing
l'hombre, while some friends were with his daughter. At about
three o'clock the waiter came with the news that the sick girl had
just died. The guests began to whisper and Bahrdt realized that
something had happened. Completely self-possessed, he gave his
cards to someone, got up, and went out. At the stairs some friends
came to meet him with the sad news and took him into the dead
girl's room. After a quarter-hour he came back and calmly asked
for his cards. The student who had taken his place at the card table
said, *"Herr Doktor,* in your absence I have lost eight *Groschen."*
"Oh," said he with some indifference, "I have lost everything that
was most precious to me in the world." Then he sat down again
and continued the game without distraction.

The funeral became the occasion of a grotesque and semitragic
scene. Bahrdt had expressed his feelings of grief and loss in writing,
and he placed the paper at the feet of the dead girl where she was
lying in her open coffin. An art dealer from Halle received permission to make a copy, but under the condition that it was not
for publication. But the man immediately ignored this stipulation
and had it printed. When the coffin was being borne to the burial
place, which was in the middle of the vineyard, there stood a boy
with the printed copies, which he sold in large numbers, for there
were about four hundred students in attendance, as well as a good
many others. When Bahrdt learned what was happening, he immediately had the remaining copies taken away from the boy, but
as soon as the art dealer heard of this he went to Bahrdt to ex-
postulate with him, for his money-making scheme was about to fail.
When the art dealer was shown the door by Bahrdt he flew into a
fury, wheeled around and struck Bahrdt, who was so taken aback
by this unexpected assault that he did nothing to defend himself.
Christine and the waiters, however, ran up and drove the man

away. The news of the encounter soon spread among the students present, who became enraged and sent out searching parties to lay hold of the art dealer. This they very soon did and brought him back in triumph from Halle. Thus the art dealer came back to the tavern escorted by several hundred indignant friends of Dr. Bahrdt. As he approached Bahrdt, he was forced to remove his hat and behave as though he were in the presence of his judge. After some debate it was decided that he would have to kneel before Bahrdt and ask his pardon. All reluctance to do so was overcome by threats to punish his refusal by a beating. Bahrdt accepted the apology, the students broke out into cheers, and Bahrdt offered the man a glass of lemonade, the only thing that the several hundred guests had not consumed.

> From this event, [writes Benkowitz] it can be seen how great was the students' affection for Doctor Bahrdt. And it was really impossible not to be fond of the man and hold him in esteem if one knew him only socially, even though on the other hand everyone was well advised to enter into no serious connections with him of a sort that required strict probity and firm principles.

From the day of his daughter's death, Bahrdt's health began to fail. The earliest symptom was a throat irritation, but gradually his entire organism began to suffer and deteriorate. He consulted a great many physicians, but he never followed the prescription of any one of them faithfully, for he had not lost faith in his own ability to make a medical diagnosis and effect a cure. But in medical matters, as he himself once said, he would have, if he had become a physician, been as great a heretic as he was in theological matters. The consequence was that he poisoned his system by treating himself with mercury in various forms, this being a remedy which he considered a panacea. Finally he wrote a dispirited letter to Professor Juncker, asking him for a visit. Juncker took charge of the case and cared for Bahrdt until his death. Afterward he wrote a history of the disease,[10] which is the chief source of our knowledge of Bahrdt's last days.

When Juncker took charge, he found Bahrdt suffering from an advanced case of mercurial poisoning. His mouth was swollen and abscessed, so that his speech was badly impaired. For some weeks he had been having attacks of hectic fever and various other troubles, but the rest of his body had not been affected by ulcers or abscesses, so that the prevalent rumor, that Bahrdt was ill of a venereal disease, was, according to Juncker, who also performed an autopsy, not true.

At first Juncker's treatment seemed to alleviate Bahrdt's sufferings somewhat, and he began to feel rather more hopeful and cheerful, but Juncker saw indications that the disease was to prove fatal and thus informed various persons. When this report reached Bahrdt he wrote to Juncker and implored him to tell him everything he knew or suspected.

I can die [he wrote] without physicians and parsons. But I still have many arrangements to make before I die in order not to cause my family serious difficulties. I will compose myself and thus endure it more easily than if death comes unexpectedly.

When Juncker informed him in writing of what the symptoms were by which he would know that his end was approaching, he was content, and as soon as he felt these symptoms he set up his last will.

On the sixteenth of April 1792, he completely lost the power of speech, and he now had to communicate his thoughts and wishes in writing. On the twenty-second the hitherto intermittent fever became constant, a certain sign of approaching death, but Bahrdt did not yet suffer so greatly as to fear his speedy end. In the evening, however, he sent for opium from the apothecary's shop, in order to take increased doses in liquid form. Undoubtedly he had in mind to take enough to give him a painless end in his sleep as he had not so long before done for his daughter.

Only a few hours before his death, when his pulse and vitality were at a very low ebb, and the fever was very high, he showed plainly that his mind was clear and active. He answered several questions precisely, made a careful selection of various refreshments that were offered and wrote coherently. In writing he requested a friend, one Bispink, to assure him that he would make provision for Christine, indicating that such assurance was all he needed to be able to meet his end calmly. He remained without anxiety of mind or pain of body until the evening of the twenty-third of April about eleven o'clock. At that time he asked for pen and paper and wrote the words "Jetzt schlafe ich ein" and died,

Appendix

DR. CARL FRIEDRICH BAHRDT:
THE DECAY OF A REPUTATION

AFTER SOME debate with myself, I have decided against calling the present essay, "The Denigration of Dr. Bahrdt, or Clichés Triumphant." But the rejected title has some merit, as I hope will be demonstrated in the following brief history of the idea which has grown to be the standard and accepted view of this once widely known champion of the German Enlightenment.

In order to understand how the image of such a controversial and multi-faceted personality could be so simplified that many scholars and historians feel they are doing Dr. Bahrdt no injustice by dismissing him with a cliché, it may be illuminating to recall that when a song or poem becomes a *Volkslied,* then everybody knows the song, but nobody remembers who wrote it. Thus, perhaps, the *Volkstheologie* of Dr. Bahrdt has blotted out remembrance of the fact that he was one of the forceful shapers of that very *Volkstheologie.* The decay of his reputation seems to show that as the rationalistic and critically evaluative attitudes toward the Bible and religion, of which Bahrdt, next to Lessing and Nicolai, was the most forceful and effective champion in Germany, lost their shock value and became so commonplace that they were no longer associated with any particular thinker or writer, the picture of him which gradually gained all but universal acceptance was the totally black one which had been drawn by his orthodox enemies, the people whose beliefs and principles had been made untenable by the now anonymous views of Bahrdt.

Incidentally, while it would be audacious to assert that I have read and noted all references to Bahrdt made in histories of literature and civilization since his death in 1792, it will be safe to say

327

that enough have been found to establish the general outline, at least, of the history we are undertaking. At any rate, there is no gainsaying that for somewhat more than fifty years opinion has been nearly unanimous and that Bahrdt, once one of the most controversial figures of the *Aufklärung,* has become perhaps the least controversial of them all. The biographical study to which this essay is appended has attempted to portray Dr. Bahrdt in the cross fire of opinion and controversy. It may be of interest now to trace the development of the Bahrdt legend after his death.

"The evil that men do lives after them; The good is oft interred with their bones." One is tempted to make these lines the motto and summary of the history of Bahrdt's reputation. It would not be strictly true, however: the extensive obituaries in Schlichtegroll's *Nekrolog*[1] do not present a picture of unrelieved evil. It is interesting to note that while Bahrdt was considered important enough to merit two articles, with a total of 238 pages, Mozart, who had died the previous year, was accorded only about thirty pages. The account in Schlichtegroll is sober and thorough; it explores and tries to clear up confusing and contradictory stories about Bahrdt and to arrive at a balanced view. Thus, in the discussion of Bahrdt's directorship of the Philanthropinum at Marschlins, it reports his undeniable shortcomings, but it also states that one cannot, without being unjust, deny that Bahrdt had applied himself to the moral betterment of his pupils and had cured some of them of certain failings. Furthermore, it was much to Bahrdt's credit that the pupils had respect and love for him and exerted themselves to win approval and praise from him. Schlichtegroll even goes so far as to put in some appreciative words about Bahrdt as an innkeeper and as a friend, quoting close associates of long standing. Thus, the *Nekrolog,* while giving full credence to many of the scandalous stories about him, views him with mixed favor and asserts about him that he played a most remarkable role and that, both by what he did and by what he wrote, he had a very significant influence upon his century.

Two years later, in 1794, there appeared an official history of the University of Halle[2] in which, of course, an account had to be given of Bahrdt and his relations, sometimes friendly and sometimes hostile, with Semler. This is a very mild report. The author, J. C. Förster, a professor of the University, is discreet to the point of concealing and suppressing information.

Not so discreet, however, is a pamphlet [3] written two years later by the man who had taught the classical languages in the school at Marschlins during Bahrdt's directorship. This book was dedicated to Rudolph von Salis and was written to vindicate Ulysses von Salis, the founder of the Philanthropinum at Marschlins. Its author, J. G. P. Thiele, maintains that Bahrdt did practically nothing in Marschlins except to conduct teaching games from time to time and that he very seldom put in an appearance at the school, being extraordinarily lazy. The whole pamphlet is a series of denunciations and a categorical denial of any redeeming feature in Bahrdt's character or work.

In 1805 another history of the University of Halle appeared.[4] This is a much more thorough and detailed account than Förster's and more critical of Bahrdt. But even so, its author, Hoffbauer, admitted that Bahrdt was a very popular and interesting lecturer, who stimulated hundreds of students to pursue his subjects further.

By 1821, a generation after Bahrdt's death, sober and responsible scholarly opinion of Bahrdt's character and accomplishments had not changed much from the view accepted by the *Allgemeine deutsche Bibliothek* and Schlichtegroll. A detailed and extensive article on Bahrdt appeared in the ambitious encyclopedia of Ersch and Gruber,[5] written by Karl Christian von Gehren with a long footnote, actually an article in itself, by H. A. Erhard. This footnote corroborates the stories of Bahrdt's frivolous life at the University of Erfurt. Gehren, however, is much milder in his judgment of Bahrdt than is Erhard. Speaking of Bahrdt's own Philanthropinum in Dürkheim he observes that, although the entire institute left much to be desired, especially with respect to the teaching staff, which had been so hastily and carelessly assembled, it still cannot be denied that some pupils made excellent progress there in their moral and academic training and that Bahrdt, as the director, enjoyed the respect and affection of many of them. In his discussion of the edict which suspended Bahrdt from performance

of ecclesiastical duties, and which led to the ultimate failure of
the school, Gehren accepts it as a fact that *Hofrat* Rühl, Bahrdt's
enemy, did not forward to the Imperial Court in Vienna the petition for clemency in Bahrdt's case, which his master, Count
Karl of Leiningen-Dachsburg, had commanded him to direct to
that court. Moreover, Gehren feels that it redounded to Bahrdt's
honor that he did not recant and become a traitor to truth in order to maintain his position, though, to be sure, the publication
of his credo at this time was most ill considered. Gehren, although
an active and distinguished clergyman, insists that many of Bahrdt's
popular theological works, including even his translation of the
New Testament, were positive accomplishments. Furthermore,
even though the accusation can with justice be levelled at Bahrdt
that the imprudence and arbitrariness with which he frequently
treated religion, the Bible, and Christianity were offensive and
even harmful to thousands of people, there can be no doubt that
he dealt a mortal blow to the blind belief in the old theological
system and exposed the untenability of that part of prevailing
doctrine that consisted of empty forms.

Nearly half a century was to pass before a comparably thorough
and generous estimate of Bahrdt was written. This is Gustav
Frank's careful and critical biographical study, which appeared
in 1866 and to which more particular reference will be made later.
The discussions of Bahrdt which lie between these two evaluations
are not as stereotyped and empty as the references to him made
after 1900, but the tendency to dismiss him with an unoriginal
cliché of moral indignation began to grow during that time and
received strong impetus from the pronouncements of Robert
Prutz and Hermann Hettner toward the end of this period, as
we shall see as we resume our chronological review.

In 1827, August Koberstein,[6] discussing various autobiographies
of the late eighteenth century which resemble picaresque novels
but exceed them in interest, calls Bahrdt's *Geschichte seines Lebens*
a remarkable book for the light it sheds on contemporary conditions. Bahrdt himself Koberstein calls a shallow rationalist,
frivolous and notorious *(berüchtigt)* . After this characterization
he gives an objective and unimpassioned account of his life. Wolf-

gang Menzel, however, as may be expected of one of his crusading spirit, was far from unimpassioned in the account of German literature which he wrote the following year.[7] He gives an inaccurate description of Bahrdt's suspension from office and condemns him roundly. Nonetheless, he calls him a martyr for what he believed to be the truth and thus, far more worthy of sympathy than the modern crawling and hypocritical rationalists—an interesting variation on a theme we have already noted.

In 1831 Heinrich Doering published a survey of German theologians of the eighteenth and nineteenth centuries.[8] His conclusion is that although there was a great disharmony between Bahrdt's teachings and his life which had certain bad results, nevertheless he scattered many seeds which sprang up and bore good fruit. He inflicted a mortal wound upon blind faith in the doctrinal system by demonstrating the untenability of many propositions of the accepted dogma. His rare natural gifts and his vivid easy style made him one of the most influential, though not most original, theologians.

G. G. Gervinus's interest in Bahrdt is more literary than moral or theological. In his book,[9] written in 1841, he makes the same comparison which Koberstein had made of Bahrdt's autobiography to the picaresque novel and justly points out many similarities between Bahrdt and the hero of Nicolai's novel, *Sebaldus Nothanker*. He makes the shrewd observation that Bahrdt really succeeded in nothing except in seeing himself but without gaining the slightest sense of what a horrible example his life constituted. Nonetheless Gervinus feels that Bahrdt was badly persecuted by his enemies in the church just as Sebaldus was, and he sees a further parallel between the fictional character and the real one in the fact that their spirit was not broken by so much adversity. He makes a further interesting parallel between Bahrdt and Jung Stilling: they both had a belief in a special Providence and were frequently saved from extremes of distress by remarkable bits of luck.

In 1846 there appeared a *Bibliothek der deutschen Aufklärer* under the name of Martin von Geismar,[10] the purpose of which was to recall to everyone's mind how great a debt was owed the Enlightenment. This book is valuable because it contains reprintings of a good many documents which would otherwise be hard to come by, but in its praise of Bahrdt it is just as uncritical as any of the stereotyped condemnations which we will note later. In the biographical introduction, for example, the scandal in Leipzig is brushed aside as being relatively innocent, and Bahrdt's whitewashed account of his doings is unthinkingly accepted. The picture of Bahrdt presented in this book is that of a noble champion of liberal thought, an innocent victim of fanatical bigotry. So far as I know, this is the only account of Bahrdt that is full of unmixed praise, although there is another book, that by Ludwig Noack, written eleven years later, which had a similar antireligious point of view.

The aesthetic-critical presentation of German literature, which Joseph Hillebrand promises in the title of his book,[11] would lead one to expect an approach similar to that in Gervinus's book, which had appeared six years before. But Hillebrand discusses Bahrdt rather as a part of the philanthropinical movement, in which, he says, there was much good despite the fact that it was associated with this rationalistically frivolous and dissolute character. It was this empty and frivolous theological rationalism, says Hillebrand, that Goethe pilloried, but despite the emptiness of his teachings Bahrdt did much to promote the spread of the so-called "French atheism." Hillebrand, incidentally, was not the first to decry rationalism, now growing in disfavor with those aptly named prophets in reverse, the scholars and historians, as a corrupting influence imported from France: Hillebrand's remark sounds like an echo of Wolfgang Menzel's thunderous denunciations of the degenerate French. Nonetheless, Hillebrand seems to feel that Bahrdt owes his fame, such as it is, to being persecuted by churchmen, both the orthodox and the conservative liberals.

The next mention of Bahrdt occurs in a book on Lessing written in 1853 by T. W. Danzel and G. E. Guhrauer,[12] in which the latter mentions him briefly and describes him as being notorious (*berüchtigt*) and sensational. Shortly after this, in 1855, Bahrdt was given much space in Ludwig Noack's book on freethinkers in religion.[13] This book was written in the interest of religious enlightenment and is antidogmatic in its purpose. Noack says of Bahrdt:

To undermine faith in the divine origin of Christianity and to expose the nullity of divine revelation which depends upon miracles and prophecies was the aim of the notorious (*berüchtigt*) Doctor Bahrdt.

Then follow a few bibliographical data and an account, partly paraphrase and partly direct quotation, of Bahrdt's creed. Noack utters no further word either of praise or condemnation. Words of condemnation, however, abound in another book from the same year, F. C. Schlosser's world history.[14] Schlosser and his collaborator, G. L. Kriegk, are apparently on the side of Enlightenment, but they must have feared for the consequences if they had not adopted a tone of moral indignation when writing about Bahrdt in a book intended for the German people. He is described as being without a conscience, sunk in the depths of depravity, ruled only by greed and sensuality. Nonetheless he left his mark on the century, an embarrassing fact which had to be explained by an appeal to the *Zeitgeist*. The explanation is simply that the spirit of the times so ardently demanded liberation from the fetters of orthodoxy that Bahrdt needed only to lift his voice in harmony with the *Zeitgeist* to be praised as a man of talent and a martyr for the Enlightenment. Besides, the party of orthodoxy persecuted him in a very stupid and even unjust way: the legalities were not observed in his suspension from office. As may not be surprising in a compendium of world history, there is little evidence that either Schlosser or Kriegk had any firsthand knowledge of Bahrdt. And, indeed, there is no compelling reason why the authors of such a history should know anything about Bahrdt at first hand. One would merely question the appropriateness of the vehement condemnation in the absence of such knowledge.

About this same time (1856), however, there appeared an article by Robert Prutz in *Raumers Historisches Taschenbuch,* later incorporated in a collection of essays,[15] which does reveal some firsthand knowledge and shows the same solicitousness for the moral welfare of the reading public. In fact, this essay, which is the story of Bahrdt's early years, was written, so Prutz says, as a warning against that limited and narrow type of enlightenment which Bahrdt represents and as an encouragement to honest and devoted friends of liberty. Since the time of the Reformation, says Prutz, no other theologian has been so widely known as Bahrdt, whose name guaranteed a ready sale of any book by or about him. But he ended his career in a sewer of dirt, misery, and decay, and has since remained in almost total oblivion, from which Prutz now proposes to exhume him and expose the horrid remains to public view. He hints that by so doing he will, as it were, hold the mirror up to certain unnamed contemporaries, who were presumably exploiting the current demand for political liberation as Bahrdt exploited the need for religious liberation in his day. The description of Bahrdt's life which follows this is a superficial and derivative account, from which it is not possible to gain any real insight into Bahrdt and his times, although it is evident that Prutz has read the autobiography at least, for he depends very much upon it. The impression made by Prutz is that all his moral protestations constitute a cloak for journalistic sensation-mongering. One suspects, however, that his essay, especially since its point of view was also expressed by Hermann Hettner, did much more to fix Bahrdt's reputation than did the subsequent sound and authentic studies by Frank, Schreiber, Keller, and Diehl, which will be mentioned in their turn.

The year 1862 can almost be said to have been a Bahrdt year: not only did Prutz's essay appear in book form, but Bahrdt received some passing attention in two other books, one by August Boden[16] and the other by Hermann Hettner.[17] Boden's book was written as a refutation of a previous attempt by one Röpe to defend Johann Melchior Götze. Röpe had made it out to be a positive merit of Götze that he permanently labeled Bahrdt's New Testament as a deliberate falsification and sacrilegious profanation of the Word of God, as Goethe also clearly labeled it in his satire. Boden points out, however, that Goethe's criticism was directed only at the incapacity of modern shallow rationalism to grasp the spirit of Biblical antiquity. And indeed, he continues, in 1773, the year of Götze's attack on Bahrdt's New Testament, Götze was already a low character, whereas Bahrdt had not yet sunk to the baseness which one usually associates with him. To substantiate this partial rehabilitation of Bahrdt for his own purposes, Boden quotes a review in the *Frankfurter gelehrte Anzeigen* for the ninth of November 1773. Amusingly enough, Bahrdt himself was the editor of this journal at this time. Rehabilitation of Bahrdt, however, was not the intention of Hermann Hettner, who assumed a tone of moral indignation in writing about him. To be sure, says Hettner, he had a good head, but he was a debauched fellow, who basely confessed that he might have remained in the orthodox camp all his life if he had not been persecuted by the heretic-hunters. He made some noise in the world because of his dissolute and adventurous life and rowdy character, and opponents of the Enlightenment have imputed to this whole movement what was really only the guilt of the individual. Furthermore, Bahrdt's position on New Testament criticism was essentially that of Semler, at least until he came to Halle, only clumsier and more impertinent. In Halle he gave up not only all belief in Revelation and actually, in a vague way and for the first time, suggested the possibility of a mythological interpretation of the New Testament, but he gave up all claim to decency by degrading himself to the level of a common tavernkeeper.

This was not the view of Friedrich W. Ebeling in his history of comical literature in Germany, first published in 1864.[18] Ebeling feels that however little nobility of spirit Bahrdt may have had, his extraordinary activity and influence made him one of the most important men of the eighteenth century. Ebeling devotes a little over twenty pages of his book to considering Bahrdt as a satirist, but although he calls for a thorough and impartial biography of Bahrdt, he does not himself attempt a rehabilitation of his character and achievements such as he wrote for Klotz. He makes it perfectly plain, however, that he considers everything that had been written about Bahrdt to be inadequate and distorted and that a fair estimate of him would do much to make possible a fairer understanding of his age. He added that a sound biography of Bahrdt could not be written by a theologian, for a theologian could produce only a caricature.

This assertion was something of a challenge to Gustav Frank, who was indeed a theologian and who wrote, in 1866, a sound and thorough study of Bahrdt.[19] He also wrote the article in the *Allgemeine deutsche Biographie*. Frank's study is a detailed, precise, and critically evaluative synopsis of Bahrdt's life and character. Frank was fully aware of Bahrdt's weaknesses and failings, but the picture he presented is far from being completely black. He knew all the primary and secondary sources that were available to him and formed his own opinion of Bahrdt's accomplishments and character, an opinion that is much closer to the estimate of the article in the Ersch and Gruber encyclopedia than to the estimate of Robert Prutz. Frank, for example, cites Bahrdt's discussion of Roennberg's defense of the legal status of the Symbolic Books as a manifestation of moral courage. As for the cliché of notorious (*berüchtigt*), which, as we have seen, had come to be a stock epithet applied to Bahrdt (as indeed, it still is), Frank feels that it was the publication of his credo which really made him sensationally notorious, for after that any book about him had a wide sale, and people did not hesitate to defame him for the sake of gain. It is Frank's conclusion that Bahrdt was not proscribed because of his morals or lack of them but because of his heterodox views, even though these views were no longer offensively new at the time he professed them.

Frank's article seems to have had very little influence on subsequent studies and estimates of Bahrdt. Thus J. Leyser, who was *Protestantischer Stadtpfarrer und königlicher Distrikts-Schulinspektor zu Neustadt a.d.H.*, very soon afterward (1867) published an interesting and informative little book on Bahrdt and his relation to the philanthropinical movement.[20] In the preface to the first printing he expresses admiration for the brilliant description of Bahrdt by Robert Prutz, but he also acknowledges indebtedness to good early sources such as Schlichtegroll. The preface to the second printing acknowledges a great debt to Hermann Hettner, through reading whose work he says he had come to a better understanding of the German Enlightenment and the popular philosophers. It is not surprising, all things considered, that Leyser sees in the background of Bahrdt's adventures the finger of Him who composes the history of the world for precept and admonition. Nonetheless, the tone of Leyser's work is not violently abusive, and it does not resort to clichés and unthinking use of secondhand material. It contributes something to our knowledge of Bahrdt's life and makes a critical and amusing appraisal of Bahrdt as an educator. This it does by developing a parallel between Bahrdt's methods of teaching, as we know them from his own writings and other contemporary accounts, and the methods of instruction described in Schummel's *Spitzbart, eine komitragische Geschichte für unser pädagogisches Jahrhundert* (1779).

Occasionally books written outside Germany made mention of Bahrdt. Dr. E. P. Evans, professor at the University of Michigan, produced a derivative history of German literature,[21] written in German, in which he says of Bahrdt merely that he degraded Wieland's hedonism to bestial vulgarity. G. A. Heinrich,[22] professor of foreign literature on the faculty of letters at Toulon, mentions Bahrdt as one of the chief promoters of deism in Germany, gives a few biographical data inaccurately, says that he had a life full of adventure and misfortune, that his autobiography is "fort curieuse pour consulter pour l'histoire de ce temps," and characterizes him as a narrow rationalist. A book appeared in England three years later (1873), written by Gostwick and Harrison,[23] who wished to denounce Bahrdt but defend rationalism:

The last-named author [Bahrdt] stood almost alone as an indecent, burlesque polemic. . . . This may suffice to indicate that there was an upper and lower school of rationalism.

One French book, however, which we may well consider in this connection, although it should, chronologically, be discussed later, was a substantial and informed study of the philanthropinical movement by A. Pinloche.[24] The résumé of Bahrdt's life, with especial attention paid, of course, to his activity in Marschlins and Heidesheim, is based upon firsthand knowledge of the important documents, except for the biographical study of Gustav Frank, and it quotes extensively from Bahrdt's autobiography. By skilfully emphasizing certain facts and passing lightly over others but without uttering bombastic denunciations, Pinloche paints a devastating and amusing picture of Bahrdt, whom he considers "un fourbe et un malhonnête homme," who had the worst possible qualifications to be an educator. The partial justice of this judgment must be admitted, but it should be added that Pinloche makes no attempt to understand Bahrdt as a complex human being, and is, understandably, not concerned with those manifestations of a certain kind of integrity which were mentioned by Gehren and Frank, among others. Neither does he attempt to explain why Bahrdt persisted in his increasing hostility to orthodox and even liberal faith when it was so plainly to his proven disadvantage to do so. Surprisingly enough, however, his final judgment of Bahrdt is far from being wholly condemnatory:

he does have one single merit, that of having struggled and suffered in the cause of progress, and this alone assures him of an honorable place in the history of civilization, although he can have no claim whatever to a similar place in the more limited history of education.

Meanwhile, the tradition of merely abusing Bahrdt without knowing anything about him kept gaining momentum within Germany. Heinrich Kurz's history of German literature,[25] apparently echoing previous opinion, finds that Bahrdt's writings gave full expression to his base nature but also contained many things worth considering and that his autobiography, untrustworthy though it is, is a pleasant, easy source of information about life in the later eighteenth century. About Bahrdt himself, however, Kurz has nothing good to say:

he was one of the chief representatives of shallow enlightenment, completely lacking in nobility of mind, a base character who put the sublime teachings of Christ into the most modern and superficial rationalistic language.

Daniel Sanders, in his history of German literature,[26] merely mentions Bahrdt as having undergone a metamorphosis from an orthodox hypocrite to an unbelieving preacher of the Enlightenment, and Karl Borinski, in his history of German literature,[27] makes only a disparaging allusion to Bahrdt. And the entries in two ecclesiastical encyclopedias [28] from about this time were completely negative and denunciatory; the writers seem to have accepted Robert Prutz as their authority. Not all references to Bahrdt made during these years were merely passing allusions, however: in 1887 Waldemar Kawerau made him the subject of a journalistic essay in *Die Grenzboten*.[29] The essay is wholly condemnatory and almost completely derivative. Kawerau quotes Hettner with approval and in part, without acknowledgment, and makes several untrue assertions, aside from the questionable sweeping analysis of Bahrdt's character as being entirely composed of crudest sensuality and cool calculation. Thus, Bahrdt, who was of course notorious (*berüchtigt*), is said to have taken up and discarded his theological convictions as though they were gloves and to have been broken inwardly and outwardly when he arrived in Halle in 1779—statements contrary to all objective evidence. But Kawerau makes an interesting attempt to explain Bahrdt's character, suggesting that he was driven by an irresistible compulsion to baseness. Thus, he calls the purchase of the vineyard a last desperate, bankrupt step, designed to cast away the final vestige of dignity and modesty and defiantly to expose his degradation to public view. This is a suggestion that would be more acceptable if we did not know that Bahrdt had always been interested in practical domestic and culinary things and that he performed such tasks and duties with pleasure and quite matter-of-factly. Equally shallow and journalistic is the judgment of Erich Schmidt, who in his book on Lessing[30] from about the same time (1892), excoriates Bahrdt freely whenever he has occasion to mention him. He even has praise for Götze's attack upon him, though with the reservation that Götze's cry for suppression of Bahrdt's New Testament by censorship was perhaps a bit extreme. Indeed, one suspects that Schmidt would not have made this concession if he had not been, so to speak, precommitted by Lessing. Schmidt's basic judgment was that the disgusting Bahrdt was a caricature of all criticism and enlightenment.

Although the judgments of Hettner, Prutz, and Schmidt seem to have done a great deal to establish a standard view of Bahrdt, some deviations from this now continued to appear. For example, three sound specialized studies of Bahrdt were published after Schmidt's book was printed. One by Albert Schreiber was concerned with the Philanthropinum in Heidesheim.[31] It gives a good account of that episode and, being based upon a study of materials in the archives of the House of Leiningen, presents much previously unknown factual material. Schreiber's judgment of Bahrdt is that he was very talented but morally unstable, clever and ingenious but often clumsy and crude, adroit and versatile but superficial and unsteady, active and enterprising but frivolous and impetuous, "mit einem Wort, ein Talent, aber kein Charakter." In 1899

J. Keller, who had occupied himself very intensively with local history in Bünden, especially with the history of education and the part played in it by Ulysses von Salis and Isaak Iselin, published a very careful and detailed study, with new information, of the Philanthropinum in Marschlins.[32] Keller had real admiration for Salis, or at least for his intentions, even though he recognized that Salis had an unwarranted confidence in ideas and plans and, accordingly, was not skilled in his judgment and direction of people. Although Keller is severe in his judgment of Bahrdt, he does not make him wholly responsible for the failure of Marschlins but attributes some part of the blame to Salis, part to detractors and enemies within the country, part to poor management, part to the unwholesome location. He also makes it clear that the personal relations between Salis and Bahrdt would have been very difficult even if Deinet, the publisher of the *Frankfurter gelehrte Anzeigen,* had not, as he did, spoiled them from the very beginning by destroying Salis's confidence in Bahrdt. And besides, even though Keller is certainly not partial to Bahrdt, he is careful to cite good contemporary opinions of him, such as have already been mentioned in this essay.

In the interval between the appearance of these two studies and the third, there were published in Giessen in 1905 two books which were mainly concerned with Semler and which therefore had to deal with Bahrdt. Both writers, who were theologians, really knew something about Bahrdt and both of them, quite naturally, rejected and censured him, but not, be it noted, on the basis of hearsay.

Of the two, Zscharnack's study of Lessing and Semler[33] is the less direct in passing judgment on Bahrdt. Zscharnack is content rather to explain Semler's point of view, which he takes as his own. Thus there is no blind and empty vituperation in his book. As for Gastrow, he too adopts Semler's viewpoint but is more outspoken in his discussion[34] of Bahrdt's strength and weakness. He acknowledges the candor of Bahrdt's confession of faith and calls it the most consistent and complete summary of the religious principles prevailing in the circles of the radical Enlightenment.

Only the tenacious energy and disregard of every consideration with which he championed the ideals of the Enlightenment, [writes Gastrow] together with a forceful style and biting sarcasm, which depended upon his temperament and natural gifts, enabled the most advanced among those who shared his views to overlook his inward emptiness and to feel a certain sympathy with him, especially in the difficult situation in which he found himself at that time and which made him seem a martyr of the Enlightenment despite his serious moral defects, which were the result of his boundless vanity, unrestrained sensuality, and base thirst for pleasure and gain.

The third of the careful special studies of Bahrdt just mentioned was an investigation of his career in Giessen, based on original sources, by Wilhelm Diehl, which appeared in 1912.[35] Diehl is no more partial to Bahrdt than Keller is, but his account is detailed, factual, and objective, and makes it plain that Bahrdt had determined active enemies from the first, including F. K. von Moser, and that Bahrdt was fighting to maintain his influence and standing. Diehl's essay is a description of a struggle for power, with all its rivalry and intrigue, that sounds very modern and, one is tempted to say, normal in a German university, if not elsewhere.

The last of this rather long series of informed accounts of Bahrdt appeared in 1913 in Albert Schweitzer's monumental *Geschichte der Leben-Jesu Forschung*.[36] After a brief and objective sketch of Bahrdt's life, Schweitzer goes on to discuss the *Briefe über die Bibel im Volkston* and the *Ausführung des Plans und Zwecks Jesu,* the first of the fictional lives of Jesus. It is Schweitzer's view that Bahrdt's representation of the life of Jesus has been judged too harshly. There are passages in it of genuine deep feeling, especially in the recurrent remarks about the relationship between faith in miracles and true faith. And the comments on Jesus' teachings are not always banal, says Schweitzer, but in its totality the story is formless and unaesthetic and the dialogues are excessively long. Moreover the invented characters who appear in the story are confusing. The rest of the discussion is devoted to a synopsis of Bahrdt's books.

Despite the appearance of these five balanced and authentic discussions of Bahrdt, the tide of uninformed condemnation was setting so strongly that apparently no sober estimate could be heard. Oehlke, in his book on Lessing,[37] even echoes Erich Schmidt's approval of Götze in his attack on Bahrdt, and Bartels[38] in the same year (1919) dismisses him as being not especially respectable, although he admits that Bahrdt's autobiography is of some consequence for the study of cultural history. Even Felix Hasselberg, who edited the autobiography[39] in 1922 and who certainly knew the literature, quotes Erich Schmidt's opinion with approving agreement in his preface. But, and this is both amusing and suggestive, Hasselberg echoes and combines practically everything that had been said about Bahrdt and accepts almost all the clichés. Bahrdt, he says, was one of the most remarkable and notorious (*berüchtigt*) personages of the eighteenth century, about whom an abundance of material has been accumulated, so that final judgment may be passed upon him. This judgment is negative. To be sure, it cannot be denied that Bahrdt had great natural gifts, was quick to learn and comprehend, possessed extraordinary intellectual flexibility, had remarkable powers of rhetorical persuasiveness, and that he could be a charming and entertaining companion. But all these positive qualities were completely obscured: as a scholar he was a bungler who could only debase the pure gold of others' coinage; he never knew honest devotion to a task he had set himself; he never pursued a moral or intellectual goal for its own sake but always for the sake of material advantage and for the sake of appeasing his conceit and thirst for distinction. His private life was highly immoral and in violent contrast to his activity as a clergyman and a pedagogue. He speculated with the great ideas of his age and damaged the great cause of the Enlightenment much more than he advanced it. He has no real significance in the history of German civilization, and it cannot be regretted that he is now scarcely known even by name.

Hasselberg was the last, so far as I know, to occupy himself intensively with Bahrdt, and almost the last to know anything about him at first hand. Konrad Burdach,[40] however, was another who really knew something about Bahrdt. His researches on the Halle of Bahrdt's day and his interest in Kindleben, a questionable contemporary and, in a sense, competitor of Bahrdt in Halle, attest to that fact. Burdach, who lumps Bahrdt with Kindleben and Laukhard as a wretched trio of rationalistic literary and academic debauchery in Halle, seems to identify himself so closely with the University as to condemn them as though they were still living to disgrace the Alma Mater. Of the three he allows some merit only to Kindleben because of the latter's interest in popular and student language and student songs. In 1928, three years after Burdach's *Vorspiel*, Elisabeth Heimpel-Michel published an historical and systematic study of the Enlightenment,[41] which refrains from making any judgment at all about Bahrdt's character but merely assesses his ideas, as summed up in his (Bahrdt's) book *Über Aufklärung und deren Beförderungsmittel* (Leipzig, 1789) as exemplifying, shallow and narrow as they are, the transition to rigid *Kleinbürgertum*. This was followed in 1929 by Karl Aner's masterful summary,[42] which takes precisely the opposite view from Zscharnack and Gastrow on the question of Semler's attitude towards Bahrdt's confession of faith, which, Aner points out, upheld the identical positions that Semler had defended in his book on the canon and elsewhere. Semler's attack on Bahrdt's confession was possible only by means of the worst sort of hairsplitting sophistry, says Aner—a fact which should not be obscured because Bahrdt was a morally questionable personality.

More recent literary historians have with few exceptions been content to characterize Bahrdt by ready-made clichés. In 1930 Paul Wiegler[43] called him a charlatan of rationalism and abused him in other ways although he did give a straightforward account of his life and indicated that he had at least read Bahrdt's autobiography. In 1937 Werner Milch[44] published a study of Zimmermann and Obereit that shows only a superficial acquaintance with Bahrdt and contains some errors of fact. For instance, Milch says that Bahrdt had no compunctions about shifting his position as a scholar and that he was imprisoned for two years. The facts are that Bahrdt proceeded steadily along the road to Enlightenment, as he saw it, and that his prison term was cut to one year. Furthermore, Milch asserts but does not and cannot prove that

Bahrdt's appointment to Halle was the result of obscure machinations. Walter Linden, in his book[45] of the same year, merely
mentions him as an *Aufklärer,* the target of Goethe's satire. Josef
Nadler's lengthy work,[46] published in 1938, is most vituperative:
Bahrdt was a consummate freethinker, hypocrite, and actor in
the pulpit, a plagiarist and a desecrator of what people hold most
sacred, and his autobiography is one of the most notorious
(*berüchtigt*) things ever written by a German. In 1949 Helmut
Prang[47] expressed similar sentiments rather more aesthetically:
Bahrdt is notorious (*berüchtigt*) rather than famous, and his
autobiography, although interesting as a document of social history, is, because of its unnecessary candor, at times quite embarrassing. About the same time Heinrich Meyer also had occasion to
mention Bahrdt in his challenging biographical study of Goethe.[48]
This is one of the very few recently published opinions of Bahrdt
that dispenses with clichés and, within brief compass, tries to be
just to Bahrdt as a human being and as a popularizer—albeit unsuccessful—of the New Testament. On the one hand, according to
Meyer, Bahrdt was the victim of the hatred and persecution of
the clergy, and on the other, he was the victim of the literary and
stylistic revolution, the revolution of feeling, so powerfully abet-
ted, if not actually wrought, by Goethe, that his translation had
become impossible even before it appeared. Another study, by
F. Sengle, of a contemporary and even briefly a close associate of
Bahrdt, Wieland,[49] written about the same time as Meyer's book
on Goethe, uses the familiar clichés to describe Bahrdt. He was
berüchtigt, of course, and the very fact that he was appointed to
the faculty at Erfurt was a bad omen for Wieland's attempted
reform of the University, for he was a shallow and impertinent
rationalist who was opposed not only by the young Goethe but
by responsible representatives of the Enlightenment also. Sengle
does, however, discuss Wieland's efforts to keep Bahrdt in Erfurt
and quotes his opinion of Bahrdt as one of the men who did honor
to the University. F. J. Schneider's book[50] of 1952 merely mentions Bahrdt in connection with Goethe as "ein unverständiger
Bibelinterpret." (The difference between this statement and
Meyer's on the same point is startling.) Bruno Sauer's biographical

sketch of Bahrdt in the *Neue deutsche Biographie*[51] is another one of the infrequent recent notices of Bahrdt that are informed rather than merely prejudiced. Sauer sums him up as a personality of internal contradictions, capable of feeling enthusiasm and of arousing it, but on the other hand, as superficial, quarrelsome, and morally unstable. He says of the autobiography that it is often untruthful but still readable as a socio-historical and psychological document. The nadir in the downward progression we have traced is probably reached in Wolfgang Pfeiffer-Belli's history of German literature.[52] This author considers even Bahrdt's autobiography an affront to the reading public, which can surely derive neither pleasure nor profit from the detailed account of the disorderly life of this "enlightened" sham theologian. And, finally, the remarks with which Heinrich Schneider accompanies his publication of a recently discovered letter of Bahrdt to George Washington[53] make some attempt to give Bahrdt the benefit of the doubt, but the thumbnail sketch of him which Schneider finally leaves with the reader is almost completely black. According to Schneider, Bahrdt had "an abominable reputation which was in every way deserved," and he was "one of those who are a disgrace to every cause they join."

Something should be said, perhaps, about the books and special studies which do not mention Bahrdt at all. A complete list of them would be almost interminable, but it would include well-known books by such scholars as Scherer, Vogt and Koch, Biese, Francke, Robertson, Ermatinger, Strich, Korff, Köster, Eloesser, Walzel, Dilthey, and Cassirer. Such a list would also show that, as the figure of Bahrdt has slipped farther and farther into ignominious obscurity, the tendency to ignore him completely has been growing. This is, of course, natural and understandable, even perhaps justifiable. It may also be inevitable, in view of a certain tendency on the part of some scholars to view the progress of history as a dialectic of leading ideas and the men and women of history as material emanations of those ideas. And so Dr. Bahrdt, who was originally a human being with his secrets and his mysteries, became a mythical hero of contradictory aspects, some dreaded and some revered, but gradually he lost status until now he is no longer even a myth but lives on only as an epithet of opprobrium: *Der Berüchtigte Doktor Bahrdt,* reduced by the mythopoeic force of partisanship to a shadow that once led an unreal existence in the far reaches of the Enlightenment.

Notes

CHAPTER I

1. This is a rather vexing point. Bahrdt says on page 74 of his autobiography that he was not quite fourteen years old when he entered the famous Schulpforta after leaving the Nikolaischule. If this is true, and if the year of his birth was 1740, he entered Schulpforta in 1754; if he was born in 1741, he entered in 1755; no later, in any case. Assuming the latter date, he must have been in the Nikolaischule from 1754 to 1755, no later. But Reiske's autobiography (*D. Johann Jakob Reiskens von ihm selbst aufgesetzte Lebensbeschreibung*) states that he became rector about the middle of 1756. There seem to be three possible explanations: (1) Bahrdt was not born in 1740 or 1741 but in 1742, and this assumption barely suffices to explain his presence in the Nikolaischule during any substantial part of Reiske's rectorate. (2) Reiske was not rector when Bahrdt was a pupil at the school; this might mean that Bahrdt, knowing Reiske as rector from later years, suffered an actual loss of memory on this point, or that he pretended that Reiske was rector at the time in order to make a *bon mot* at his expense. (3) Bahrdt, wittingly or unwittingly, made himself out to be younger than he actually was when he entered Schulpforta. This is probably the most plausible explanation, since he is vague and inaccurate about his age at this time. Thus, if he was nearly fourteen upon entering Pforta and spent two years there (page 110 of the autobiography, *Dr. Carl Friedrich Bahrdts Geschichte seines Lebens, seiner Meynungen und Schicksale. Von ihm selbst geschrieben*), he must have been nearly sixteen when he left to enter the University. But on page 115 of the autobiography he states that he was not quite fifteen years old when he became a university student. It seems likely that he is trying to impress the reader with his precocity and thus exaggerates his youth and innocence.

2. Reiske never attained a more eminent post than the rectorship, although, of course, professorships fell vacant which would have allowed him to make a far greater contribution to his world than he was able to make as a misplaced pedagogue. But the academic powers were against him, eccentric and hypochondriac as he was, and saw to it that their own favorites received the posts that he coveted. Thus, when Gesner, the professor of classical philology at Göttingen, died, Reiske was the logical candidate to succeed him, but the appointment was blocked by J. D. Michaelis, the Orientalist and Old Testament scholar of Göttingen, and J. A. Ernesti, the

classical philologist and theologian of Leipzig. Incidentally, the man who temporarily succeeded Gesner at Göttingen was Christian Adolf Klotz, who had only recently been taught by Reiske. Klotz went to Halle when the chair at Göttingen fell permanently (in 1763) to Ernesti's pupil, Heyne, who added lustre to the University of Göttingen for many years until it was dimmed by the virulent attacks made upon him by his own pupil, Johann Heinrich Voss, author of the famous translations of Homer. Reiske died in 1774, attended by Ernestine Christine, whom he had trained to help him in his research and who edited and published his posthumous works, including an autobiographical book, thirty pages of which are devoted to a list of his writings.

3. *Cf.* Schlichtegroll's *Nekrolog auf das Jahr 1792* (1793); *Allgemeine deutsche Bibliothek CXI* (Kiel, 1792), pp. 559–618; D. Pott, *Leben, Meynungen und Schicksale D. Carl Friedrich Bahrdts;* A. Pinloche, *La Réforme de l'Education en Allemagne au Dix-huitième Siècle.*

CHAPTER II

1. Wolff's orthodox and pietistic confreres at the University of Halle were not only dismayed by his views; they had also undertaken to suppress them by having them declared heretical and their author silenced or dismissed. To this end they did what Bahrdt's colleagues later did to him (it must have been a fairly widespread practice among theologians): they sent spies into his lectures to collect evidence against him. Wolff was apparently not daunted. In fact, he publicly gave his enemies the pretext they sought to denounce him: he declared in an official lecture, "De Sinarum Philosophia Practica," that the ethics of Confucius were similar to his own, and he concluded from this that human bliss was attainable even without revelation. It is likely that there would have been no serious consequences for Wolff, since he was favorably regarded by Frederick William I, whose greatest passion was the army and who would probably have cared very little for the theologians' cries of "Heretical Determinism." But when certain practical consequences of Wolff's determinism were pointed out to him by friends of the Pietistic professors at Halle, namely that his tall grenadiers could not justly be punished for desertion, because their running away was in the divine order of things, the King saw that heterodoxy constituted a manifest danger to his regime, and so he banished Wolff. In fairness it must be added that some years later the King recognized that he had done Wolff an injustice and desired to recall him. It was, however, left for his

son, Frederick the Great, to restore Wolff to his position at the University of Halle (1740), covered with honors but no longer popular as a lecturer: he had ceased to be avant-garde because his ideas were finding general recognition. The University of Halle, however, under the aegis of Frederick, became and remained a stronghold of the Enlightenment.

2. "... acutissimus Crusius, quem inter Germaniae, non dicam philosophos, sed philosophiae promotores profiteor vix cuique secundum." *Immanuel Kants Werke.* Vol. 1, p. 404.

3. Perhaps this is not too far removed from the rationalization of the Trinity which we find in Lessing's *Erziehung des Menschengeschlechts:* the idea of the Trinity has as its purpose to assist the human mind to comprehend that God cannot possibly be one in the sense that finite things are one, but that his oneness must be a transcendental oneness which does not exclude a sort of plurality. Thus if God has the most perfect idea of himself, then the idea must contain everything of himself, be a second Person or the Son, and the harmony existing between God and his idea of himself is the Holy Spirit.

4. It may be questioned whether this was true, since, as we shall see, *Fausts Höllenzwang* was one of the books he desperately missed when he had to flee from Dürkheim to Halle.

CHAPTER IV

1. Degenhardt Pott, *Leben, Meynungen und Schicksale D. Carl Friedrich Bahrdts aus Urkunden gezogen.* This biography is far from being thoroughly reliable. Pott played up the sensational aspects of Bahrdt's career in order to ensure a good sale. For instance, Pott repeats the story, which is not credited by most investigators, that as a student Bahrdt enlisted as a soldier, a step that was generally, and with good reason, regarded as proof of moral bankruptcy. This is amply borne out in the career of Bahrdt's contemporary F. C. Laukhard, a dissolute journalist, who did take that desperate step and wrote about it in his autobiography.

2. Teller, like Bahrdt at this time, was a disciple of Crusius, but unlike Bahrdt, remained a champion of orthodoxy to the end of his days. His brother, Wilhelm Abraham, however, distinguished himself in the cause of the Enlightenment both through his writings and by virtue of his official position in Berlin.

3. Carl Renatus Hausen, *Leben und Character Herrn Christian Adolph Klotzens.* In the days of their friendship Klotz and Hausen agreed that

whichever of the two lived the longer would write a truthful biography of the other. Relations between them became strained a few years before the end of Klotz's short life, apparently because Klotz felt that Hausen, who owed his position in Halle to Klotz, was becoming his rival at the University. It may be for this reason that Hausen's biography, far from flattering its subject, painted so devastating a picture of him that Goethe, reviewing the book in the *Frankfurter Gelehrte Anzeigen* for 1772 (XXXIII), exclaims, "Poor Klotz, in what a pitiable condition you are laid out before the public. . . . We do not wish to quote any further, we have more Christian charity than Herr Hausen, [even though] we are critics."

For a more charitable view of Klotz see F. W. Ebeling, *Geschichte der komischen Literatur in Deutschland seit der Mitte des 18. Jahrhunderts,* I, especially p. 390 ff. Ebeling maintains (I, p. 425) that Bahrdt sought help from Klotz in the first instance and also quotes a letter from Riedel to Klotz (p. 398), which suggests that Klotz knew nothing in advance of Riedel's appointment to Erfurt.

4. Pütter, *Gelehrtengeschichte von Göttingen* (I, p. 187).

5. It was none other than Johann Heinrich Voss, Heyne's pupil and detractor, who first pointed out the parallel between Heyne and Klotz in a letter to F. A. Wolf.

6. One instance in which Klotz's influence was effective, and perhaps also questionable, was the case of one of the poets of the *Göttinger Dichterbund,* Gottfried August Bürger, still well known for his songs and ballads, particularly "Lenore," with its compelling, if obvious, rhythm and weird atmosphere. Bürger had come to Halle as a sixteen-year-old student and fallen under the influence of Klotz, who encouraged him in his poetic efforts, particularly a translation of the late Latin poem "Pervigilium Veneris." Later Bürger left Halle for Göttingen at the insistence of his grandfather, who feared that the association with Klotz encouraged licentiousness in the young man, but even there Klotz's influence persisted, for Bürger was lodged in the somewhat doubtful house of Klotz's mother-in-law. *Cf.* Robert Prutz, *Der Göttinger Dichterbund,* pp. 207–10.

7. He was already editing the *Acta Litteraria* and the *Neue Hallische Gelehrte Zeitungen.*

8. Meusel became a very fine bibliographer. His *Das gelehrte Teutschland oder Lexikon der jetzt lebenden teutschen Schriftsteller* is still a useful reference work, although much of its material has been reworked in Goedeke's *Grundriss.* More will be said about Riedel later in this chapter.

CHAPTER V

1. Georg Gottfried Volland, *Beiträge und Erläuterungen zu Herrn Doctor Carl Friedrich Bahrdts Lebensbeschreibung, die er selbst verfertigt.*

2. It should not be supported that this procedure was unusual among Bahrdt's contemporaries and colleagues. For example, Pütter, who was eventually chosen to write the academic history of Göttingen rather than Klotz, married, at the suggestion of friends, a girl with whom he had no personal acquaintance at all. And the illustrious Semler jilted a young lady "whom he deeply admired" for the daughter of his landlady, to whom he was in debt. This marriage not only relieved Semler of his embarrassment, but it also enabled him to launch his academic career fittingly.

In this respect, that he suffered so deeply that he finally rebelled against his rationally concluded marriage of convenience, Bahrdt was not a child of his age.

CHAPTER VI

1. The six Symbolic Books are: the Large and the Small Catechisms of Martin Luther, the Augsburg Confession and the Apology to the Same, the Schmalkaldic Articles, and the Formula of Concord.

2. The story is told that Bahrdt gave his diploma to Riedel as security for a loan of three hundred *Taler*. When Riedel sailed down the Danube to Vienna to accept a promising appointment there—it turned out to be a great disappointment because Jordan Simon denounced Riedel to Maria Theresa—he tore the diploma into pieces, which he scattered on the water with the observation: "Bahrdt owes me a great deal: because of me his name will get at least as far as the Black Sea."

3. See the article by Seuffert, "Wielands Erfurter Schüler vor der Inquisition."

4. Hermann Hettner, *Geschichte der deutschen Literatur im achtzehnten Jahrhundert.* Teil II, p. 181, called this observation a "despicable admission" [*schnödes Geständnis*]. It is hard to understand why this admission should be particularly despicable unless it be on the assumption that literature and ideas should unfold through the workings of a pure process of dialectics, free from the taint of personal experience. Hettner and Erich Schmidt, it may be remarked, probably did more than any other literary historians to draw the simple all-black picture of Bahrdt which is now so generally accepted as standard.

5. The vignettes that adorn the title pages of many of Bahrdt's books are quite wonderful in their combination of intentional and unintentional humor. Each of the four parts of the autobiography, for example, is preceded by such a vignette which illustrates a salient point in the following narrative. The most hilarious of them is probably on the title page of the third part. The scene is the home of the magnanimous Jew, Löw Bär Isak, who has just given Bahrdt money, clothes, and a ring to make a worthy showing in London. Bahrdt, holding Löw Bär Isak's hand in his left, has raised his right hand to invoke a blessing upon his benefactor. The new clothes are draped over a table, and in the background Löw Bär Isak's lovely daughter, hot tears rolling down her cheeks, is sitting at a piano in the corner as she sings a song of farewell to the intrepid Bahrdt on his way to far-off England.

6. In the autobiography Bahrdt gives the reference as I Timothy 4:18. This is an error.

7. *Handausgabe der Hexapla des Origenes* (Leipzig und Lübeck, 1769-1770).

8. *Neue theologische Bibliothek,* X, pp. 423 ff., 521 ff.

9. Erfurt, 1770.

10. Erfurt, 1770–1771.

CHAPTER VII

1. F. C. Laukhard, in his *Beyträge und Berichtigungen zu Herrn Karl Friedrich Bahrdts Lebensbeschreibung in Briefen eines Pfälzers,* says that this story cannot be true, for there was no prayer bell either in Giessen or in all Hessen-Darmstadt. Laukhard also defends Benner explicitly against Bahrdt's characterization. But it must be pointed out that Laukhard was a most unsavory and untrustworthy character and that this book was written to capitalize on the great popularity of Bahrdt's autobiography. The *Allgemeine deutsche Bibliothek* (CXI, p. 559) dismissed Laukhard's book on Bahrdt as merely sensation-mongering.

2. The chief authority for this account is Wilhelm Diehl, "Beiträge zur Geschichte von Karl Friedrich Bahrdts Giesser Zeit." Diehl prints a good many letters and official documents affecting the case.

3. It is a very interesting fact that neither at Erfurt nor at Giessen did Bahrdt's opponents seek to disqualify him on the grounds of loose living. It was F. K. von Moser, who returned to Hessen-Darmstadt as Minister of State in 1772, who injected this note into the debate. So far as the records

show, the orthodox clergy were not concerned with this aspect of the matter or with anything except conformity to the Symbolic Books.

4. In the minutes of the theological faculty, Benner as dean made the following entry: "Academia meis monitis accessit."

5. Discussed and printed in Wilhelm Stieda, *Erfurter Universitätsreformpläne im 18. Jahrhundert.*

6. The text is given in Boxberger's "Wielands Professur in Erfurt."

CHAPTER VIII

1. F. C. Laukhard, *Magister F. Ch. Laukhard's Leben und Schicksale.*

2. The Chancellorship seems to have been a continuing administrative office charged with executing the decisions of the University and decrees of government.

3. Laukhard, in his *Beyträge und Berichtigungen zu Herrn Karl Friedrich Bahrdt's Lebensbeschreibung in Briefen eines Pfälzers,* asserts that this is a lie and that Bahrdt does not possess a single letter from the Landgravine. Laukhard's testimony is unreliable, however. In Degenhardt Pott's collection of letters written to Bahrdt by famous people, published in Leipzig in 1798, there is a letter from Karoline to Bahrdt, dated Darmstadt, May 28, 1772, which is couched in very friendly terms and expresses her admiration for a collection of his sermons and her agreement with his general position as expressed in his other writings. She also urges him to be more cautious and mild-tempered. That Karoline should find herself in agreement with the "enlightened" views of Bahrdt is not surprising in this friend of Frederick the Great. If more testimony were needed to the fact that Bahrdt enjoyed the protection of the Landgravine, it can be found in the words of Bahrdt's enemy Moser to the Privy Council. See Chapter X, page 90, and note 15 to that chapter.

4. Although Ludwig was dominated even in his early days, and later beyond the point of folly, by his passion for soldiering, he seems to have had little taste for war itself and missed his young wife sorely when he was in the field. On one occasion he urged her to join him at his headquarters. Karoline replied: "Vous savez combien je Vous suis attachée et que les moments les plus chers pour moi sont ceux, que je passe avec Vous, mon aimable prince, mais si Vous voulez bien penser au tort que cela ferait a ma réputation . . . je crois qu'alors Vous verrez Vous même combien l'entreprise est difficile." (*Briefwechsel der "Grossen Landgräfin" Caroline von Hessen,* ed. P. A. F. Walther II, p. 9.) A little later (winter 1742) he let her know that he was

thinking of giving up his commission in the French army and coming back to her. To this suggestion she replied: "Vous m'assurez, cher prince, que peut être pourriez-Vous venir sans que le devoir ni Votre gloire en souffre. Je vous laisse à juger, si une pareille espérance m'est indifférente; ne fût-ce pour huit jours, je serais contente, mais, malgré mon empressement à Vous embrasser, Votre gloire, Dieu le sait, m'est encore bien plus chère que ma propre satisfaction." (Walther, *Briefwechsel*, II, p. 11.)

5. Walther, *Briefwechsel*, I, p. 282.

6. Even in Pirmasens Ludwig was not spared occasional supernatural visitations, although he sought to avoid them by staying up all night in the company of his court officials and going to bed only at dawn. For example, according to an entry in his diary, the death of the Landgravine was announced to him by a great noise in his drum-room, as though all the portraits were falling down from the walls.

The ability to see ghosts seems to have been an hereditary affliction in Ludwig's family, dating back to 1637, when the spirit of the poisoned Landgrave Wilhelm V of Kassel appeared to Ludwig's great-great-grandfather, Georg II. Ludwig's daughter Karoline was also credited with possessing the unhappy gift.

7. Quoted in August Eberlein's dissertation, *Landgraf Ludwig IX und seine Pirmasenser Militärkolonie*, p. 29.

8. One of these notes reads: "NB! Nunmehro finde ich noch zu erinnern, dass der Cantzler Otto über dieser Ordre gestorben nunmehro ich keinen andern darüber setzen werde, also ich ganz allein dieses Etablissement, so wie zu Freystätt denen Catholischen ihr Exerzitium erlaubt, also ich den Reformierten in Pirmasens erlaubt. Derjenige, welcher hier über etwas einwenden wird, dem will ich eine harte Ahndung vorbehalten, sollte es auch die Regierung selber seyn." (Eberlein, *Landgraf Ludwig IX*, p. 30.)

9. *Der Herr und der Diener geschildert mit patriotischer Freyheit.*

CHAPTER IX

1. By Wilhelm Diehl, "Beiträge zur Geschichte von Karl Friedrich Bahrdts Giesser Zeit."

2. *Der Herr und der Diener*, pp. 157–58.

3. *Cf.* K. Witzel, "Friedrich Carl von Moser. Ein Beitrag zur hessendarmstädtischen Finanz-und Wirtschaftsgeschichte am Ausgang des 18. Jahrhunderts."

4. *Cf.* Georg Zimmermann, *Johann Heinrich Merck, seine Umgebung und Zeit;* Richard Loebell, *Der Anti-Necker J. H. Mercks und der Minister Fr. K. v. Moser;* Helmut Prang, *Johann Heinrich Merck, Ein Leben für Andere.*

5. Wilhelmine, known after her marriage as the Grand Duchess Natalie, died in 1776 from the effects of childbirth.

6. Karl Wagner, *Briefe aus dem Freundeskreise Goethes,* pp. 220 ff. quoted by Eduard Vehse, *Geschichte der deutschen Höfe.*

Merck is guilty of a misstatement in quoting the Landgravine's testament. In it she mentioned no one by name but said merely that she forgave her enemies, if she had any, and traitors ("Je pardonne à mes Ennemis, si j'en ai, et aux traîtres"). There is general agreement, however, that by "traitors" she meant Moser and that he had indeed attempted to create some discord between her and the Landgrave, as is evidenced by a passage from a letter she wrote to Ludwig on January 29, 1774, not long before her death. In it she says, "I repeat, I can regard that man only as my cruelest enemy, who designed to make me suspect in your eyes, and I will never forget the proof of your regard [for me] which you gave me, my dear Landgrave, on that occasion. You know people better than I know them. I will always repeat that to myself." (Quoted in Walther, *Briefwechsel.*)

An interesting light is thrown upon the whole affair by a letter from Baron Grimm to Karoline, which is also reproduced in Walther, *Briefwechsel:*

"Sarskozelo [*sic*]
24 Février 1774

. . . . J'ai reçu ici en deux fois vingt-quatre heures les lettres de V.[otre] A.[ltesse], du 29 Décembre et du 23 Janvier, la première par Mr. [*sic*] de Dybow qui a été fait Gentilhomme de la Chambre, à son retour, et l'autre par la poste. Les deux lettres m'ont, sans doute, rassuré, mais la dernière avoit bien de quoi m'affliger de nouveau. L'Impératrice, instruite par Madame la Grande Duchesse [Wilhelmine] de toutes les découvertes que V. A. avoit faites à Son retour sur le compte d'un homme [Moser] qui lui parassoit attaché, m'en avoit parlé. Ces découvertes sont très affligeantes. Mon Dieu, que les hommes sont plats et bêtes, et pour quelles fadaises ils mettent leur honneur et leur probité au jeu! Je découvris quelques jours avant le départ de celui-ci qu'il avait de l'humeur. Je pensois que quelque boîte, quelque bijou, comme un souvenir des bontés de l'Impératrice, auroit pu calmer cette humeur un peu âcre. Il ne pouvoit digérer de n'être pas mieux traité que tout autre ministre étranger, et il répétoit toujours avec aigreur qu'on savoit ici faire une différence convenable entre l'homme du Landgrave et les hommes de Madame la Landgrave [Merck and Schrautenbach], en refusant tout au premier et accablant les autres de toutes les graces possibles. Je marquai à Mr. [*sic*] de Rathsamhausen mon inquiétude sur cette disposition d'âme et sur le mal qu'elle pourroit produire à Pirmesens [*sic*]; mais celui-ci me rassura entièrement, en me disant que l'autre était trop honnête homme pour se livrer à un ressentiment si frivole. J'étois donc tranquille. L'Impératrice m'a appris depuis qu'il avoit voulu entrer ici à son service, et qu'elle lui a refusé le titre de conseiller privé qu'il lui avoit fait demander. Voilà, peut-être, le véritable grief." Grimm then goes on to warn Karoline against forgiving and trusting Moser and expresses the surmise that Moser may soon wish to leave the service of Hessen-Darmstadt for that of Hessen-Kassel.

7. Karl August was one of those who hated Moser and rejoiced at his downfall. In one of his letters he characterizes Moser as "ein goldene Dosen und Uhren-Fresser." Goethe was ambivalent in his attitude, recognizing Moser's questionable character but hoping that some positive employment might be found for his great talent. In *Dichtung und Wahrheit* he speaks well of him.

8. Gustav Frank, "Dr. Karl Friedrich Bahrdt. Ein Beitrag zur Geschichte der deutschen Aufklärung."

9. An article in the New York *Times* with the dateline Milwaukee, February 11, 1956, discusses the recent heresy trials of three pastors of the Northwest Synod of the United Lutheran Church in America. The charges in all three cases were similar: the pastors had publicly denied the virgin birth of Christ, the physical resurrection of Jesus, the bodily presence of Christ in the communion elements, and the historical authenticity of miracles. It should be added, however, that the same article quotes prominent Lutheran theologians to the effect that "the position that an errorless Bible is untenable is surely accepted in wide areas of our church. Those who would contend to the contrary and would uphold fundamentalism have definite problems."

CHAPTER X

1. "Was übrigens die Hauptsätze des Bahrdts betrifft, so bin Ich darinnen mit ihm einig, dass durch die bisherige [*sic*] Schuhl-Füchsereyen derer Geistlichen vieles in die Religion gemischet worden, welches nicht Biblisch seyn mag." Quoted in Wilhelm Diehl, "Beiträge zur Geschichte von Karl Friedrich Bahrdt's Giesser Zeit."

2. *Vorschläge zur Aufklärung und Berichtigung des Lehrbegriffs unserer Kirche* (1771).

3. Benner's book did not mention Bahrdt by name, thus complying with the letter of ordinances which forbade university colleagues to publish polemical writings against each other over their names. Benner's friends and former pupils, however, were under no such restraint, as can be seen from the following partial list of publications against Bahrdt from the year

1772: (1) H. E. Teuthorn, Pfarrer in Biedenkopf, *Abgenöthigter Beweis dass die Lehrer der evangelischen Kirchen und Schulen besonders in Hessen keine Mitbrüder des Herrn Dr. Bahrdt weder sind noch sein können* (Frankfurt) ; (2) J. G. G. Schwarz, *Abhandlungen für die Reinigkeit der Religion, eine Anzeige einiger der gegen die Heilsordnung und Religion der Christen überhaupt streitenden Irrthümer Herrn Bahrdts* (Frankfurt) ; (3) J. A. Keyser, Pfarrer in Massenheim, *Das gerettete Eden von den falschen Erklärungen des Dr. Bahrdten Freundes* (Frankfurt).

4. *Freie Betrachtungen über die Religion für denkende Leser* (Halle, 1771).

5. *Quae vera notio vocabulis* νόμος, γράμμα, πνεῦμα, ἔργα *in N. T. libris subjecta sit* (Giessen, 1771). *De precibus quas in nomine Jesu facere iubentur novae societatis statores ad Joh. XIV, 13* (Giessen, 1771).

6. "Allein die höchste Zufriedenheit Ew. Hochfürstl. Durchl. mit allen meinen Handlungen liegt mir zu sehr am Herzen, als dass ich mich eher zu etwas entschliessen sollte, bevor Höchstdieselben mir gnädigste Verhaltungsbefehle ertheilet, und mir entweder das Stillschweigen oder das öffentliche Antworten werden anbefohlen haben." Quoted by Diehl.

7. This was the recommendation of the Privy Council. Ludwig, in accepting the recommendation, wrote the following characteristic lines: "Placet der Antrag, mit dem Zusaz, dem Bahrdt zu bedeuten, es seye dieses Verfahren weder christlich, rühmlich, anständig, noch theologisch, und er solte doch nicht Jedermann zum Feind sich machen, da Er schon die ganze Universität gegen sich hat: der Obris Müller ist sodann zu disponieren sich mit dieser Satisfaction zu begnügen." Quoted by Diehl.

8. Schulz did, indeed, marry Benner's daughter, perhaps, as Bahrdt says, "ihrer seltenen Fleischigkeit halber," but surely for the sake of her father's money. It must have been galling in the extreme to Benner to see his daughter married to an *Aufklärer,* who opposed everything that he, Benner, so tenaciously defended.

9. It was Schulz who succeeded, where Bahrdt failed, in opening up the University of Giessen to "enlightened" ideas, for he made it his business to influence the students directly. The seminary for preachers was just one of his activities, but one that nearly cost him his position. In 1775 the government opened an investigation of his beliefs, the orthodox party denounced him as an outright heretic, and in 1777 he was deprived of his professorship on the theological faculty and of the directorship of the preacher's seminary. He was, however, allowed to remain on the philosophical faculty and eventually stirred up such partisanship among the students, who were quite naturally interested in new, or at least unorthodox, ideas that he was gradually permitted to extend his lectures into fields close to theology. The dismissal of Moser (1780) and the death of Schulz's father-in-law Benner (1782) removed the main obstacles to his eventual triumph. Even before Benner's death he addressed a petition to Hesse, saying that "when in the

year 1776 he was the victim of Herr von Moser's oppression and had to desist from lecturing on dogmatics and give up his position as a theologian, the University had over eighty students of theology; now, scarcely more than ten." He went on to predict that if he were allowed to lecture on dogmatics again, the number of students would soon rise to the old number. After Benner's death he re-addressed his petition to the Landgrave, and on the sixth of August 1782, he was made *Professor ordinarius* of theology. From then on, his way was clear to all positions of highest influence on ecclesiastical and educational matters, which he did much to reform in the spirit of the Enlightenment.

10. Bahrdt himself had been invited by Merck to contribute to the journal, and he had accepted, as is indicated by the fact that Deinet on February 8, 1772, lists him as a contributor. A week later, however, Deinet wrote to Raspe that Bahrdt would have to be dropped because it was obvious from his articles that he had enemies. *Cf.* Max Morris, *Goethes und Herders Anteil an dem Jahrgang 1772 der Frankfurter gelehrten Anzeigen.*

11. Ouvrier's interpretation was so foolish that even Benner had to admit that Bahrdt was right.

12. In an outline of homiletics which Bahrdt wrote at this same time, he says: "I for my part value fine elocution and action so much that I have long cherished the wish that a few good actors might be employed in every country who would train the students of theology." It is, of course, to this suggestion that Goethe alludes in *Faust* I.

13. The language of Moser's memorandum to the Privy Council reveals his own vindictiveness: "Anligendes—Blat der Frankfurter Gelehrten Zeitung N. II zeiget, auf welche hämische, persönlich injuriöse und vor die gesamte Universität beleidigende Art das nach vorgängiger Censur gedruckte Programma des H. Prof. Schulzen wegen des zu errichtenden Prediger Seminarii vor dem Publico angeheftet worden. In dem fernern N. IV wird mit dem Weynachts-Programm H. Sup. Ouvrier nicht viel besser umgesprungen. Ich habe sehr nahe und gesicherte Spur, daz diese anzapfende und Pasquillenmässige Recensionen von einem Professore in Giessen selbst herkommen, der ohngeachtet des so ernstlich anbefohlnen Stillschweigens nicht ohne Zanck und Hader leben kan, und da er innerhalb der Mauern schweigen muss, auswärts sein Müthgen zu kühlen sucht. Ich glaube, dass in der Sorgfalt vor die academische Polizey, dem guten Nahmen der misshandelten Männer und der Ehre der Universität selbst schuldig seyen, diesem Muthwillen (dann die Petulanz nicht eines Pedanten, sondern eines gelehrten Bon vivant leuchtet überall durch) in Zeiten zu stemen und wann der Thäter entdeckt worden, es gegen ihn als einen Stöhrer der öffentlichen academischen Ruhe condigne zu ahnden." Quoted by Diehl.

14. Ludwig's words are, as so often, worth quoting: "An das Geheime Raths Collegium, Mir ist von denen vorgeblichen Beschwerden noch nichts bekannt. Solten aber solche einlauffen, so werde Ich Mich nicht darum

bekümmern, sondern Ich werde die Entscheidung dieser gelehrten Grillen denen Feder Kriegern überlassen. Dem Vernehmen nach gehen die beyde Kriticken gegen den Ouvrier und Schulz, und ohngeachtet Ich davon nicht urtheilen kan, so ist doch soviel gewiss, dass ich den Bahrdt, den ich selbst gesprochen, vor einen Mann halte, der den Ouvrier weit übersiehet, und der mehr Wiz und Gelehrsamkeit im kleinen Finger hat, als Ouvrier im ganzen Leibe." Quoted by Diehl.

15. In his report to the Privy Council, Moser said: "Was ich vermuthet, ist geschehen, dass H. D. Bahrdt, der auf die Gnade beyder Durchlauchtigsten Herrschafften trotzt, all seine Gauckelkünste anwenden würde, um sich der verdienten Ahndung der Gesetze—zu entziehen." Quoted by Diehl.

CHAPTER XI

1. This is apparently still a controversial theological question. Hugh T. Kerr writes in his article on redemption in *A Handbook of Christian Theology* that although theologians are virtually unanimous that redemption involves God's gracious saving love in Christ for sinful mankind, there is difference of opinion among them as to how this is effected and what it means.

2. J. G. Töllner (1724–1774), professor at the University of Frankfurt an der Oder, author of, among other things, *Unterricht von symbolischen Büchern überhaupt* (1769) and *Der tätige Gehorsam Jesu Christi* (1768), gave widely acclaimed expression to the "moral influence" as opposed to the "satisfaction" theory of redemption. The letter referred to is printed in *Briefe angesehener Gelehrten, Staatsmänner, und anderer, an den berühmten Märtyrer D. Karl Friedrich Bahrdt,* ed. Degenhardt Pott, Teil I, pp. 110–16.

3. Where Luther has *Versöhnung,* and the King James Bible has "propitiation," Bahrdt has *Gottgefälligmachung.*

4. Bahrdt is not exact in his references: he gives the passage as Romans 9, but the language he quotes is Romans 11:11.

5. Again Bahrdt is inexact in his quotation and makes the passage refer to the Apostles in general.

6. *E.g.* Titus 2:14, "[Jesus Christ] who gave himself for us, that he might redeem us from all iniquity, and purify unto himself a people for his own possession, zealous of good works."

7. *Entwurf einer unpartheyischen Kirchen Geschichte Neuen Testaments* (Frankfurt am Main, 1773).

8. Thus Ernesti in a letter dated December 13, 1771.

9. In this context *pragmatisch* has the rather technical meaning of treating the facts of history in their connection with each other as cause and effect and with reference to their practical lessons.

10. At this point there is evident the inconsistency in Bahrdt's thinking on the subject of redemption with which we are already familiar. Here he has not given up the idea that the righteousness of Christ in his obedience to God's will is imputed to all mankind. At the same time Bahrdt considers Christ's death an inspiration and a guarantee of the truth of his message which man must follow to become free of sin.

11. This is one of the standard "enlightened" views of St. Augustine. For instance, Johann Friedrich Wilhelm Jerusalem, the father of the prototype of Goethe's Werther, as early as the year 1747, wrote to Gottsched that he bore Augustine and Jerome a grudge for being so unjust to Pelagius, and in the posthumous writings of Jerusalem there is a passage which inveighs against the "nonsense of the bilious Augustine" and in which the questions are asked: "Where is it written that men are to be damned because of their inborn depravity? Where, that men who live outside the Christian church, that heathens, that unbaptized children are to be damned? Where, finally, that, according to the most dreadful of all ideas, God has actually resolved from eternity to damn some people?" Quoted by Karl Aner, *Die Theologie der Lessingzeit*, p. 162.

12. *Predigten zur Paraphrase des Neuen Testaments* (Riga, 1773).

13. *Kritiken über die Michaelis'sche Bibelübersetzung* (Frankfurt, 1773).

14. *Die neusten Offenbarungen Gottes in Briefen und Erzählungen verdeutscht durch D. Carl Friedrich Bahrdt* (Riga, 1773).

15. The Greek, it may be pointed out, says merely κάλαμον συντετριμμένον οὐ κατεάξει καὶ λίνον τυφόμενον οὐ σβέσει.

16. Karl Aner, *Die Theologie der Lessingzeit*, p. 206.

17. It may be interesting to compare Bahrdt's version of the Lord's prayer with one written a good many years earlier by Benjamin Franklin.

Bahrdt: "Gott! Vater der Menschen! erfülle unser aller Herz mit Ehrfurcht gegen dich, als das allervollkommenste Wesen. Gründe und erweitere dein Reich, welches da ist, wo durch deinen Geist Weisheit und Tugend blühen. Lehre uns alle im Gehorsam gegen deine Gebote und in der Ergebung in deinen Willen unsere Ruhe und Glückseeligkeit finden. Befreye uns durch deine liebreiche Vorsorge von ängstlichen Sorgen für die Zukunft. Verzeihe uns wenn wir von Sünden übereilt werden, wie wir auch unsern Nebenmenschen gern alle Beleidigungen vergeben wollen. Lass uns in Stunden, wo wir zur Verleugnung der Wahrheit oder der Tugend gereizet werden, nicht unterliegen. Errette uns von allem was uns wahrhaftig unglücklich macht. Auf dir steht unser Vertrauen: Denn du bist unser Herr, du bist mächtig; du bist der Besitzer aller Schätze des Himmels und der Erden; du bist es und bleibst es in alle Ewigkeit, Amen."

Franklin: "Heavenly Father, may all revere thee, and become thy dutiful children and faithful subjects. May thy laws be obeyed on earth, as perfectly as they are in heaven. Provide for us this day, as thou hast hitherto daily done. Forgive us our trespasses and enable us to forgive those who offend us. Keep us out of temptation and deliver us from evil."

Despite the additions and interpolations of the pulpit orator Bahrdt, the similarity in outlook is marked, especially in Franklin's justification of his proposed changes, for example, substituting "May all revere thee" for "Hallowed be thy name." "This seems to relate to an observance among the Jews not to pronounce the proper or peculiar name of God, they deeming it a profanation so to do. We have in our language no *proper name* for God; the word *God* being a common or general name, expressing all chief objects of worship, true or false. The word *hallowed* is almost obsolete. People now have but an imperfect conception of the meaning of the petition." Quoted in *In God We Trust*, ed. Norman Cousins, p. 21. See Aner, *Die Theologie der Lessingzeit*, p. 363 for a Kant-Fichtean parallel.

18. J. M. Götze, *Beweis, dass die Bahrdt'sche Verdeutschung des Neuen Testaments keine Übersetzung, sondern eine vorsätzliche Verfälschung des Wortes Gottes sei.*

19. Lessing's defense of Bahrdt appeared in his *Anti-Goeze*, I; in the Lachmann-Muncker edition in vol. XIII, p. 143.

20. *Allegemeine deutsche Bibliothek*, Anhang zu dem 13. bis 24. Bande (1777).

21. 1774. It can be found in the Weimar edition of Goethe's works 1. Abteilung, XVI, 105–10.

22. "Da Kam mir ein Einfall von ungefähr, So redt' ich, wenn ich Christus wär."

Goethe writes in *Dichtung und Wahrheit* that Bahrdt seemed to take this criticism good-naturedly enough, that he came to see Goethe and wished to establish friendly relations. It seems plain that Bahrdt recognized Goethe's superior qualities, but he never quite forgave him the slap; in his *Allgemeine theologische Bibliothek* (II, p. 323) he writes that the "Prolog" and the farce "Götter, Helden und Wieland" reveal Goethe's misanthropy and malice, and in the *Kirchen- und Ketzeralmanach* (p. 66) he writes, "In theology he goes his own way, as do all geniuses. He is too shrewd to defend the religion of the Götzes and the Seilers and too proud to join the reformers. Therefore, together with Herder and a few others he has set out on his own middle course and doled out slaps right and left to both orthodox and heretics."

CHAPTER XII

1. Printed in *Kösters Neueste Religionsbegebenheiten für das Jahr 1792.*
2. Scheben was at that time *kaiserlicher Büchercommissarius.*
3. It might be pointed out that some of the greatest German wines, Leisten-wein and Steinwein, grow on the slopes of the mountain leading up to the ancient residence of the bishops of Würzburg.
4. J. H. von Gerstenberg, *Versuch den katholischen Lehrbegriff zu vertheidigen, von einem Protestanten.* According to Bahrdt this was really an attempt to demonstrate the absurdity of all positive religions by seeming to defend the most absurd one.
5. *Toleranzbrief an die oberhessische Geistlichkeit; Sendschreiben eines Predigers im Elsass an seinen in Giessen studirenden Sohn über des Dr. Bahrdt Neueste Offenbarungen.*
6. Quoted by Gustav Frank in his account of Bahrdt in *Raumers historisches Taschenbuch* for 1866.
7. The report concludes with these lines not unworthy of a Catullus or a Juvenal:

> Ravola, tu pathicae Rhodopes inceste subactor,
> Digne decem raphanis mugilibusque decem.
> Sive his si terebris nondum tua facta piasti,
> Digne decem Gyaris Anticyrisque decem.
> Quin etiam annales Volusi, tua crimina prostant,
> Te lambis, reliquos salva ibi dente petis,
> Exercens rabiemque canis, veneremque caninam,
> Turpiter ostendis parte ab utraque canem.
> Ortum furva tibi bilis succusque cicutae,
> Et colubri sanies hippomanesque dedit.
> Redde hominem, si forte potes, scelerique minantem,
> Hunc quoque tu laceras, disce timere Deum.

Quoted in Drews, "Das Eindringen der Aufklärung in der Universität Giessen."

CHAPTER XIII

1. In his article, "Das rhätische Seminar Haldenstein-Marschlins." Keller is the author of a second very illuminating article, "Das Philanthropinum in Marschlins." Keller is an able defender of Ulysses von Salis.

2. Basedow seems to have been indebted for some of his ideas to the French educator La Chalotais.

3. *Inusitata et optima honestioris juventutis erudiendae Methodus* (Kiel, 1752).

4. *Vorstellung an Menschenfreunde und vermögende Männer über Schulen und ihren Einfluss auf die öffentliche Wohlfahrt. Mit einem Plane eines Elementarbuchs der menschlichen Erkenntnis.*

5. Second edition, Leipzig, 1783; third edition, Stuttgart, 1849. A translation into French by Huber appeared in Leipzig in 1774, bearing the title *Manuel élémentaire d'éducation, ouvrage utile à tout ordre de lecteurs, en particulier aux parents et aux maîtres, pour l'éducation des enfants et des adolescents, et qui renferme une suite de toutes les connaissances nécessaires.*

6. For instance, Goethe, who approved of much of the *Elementarwerk*, in the fourteenth book of the third part of *Dichtung und Wahrheit* lays his finger on the unnatural conceptualistic structure of the book. "I did not like," he writes, "that the drawings in his *Elementarwerk* were more distracting than the objects themselves, for in the actual world only possible things appear in juxtaposition, and it has therefore, notwithstanding all its variety and apparent confusion, something ordered in all its parts. But the *Elementarwerk* splits it up completely, by putting together things which in the world are never seen together, only for the sake of the logical connection. For this reason it lacks the advantages of sensuous method, which we must concede to similar works of Amos Comenius."

This passage occurs in a rather lengthy and entertaining description of Basedow as Goethe got to know him during the summer of 1774 when he travelled extensively in the company of Basedow and Lavater: "Propheten rechts, Propheten links/Das Weltkind in der Mitten."

7. *Das in Dessau errichtete Philanthropinum, eine Schule der Menschenfreundschaft und guter Kenntnisse für Lernende und junge Lehrer, Arme und Reiche; ein Fidei-Kommiss des Publikums zur Vervollkomnung des Erziehungswesens aller Orten nach dem Plane des Elementarwerks, den Erforschern und Thätern des Guten unter Fürsten, menschenfreundlichen Gesellschaften und Privatpersonen empfohlen.*

8. Goethe's vivid description of Basedow's pestilential pipe-smoking and eccentric mode of life tends to confirm this account. A brief passage is worth citing: ". . . I always spent part of the night with Basedow. The latter never went to bed but dictated without ceasing. Sometimes he threw himself on a couch and took a nap while his tyro, pen in hand, calmly remained seated and was ready to resume writing instantly, as soon as Basedow was half awake and gave free rein to his thoughts. All this went on in a tightly closed room filled with clouds of tobacco and tinder smoke." The tinder smoke resulted from a mixture of Basedow's own making, which Goethe says he threatened to give the scientific classification, *Basedowscher Stinkschwamm.*

9. This charge may very well be entirely false and slanderous. It has certainly been denied vehemently by various people, notably J. G. P. Thiele, an

instructor in the Philanthropinum, in his little book, *Dr. Bahrdt in Marschlins,* which is respectfully dedicated to Rudolf von Salis of Haldenstein. That Mme Bawier's relation to Salis was something more than that of mere employee is, however, plainly indicated by the fact that at the end of a letter written by Salis to Lavater on June 3, 1776, piteously imploring Lavater to hasten to Marschlins to aid and console him, there are two postscripts, one of them written by Salis's wife and the other by Judith Bawier, who wrote, "Kommen Sie, Lavater, ich bitte Sie um Gotteswillen. Ach kommen Sie." (Quoted in Keller, "Das Philanthropinum in Marschlins.")

10. Most accounts agree on this, and it is a matter of record that the school was visited by epidemics of serious illness.

CHAPTER XIV

1. Schlichtegroll's *Nekrolog auf das Jahr 1792,* p. 145 ff.

2. Dr. Amstein was the only member of the original staff for whom Bahrdt expresses any regard. Amstein left the school during Bahrdt's year as Director because he was in love with Hortensia, Salis's sister, of whom Bahrdt also speaks in the highest terms. Amstein and Hortensia were later married despite the class barrier, which had made Amstein feel he could make no acceptable claim to her hand.

3. Quoted in Keller, "Das Philanthropinum in Marschlins."

4. Ibid.

5. See Note 9 to Chapter XIII. Some of Thiele's work had come to the favorable attention of Bahrdt, who invited him to contribute to the *Allgemeine theologische Bibliothek* (Mitau, 1774), a critical journal which he edited together with sixteen others, including Lavater, Pfenninger, and Urlsperger. Bahrdt was responsible for the first four volumes only. When Bahrdt accepted Salis's invitation to become Director of the Philanthropinum, he recommended Thiele for a position there. Of Thiele he says that he was very widely read and possessed the gift of combining and comparing various bits of information in a highly original way. In person and manner he was also extremely original. "Herr Thiele," he says, "never made a single movement of his limbs and muscles as other people do. When, for example, he bowed in greeting to someone, he first came to a halt in a flash, then he suddenly shot up to that person at high speed and, with his body rigid, stopped again very close to him so that he almost touched his chest with his own, pushed his head out at him, assuming the most roguish expression, and then quickly dropped his head as though he wished to sight down the other person's arms, and thus he remained standing, engaged in conversation."

6. *Philanthropinischer Erziehungsplan oder vollständige Nachricht von dem ersten wirklichen Philanthropin zu Marschlins* (Frankfurt am Main, 1776).

7. That Salis actually ordered Bahrdt to fill the book with falsehoods has been hotly disputed, and the charge cannot be proved any more than it can be disproved. It is a fact, however, that when the book was published, the preface was signed Ulysses von Salis. Salis wrote to Lavater on the sixth of February 1776 that Bahrdt, who believed that the prospectus would bring him great credit, bore responsibility for the whole thing; nevertheless there was much in the book that was trivial, shallow, and incorrect. "I must be satisfied," he went on, "to strike out what is contrary to my principles in ethics and religion and then, by means of the foreword which I will sign, save my own credit and the credit of the school so far as possible." Quoted by Keller, "Das Philanthropinum in Marschlins."

8. The chapter headings are: I. Concerning the Special Features of a Philanthropinum and the First Principle of Philanthropinical Education; II. Body Building; III. Training in Conduct; IV. Concerning Philanthropinical Instruction in Its Entire Scope; V. Concerning the Socratic Method of Instruction; VI. Concerning the Ennobling of the Soul by Virtue; VII. Philanthropinical Code [the rules and regulations which had so incensed Salis]; VIII. Concerning Punishments; IX. Concerning Rewards; X. Court, Senate [*i.e.,* self-government of the school]; XI. Philanthropinical Religious Services; XII. Concerning All Kinds of Philanthropinical Games; XIII. Discipline [written by Salis]; XIV. List of All Expenses Which the Various Classes of Philanthropinical Pupils Are Required to Meet [written by Salis]; XV. Author's Epilogue.

9. The importance of a healthy body and sound sense-organs is, of course, explicit in the systems of Locke and Rousseau among others, but it must probably be admitted that the philanthropinical schools, by putting the theory into practice, helped much to secure acceptance of more "natural" styles of dress and modes of living for school children, and to make possible the general modern acceptance of Juvenal's maxim "Orandum est, ut sit mens sana in corpore sano."

10. Here Bahrdt was describing actual practice as is confirmed by Thiele, who wrote of the practice with ironical contempt. One wonders whether Bahrdt's great emphasis on field trips may not have been suggested to him by previous conversations with his friend Baumer in Giessen.

11. Perhaps it should be pointed out, however, that there were other successful educational reformers. Before Basedow and Bahrdt there was *Abt* Jerusalem, who had travelled part way along the same road. And two very influential teachers in addition to Wolke were at one time associated with Basedow. One was Christian Gotthelf Salzmann, who founded a model school in Schnepfental, and the other was Joachim Heinrich Campe, the tutor of Wilhelm and Alexander von Humboldt, whose *Allgemeine Revision des gesammten Schul- und Erziehungswesens* in sixteen volumes was a widely read encyclopedia of pedagogical theory. The first contribution received by

Campe was an essay on the purpose of education ("Über den Zweck der Erziehung") by Bahrdt.

12. Schlichtegroll's *Nekrolog auf das Jahr 1792*.

CHAPTER XV

1. Correspondence in Pott, *Briefe*.

2. To the indignation of Bahrdt's Lutheran confreres this child was baptized in the Reformed church. During his stay in Switzerland he was a regular communicant of the Reformed church, being, as he says, afflicted by the acute *indifferentismus crassus*. The child died not long after the family reached Dürkheim. Bahrdt records the event with what is perhaps the most offensively cynical remark in his autobiography: "Fifteen years earlier I might have persuaded myself that the omission of Lutheran baptism could have been partly to blame."

3. Albert Schreiber: "Der Zusammenbruch des Dr. Bahrdtschen Philanthropinums in Heidesheim."

4. Bahrdt, however, says that Rühl was really incompetent, that he was not thoroughly grounded in law, but only made use of the opinions which he obtained from *Hofrat* Pütter in Göttingen. Moreover, says Bahrdt, he had no professional competence in any field whatever, least of all in philosophy, and even his French, of which he was inordinately proud, was, in the opinion of experts, execrable.

CHAPTER XVI

1. In his *Kirchen- und Ketzeralmanach* (1781) Bahrdt speaks very appreciatively of Lavater's warmth of heart and human goodness, and very indulgently and understandingly of the admixture of vanity in his personality. But, he says, Lavater's enthusiasm simply swept away his capacity for seeing things in perspective, so that he would uncritically accept as actual or true anything he hoped might be true. Besides, Lavater was poorly grounded in Greek and biblical philology.

2. The field of motivation of human conduct proved to be very fruitful for Bahrdt, and it was not long before he hit upon the idea that specific actions must be caused by specific motives and that a person's behavior can be brought into conformity with moral law by a counsellor who understands these motives and who can remove the harmful ones and fortify the good ones. Bahrdt himself saw the resemblance of his practice to that of the physician, as is evident in the following passage, which might be acceptable to some modern reformers and penologists: "Thus in time was evolved my own special therapy which is completely missing from the ordinary systems of ethics, which advocates a special cure for every illness (for I soon hit upon the idea of treating all sins and vices as diseases), and which answers such questions as how, by what means, exercises, preventatives, *etc.* the avaricious man may be weaned from his avarice, the obstinate man from his obstinacy, the lazy man from his laziness, *etc.* and the illness thus be radically cured." Bahrdt, *Geschichte seines Lebens,* III, p. 56.

3. *Erste Nachricht an das Publikum von Errichtung eines Leiningischen Erziehungshauses oder dem wirklichen dritten Philanthropin auf dem hochgräflichen Schlosse zu Heidesheim im oberrheinischen Kreise* (1776). This announcement appeared also in a French translation by Rühl. In 1777 Bahrdt published a *Zweite Nachricht.*

4. It should be pointed out here that a few years later, when Bahrdt was in serious trouble, Nicolai was magnanimous enough to give him moral and material support.

5. A clear statement of this problem may be found in Adolph *Freiherr* von Knigge's *Über den Bücher-Nachdruck.* Knigge, who was a kind of Emily Post of his day, was later involved, through no fault of his own, in the scandal which resulted from Bahrdt's quarrel with Zimmermann, the internationally renowned physician and popular philosophizer.

6. Cf. *Allgemeine deutsche Bibliothek* CXI¹, a review of Bahrdt's autobiography, p. 559 ff.

7. Schlichtegroll's *Nekrolog auf das Jahr 1792,* p. 168 ff.

CHAPTER XVII

1. In Campe's *Allgemeine Revision des gesammten Schul- und Erziehungswesens,* Teil I, pp. 3–124.

2. Cf. *Kösters Neueste Religionsbegebenheiten für das Jahr 1792,* pp. 79–85.

3. The dissolute F. C. Laukhard, in his book of memoirs, *Magister F. Ch. Laukhard's Leben und Schicksale,* is explicit on this point. Laukhard, who

was a native of the Palatinate, tried for a while to obtain a church in the region with indifferent success. He records a conversation with *Inspektor* Bierau of Alzey (the district which experienced a sudden spurt in population growth as a result of the dedication of Bahrdt's Philanthropinum), in which Bierau explained the secret of success in a clerical career. "My friend," he said in effect, "guzzle as much as you wish, produce bastards, fight and brawl; in brief, indulge in all excesses you may care to. But do not become known as a freethinker. Fornication and adultery are acceptable; heresy is not."

4. *Cf.* Pott *Briefe,* Teil II, 186–87.

5. *Cf.* Pott *Briefe,* Teil II, 253–55.

6. Sigmund felt himself to be next in command to Bahrdt and sometimes enforced his pretensions to authority by the power of his fists. It is reported that once, when the professor of philology told Sigmund openly that he was a professor in name only and in reality nothing but a distiller and grease maker, Sigmund, who at the moment happened to be repairing a pupil's shoe, threw the shoe and hit his colleague on the head. The philologist grabbed up a whitewash brush and began to belabor Sigmund with it, but he was soon thrown to the ground. The two were then separated with some difficulty.

Laukhard, in his *Beyträge und Berichtigungen zu Herrn Karl Friedrich Bahrdt's Lebensbeschreibung in Briefen eines Pfälzers,* has a comical scene satirizing Bahrdt, his school, and the ignorance of the teachers. This kind of pedagogical satire was familiar to Laukhard and his contemporaries from a kind of novel by Johann Gottlieb Schummel called *Spitzbart, eine komitragische Geschichte für unser pädagogisches Jahrhundert,* which had Basedow and his following as its main target. Laukhard combined school scenes from *Spitzbart* with the examples of Socratic method which Bahrdt had published to produce something which is both amusing and partially authentic.

Lehrer: Nun Musje Karl, merken Sie auf!—Hören Sie nicht?

Karl: (Spielt mit einer Karte, welche er nach den Farben rangirt.)

Lehrer: Nun liebes Karlchen, legen Sie doch die Karte weg.

Karl: (Wie oben)

Lehrer: (Reisst ihm die Karten aus der Hand) Ich will Sie schon attent machen—Wo ist die Grammatik?

Karl: (Lacht)

Lehrer: Wo ist die Grammatik?

Karl: (Lacht noch ärger und pfeift sich eins.)

Lehrer: Musje Karl, wenn Sie die Grammatik nicht herbeischaffen, und lernen, so sollen Sie diesen Nachmittag hübsch zu Hause bleiben. Wir spaziren nach Grünstadt, da ist das hübsche Luischen, wenn Sie vernünftig sind, so kommen Sie mit.

Karl: (springt freudig auf, holt die Grammatik und schlägt auf.) Hier ist die Letz (Lection). Der Doktor Bahrdt (welcher die Zeit über an der

Thür gestanden, und alles mit angehört hatte, tritt herein). Recht so, lieber Herr Professor! So muss man die Kinder durch Vorspiegelung von künftigen Vergnügen zum Gehorsam bringen—das stimmt ganz in meinen Plan: fahren Sie so fort (geht ab).

Lehrer: Nun liebstes, goldnes Karlchen, wo stehen wir dann?

Karl: Hier.

Lehrer: Aha in der dritten Deklination. Also deklinieren Sie *dos*.

Karl: *Numerus singularis Nominativus dos* die Morgengabe, *Gen. dossis Dat. dossi, Acc. dossem, Voc. dos, Abl. dosse, Pluralis Nom. dosses, Gen. dossum, Dat. dossibus, Accus. dosses, Abl. dossibus.*

Lehrer: Schön liebes Karlchen; aber machen Sie einmal das Buch zu. Sie müssen nicht immer das Schema ansehen. Machen Sie das Buch zu und deklinieren Sie einmal ein anderes Wort in *os*. Halt welches, (besinnt sich). Ja deklinieren Sie *bos* der Ochse.

Karl: *Bos* der Ochse *bossis, bossi,* (stockt).

Lehrer: Nun *dos dossem*, also *bos?*—

Karl: *bossem bos bosse. Plur* . . .

Lehrer: Nun, *dosses* also?

Karl: *bosses, Gen. bossorum.*—

Lehrer: Ach was, *bossorum!*—*bossum*, mein liebes Karlchen, *bossum* heisst es.

Sigismundus: (Hatte an der Thüre gehorcht, und kam nun mit schrecklichem Gelächter in die Stube). Ha, ha, ha—da machen Sie schön Zeug, Herr Kollege. Pfui, können Sie nicht dekliniren. Ha, ha, ha, *Bos, Bossis!* Das wäre schön, *Bos* geht wie *os*. Ich wills Ihnen vordekliniren; *bos* der Ochse, *boris* des Ochsen, *bori borem bos bore. Plur. bores borum boribus.* Sehn Sie! (geht mit triumphirender Miene ab.)

Karl: (nimmt seine Karten und läuft fort)

Lehrer: Hol der höllische Satan den verfluchten Wagenschmierfabrikanten (schiebt ab).

Although Laukhard probably does very little injustice to the abilities of the teachers, he is seriously astray in one respect. In Dr. Bahrdt's system the inflections were not learned by rote memorization but by the modern "pattern" system, as Bahrdt explains in his *Erziehungsplan*. Verb forms, for example, were supposed to be taught by a series of questions and answers such as the following: Lehrer: Quid heri in ambulacro faciebas? Schüler: Garriebam. L.: Quid ego tecum? Sch.: Garriebas. L.: Quid ille? Sch.: Garriebat. L.: Quid hodie in eodem loco agemus? Sch.: Garriemus, etc., etc.

7. Böhme's story is quoted in Schlichtegroll's *Nekrolog. Nachträge und Berichtigungen 1790, 1791, 1792, 1793. Supplement Band.*

What sort of man was this preacher of the Reformed church? Debauched, lewd, and unprincipled as most writers who have occasion to mention him say Bahrdt was? Or was there perhaps something about Bahrdt which could capture and hold the esteem of a good and upright man? Fortunately, we have an account of Böhme in Schlichtegroll's *Nekrolog auf das Jahr 1794,* which may well be cited here.

The article in Schlichtegroll is unequivocal in its praise of Böhme as a man of exemplary character. The writer begins by saying that he has consulted a great many very different people and found that there was complete unanimity in their estimate of him as one of the best and most virtuous people, a man who, they all agreed, exhibited a very great number of excellent qualities. The facts of his career are unimportant and simple— he died as pastor of the Heiliggeistkirche in Heidelberg, his father's old church—but he exerted a sound and benevolent influence upon everyone who knew him.

Exact and prompt in the performance of all his official duties, he was warm and friendly, loved good food and drink, decent laughter, and stimulating conversation. Most of all he enjoyed making excursions into the countryside, taking with him a basket of food and a bottle or two of wine, building and tending a camp fire, and chatting with one or two good companions. In the matter of religious faith he had adopted an enlightened outlook merely because sound common sense necessarily rejected as absurd such matters of dogma as eternal damnation and exclusive salvation. He therefore admired Bahrdt's learning, the force of the arguments with which Bahrdt could by appeal to history and philology demonstrate the natural explanation of so much that mere common sense could not accept. Böhme therefore learned much from Bahrdt, but at the same time he exercised upon him a wholesome and restraining influence, for Bahrdt apparently respected his friend for his sincerity, his honest facing up to facts, his decency. In Böhme, as in Baumer, Doctor Bahrdt apparently felt and responded to simple and unaffected honesty, the unclouded outlook of the man who deals with the objective.

CHAPTER XVIII

1. It is odd that Bahrdt mentions Triest as favorably as he does, for the latter had written a pamphlet, *Der wahre Character des Herrn Doctor C. F. Bahrdt. In vertrauten Briefen geschildert von einem Niederländischen Bürger an seinen Freund in London,* which was anything but complimentary to Bahrdt.

Triest's son was one of the first pupils to be enrolled in the Philanthropinum. Bahrdt describes him as grotesquely fat and lazy, wrapped up in a sevenfold layer of clothing that required two hours to put on. Bahrdt was the guest of Triest in Amsterdam and entertained him at Heidesheim in 1779. In the pamphlet mentioned above, Triest described conditions in the school as intolerable. As an example he reports that no sooner had he lain down to sleep than he was assailed by a "legion of dark brown aerialists."

2. His motive in writing this bit of fiction was, of course, to strike at the claim of positive religions to be the revealed and unique pathway to salvation, for here was a Jew, a lost soul, who exhibited more than merely Christian virtue. Exclusion of a Löw Bär Isak from the Kingdom of Heaven was palpable nonsense. The figure of the noble Jew and the consequences for theology to be drawn from this figure were, of course, familiar to Bahrdt from Lessing's *Nathan*.

3. Assuming that there is some truth in this tale, one very naturally wonders just why Bahrdt did not accept this way out of his difficulties. The idea must have appealed to his sense of the bizarre and sensational, and if, as his enemies insisted, his conduct was governed entirely by base self-interest, this was as good a way as any to gratify his wants. It seems at least possible that he simply could not bring himself to profess faith in something he considered absurd.

4. Bahrdt asserts that he quickly learned enough English to get along without an interpreter, but the few English phrases which he puts into his narrative at this point make his assertion very doubtful.

5. *Johann Reinhold Forsters und Georg Forsters Reise um die Welt in den Jahren 1772–1775* (English version 1777, German version 1779).

6. In his autobiography Bahrdt made Wendeborn the leading figure in a bit of semifiction, just as he did Löw Bär Isak and for comparable polemical reasons. England, as we have seen, was made to appear the home of honesty, simplicity, uprightness, and liberty, both personal and political, a land where sexual behavior was a completely individual matter, where there was, to be sure, extraordinary license and opportunity for voluptuous satisfactions, but where such matters were taken completely for granted and never made the occasion for censure and gossip. It was thus possible, says Bahrdt, for Pastor Wendeborn, who was surely the most upright, blameless, and sober of men, to personally acquaint our errant doctor of theology with the English form of prostitution, perhaps somewhat as a modern social worker might guide a distinguished visitor on a tour of scientific investigation.

This excursion was undertaken, says Bahrdt, because he thought he had noticed a certain decency and modesty in the behavior of the common prostitute. Wendeborn confirmed him in this suspicion and suggested that Bahrdt really ought to see for himself how superior these vilest of creatures in England were to their coarse and brazen German counterparts. Bahrdt agreed, and so the two divines went strolling one evening in Covent Garden to make their observations. Every two or three steps they were accosted by one or more of these elegantly dressed women, who said to them, "Mei Dier gib mi Glas Wein," and when they received no answer simply moved on in silence. "When at length we noticed a group of three such girls who seemed especially beautiful to us, at the aforementioned greeting we raised our arms, and in a moment we were all five engaged arm in arm in a very pleasant conversation. Wendeborn talked with them on the subject of British liberty, and the girls talked like male Britons. In the principal streets almost every other house is dedicated to Venus. We entered one at random. A waiter came up to us with two candles and asked whether we required a private room. Upon receiving our affirmative answer he opened a room on the first floor which was hung with the most valuable tapestries, furnished very beautifully, and equipped with beds. Wendeborn ordered a pint of wine. We seated ourselves. The former subject of conversation was renewed. The girls spoke like ladies of quality. Not a word, not a look, that could occasion an unseemly thought. Pastor Götze could have been one of the group sitting there without taking or giving offense. Wendeborn filled the glasses. The girls finished the pint. About a quarter of an hour passed, which we spent in very polite conversation. Finally we arose. The girls thanked us. Wendeborn paid two shillings. And we left our ladies without having heard a single indecent word from them."

When this story came to Wendeborn's attention he vigorously denied it (*Hamburgischer Correspondent,* May 6, 1791). Several years later in his book of memoirs (*Erinnerungen aus meinem Leben,* Hamburg, 1813) he again denied it, and there is an account of the matter in the *Neueste Religionsbegebenheiten* for 1791. There is no reason to doubt that Bahrdt made up the story for its polemical and sensational effect.

It was also obviously for sensational effect that he added another anecdote about a visit to a more exclusive and magnificent house of entertainment. An anonymous friend escorted him to a villa in a remote section of the city. They were admitted by one servant in livery and ushered into a splendid salon by another. This room was long and narrow, richly furnished, and had fireplaces adorned with gilt and mirrors at either end. Around each fireplace was a group of eight or ten extremely beautiful, nude young women with whom Bahrdt exchanged a few pleasantries, keeping always within the limits of decency. After a short time, Bahrdt, who felt he could not afford to take full advantage of the opportunities offered by the place, insisted on leaving. On the way out the spectator's fee of half a guinea was required. Full participation would have cost three.

The moral of these stories is that standards of decency and personal behavior are entirely a matter of convention.

CHAPTER XIX

1. His *Literarisches Correspondenz- und Intelligenzblatt* had been transformed into a *Pädagogisches Wochenblatt* (Heidesheim, 1778).

2. *Gutachten zweier theologischen Facultäten, der würzburgschen und göttingschen, auf allerhöchsten Befehl seiner Kaiserlichen Majestät über die Übereinstimmung Herrn Dr. Bahrdt's zu Heidesheim mit den reichsgesetzmässigen Lehrsystemen ausgefertiget.*

3. *Unterthänigstes Gutachten wegen der jetzigen Religionsbewegungen, besonders in der evangelischen Kirche, wie auch über das kaiserliche Commissionsdekret in der Bahrdtischen Sache.*

4. (a) Anonymous. *Von der Gerichtsbarkeit der höchsten Reichsgerichte in geistlichen Sachen, bei Gelegenheit des neuesten Dr. Bahrdt'schen Rechtsfalls* (1779).

(b) G. L. Böhmer, *Oratorio de Jure cognoscendi et statuendi de tolerandis his, qui communes religionum in Germania approbatarum doctrinas publice impugnant* (Göttingen, 1779).

(c) C. H. Geisler, *De iudicio super Religione aliorum ferendo Disputatiuncula* (Marburg, 1779).

5. *Anmerkungen über die Schrift unter dem Titel: Von der Gerichtsbarkeit der höchsten Reichsgerichte in geistlichen Sachen* (Frankfurt und Leipzig, 1779).

6. "Der Fürst von Leiningen verwendete sich selbst für seinen Superintendenten in einem Vorschreiben an den Kaiser Joseph, das gewiss nicht fruchtlos gewesen seyn würde, und befahl dem Hofrath Rühl, es nach Wien zu befördern; aber weder dieses, noch eine Bittschrift der Gemeine in Dürkheim an den Kaiser, wurde dem Oberhaupt des Reichs übergeben." Schlichtegroll's *Nekrolog auf das Jahr 1792*, p. 177. Gehren, in his article on Bahrdt in Ersch und Grubers *Allgemeine Encyclopädie der Wissenschaften und Künste*, Teil VII, p. 129, writes to the same effect. There is no reason to doubt that Rühl was capable of such insubordination, and the probability is strengthened by the fact that Bahrdt seems to have been unaware of what we may suppose really happened: he says nothing about such a possibility in his autobiography.

7. In doing this he was undoubtedly aware that he was following the example of Laelius Socinus (1525–1562), whose heretical teachings were sympathetic to him.

8. *Glaubensbekenntnis, veranlasst durch ein kaiserliches Reichshofrathsconclusum* (1779). A preliminary form had already appeared in the twelfth number of Bahrdt's *Literarisches Correspondenz- und Intelligenzblatt*.

9. Goedeke lists fifteen refutations and attacks, of which the most significant were Johann Salomo Semler's *Antwort auf das Bahrdtische Glaubensbekenntnis* and *Das Bahrdt'sche Glaubensbekenntnis widerlegt von Dr. J. S. Semler nebst den beiden Gutachten der theologischen Facultäten*

zu Würzburg und Göttingen über das Bahrdt'sche Neue Testament im Auszuge.

10. See appended essay on the history of Bahrdt's reputation.

11. John 10:34–36: "Jesus answered them [the Jews], Is it not written in your law, I said, ye are gods? If he called them gods, unto whom the word of God came (and the scripture cannot be broken), say ye of him, whom the Father sanctified, and sent into the world, Thou blasphemest; because I said, I am the Son of God?" The passage Jesus quotes from Hebrew scripture is Psalm 82:6.

CHAPTER XX

1. The school very soon collapsed completely. Rühl quarreled with his associates, and both teachers and pupils (those who were still there) left him.

2. In a letter dated the thirteenth of June 1779, Heres, who had previously written to Bahrdt, earnestly and sadly reproaching him for irresponsible and reckless conduct and urging him to mend his ways in all respects, explained how Rühl had contrived to make Bahrdt flee, thus driving him into the trap which Rühl had set for him in Dienheim. "I made inquiries," writes Heres in an excited jumble of disjointed sentences, "and found out—draw a deep breath, for you are about to read something that does honor to a devil, which could turn you to stone—I found out that the whole thing was designed to destroy you completely; that Rühl's affirmation that you were in danger of arrest [*dass die Versicherung R. vom Arrest*] was a pretense to frighten you and to make you leave out of fear; and that in order to dupe you completely he directed that you be paid four hundred florins, which, however, you were forced to accept in Dienheim; that the Count did indeed wish you to have the four hundred florins but knew nothing of the affair; that his [*i.e.,* Rühl's] assurance that he would publish in the newspaper that you were leaving with the Count's consent was a lie of which the Count knew nothing and which will certainly not be done; that some hours after your departure R. had the people informed that you would not come back and were in Dienheim; that it was his will and intention to have you arrested there because he could not do anything to you inside the country because of the Count; the Society [*ökonomische Gesellschaft*] would not have done it either, but would on the contrary have given you money, clothes, and linens for the trip if you had told them in advance that you had to and intended to leave; that he induced you to hide your possessions so that he would be able to charge you with criminal breach of trust; in brief, I found out that the

fellow is a devil who lured you into his trap." Pott, *Briefe*, Teil III, pp. 18–19.

3. Bahrdt did, of course, try to hide various things, some of which were his and some of which were not, in the palace at Heidesheim, hoping that some friend could send them on once he had become established in Halle. These effects were discovered, however, and put up at auction along with the rest of the inventory of the now bankrupt *ökonomische Gesellschaft*. There is a very interesting detailed account of these proceedings by Albert Schreiber in *Rheinische Blätter für Erziehung und Unterricht*, pp. 411–40.

CHAPTER XXI

1. Dated Berlin, August 11, 1779. To be found in Pott, *Briefe*, Teil II, p. 67.

2. Pott, *Briefe*, Teil II, p. 57.

3. *Neologie* and *Neologen* are terms which were current at the time of which we are writing to designate an outlook and a class of theologians and other scholars in contrast to the orthodox and conservative *Paläologen*. Karl Aner, in his book *Die Theologie der Lessingzeit*, makes a careful distinction among three stages in the progress of the *Aufklärung: Wolffianismus, Neologie*, and *Rationalismus*. Aner distinguishes these three stages according to the relationship between reason and revelation which his analysis finds to inhere in the logical substructure of the thought of the men representing these stages. Thus, *Wolffianismus* allows reason and revelation a peaceful coexistence within its system. But *Neologie* rejects whatever seems to it to be contrary to reason, that is, most of the specific content of Biblical revelation, without, however, rejecting the concept of revelation. The concept of revelation which it accepts is not historical but rational, and thus the content of revelation consists of those universal truths which reason is bound to discover. *Rationalismus* carries the process further and discards the notion of revelation as disclosure of truth by a power external to man but accepts the content of revelation, *i.e.*, the truths discoverable by reason or reason itself. Aner represents this systematically in the following formula in which $V = Vernunft$ and $O = Offenbarung$.

$$Wolffianismus = V + O$$
$$Neologie = V + O^{begriff} - O^{inhalt}$$
$$Rationalismus = V = O^{inhalt} - O^{begriff}$$

Needless to say, the charges of neologism brought against Starck (or Bahrdt) did not presuppose this analysis.

4. See Felix Eberty, *Geschichte des preussischen Staats,* Teil V, p. 325. Also Jean Blum, *J.-A. Starck et la Querelle du Crypto-Catholicisme en Allemagne 1785–1789.*

5. The complete title of the book is *Theoduls Gastmahl oder über die Vereinigung der verschiedenen christlichen Religions-Societäten.* The title page bears the motto: "Unus Dominus, una Fides, unum Baptisma, unus Deus et Pater omnium, qui est super omnes, et per omnia in omnibus nobis! Paulus Ep. ad Ephes. Cap. IV. 5.6." The book reports the conversation of the guests at Theodul's symposium. One of the prominent speakers is Odilo, the old former abbot of St. Appolinar, who has just returned from France. At the end of the book (p. 270 ff.) Odilo expresses the view that Protestantism has been so undermined and debilitated by the spirit of tolerance and indifferentism that it would have died out if princes and heads of government, realizing that human society depends on a positive religion, had not supported it in order to maintain themselves. But since it is impossible for Protestantism to form a united religious body under the authority of a single head, the princes and chiefs of government will eventually be forced to bring about a union with the Catholic church. The Protestant members of the symposium are impressed by his words, even though not convinced, and the discussion is concluded with a fraternal handshake. To the editor of the *Allgemeine deutsche Bibliothek* and his collaborators, at any rate, it was clear that the Catholic church was singing the siren song of union and toleration in order to bring the Protestants back into the fold. See *Allgemeine deutsche Bibliothek,* LXI, p. 361.

6. Pott, *Briefe,* Teil II, 64–66.

7. Starck's fancying himself in the role of mover of men and of a power behind the scenes was apparently a part of his love of mysteries and mystification. For instance, he wrote a book about ancient and modern mysteries including Masonry, *Über die alten und neuen Mysterien,* and when he was openly accused of crypto-Catholicism, he wrote in reply a book which is equally astounding for its length and its ambiguity. This work, which ran to 1597 pages in three volumes and several appendices plus a *Vorrede* bears the title: *Johann August Starck, der heil. Schrift Doctor, Hochf. Hessen-Darmstädtischer Oberhofprediger, Consistorialrath und Definitor, über Kryptokatholicismus, Proselytenmacherey, Jesuitismus, geheime Gesellschaften und besonders die ihm selbst von den Verfassern der Berliner Monatsschrift gemachte [sic] Beschuldigungen mit Acten-Stücken belegt.* His purpose is stated and his tactics can be studied in these excerpts from the *Vorrede:* "Nach diesen Überzeugungen meines Herzens hätte ich also auf alle meine Person angehenden Anfälle dem Publikum nichts oder nur sehr wenig sagen sollen. Ich bin aber protestantischer Theolog [true], und nach dem Eide, den ich meiner Kirche [Roman Catholic] geleistet, verbunden, das beste derselben [the Catholic Church] zu befördern, und allen ihr drohenden Nachtheil nach meinen geringen Kräften abzuwenden. Und nach dieser mir

obliegenden Pflicht habe ich viel recht viel zu reden. . . . Man wird um so viel mehr mich zu einem heimlichen Päpstler, ja Gott weiss, wozu nicht alles machen. Das kümmert mich nicht: bin ich doch alles dieses nicht [not *all* those things but only one of them]; und kann man ärgere Dinge von mir sagen, als man bereits gesagt . . ."

8. And Scripture does not support what reason rejects, for in Eberhard's view the only passage that might make his conclusion seem doubtful is Matthew 25:46, "And these shall go away into everlasting punishment: but the righteous into life eternal." Although he recognizes the seriousness of the difficulty posed by this passage, he nevertheless rejects the notion of eternal punishment, on the principle that the validity or non-validity of certain portions of Scripture can be judged only on the basis of reason.

9. Berlin und Stettin bey Friedrich Nicolai, 1772.

10. The passage cited is from *De Doctrina Christiana*, Book II, chapter 28: ". . . omnes Domini nostri Jesu Christi sententias, quas mirari et praedicare cogebantur de Platonis libris eum didicisse, quoniam longe ante humanum adventum Domini Platonem fuisse, negari non potest." It should be pointed out, however, that Augustine feels a more likely explanation to be that Plato had been in Egypt and learned "our" ideas there from Jeremiah.

CHAPTER XXII

1. It should be remembered, of course, that Semler was not the only scholar to employ the method of interpreting a document in relation to its historical and cultural background. C. G. Heyne at the University of Göttingen, for example, did much pioneer work in this field. Heyne came to recognize the myths and legends of classical literature not as purple patches sewn upon what might otherwise have been a mere drab fabric but as the natural and inevitable outgrowth of a metaphorical and mythopoeic mode of thought peculiar to an immature stage of human mentality, an idea which, as is well known, was popularized by Herder and has had an influential history to the present day. For an account of how Heyne's concept of mythological thinking was applied first to the Old Testament by J. G. Eichhorn and J. P. Gabler and then to the New by G. L. Bauer, see Christian Hartlich and Walter Sachs, *Der Ursprung des Mythosbegriffes in der modernen Bibelwissenschaft.*

2. How obsessive was Semler's drive to view everything under a dual aspect may be seen in his book *D. Joh. Sal. Semlers hermetische Briefe wider Vorurtheile und Betrügereyen.* According to this book there is in addition to the usual public science of chemistry a secret, hermetic chemistry which

Semler would like to call "die freie Privatchymie, die himmlische, olympische, elementarische oder die innerliche feuchte, nasse, unbekannte Chymie." This is a science which is unknown and must be kept from the vulgar, immoral, and irreligious. But for the right people it will reveal invisible gold. There is an extensive review of this book in the *Allgemeine deutsche Bibliothek,* LXXXVIII,[2] p. 481 ff., in which the reviewer speaks also of how sensitive Semler had become to criticism of his work.

Apropos *die freie Privatchymie,* it is recorded in the article on Semler in Schlichtegroll's *Nekrolog* that during the latter years of his life, as his interest in alchemy grew, he at regular intervals perused the volumes of the alchemistic library which he had accumulated in his privy.

3. Quoted in Paul Gastrow, *Johann Salomo Semler in seiner Bedeutung für die Theologie.*

4. *Beantwortung der Fragmente eines Ungenannten insbesondere vom Zweck Jesu und seiner Jünger.*

5. *Beantwortung,* pp. 267–69.

6. ". . . die Absicht dieser neuen Bestimmung (Vater, Sohn u. heil. Geist sind drey Personen in Gott) hat einen blos äusserlichen Endzweck, die Unterscheidung der Christen in zweierley äusserliche Parteien; welche aber beide den Grund, die Grundbegriffe des innerlichen Christtums, und der eigenen Seligkeit, die sie dem Vater, Sohn und heil. Geist unter verschiedenen Nebenvorstellungen denken, gleich gewis schon gemein behalten." *Beantwortung,* p. 57.

7. See Waldemar Oehlke, *Lessing und seine Zeit,* II, p. 360.

8. Semler's *Beantwortung der Fragmente eines Ungenannten* appeared on March 1, 1779; the decree by which Bahrdt was removed from his office was published March 27, 1779; the *confessio fidei* was made within two months thereafter; Bahrdt arrived in Halle on May 28, 1779.

9. Unpublished letters from Eberhard to Nicolai, cited by Aner, *Theologie der Lessingzeit,* pp. 103–6.

10. Trapp remained in this post until 1782. Upon his departure Bahrdt sought to move heaven and earth to succeed him, but by this time Zedlitz had become convinced that Bahrdt's discretion could not be trusted and pointed out that neither his record of failure as an educator nor his persistent importunity, could recommend him for the position which he requested. See Pott, *Briefe,* Teil III, p. 54.

11. *D. Joh. Sal. Semlers Antwort auf das Bahrdtische Glaubensbekenntnis.*

12. Aner, *Die Theologie der Lessingzeit,* p. 103 ff.

13. Berlin, 1779.

14. *Allgemeine deutsche Bibliothek,* XLIII.[1]

CHAPTER XXIII

1. Albert Schweitzer, *Geschichte der Leben-Jesu-Forschung*. On page 38 Schweitzer points out that the popular fictionalized lives of Jesus by Bahrdt and Venturini (*Natürliche Geschichte des grossen Propheten von Nazareth* (Bethlehem, *i.e.*, Copenhagen, 1800–1802), were the first attempts to pose and solve the critical problems involved in writing a biography of Jesus: "Sie sind die ersten," says Schweitzer, "welche sich nicht mit der einfachen Aufzählung der Perikopen begnügen, sondern den inneren treibenden Zusammenhang der Ereignisse und Erlebnisse Jesu begreifen wollen."

2. Pott, *Briefe*. Other letters cited in this chapter are also to be found here.

3. On the twentieth of June 1781, Heres writes: "Der Brief Ihres Hannchen [Bahrdt's daughter] hat mich sehr gefreut. Ist wirklich Ihre liebe Frau kränklich? Neulich sagte man mir, Sie wäre in Mühlhausen. O thun Sie doch alles, dem würdigen Weibe das Leben angenehm zu machen.

Grüssen Sie und herzen Sie alle Ihre lieben Kinder, besonders Ihre liebe Frau von Ihrem Heres."

4. See details in Schlichtegroll's *Nekrolog. Nachträge und Berichtigungen 1790, 1791, 1792, 1793, Supplement Band.*

5. See Heinrich Schneider, "D. Karl Friedrich Bahrdt's Letter to Washington."

6. This account is confirmed by Johann Christian Hoffbauer, who had the title of *Ordentlicher Professor der Philosophie* at Halle, in his book *Geschichte der Universität zu Halle bis zum Jahre 1805*, p. 360 ff. Hoffbauer knew Bahrdt personally and went to some of his lectures. He is the authority for the correctness of the estimates here given of the attendance at Bahrdt's lectures.

7. It may be of interest to compare a passage from Tacitus' *Annals* II, 71, the death of Germanicus, with Bahrdt's version. An examination of the two passages will show that Zedlitz and the reviewers whom Meusel cited were right in their praise of Bahrdt's skill as a translator. The rhythms, the emphasis, the pregnant earnestness of the Latin are captured in a German of notable clarity and felicity. Parenthetically it may be observed that Bahrdt's style here was in great contrast to the style of the most important comparable contemporary translation which could have served as a model, Reiske's *Thucydides*, which was generally held to be a stylistic atrocity.

Tacitus wrote: Caesar paulisper ad spem erectus, dein fesso corpore, ubi finis aderat, adsistentis amicos in hunc modum adloquitur. Si fato concederem, iustus mihi dolor etiam adversus deos esset, quod me parentibus, liberis, patriae intra iuventam praematuro exitu raperent; nunc scelere Pisonis et Plancinae interceptus ultimas preces pectoribus vestris relinquo: referatis patri ac fratri quibus acerbitatibus dilaceratus, quibus insidiis circumventus miserrimam vitam pessima morte finierim. Si quos spes meae, si quos propinquus sanguis, etiam quos invidia erga viventem movebat, inlacrimabunt quondam florentem et tot bellorum superstitem muliebri fraude cecidisse. Erit vobis locus querendi apud senatum, invocandi leges. Non hoc pracipuum amicorum munus est, prosequi defunctum ignavo questu, sed quae voluerit meminisse, quae mandaverit exequi. Flebunt Germanicum etiam ignoti: vindicabitis vos, si me potius quam fortunam meam fovebatis. Ostendite populo Romano divi Augusti neptem eandemque coniugem meam, numerate sex liberos. Misericordia cum accusantibus erit fingentibusque scelesta mandata aut non credent homines aut non ignoscent. Iuravere amici dextram morientis contingentes spiritum ante quam ultionem amisuros.

Bahrdt's version runs: Caesar genoss anfangs einigen Trost der Hofnung, aber bald erlag sein Körper und—da das Ende sich nahte, sprach er so zu seinen umstehenden Freunden. Stürb' ich den Tod der Natur, so könnte ich doch mit Recht auch über die Götter jammern, dass sie mich den Eltern, den Kindern, dem Vaterland, noch Jüngling, durch zu frühen Tod entrissen; aber so muss ich, durch die Ruchlosigkeit des Piso und der Plancina aus meiner Laufbahn gerissen, euren Herzen meine letzte Bitte zurücklassen; gebt Aufschlus dem Vater und Bruder, mit was für Kränkungen zermartet, mit welcher Hinterlist berückt, ich mein elendes Leben mit dem schlechtesten Tode habe enden müssen. Beweinen werden's alle, denen ich durch meine Aussichten, oder als Verwandter, ja selbst als Gegenstand des Neides wichtig war, dass ein Mann weiland im Schoss des Glücks, der so viel Feldzüge überlebt hat, durch Weiberlist fallen musste. *Ihr*—habt Recht beim Senat zu klagen, die Gesetze anzurufen. Nicht ist dies das grosse Werk der Freundschaft, den Verstorbenen mit thatlosen Klagen zu begleiten, sondern das ist's: seinen Willen im Herzen haben und seine Aufträge vollziehn. Auch Unbekannte werden den Germanicus beweinen, *rächen* müsst ihr ihn, wofern ihr meine Person, nicht etwa nur mein Glück geliebt habet. Zeiget dem römischen Volk sie—des himmlischen Augusts Enkelin, sie, meine Gemahlin. Zählet ihm sechs Kinder vor. Das Mitleid wird für euch, meine Kläger, sprechen; und das Vorgeben verruchten Befehls wird die Welt nie glauben oder doch nie vergeben. Die Freunde schwuren—den Sterbenden bei seiner Rechten fassend—dass sie eher ihr Leben als die Rache aufgeben wollten.

Despite Bahrdt's failure to force his translation upon all the schools in Prussia, his *Tacitus* had some success. Goedeke lists the following editions: *Des Tacitus Annalen 1. und 2. Buch; ein Probestück für Kenner* (Dessau, 1780). *C. Tacitus sämmtliche Werke übersetzt* (Halle, 1781) II; 2. Auflage III (Wien und Prag, 1801). Also under the general title *Sammlung der classischen, römischen und griechischen Geschichtschreiber Bd. I übersetzt von Dr. K. F. Bahrdt* (Halle, 1781).

8. *Magazin für Prediger, oder Sammlung neu ausgearbeiteter Predigtentwürfe über die sonn-und festtäglichen Evangelien und Episteln, sowie über freie Texte auf Casualfälle*, 12 vol. (Züllichau, 1782–1791).

9. *Griechisch-deutsches Lexikon über das Neue Testament, nebst einem Register über Luther's deutsche Bibel, welches auch Ungelehrte in den Stand*

setzt, dies Wörterbuch zu gebrauchen und sich über Dunkelheiten der deutschen Bibel Raths zu erholen (Berlin, 1786).

10. *Über den Versöhnungstod Jesu Christi.*

11. *Apologie der Vernunft durch Gründe der Schrift unterstützt in Bezug auf die christliche Versöhnungslehre* (Basel, 1781). Goedeke lists the title as *Apologie der gesunden Vernunft* etc. The copy which I have used does not include the adjective.

12. *Kirchen- und Ketzeralmanach aufs Jahr 1781* (Häresiopel, *i.e.*, Züllichau, *Im Verlag der Ekklesia pressa*). *Zweites Quinquennium, ausgefertigt im Jahre 1787* (Gibeon, *i.e.*, Berlin, gedruckt und verlegt bei Kasimir Lauge). The so-called *Zweites Quinquennium* provoked Bahrdt's friend Trapp to the publication of a pseudonymous satirical epistle to him: *Epistel an den Verfasser des 2. Quinquenniums vom Kirchen- und Ketzeralmanach. Ecce iterum Crispinus!*, in which he severely took Bahrdt to task for offending and injuring people indiscriminately. Some of the lines are: "Welcher Kukuk hat ihn geheissen/ Sich mit der ganzen Welt 'rumzubeissen?/Und seiner Lehre wird niemand hold/Wenn er damit tändelt wie Kinder mit Gold,/Wovon der Werth sie minder rührt,/Als dass es blank ist und brilliert;/Wenn besser durch sie er ist um kein Haar,/Als da er in Leipzig Magister noch war/Und als ein orthodoxer Bengel/An Crugott wurde zum Satansengel." The entire bit of doggerel was reprinted in the *Allgemeine deutsche Bibliothek*, LXXVI², pp. 586–92. Trapp had previously written a very effective satire against Bahrdt's enemies on the theological faculty of Halle, but Bahrdt had been indiscreet enough to reveal that Trapp was the author. Hence Trapp's castigation of Bahrdt.

13. *Appellation an das Publikum wegen einer Censurbedrückung, das Systema theologicum betreffend, welches zu Ostern erscheinen wird.*

14. *Theologischer Beweis, dass der Doctor Bahrdt schuld an dem Erdbeben in Kalabrien sei. Der Hochwürdigen theologischen Facultät in Halle demüthig zugeeignet von Simon Ratzeberger dem jüngern, weiland Herausgeber des berühmten Vademekums für lustige Leute.* Reprinted in Martin von Geismar, *Bibliothek der deutschen Aufklärer des achtzehnten Jahrhunderts* (Leipzig, 1846).

15. *Über das theologische Studium auf Universitäten. Sr. Excellenz dem königlichen Staatsminister und Obercurator Freiherrn von Zedlitz gewidmet* (Berlin, 1785).

CHAPTER XXIV

1. Johann Jakob Hess, *Geschichte der drei letzten Lebensjahre Jesu.* This book is mostly a Gospel paraphrase.

2. *Kleine Bibel;* I: *Geschichte von Erschaffung der Welt bis auf die Zerstörung Jerusalems durch die Römer;* II: *Glaubens-und Sittenlehren, erbauliche Gesänge und eine erbauliche Geschichte aus dem Buche Hiob entnommen* (Berlin, 1780). The idea of an abridged version had already suggested itself to Semler, who felt that such a book would be very useful.

3. *Briefe über die Bibel im Volkston. Eine Wochenschrift von einem Prediger auf dem Lande.* 5 Quartale (Halle, 1782–1783).

4. This conjecture is one of the very earliest applications to the New Testament of C. G. Heyne's great achievement, recognition of myth as the form of thought and expression peculiar and necessary to the early stages of human development. *Homo mythicus,* having no knowledge of the true causes of things, inevitably resorted to a *sermo mythicus* which explained things by supposing the intervention of gods and demons. Heyne's publications on classical mythology—he did not view the Bible *sub specie mythologiae*—date back to 1763, but the definitive formulation of his principle appeared as late as 1783 in his edition of Apollodorus: *A mythis omnis priscorum hominum cum historia tum philosophia procedit.* Heyne's pupil J. G. Eichhorn made the application of Heyne's principle to the Old Testament in 1779 in his anonymously published *Urgeschichte,* which had little influence until it was republished between 1790 and 1793 by Eichhorn's pupil J. P. Gabler. Gabler, in his inaugural address at the University of Altdorf in 1787, asserted the complete autonomy of biblical theology as a scholarly discipline, proclaiming the dependence of dogma upon exegesis rather than, as thitherto, the dependence of exegesis upon dogma. The enunciation of this principle was in effect a declaration of the intent and the right to lay bare the mythical elements of the New Testament. Bahrdt, whose conjecture about the mythological character of the Gospels dates from 1782, was apparently unaware of the far-reaching consequences of his insight, and he was not enough of a philologist to embark upon the truly epoch-making task to which Eichhorn and Gabler systematically addressed themselves, chiefly in their journals. For Bahrdt, the naive polemicist, the important thing was to recreate Jesus in Bahrdt's image, to make of him an enlightened moralist, and not to understand him from within. The local, temporal, and mythical elements were to be separated from the rational and moral elements, which alone were eternal, universal, and hence of religious significance. Bahrdt's position is, of course, a crude prefiguration of Bultmann's program of demythologizing. See Christian Hartlich and Walter Sachs, *Der Ursprung des Mythosbegriffes in der modernen Bibelwissenschaft.*

5. *Über die alten und neuen Mysterien.*

CHAPTER XXV

1. *Standrede am Sarge des weiland Hochwürdigen und Hochgelahrten Herrn Johann Melchior Götze, gehalten von dem Kanonikus Ziegra* (Hamburg [Berlin], 1786).

2. J. F. Stadelmann, *Standrede am Sarge des weiland hochgelahrten Herrn Carl Friedrich Bahrdt. Eine Parodie* (Berlin, 1787).

3. The texts of this message and of other documents relating to the Union are largely reproduced in Martin von Geismar, *Bibliothek der deutschen Aufklärer.* Also in Bahrdt's *Geschichte und Tagebuch meines Gefängnisses nebst geheimen Urkunden und Aufschlüssen über die Deutsche Union* (Frankfurt am Main, 1790).

4. *Über Aufklärung und deren Beförderungsmittel* (Leipzig, 1789). The last article in the book is, according to Goedeke, by Professor Weber in Büzow.

5. There were other well-known definitions by Mendelssohn, J. J. Engel, J. A. Eberhard, Wieland, J. G. Schlosser.

6. *Mehr Noten als Text oder die Deutsche Union der Zweiundzwanziger, eines neuen geheimen Ordens zum Besten der Menschheit. Aus einem Packet gefundener Briefe zur öffentlichen Schau gestellt durch einen ehrlichen Buchhändler* (Leipzig, 1789).

7. *Nähere Beleuchtung der deutschen Union* (1789).

CHAPTER XXVI

1. G. G. Volland, *Beiträge und Erläuterungen zu Herrn Doctor Carl Friedrich Bahrdts Lebensbeschreibung, die er selbst verfertigt.*

2. *Ala Lama, oder der König unter den Schäfern. Auch ein goldener Spiegel.* 2 vol. (Halle, 1790).

3. C. F. Benkowitz, in his essay "Doktor Bahrdt auf seinem Weinberg," writes: "Die Töchter des Doktors sah man nur sehr selten, und sie führten eine äuserst sittsame und eingegozene Lebensart." And Gustav Frank, on pages 306 and 307 of his sketch of Bahrdt writes, "Ebenso erzählt der neugierige Dressel in seinen 'Reisen,' der selbst in Bahrdt's Küche seine Augen schweifen liess: Ich konnte nichts entdecken, was auch nur einen Schein von unmoralischen Anlagen verrathen hätte. Einmal begegnete mir eine von seinen Töchtern, die aber ein bescheidenes, mehr schüchternes als freches Wesen in ihrem Vorbeigehen bewies, und sich still in eine Nebenstube zu ihren Geschwistern verfügte."

4. One of a total of three which she bore to Dr. Bahrdt.

5. What Bahrdt has to say about his legitimate children is not without interest. Mariane was his favorite: talented and quick to learn, she was not only skilled in needlework and the culinary arts but was apparently a good pianist and gained considerable recognition in Halle as a singer. The second girl was more temperamental. "Every nerve was feeling and passion. I was often worried how to control this fiery nature without suppressing it. Her heart is noble and full of good will." The youngest was more practical and felt really happy when she was busy with household chores, sweeping, washing, scouring floors, cooking, drawing beer, and so on. Three boys were born in the marriage. All died in infancy, but the youngest was Bahrdt's "sweetest hope, because it seemed to be a strong and healthy child. But the choice of wet nurse caused this hope to fade also. Various young, healthy persons applied, but my dear wife thought they were all too attractive. Finally her choice fell upon an old crone, in whose arms the child declined every day until finally the doctor was summoned and pointed out to us too late that the child had starved at her breast."

6. A. Riem, *Über Aufklärung, ob sie dem Staate, der Religion oder überhaupt gefährlich sey und seyn könne? Ein Wort zur Beherzigung für Regenten, Staatsmänner und Priester. Ein Fragment.* P. Villaume, *Freymüthige Betrachtungen über das Edikt vom 9. Juli 1788, die Religionsverfassung in den Preussischen Staaten betreffend.*

7. G. Hufeland, *Über das Recht protestantischer Fürsten, unabänderliche Lehrvorschriften festzusetzen und über solche zu halten.*

8. J. S. Semler, *Verteidigung des Königlichen Edikts vom 9. Juli 1788 wider die freimütigen Betrachtungen eines Ungenannten.*

CHAPTER XXVII

1. *Das Religions-Edikt. Ein Lustspiel in fünf Aufzügen. Eine Skizze von Nicolai dem Jüngern* (Thenakel, 1789). "Gedruckt durch Joh. Mich. Bengel." The publisher was in reality Bahrdt's associate in the German Union, Wucherer in Vienna.

2. Bahrdt himself was satirized in a publication called *Der dritte und vierte Aufzug des Lustspiels das Religions-Edikt. Vollendet durch Nicolai den Jüngeren* (Thenakel, 1789). "Gedruckt durch Johann Michael Bengel." Foreword "An den Erz-Ketzer Herrn Dr. Bahrdt in Halle, dermalen in der Klemme."

3. Woellner and Blumenthal had become friends during their student days, and the rumor was current that Blumenthal had had a hand in the composition of the Edict. Paul Schwartz, *Der erste Kulturkampf*, pp. 144–46, quotes letters from Blumenthal to Woellner which, while far from conclusive, certainly support the supposition that the rumor was true.

4. Schulz was an outspoken champion of "enlightenment" and became a martyr of his own convictions, which were strongly critical of church and clergy.

5. *Commentar über das königlich preussische Religions-edict*. Sr. Excellenz dem Herrn Staatsminister von Wöllner zugeeignet (Amsterdam [*i.e.*, Halle], 1788).

6. Quoted in Schwartz, *Kulturkampf*, p. 150.

7. *Geschichte und Tagebuch meines Gefängnisses nebst geheimen Urkunden und Aufschlüssen über die Deutsche Union* (Frankfurt am Main, 1790).

8. *Apologismos an das bessere Publicum.*

9. *Leben, Meynungen und Schicksale D. Carl Friedrich Bahrdts aus Urkunden gezogen.* The first part was the only one published.

10. *Alvaro und Ximenes. Ein spanischer Roman* (Halle, 1790). *Leben und Thaten des weiland hochwürdigen Pastor Rindvigius. Ans Licht gestellt von Kasimir Renatus Denarée, Oberpastor zu Ochsenhausen*, 2 vol. (Ochsenhausen [Friedrich in Liebau], 1790), auf Kosten der Familie. *Geschichte des Prinzen Yhakanpol, lustig und zugleich orthodox-erbaulich geschrieben von dem Magister Wramschowsky, mit einer Vorrede vom Doktor Hofstede, Grossinquisitor* (Adrianopel [Halle], 1790).

11. He represents her as a lazy and extravagant Indian woman who had bought an excellent female slave of whom she became so jealous that her husband was forced to move to the country in order to limit his wife's mischief-making.

12. According to Gustav Frank, Dr. Reimarus is meant.

CHAPTER XXVIII

1. Werner Milch, *Die Einsamkeit. Zimmermann und Obereit im Kampf um die Überwindung der Aufklärung*, pp. 90–92.

2. *Über Friedrich den Grossen und meine Unterredungen mit ihm kurz vor seinem Tode.*

3. The *Allgemeine deutsche Bibliothek* for 1792 (CXII [2]), in a general review of the controversy stirred up by Zimmermann, points out that in the

opinion of a good many physicians Bahrdt's criticism of the medical treatment and his own suggestion were correct.

4. This account is dependent on the findings of Rudolf Ischer in his *Johann Georg Zimmermanns Leben und Werke.*

5. *Erklärung des Verfassers Dr. Bahrdt mit der eisernen Stirn* (Königsberg, 1791).

CHAPTER XXIX

1. *Katechismus der natürlichen Religion als Grundlage eines jeden Unterrichts in der Moral und Religion, zum Gebrauche für Ältern, Prediger, Lehrer und Zöglinge* (Halle, 1790).

2. *Zeitschrift für Gattinnen, Mütter und Töchter* (Halle, 1791).

3. *Auszug aus Dr. Martin Luther's Tischreden, mit Anmerkungen von Dr. K. F. Bahrdt* (Halle, 1791).

4. *Anekdoten und Charakterzüge, Aus der wahren Geschichte für Liebhaber des Vademecums und ernsthafte Leser. Ein Nachlass von Dr. Karl Friedrich Bahrdt* (Germanien [*i.e.,* Halle], 1791).

5. Quoted by Gustav Frank, "Dr. Karl Friedrich Bahrdt. Ein Beitrag zur Geschichte der deutschen Aufklärung."

6. *Über symbolische Bücher in Bezug aufs Staatsrecht* (Rostock, 1789).

7. *Prüfung der Roennberg'schen Schrift über symbolische Bücher in Bezug auf das Staatsrecht* (1791).

8. *Prüfung der Schrift des Hofraths Roennberg über symbolische Bücher in Bezug aufs Staatsrecht. In Briefen von K. F. Bahrdt* (Halle, 1791).

9. "Doktor Bahrdt auf seinem Weinberg."

10. *Etwas über die Weinbergskrankheit des verstorbenen Dr. Bahrdt und ähnlicher noch lebender Kranken.*

APPENDIX

1. Schlichtegroll, *Nekrolog auf das Jahr 1792;* also *Nachträge und Berichtigungen 1790, 1791, 1792, 1793, Supplement Band.*

2. J. C. Förster, *Übersicht der Geschichte der Universität zu Halle in ihrem ersten Jahrhunderte.*

3. J. G. P. Thiele, *Dr. Bahrdt in Marschlins.*

4. J. C. Hoffbauer, *Geschichte der Universität zu Halle bis zum Jahre 1805.*

5. Ersch und Gruber, *Allgemeine Encyclopädie der Wissenschaften und Künste,* Teil VII.

6. A. Koberstein, *Geschichte der deutschen Nationalliteratur.*

7. W. Menzel, *German Literature.*

8. Heinrich Doering, *Die gelehrten Theologen Deutschlands im 18. und 19. Jahrhundert.*

9. G. G. Gervinus, *Geschichte der poetischen Nationalliteratur der Deutschen.*

10. Martin von Geismar (E. Bauer), *Bibliothek der deutschen Aufklärer des achtzehnten Jahrhunderts.*

11. J. Hillebrand, *Die deutsche Nationalliteratur seit dem Anfange des achtzehnten Jahrhunderts, besonders seit Lessing, bis auf die Gegenwart, ästhetisch-kritisch dargestellt.*

12. T. W. Danzel und G. E. Guhrauer, *Gotthold Ephraim Lessing, sein Leben und seine Werke.*

13. L. Noack, *Die Freidenker in der Religion, oder die Repräsentanten der religiösen Aufklärung in England, Frankreich und Deutschland.*

14. F. C. Schlosser, *Weltgeschichte für das deutsche Volk.* Neunter Teil. *Geschichte des achtzehnten Jahrhunderts.*

15. R. Prutz, "Karl Friedrich Bahrdt's Jugendgeschichte."

16. A. Boden, *Lessing und Goeze. Ein Beitrag zur Literatur-und Kirchengeschichte des achtzehnten Jahrhunderts. Zugleich als Widerlegung der Röpeschen Schrift: Johann Melchior Goeze, eine Rettung.*

17. H. Hettner, *Geschichte der deutschen Literatur im achtzehnten Jahrhundert.*

18. F. W. Ebeling, *Geschichte der komischen Literatur in Deutschland.*

19. G. Frank, "Dr. Karl Friedrich Bahrdt. Ein Beitrag zur Geschichte der deutschen Aufklärung."

20. J. Leyser, *Karl Friedrich Bahrdt, der Zeitgenosse Pestalozzi's, sein Verhältnis zum Philanthropinismus und zur neuern Pädagogik. Ein Beitrag zur Geschichte der Erziehung und des Unterrichts.*

21. E. P. Evans, *Abriss der deutschen Literaturgeschichte.* Evans was accused by Gustavus Fischer of having stolen the work from lectures delivered by Professor W. Müller, of the University of Göttingen, according to the *Globe and Evening Press* of New York for Wednesday, 16 February 1870.

22. G. A. Heinrich, *Histoire de la Littérature Allemande.*

23. J. Gostwick and R. Harrison, *Outlines of German Literature.*

24. A. Pinloche, *La Réforme de l'Education en Allemagne au Dix-huitième Siècle.*

25. H. Kurz, *Geschichte der deutschen Literatur.* Siebte unveränderte Auflage (Leipzig, 1876).

26. D. Sanders, *Deutsche Literaturgeschichte.*

27. K. Borinski, *Geschichte der deutschen Literatur.*

28. Lichtenberger, *Encyclopédie des Sciences Religieuses;* Wetzer und Welte, *Kirchenlexikon.*

29. W. Kawerau, "Karl Friedrich Bahrdt. Ein literarisches Charakterbild."

30. E. Schmidt, *Lessing, Geschichte seines Lebens und seiner Schriften.*

31. A. Schreiber, "Der Zusammenbruch des Dr. Bahrdtschen Philanthropinums in Heidesheim."

32. J. Keller, "Das Philanthropinum in Marschlins." Keller had already published an account of the founding of the school: "Das rhätische Seminar Haldenstein-Marschlins."

33. Leopold Zscharnack, *Lessing und Semler.*

34. Paul Gastrow, *Johann Salomo Semler.*

35. W. Diehl, "Beiträge zur Geschichte von Karl Friedrich Bahrdts Giesser Zeit."

36. Albert Schweitzer, *Geschichte der Leben-Jesu Forschung.*

37. W. Oehlke, *Lessing und seine Zeit.*

38. A. Bartels, *Geschichte der deutschen Literatur.*

39. F. Hasselberg ed. *Dr. Carl Friedrich Bahrdt. Geschichte seines Lebens, seiner Meinungen und Schicksale.*

40. K. Burdach, *Vorspiel. Gesammelte Schriften zur Geschichte des deutschen Geistes.*

41. E. Heimpel-Michel, "Die Aufklärung. Eine historisch-systematische Untersuchung."

42. Karl Aner, *Die Theologie der Lessingzeit.*

43. P. Wiegler, *Geschichte der deutschen Literatur.*

44. W. Milch, *Die Einsamkeit. Zimmermann und Obereit im Kampf um die Überwindung der Aufklärung.*

45. W. Linden, *Geschichte der deutschen Literatur.*

46. J. Nadler, *Literaturgeschichte des deutschen Volkes, Dichtung und Schrifttum der deutschen Stämme und Landschaften.*

47. H. Prang, *Johann Heinrich Merck. Ein Leben für Andere.*

48. H. Meyer, *Goethe. Das Leben im Werk.*

49. F. Sengle, *Wieland.*

50. F. J. Schneider, *Die deutsche Dichtung der Gegenwart.*

51. *Neue deutsche Biographie.*

52. W. Pfeiffer-Belli, *Geschichte der deutschen Dichtung.*

53. H. Schneider, "D. Karl Friedrich Bahrdt's Letter to George Washington."

Selected Bibliography

Imaginative and other works of Bahrdt's well-known contemporaries, unless of special interest, are not mentioned here. Neither are Bahrdt's own writings, a list of which may conveniently be found in Goedeke's *Grundriss*. Special mention, however, should be made of Bahrdt's autobiography, *Dr. Carl Friedrich Bahrdts Geschichte seines Lebens, seiner Meinungen und Schicksale. Von ihm selbst geschrieben* (Berlin: Friedrich Vieweg, 1790–1791), a vastly entertaining, informative, and misleading book.

Die Allgemeine deutsche Bibliothek. Berlin und Stettin, 1765–1792. Kiel, 1792–1796.

Die Allgemeine deutsche Biographie. Leipzig, 1875–1912.

Almanach der Bellettristen und Belletristinnen fürs Jahr 1782. Ulietea.

ANER, KARL. *Der Aufklärer Friedrich Nicolai.* Giessen, 1912.

———. *Die Theologie der Lessingzeit.* Halle, 1929.

BARTELS, A. *Geschichte der deutschen Literatur.* Berlin und Hamburg, 1943.

BASEDOW, JOHANN BERNHARD. *Das Elementarwerk, ein Vorrath der besten Erkenntnisse zum Lernen, Lehren, Wiederholen und Nachdenken.* Dessau, 1774. Reprinted Leipzig, 1909.

———. *Das in Dessau errichtete Philanthropinum, eine Schule der Menschenfreundschaft und guter Kenntnisse für Lernende und junge Lehrer, Arme und Reiche; ein Fidei-Kommiss des Publikums zur Vervollkomnung des Erziehungswesens aller Orten nach dem Plane des Elementarwerks, den Erforschern und Thätern des Guten unter Fürsten, menschenfreundlichen Gesellschaften und Privatpersonen empfohlen.* Leipzig, 1774.

———. *Vorstellung an Menschenfreunde und vermögende Männer über Schulen und ihren Einfluss auf die öffentliche Wohlfahrt. Mit einem Plane eines Elementarbuchs der menschlichen Erkenntnis.* Hamburg, 1768.

BAUER, F. C. *Lehrbuch der christlichen Dogmengeschichte.* Leipzig, 1867.

BAUSER, F. *Geschichte der Moser von Filseck.* Stuttgart, 1911.

BENKOWITZ, C. F. "Doktor Bahrdt auf seinem Weinberg," *Deutsche Monatsschrift.* Berlin, October 1792.

BENNER, J. H. *Pflichtmässige Erwägungen, die Religion betreffend.* Giessen, 1772.

BENZ, RICHARD. *Die Zeit der deutschen Klassik.* Stuttgart, 1953.

BERGER, ARNOLD E. "Die Entwicklung der Aufklärungsideen in Westeuropa," *Jahrbuch des freien deutschen Hochstifts.* Frankfurt am Main, 1911.

BIEDERMANN, KARL. *Deutschland im achtzehnten Jahrhundert.* Leipzig, 1854.

390   *Bibliography*

BIEREYE, JOHANNES. *Erfurt in seinen berühmten Persönlichkeiten.* Erfurt, 1937.

BLUM, JEAN. *J.-A. Starck et la Querelle du Crypto-Catholicisme en Allemagne, 1785–1789.* Paris, 1912.

BOCK, A. "Friedrich Karl von Moser, der Herr und der Diener, 1759," *Literar-historisches Taschenbuch,* ed. R. E. PRUTZ, 1846.

BODEN, AUGUST. *Lessing und Goeze. Ein Beitrag zur Literatur- und Kirchengeschichte des achtzehnten Jahrhunderts. Zugleich als Widerlegung der Röpeschen Schrift: Johann Melchior Goeze, eine Rettung.* Leipzig und Heidelberg, 1862.

BÖHM, BENNO. *Sokrates im achtzehnten Jahrhundert.* Leipzig, 1929.

BOEHN, MAX VON. *Deutschland im 18. Jahrhundert.* Berlin, 1921.

BOPP, PHILIPP. "Die grosse Landgräfin. Bild einer deutschen Fürstin des 18. Jahrhunderts," *Raumers historisches Taschenbuch.* Dritte Folge, IV (1853), 535–73.

BORINSKI, K. *Geschichte der deutschen Literatur. (Seit dem Ausgang des Mittelalters. Deutsche Nationalliteratur CLXIII².)* Stuttgart, 1892-1894.

BOXBERGER, R. "Wielands Beziehungen zu Erfurt," *Jahrbücher der königlichen Akademie gemeinnütziger Wissenschaften zu Erfurt.* Neue Folge, Heft VI (1870).

——. "Wielands Professur in Erfurt," *Jahrbücher der königlichen Akademie gemeinnütziger Wissenschaften zu Erfurt.* Neue Folge, Heft VI (Erfurt, 1870).

BRAEKER, ULRICH. *Lebensgeschichte und natürliche Abentheuer des armen Mannes in Tockenburg.* Zürich, 1789. Reprinted Zürich, n.d.

BRÄSS, H. W. D. *D. Carl Friedrich Bahrdts Unruhiges Leben und schmerzvoller Tod. Als Anhang Auszug aus Dressels Reisen.* Halle, 1792.

BRÄUNING-OKTAVIO, H. *Beiträge zur Geschichte und Frage nach den Mitarbeitern der Frankfurter Gelehrten Anzeigen vom Jahre 1772.* Darmstadt, 1912.

——. "Bemerkungen zu den Frankfurter Gelehrten Anzeigen," *Euphorion,* XVI⁴ (1909).

BRANDES, J. CHR. *Meine Lebensgeschichte.* Berlin, 1799–1800.

BRINITZER, CARL. *G. C. Lichtenberg, die Geschichte eines gescheiten Mannes.* Tübingen, 1956.

BRONOWSKI, J., and BRUCE MAZLISH. *The Western Intellectual Tradition.* New York, 1960.

BRÜGGEMANN, FRITZ. *Der Anbruch der Gefuhlskultur in den fünfziger Jahren.* Leipzig, 1935.

——. "Der Kampf um die bürgerliche Welt- und Lebensanschauung in der deutschen Literatur des 18. Jahrhunderts," *Deutsche Vierteljahrsschrift,* III (1925).

——. *Das Weltbild der Aufklärung.* Leipzig, 1930.

BRUNSCHWIG, HENRI. *La Crise de l'Etat Prussien à la Fin du XVIIIᵉ Siècle et la Genèse de la Mentalité Romantique.* Paris, 1947.

BURDACH, K. *Vorspiel. Gesammelte Schriften zur Geschichte des deutschen Geistes.* Halle, 1926.

BUSCHE, H. VOM. *Friedrich Carl Freiherr von Moser.* Stuttgart, 1846.

CAMPE, JOACHIM HEINRICH. *Allgemeine Revision des gesammten Schul- und Erziehungswesens.* Hamburg, 1785–1791.

COUSINS, NORMAN, ed. *In God We Trust.* New York, 1958.

DANZEL, T. W., und G. E. GUHRAUER. *Gotthold Ephraim Lessing, sein Leben und seine Werke.* Leipzig, 1853.

Des Freiherrn C. Fr. von Moser Dienst-Jahre in dem Fürstl. Hessen-Darmstädtischen betreffend. Als erläuternde Anmerkungen und Berichtingungen zu des Herrn Professor Reus Schrift über diesen Gegenstand. Bebenhausen, 1789.

DIEHL, WILHELM. "Beiträge zur Geschichte von Karl Friedrich Bahrdts Giesser Zeit," *Archiv für hessische Geschichte und Altertumskunde,* Neue Folge, VIII (Darmstadt, 1912).

DOERING, HEINRICH. *Die gelehrten Theologen Deutschlands im 18. und 19. Jahrhundert.* Neustadt an der Orla, 1831.

DREWS, PAUL. "Das Eindringen der Aufklärung in der Universität Giessen," *Preussische Jahrbücher,* CXXX (October-December, 1907), 35–59.

DÜNTZER, HEINRICH. *Christoph Kaufmann, der Apostel der Geniezeit und der Herrnhutische Arzt.* Leipzig, 1882.

EBELING, F. W. *Geschichte der komischen Literatur in Deutschland seit der Mitte des 18. Jahrhunderts.* Leipzig, 1869.

EBERHARD, JOHANN AUGUST. Letters to Friedrich Nicolai. Unpublished.

———. *Neue Apologie des Sokrates oder Untersuchung der Lehre von der Seligkeit der Heiden.* Berlin und Stettin, 1772.

EBERLEIN, AUGUST. *Landgraf Ludwig IX und seine Pirmasenser Militärkolonie.* Erlangen, 1911.

EBERTY, FELIX. *Geschichte des preussischen Staats.* Breslau, 1870.

ELSASSER, ROBERT. *Über die politischen Bildungsreisen der Deutschen nach England* (vom 18. Jahrhundert bis 1815). Heidelberg, 1917.

ERHARD, H. A. Footnote to GEHREN's article on Bahrdt in ERSCH and GRUBER, *Allgemeine Encyclopädie der Wissenschaften und Künste.* VII Teil. Leipzig, 1821.

———. *Überlieferungen zur vaterländischen Geschichte.* Zweites Heft. Magdeburg, 1827.

ERNESTI, J. A. *Ioannis Augusti Ernesti Institutio interpretis Novi Testamenti.* Leipzig, 1761.

ERSCH, J. S. *Allgemeines Repertorium der Literatur.* Jena, 1793–1807.

———. *Handbuch der deutschen Literatur seit der Mitte des achtzehnten Jahrhunderts bis auf die neueste Zeit.* Amsterdam und Leipzig, 1812.

ERSCH, J. S., und J. G. GRUBER. *Allgemeine Encyclopädie der Wissenschaften und Künste.* Leipzig, 1818–1889.

EVANS, E. P. *Abriss der deutschen Literaturgeschichte.* New York, 1869.

392   *Bibliography*

EYBISCH, H. *Anton Reiser, Untersuchungen zur Lebensgeschichte von K. Ph. Moritz und zur Kritik seiner Autobiographie.* Leipzig, 1908.

FARMAKIS, VIOLA MARINA. *K. Ph. Moritz and His Conception of the Artist.* Chicago, 1948.

FICHTE, JOHANN GOTTLIEB. *Friedrich Nicolai's Leben und sonderbare Meinungen. Ein Beitrag zur Litterar-Geschichte des vergangenen und zur Pädagogik des angehenden Jahrhunderts.* Hrsgg. von A. W. SCHLEGEL. Tübingen, 1801.

FISCHER, G. N., und A. RIEM. *Berlinisches Journal für Aufklärung.* Berlin, 1788–1790.

FÖRSTER, J. C. *Übersicht der Geschichte der Universität zu Halle in ihrem ersten Jahrhunderte.* Halle, 1794.

FÖRSTER, RICHARD. "Johann Jakob Reiske. Zu seinem 200-jährigen Geburtstag," *Neue Jahrbücher für Pädagogik,* XXXVIII (1916), p. 449 ff.

————, ed. *Johann Jakob Reiskes Briefe. Abhandlungen der Sächs. Gesellschaft d. Wissenschaften,* XVI (Leipzig, 1897), Nr. 170.

FRANK, GUSTAV. "Dr. Karl Friedrich Bahrdt. Ein Beitrag zur Geschichte der deutschen Aufklärung," *Raumers historisches Taschenbuch.* Folge 4, VII. Leipzig, 1866.

————. *Geschichte der protestantischen Theologie.* Leipzig, 1862.

————. *Geschichte des Rationalismus und seiner Gegensätze.* Leipzig, 1875.

Frankfurter Gelehrte Anzeigen. Frankfurt. 1772–1790.

FREYTAG, GUSTAV. *Bilder aus der deutschen Vergangenheit.* Leipzig, 1859–1862.

FRICKE, GERHARD. "Der deutsche Mensch der Aufklärung, *Der deutsche Mensch.* Stuttgart und Berlin, 1935.

FRICKE, GERHARD, F. KOCH, und KLEMENS LUGOWSKI. *Von deutscher Art in Sprache und Dichtung.* Stuttgart und Berlin, 1941.

GASTROW, PAUL. *Johann Salomo Semler in seiner Bedeutung für die Theologie.* Giessen, 1905.

GEHREN, KARL CHRISTIAN VON. Article on Bahrdt in ERSCH and GRUBER's *Allgemeine Encyclopädie der Wissenschaften und Künste.* VII Teil. Leipzig, 1821.

GEIGER, LUDWIG. Article on Frau Reiske. *Die Frau.* July 1898.

GEISMAR, MARTIN VON (E. BAUER). *Bibliothek der deutschen Aufklärer des achtzehnten Jahrhunderts.* Leipzig, 1846.

GEDIKE und BIESTER. *Berlinische Monatsschrift.* Berlin, 1783–1792. Jena, 1792. Dessau, 1793–1796.

GERSTENBERG, J. H. VON. *Versuch den katholischen Lehrbegriff zu vertheidigen, von einem Protestanten.* Frankfurt am Main, 1772.

GERVINUS, G. G. *Geschichte der poetischen Nationalliteratur der Deutschen.* Leipzig, 1844.

[Giessen]. *Die Universität Giessen von 1607 bis 1907. Beiträge zu ihrer Geschichte. Festschrift zur dritten Jahrhundertfeier.* Giessen, 1907.

GNÜCHTEL, ERNST. *Isaak Iselin und sein Verhältnis zum Philanthropinismus.* Leipzig, 1907.

GOEDEKE, KARL. *Grundriss zur Geschichte der deutschen Dichtung.* (Vierter Band.) Dresden: Verlag von L. Ehlermann, 1891.

GÖTZE, J. M. *Beweis, dass die Bahrdt'sche Verdeutschung des Neuen Testaments keine Übersetzung, sondern eine vorsätzliche Verfälschung des Wortes Gottes sei.* Hamburg, 1773.

GOLDFRIEDRICH, JOHANN. *Geschichte des deutschen Buchhandels vom Beginn der klassischen Litteraturperiode bis zum Beginn der Fremdherrschaft* (1740–1804). Leipzig, 1909.

GOSTWICK, J., and R. HARRISON. *Outlines of German Literature.* London and Edinburgh, 1873.

GRÄF, H. G. *J. H. Mercks Briefe an die Herzogin-Mutter Anna Amalia und an den Herzog Carl August von Sachsen-Weimar.* Leipzig, 1911.

GRENZMANN, WILHELM. *Georg Christoph Lichtenberg.* Leipzig, 1939.

GUINAUDEAU, O. *Études sur J.-G. Lavater.* Paris, 1924.

Gutachten zweier theologischen Facultäten, der würzburgschen und göttingschen, auf allerhöchsten Befehl seiner Kaiserlichen Majestät über die Übereinstimmung Herrn Dr. Bahrdt's zu Heidesheim mit den reichsgesetzmässigen Lehrsystemen ausgefertiget. Berlin und Leipzig, 1779.

[Halle]. *Geschichte des Erziehungsinstituts bei dem theologischen Seminarium zu Halle.* 1781.

A Handbook of Christian Theology. New York, 1958.

HARNACK, ADOLF. *Lehrbuch der Dogmengeschichte.* Tübingen, 1909.

HARTLICH, CHRISTIAN, und WALTER SACHS. *Der Ursprung des Mythosbegriffes in der modernen Bibelwissenschaft.* Tübingen, 1952.

HASSELBERG, F., ed. *Dr. Carl Friedrich Bahrdt. Geschichte seines Lebens, seiner Meinungen und Schicksale.* Berlin, 1922.

HAUSEN, CARL RENATUS. *Leben und Character Herrn Christian Adolph Klotzens.* Halle, 1772.

HÄUSSER, L. *Deutsche Geschichte.* Berlin, 1854.

HAZARD, PAUL. *La Crise de la Conscience Européenne.* Paris, 1935.

HEIMPEL-MICHEL, E. "Die Aufklärung. Eine historisch-systematische Untersuchung," *Göttinger Studien zur Pädagogik,* VII. Langensalza, 1925.

HEINRICH, G. A. *Histoire de la Litérature Allemande.* Paris, 1870.

HERBST, WILHELM. *Johann Heinrich Voss.* Leipzig, 1872–1876.

HESS, JOHANN JAKOB. *Geschichte der drei letzten Lebensjahre Jesu.* Leipzig und Zürich, 1768–1772, seventh edition 1823.

HETTNER, HERMANN. *Geschichte der deutschen Literatur im achtzehnten Jahrhundert,* ed. GEORG WITKOWSKI, Leipzig, 1928.

HILLEBRAND, JOSEPH. *Die deutsche Nationalliteratur seit dem Anfange des achtzehnten Jahrhunderts, besonders seit Lessing, bis auf die Gegenwart, ästhetisch-kritisch dargestellt.* Zweite, verbesserte und mehrfach umgearbeitete Ausgabe. Hamburg und Gotha, 1850.

HOFFBAUER, JOHANN CHRISTIAN. *Geschichte der Universität zu Halle bis zum Jahre 1805.* Halle, 1805.

394

Bibliography

HORRER, GEORG ADAM. *Untersuchung des Bahrdtischen Glaubensbekenntnisses.* Leipzig, 1779.

HUFELAND, G. *Über das Recht protestantischer Fürsten, unabänderliche Lehrvorschriften festzusetzen und über solche zu halten.* Frankfurt und Jena, 1788.

ISCHER, RUDOLPH. *Johann Georg Zimmermanns Leben und Werke.* Bern, 1893.

JOLIVET, A. *Wilhelm Heinse. Sa vie et son œuvre jusqu'en 1787.* Paris, 1922.

JUNCKER, J. C. W. *Etwas uber die Weinbergskrankheit des verstorbenen Dr. Bahrdt und ähnlicher noch lebender Kranken. Den Nichtärzten zur freundschaftlichen Warnung mitgetheilt von Dr. J. Ch. W. Juncker.* Halle, 1792.

KAHNIS, K. F. A. *Der innere Gang des deutschen Protestantismus.* Leipzig, 1874.

KANT, IMMANUEL. *Werke,* ed. ERNST CASSIRER. I. Berlin, 1922.

KAUFMANN, HANS-HEINRICH. "Friedrich Carl von Moser als Politiker und Publizist," *Quellen und Forschungen zur Hessischen Geschichte,* XII (Darmstadt, 1931).

KAWERAU, WALDEMAR. *Aus Halles Litteraturleben.* Halle, 1888.

———. "Karl Friedrich Bahrdt. Ein literarisches Charakterbild," *Die Grenzboten,* XLVI⁴ (Leipzig, 1887).

KAYSER, JOHANN ANDREAS. *D. Carl Friedrich Bahrdts Glaubensbekenntnis widerlegt von Orthonoëte,* 1780.

KELLER, J. "Briefe aus dem Philanthropinum in Dessau," *Kehrs Pädagogische Blätter,* XXIV.

———. "Isaak Iselins Verdienste," *Kehrs Pädagogische Blätter,* XIV.

———. "Das Philanthropinum in Marschlins," *Beiträge zur Lehrerbildung und Lehrerfortbildung,* Heft II (1899).

———. "Das rhätische Seminar Haldenstein-Marschlins," *Kehrs Pädagogische Blätter,* XII.

———. "Zur Kenntnis Leuchsenrings," *Archiv für Literaturgeschichte,* XIV (Leipzig, 1886).

Kirchen- und Ketzeralmanach auf das Jahr 1786, hrsgg. von Hauptpastor xxxx. Gera, 1785.

KNIGGE, ADOLPH, FREIHERR VON. *Über den Bücher-Nachdruck.* Hamburg, 1792.

KOBERSTEIN, AUGUST. *Geschichte der deütschen Nationalliteratur.* Fünfte umgearbeitete Auflage von KARL BARTSCH. Leipzig, 1873–1874.

Kösters Neueste Religionsbegebenheiten mit unpartheyischen Anmerkungen. Giessen, 1778–1793.

KOLDEWEY, FRIEDRICH. *Lebens-und Charakterbilder.* Wolfenbüttel, 1881.

KOTZEBUE, AUGUST VON. *Doctor Bahrdt mit der eisernen Stirn oder Die deutsche Union gegen Zimmermann. Ein Schauspiel in vier Aufzügen von Freyherrn von Knigge.* 1790.

KUGLER, FRANZ. *Geschichte Friedrichs des Grossen.* Mit 400 Illustrationen gezeichnet von ADOLF MENZEL. Leipzig, 1906.

KURZ, HEINRICH, und FR. PALDAMUS. *Deutsche Dichter und Prosaisten nach ihrem Leben und Wirken geschildert.* Leipzig, 1867.

KURZ, H. *Geschichte der deutschen Literatur.* Siebte unveränderte Auflage. Leipzig, 1876.

LAMBERT, J. H. *J. H. Lamberts deutscher gelehrter Briefwechsel,* ed. JOH. BERNOULLI. Berlin und Dessau, 1781.

LARGIADÉR, A. P. "Karl Friedrich Bahrdt und seine wahren Verdienste um die Erziehungsanstalt in Marschlins," *Kehrs Pädagogische Blätter,* XII (1883), 62–73.

LAUKHARD, F. C. *Anekdotenbuch oder Sammlung unterhaltender und lehrreicher Erzählungen aus der wirklichen Welt.* Hrsgg. v. F.C.L. Teil I. Leipzig, 1802.

――――. *Beyträge und Berichtigungen zu Herrn Karl Friedrich Bahrdt's Lebensbeschreibung in Briefen eines Pfälzers.* 1791.

――――. *Eulerkappers Leben und Leiden; eine tragisch-komische Geschichte.* Halle, 1804.

――――. *Leben und Thaten des Rheingrafen Carl Magnus, den Joseph II. auf zehn Jahre ins Gefängnis nach Königstein schickte, um da die Rechte der Unterthanen und anderer Menschen respectiren zu lernen.* Leipzig, 1798.

――――. *Magister F. Ch. Laukhard's Leben und Schicksale.* Bearbeitet von DR. VICTOR PETERSEN. Einleitung von PAUL HOLZHAUSEN. Stuttgart, 1908.

LAVATER-SLOMAN, MARY. *Genie des Herzens.* Zürich, 1939.

LECKY, W. E. H. *History of the Rise and Influence of the Spirit of Rationalism in Europe.* London, 1890.

LEITZMANN, ALBERT. *Georg und Therese Forster und die Brüder Humboldt.* Bonn, 1936.

LEUTZ, F. "Beiträge zur Geschichte der Philanthropine in Dessau und Marschlins (Der Unterricht in dem Grossherzoglichen Badischen evangelischen Schullehrerseminar in Karlsruhe, XXIX, XXX)," *Jahresberichte,* 1875–1876.

LEYSER, JAKOB. *Joachim Heinrich Campe; ein Lebensbild aus dem Zeitalter der Aufklärung.* Braunschweig, 1877.

――――. *Karl Friedrich Bahrdt, der Zeitgenosse Pestalozzi's, sein Verhältnis zum Philanthropinismus und zur neuern Pädagogik. Ein Beitrag zur Geschichte der Erziehung und des Unterrichts.* Zweite verbesserte Auflage. Neustadt an der Haardt, 1870.

LICHTENBERGER, F. *Encyclopédie des Sciences Religieuses.* Paris, 1877.

LINDEN, WALTER. *Geschichte der deutschen Literatur.* Leipzig, 1937.

LOEBELL, R. "Mephistopheles Merck," *Evangelisches Monatsblatt,* 1894. Nos. 4 and 5.

――――. *Der Anti-Necker J. H. Mercks und der Minister Fr. K. v. Moser.* Darmstadt, 1896.

――――. "Zum Kapitel Goethe ein grosser Nehmer (Goethe und J. H. Merck)," *Zeitschrift fur den deutschen Unterricht,* V (Leipzig, 1891), 770–75.

Loth, Richard. "Dr. Joh. Wilh. Baumer, der erste Sekretär der königlichen Akademie gemeinnütziger Wissenschaften zu Erfurt," *Jahrbücher der königlichen Akademie gemeinnütziger Wissenschaften zu Erfurt.* Neue Folge, Heft XXXII (Erfurt, 1906).

Lucas, J. C. D. *Carl Friedrich Bahrdts Glaubensbekenntnis veranlasst durch ein Kayserl. Reichshofrathsconclusum. Methodice beantwortet.* Leipzig, 1779.

Meier, C. J. B. *Basedows Leben, Charakter und Schriften unparteiisch dargestellt und beurtheilt.* Hamburg, 1791–1792.

Menzel, Wolfgang. *German Literature.* Translated from the German, with notes, by Thomas Gordon. Oxford, 1840.

Merck, J. H. *Schriften und Briefwechsel,* ed. Kurt Wolff. Leipzig, 1909.

Merker, P., und W. Stammler, *Reallexikon der deutschen Literaturgeschichte.* Berlin, 1925–1931.

Meusel, Johann Georg. *Das gelehrte Teutschland oder Lexikon der jetzt lebenden teutschen Schriftsteller.* Lemgo, 1783.

———. *Lexikon der vom Jahr 1750 bis 1800 verstorbenen teutschen Schriftsteller.* Leipzig, 1802–1816.

Meyer, Henrich. *The Age of the World. A Chapter in the History of Enlightenment.* Allentown, Pennsylvania, 1951.

———. *Goethe. Das Leben im Werk.* Hamburg-Bergedorf, 1949–1951.

Michaelis, Johann David. *Erklärung der Begräbnis-und Auferstehungsgeschichte Christi nach den vier Evangelien.* Halle, 1783.

Michaud, J. F. *Biographie Universelle.* Nouvelle Edition. Paris, 1811–1862.

Michel, Victor. *C.-M. Wieland. La formation et l'évolution de son esprit jusqu'en 1772.* Paris, 1937.

Milch, Werner. *Die Einsamkeit. Zimmermann und Obereit im Kampf um die Überwindung der Aufklärung.* Frauenfeld und Leipzig, 1937.

Mirabeau, Honoré Gabriel Victor Riquetti, Comte de. *De la Monarchie Prussienne sous Frédéric le Grand.* London, 1788.

Moritz, Karl Philipp. *Anton Reiser, ein psychologischer Roman (Deutsche Literaturdenkmale des 18. und 19. Jahrhunderts in Neudrucken,* ed., Bernhard Seuffert, XXIII). Heilbronn, 1896.

Morris, Max. *Goethes und Herders Anteil an dem Jahrgang 1772 der Frankfurter gelehrten Anzeigen.* Stuttgart und Berlin, 1909.

Moser, F. K. von. *Der Herr und der Diener geschildert mit patriotischer Freyheit.* Frankfurt am Main, 1759.

Müller, G. "Das Aufklärungszeitalter," *Literaturwissenschaftliche Jahrbücher der Görres-Gesellschaft,* VI (1931).

Nadler, Josef. *Literaturgeschichte des deutschen Volkes. Dichtung und Schrifttum der deutschen Stämme und Landschaften.* Berlin, 1938.

Neue deutsche Biographie. Berlin, 1953.

Neue theologische Bibliothek, ed. J. A. Ernesti. 1773–1779.

Nicolai, Friedrich. *Das Leben und die Meinungen des Magisters Sebaldus Nothanker,* ed. F. Brüggemann. (*Deutsche Literatur in Entwicklungsreihen*). Leipzig, 1938.

NICOLSON, HAROLD. *The Age of Reason*. New York, 1961.

NIEMAYER, AUGUST HERMANN. *Charakteristik der Bibel*. 1775. Neue Auflage, Halle, 1830–1831.

NITSCH, FRIEDRICH. "Die geschichtliche Bedeutung der Aufklärungstheologie," *Jahrbücher für Protestantische Theologie*, I. Leipzig, 1875.

NOACK, LUDWIG. *Die Freidenker in der Religion, oder die Repräsentanten der religiösen Aufklärung in England, Frankreich und Deutschland*. Bern, 1855.

OEHLKE, WALDEMAR. *Lessing und seine Zeit*. Munich, 1919.

O'FLAHERTY, JAMES C. "J. D. Michaelis: Rational Biblicist," *Journal of English and Germanic Philology*, XLIX, 172–81.

ONCKEN, W. *Das Zeitalter Friedrichs des Grossen*. Berlin, 1890–1892.

OST, GÜNTHER. "Friedrich Nicolais Allgemeine deutsche Bibliothek," *Germanische Studien*, Heft 63. Berlin, 1928.

PFEIFFER-BELLI, W. *Geschichte der deutschen Dichtung*. Freiburg, 1954.

PINLOCHE, A. *La Réforme de l'Education en Allemagne au Dix-huitième Siècle*. Paris, 1889.

PÖLLNITZ, KARL LUDWIG, FREIHERR VON. *Amusemens des eaux d'Aix-la-Chapelle*. Amsterdam, 1736.

———. *Lettres et mémoires du baron de Pöllnitz, contenant les observations qu'il a faites dans ses voyages, et le caractère des personnes qui composent les principales cours de l'Europe*. Amsterdam, 1744.

———. *La Saxe Galante*. Amsterdam, 1734.

POTT, DEGENHARDT, ed. *Briefe angesehener Gelehrten, Staatsmänner, und anderer, an den berühmten Märtyrer D. Karl Friedrich Bahrdt*. Leipzig, 1798.

———. *Leben, Meynungen und Schicksale D. Carl Friedrich Bahrdts aus Urkunden gezogen*. Erster Theil mit Kupfern. Leipzig, 1790.

PRANG, HELMUT. *Johann Heinrich Merck. Ein Leben für Andere*. Insel-Verlag, 1949.

PRUTZ, ROBERT. *Der Göttinger Dichterbund*. Leipzig, 1841.

———. "Karl Friedrich Bahrdt's Jugendgeschichte," *Biographische Beiträge zur deutschen Literatur-und Sittengeschichte des achtzehnten Jahrhunderts*. Leipzig, 1862.

———. *Menschen und Bücher* (Chapter VII on Bahrdt, Chapter VIII on Laukhard). Leipzig, 1862.

PÜTTER, JOHANN STEPHAN. *Versuch einer academischen Gelehrtengeschichte von der Universität Göttingen*. Göttingen, 1765.

RABANY, C. *Kotzebue. Sa Vie et son Temps, ses Œuvres Dramatiques*. Paris, 1893.

RANDALL, JOHN HERMANN. *The Making of the Modern Mind*. Boston and New York, 1940.

RATHGEBER, JULIUS. *Der letzte deutsche Fürst von Hanau-Lichtenberg. Landgraf Ludwig IX von Hessen-Darmstadt*. Strassburg, 1890.

REISKE, J. J. D. *Johann Jakob Reiskens von ihm selbst aufgesetzte Lebensbeschreibung*. Leipzig, 1783.

REUSS, J. A. *Über die Rechtssache des Freiherrn von Moser und des Herrn Landgrafen zu Hessen-Darmstadt Hochfürstlichen Durchlaucht.* Stuttgart, 1788.

RIEM, A. *Über Aufklärung, ob sie dem Staate, der Religion oder überhaupt gefährlich sey und seyn könne? Ein Wort zur Beherzigung für Regenten, Staatsmänner und Priester. Ein Fragment.* Berlin, 1788.

ROCHOW, F. E. VON. "Authentische Nachricht von der zu Dessau auf dem Philanthropin den 13. bis 15. May 1776 angestellten öffentlichen Prüfung," *Der teutsche Merkur.* May 1776.

ROENNBERG, JAKOB FRIEDRICH. *Über symbolische Bücher in Bezug aufs Staatsrecht.* Rostock, 1789.

RÖPE, GEORG REINHARD. *Johann Melchior Goeze, eine Rettung.* Hamburg, 1860.

ROSENSTEIN, I. "Friedrich Karl von Moser," *Preussische Jahrbücher,* XV (1865), pp. 228–58, 475–505.

ROTTECK, KARL VON, und KARL WELCKER. *Staatslexikon. Encyclopädie der sämmtlichen Staatswissenschaften für alle Stände.* Leipzig, 1856.

SANDERS, D. *Deutsche Literaturgeschichte.* Berlin, 1879.

SCHIEL, HUBERT. *Johann M. Sailer. Leben und Persönlichkeit.* Regensburg, 1948.

——. *Johann M. Sailer. Briefe.* Regensburg, 1952.

SCHLICHTEGROLL, FRIEDRICH. *Nekrolog.* Gotha, 1791–1806.

——. *Nekrolog. Nachträge und Berichtigungen 1790, 1791, 1792, 1793. Supplement Band.*

SCHLÖZER, AUGUST LUDWIG. *Briefwechsel, meist historischen und politischen Inhalts.* Göttingen, 1776–1783.

SCHLOSSER, F. C. *Weltgeschichte für das deutsche Volk. (Geschichte des achtzehnten Jahrhunderts, Teil IX.)* Frankfurt am Main, 1855.

SCHMIDT, ERICH. *Lessing, Geschichte seines Lebens und seiner Schriften.* Berlin, 1892.

SCHMIDT, MARTIN. "Evangelische Kirchengeschichte Deutschlands," *Deutsche Philologie im Aufriss.* Berlin, 1952–1957.

SCHNEIDER, F. J. *Die deutsche Dichtung der Gegenwart.* Stuttgart, 1952.

SCHNEIDER, HEINRICH. "D. Karl Friedrich Bahrdt's Letter to Washington," *Germanic Review,* October 1954.

——. *Lessing. Zwölf biographische Studien.* Bern, 1951.

——. *Quest for Mysteries: The Masonic Background for Literature in Eighteenth-Century Germany.* Ithaca, N. Y., 1947.

SCHREIBER, ALBERT. "Der Zusammenbruch des Dr. Bahrdtschen Philanthropinums in Heidesheim," *Rheinische Blätter für Erziehung und Unterricht,* LXIX (Frankfurt am Main, 1895).

SCHULZ, J. G. *Nähere Beleuchtung der deutschen Union.* 1789.

SCHULZE-MAIZIER, FRIEDRICH. "Wieland in Erfurt," *Jahrbücher der Akademie gemeinnütziger Wissenschaften zu Erfurt.* Neue Folge, Heft XLIV (1919).

SCHUMMEL, JOHANN GOTTLIEB. *Fritzens Reise nach Dessau.* Leipzig, 1776.

————. *Spitzbart, eine komitragische Geschichte für unser pädagogisches Jahrhundert.* Tübingen, 1779.

SCHWARTZ, PAUL. *Der erste Kulturkampf in Preussen um Kirche und Schule* (1788–1799). Berlin, 1925.

SCHWARZ, CARL. *Gotthold Ephraim Lessing als Theologe.* Halle, 1854.

SCHWEITZER, ALBERT. *Geschichte der Leben-Jesu-Forschung.* Tübingen, 1951 (sixth printing).

SCHWINGER, RICHARD. *Friedrich Nicolais Roman Sebaldus Nothanker.* Weimar, 1897.

SEILER, G. F. *Über den Versöhnungstod Jesu Christi.* Erlangen, 1778 and 1779.

SEMLER, J. S. *Abhandlung von der freien Untersuchung des Kanons.* Halle, 1771–1775.

————. *Antwort auf das Bahrdtische Glaubensbekenntnis.* Halle, 1779.

————. *Beantwortung der Fragmente eines Ungenannten insbesondere vom Zweck Jesu und seiner Jünger.* Halle, 1780.

————. *Das Bahrdt'sche Glaubensbekenntnis widerlegt von Dr. J. S. Semler nebst den beiden Gutachten der theologischen Facultäten zu Würzburg und Göttingen über das Bahrdt'sche Neue Testament im Auszuge.* Erlangen, 1779.

————. *Dissertatio de daemoniacis, quorum in Evangeliis fit mentio.* Halle, 1760.

————. *D. Joh. Sal. Semlers hermetische Briefe wider Vorurtheile und Betrügereyen.* Leipzig, 1788.

————. *Lebensbeschreibung.* Halle, 1781.

————. *Sendschreiben eines Landgeistlichen an den Herrn Professor Bahrdt in Halle. Bedenke das Ende.* Blankenburg, 1786.

————. *Versuch einer freyeren theologischen Lehrart.* Halle, 1777.

————. *Verteidigung des Königlichen Edikts vom 9. Juli 1788 wider die freimütigen Betrachtungen eines Ungenannten.* Halle, 1788.

Sendschreiben eines Predigers im Elsass an seinen in Giessen studirenden Sohn über des Dr. Bahrdt Neueste Offenbarungen. Strassburg, 1775.

SENGLE, F. *Wieland.* Stuttgart, 1949.

SEUFFERT, BERNHARD. "Wielands Erfurter Schüler vor der Inquisition," *Euphorion,* III (1896), pp. 376–89, 722–35.

SEUME, J. G. *Gesammelte Schriften,* ed. J. P. ZIMMERMANN. Wiesbaden, 1826.

SPRECHER, J. A. VON. *Geschichte der Republik der drei Bünde im 18. Jahrhundert.* Chur, 1873–1875.

SPRENGEL, E. "Johann August Eberhard," *Der neue teutsche Merkur,* IV (1809).

STARCK, J. A. *Apologismos an das bessere Publicum.* Leipzig, 1789.

————. *Freimüthige Betrachtungen über das Christentum.* Berlin, 1780.

————. *Johann August Starck, der heil. Schrift Doctor, Hochf. Hessen-Darmstädtischer Oberhofprediger, Consistorialrath und Definitor, über Kryptokatholicismus, Proselytenmacherey, Jesuitismus, geheime Gesell-*

schaften und besonders die ihm selbst von den Verfassern der Berliner
Monatsschrift gemachte [sic] Beschuldigungen mit Acten-Stücken belegt.
Frankfurt und Leipzig, 1787.

————. *Theoduls Gastmahl oder über die Vereinigung der verschiedenen
christlichen Religions-Societäten*. Frankfurt am Main, 1809.

————. *Über die alten und neuen Mysterien*. Berlin, 1782.

STEINEN, WOLFRAM VON DEN. *Das Zeitalter Goethes*. Bern, 1949.

STEINHAUSEN, GEORG, ed. *Monographien zur deutschen Kulturgeschichte*.
Leipzig, 1899–1905.

STERN, J. P. *Lichtenberg: A Doctrine of Scattered Occasions*. Bloomington,
Indiana, 1959.

STIEDA, WILHELM. *Erfurter Universitätsreformpläne im 18. Jahrhundert*.
Erfurt, 1934.

STRIEDER, F. W. *Grundlage zu einer hessischen Gelehrtengeschichte*. Göttingen,
1781–1819.

TELLER, JOHANN FRIEDRICH. *D. Carl Friedrich Bahrdts berüchtigtes Glaubensbekenntnis aus alter guter Freundschaft von Wort zu Worte berichtigt*.
Leipzig, 1780.

THIÉBAULT, DIEUDONNÉ. *Mes Souvenirs de vingt ans de Séjour à Berlin; ou,
Frédéric le Grand, sa famille, sa cour, etc*. Paris, 1804.

THIELE, J. G. P. *Dr. Bahrdt in Marschlins, ein fehlendes Füllstück zu seiner
Lebensgeschichte von einem Augenzeugen*. Zizers, 1796.

Toleranzbrief an die oberhessische Geistlichkeit. Frankfurt und Riga (actually
Hersfeld) , 1774.

TRAPP, ERNST CHRISTIAN. *Epistel an den Verfasser des 2. Quinquenniums
vom Kirchen- und Ketzeralmanach*. 1787. (Reprinted in *Allgemeine
deutsche Bibliothek*, LXXVI,[2] pp. 586–92) .

————. *Theologischer Beweis, dass der Doctor Bahrdt schuld an dem Erd-
beden in Kalabrien sei. Der Hochwürdigen theologischen Facultät in Halle
demüthig zugeeignet von Simon Ratzeberger dem jüngern, weiland
Herausgeber des berühmten Vademekums für lustige Leute*. Halle, 1785.

TRIEST. *Der wahre Character des Herrn Doctor C. F. Bahrdt. In vertrauten
briefen geschildert von einem Neiderländischen Bürger an seinen Freund
in London*. 1779. (Published anonymously; place of publication not
known.)

*Unterthänigstes Gutachten wegen der jetzigen Religionsbewegungen, besonders
in der evangelischen Kirche, wie auch über das kaiserliche Commissionsdekret in der Bahrdtischen Sache*. March 30, 1780.

VEHSE, EDUARD. *Geschichte der deutschen Höfe*. (*Geschichte der Häuser
Baiern, Würtemberg, Baden und Hessen*, XXVII.) Hamburg, 1853.

————. *Geschichte der deutschen Höfe seit der Reformation*. Hamburg,
1851–1860.

VILLAUME, P. *Freymüthige Betrachtungen über das Edikt vom 9. Juli 1788,
die Religionsverfassung in den Preussischen Staaten betreffend*. Frankfurt
und Leipzig, 1788.

VOLLAND, GEORG GOTTFRIED. *Beiträge und Erläuterungen zu Herrn Doctor Carl Friedrich Bahrdts Lebensbeschreibung, die er selbst verfertigt.* Jena, 1791.

WAGNER, JOHANN EHRENFRIED. *Schreiben eines Schulmeisters im sächsischen Gebirge an seinen Nachbar über das Bahrdtische Glaubensbekenntnis an seine Majestät den Römischen Kayser.* Frankfurt und Leipzig, 1780.

WAGNER, KARL. *Briefe aus dem Freundeskreise Goethes.* Leipzig, 1847.

———. *Merck: Briefe.* Darmstadt und Leipzig, 1835, 1847.

———. *Briefe an Johann Heinrich Merck von Göthe, Herder, Wieland und anderen berühmten Zeitgenossen, etc.* Darmstadt, 1835.

WALTHER, P. A. F. *Briefwechsel der "Grossen Landgräfin" Caroline von Hessen.* Wien, 1877.

WENDEBORN, G. F. A. Denial of Bahrdt's story of his conduct in London, in *Hamburgischer Correspondent* (May 6, 1791).

———. *Erinnerungen aus meinem Leben.* Hamburg, 1813.

———. "Erklärung gegen Herrn D. Bahrdt," *Neueste Religionsbegebenheiten.* Giessen, 1791.

WERNER, R. M. "Frankfurter gelehrte Anzeigen vom Jahre 1773," *Goethe Jahrbuch,* IV, p. 359 ff.

WETZER, HEINRICH JOSEPH, und BERNHARD WELTE. *Kirchenlexikon,* I. Freiburg im Breisgau, 1882.

WIEGAND, FRITZ. "Das Stadtarchiv Erfurt und seine Bestände," *Thüringische Archivstudien,* V (Weimar, 1953).

WIEGLER, PAUL. *Geschichte der deutschen Literatur.* Berlin, 1930.

WIELAND, C. M., ed. *Der teutsche Merkur.* Weimar, 1773–1789. *Der neue teutsche Merkur.* Weimar, 1798–1810.

———. "Ein paar Goldkörner aus Maculatur oder sechs Antworten auf sechs Fragen von Timalethes." *Der teutsche Merkur* 1789, 2. Vierteljahr.

———. "Unmaasgebliche Gedanken eines Laien über Herrn D. Carl Friedrich Bahrdts Glaubensbekenntnis," *Der teutsche Merkur,* Juli und September 1779.

WIESE, BENNO VON. "Die deutsche Leistung der Aufklärung," *Von deutscher Art in Sprache und Dichtung.* Stuttgart und Berlin, 1941.

WITZEL, K. "Friedrich Carl von Moser. Ein Beitrag zur hessen-darmstädtischen Finanz-und Wirtschaftsgeschichte am Ausgang des 18. Jahrhunderts," *Quellen und Forschungen zur hessischen Geschichte,* X (Darmstadt, 1929).

WOLFF, HANS M. *Die Weltanschauung der deutschen Aufklärung.* Bern, 1949.

Das Zeitalter des Absolutismus. (*Propyläen Weltgeschichte,* VI.) Berlin, 1931.

ZIMMERMANN, GEORG. *Johann Heinrich Merck, seine Umgebung und Zeit.* Frankfurt am Main, 1871.

ZIMMERMANN, JOHANN GEORG. *Fragmente über Friedrich den Grossen zur Geschichte seines Lebens, seiner Regierung und seines Charakters.* Leipzig, 1790.

———. *Betrachtungen über die Einsamkeit.* Leipzig, 1784–1785.

————. *Über Friedrich den Grossen und meine Unterredungen mit ihm kurz vor seinem Tode. Von dem Ritter von Zimmermann, Königlich Grossbritannischem Leibarzt und Hofrath.* Karlsruhe, 1788.

ZINCK, PAUL A. *Isaak Iselin als Pädagog.* Leipzig, 1900.

ZSCHARNACK, LEOPOLD. *Lessing und Semler.* Giessen, 1905.

Index